Marketing Management: Theory and Practice

Marketing Management: Theory and Practice

Edited by Anna Freeman

www.clanryeinternational.com

Clanrye International,
750 Third Avenue, 9th Floor,
New York, NY 10017, USA

Copyright © 2019 Clanrye International

This book contains information obtained from authentic and highly regarded sources. Copyright for all individual chapters remain with the respective authors as indicated. All chapters are published with permission under the Creative Commons Attribution License or equivalent. A wide variety of references are listed. Permission and sources are indicated; for detailed attributions, please refer to the permissions page and list of contributors. Reasonable efforts have been made to publish reliable data and information, but the authors, editors and publisher cannot assume any responsibility for the validity of all materials or the consequences of their use.

Trademark Notice: Registered trademark of products or corporate names are used only for explanation and identification without intent to infringe.

ISBN: 978-1-63240-809-9

Cataloging-in-Publication Data

Marketing management : theory and practice / edited by Anna Freeman.
    p. cm.
Includes bibliographical references and index.
ISBN 978-1-63240-809-9
1. Marketing--Management. 2. Marketing. 3. Management. I. Freeman, Anna.
HF5415.13 .M37 2019
658.8--dc23

For information on all Clanrye International publications
visit our website at www.clanryeinternational.com

Contents

Preface VII

Chapter 1   **Applying decision tree models to SMEs: A statistics-based model for customer relationship management** 1
Ayad Hendalianpour, Jafar Razmi and Arefe Rameshi Sarvestani

Chapter 2   **Evaluating impulse purchases generated by affections and advertisement effectiveness** 13
Aakash Kamble, Aatish Zagade and Nayna Abhang

Chapter 3   **The effect of corporate image on the formation of customer attraction** 21
Reza Koohjani Gouji, Reza Taghvaei and Hossein Soleimani

Chapter 4   **Investigating the impact of consumer values and advocacy behavior on buying decision satisfaction: A study through gender lens** 36
Raja Ahmed Jamil, Syed Rameez ul Hassan, Asdaq Farid and Naveed Ahmad

Chapter 5   **An empirical review of lean manufacturing and their strategies** 48
Virender Chahal and M.S. Narwal

Chapter 6   **Analytic network process (ANP) approach for product mix planning in railway industry** 64
Hadi Pazoki Toroudi, Mahsa Sadat Madani and Fatemeh Sarlak

Chapter 7   **Predicting customer's intentions to use internet banking: the role of technology acceptance model (TAM) in e-banking** 70
Samar Rahi, Mazuri Abd. Ghani and Feras MI Alnaser

Chapter 8   **Systematic model for lean product development implementation in an automotive related company** 82
Daniel Osezua Aikhuele

Chapter 9   **Critical success factors model developing for sustainable Kaizen implementation in manufacturing industry in Ethiopia** 96
Haftu Hailu, Abdelkadir Kedir, Getachew Bassa and Kassu Jilcha

Chapter 10   **Pay-What-You-Want pricing: An integrative review of the empirical research literature** 112
Torsten J. Gerpott

Chapter 11   **Analyzing the effect of customer loyalty on virtual marketing adoption based on theory of technology acceptance model** 139
Peyman Ghafari Ashtiani, Atefeh Parsayan and Moein Mohajerani

Chapter 12	**Strategic analysis of the mobile services value chain in Iran's capital market and development of a mechanism to promote it** .... 151 Bahareh Ghodoosi, Alireza Moshkforoush, Ali Abdollahi and Mohammadesmaeil Fadaeinejad	
Chapter 13	**Impact of Mobile advertising on consumer attitudes in Algeria: case study of Ooredoo** .... 163 Amina Merabet, Abderrezzak Benhabib and Abderrezzak Merabet	
Chapter 14	**The effect of firm's logo on its performance: Evidence from oil industry** .... 171 Jafar Jafari	
Chapter 15	**Integrating technology acceptance model and organizational innovativeness in the adoption of mobile commerce** .... 179 Maruf Gbadebo Salimon, Jibril Adewale Bamgbade, Ajulor Olusegun Nathaniel and Tijani A. Adekunle	
Chapter 16	**Identifying and ranking the factors affecting the adoption of biofuels** .... 195 Saeed Azizi, Fattaneh Alizadeh Meshkani and Reza Agha Mousa	

Permissions

List of Contributors

Index

Preface

Every book is initially just a concept; it takes months of research and hard work to give it the final shape in which the readers receive it. In its early stages, this book also went through rigorous reviewing. The notable contributions made by experts from across the globe were first molded into patterned chapters and then arranged in a sensibly sequential manner to bring out the best results.

Marketing management is the allocation of the resources of an organization to develop a strategy that targets potential customers with the goal of maximizing the sale of a product or service. The diverse aspects of this field include market analysis, developing strategies, forecasting sales, setting goals, planning, coordination, etc. Marketing management implements the tools of economics and competitive strategy for an understanding of the industry in which the firm's production falls. This book covers in detail some existing theories and innovative concepts revolving around marketing management. Different approaches, evaluations, methodologies and advanced studies revolving around marketing management have been presented in this book. It aims to serve as a resource guide for students and experts alike and contribute to the growth of the discipline.

It has been my immense pleasure to be a part of this project and to contribute my years of learning in such a meaningful form. I would like to take this opportunity to thank all the people who have been associated with the completion of this book at any step.

Editor

Applying decision tree models to SMEs: A statistics-based model for customer relationship management

Ayad Hendalianpour[a*], Jafar Razmi[a] and Arefe Rameshi Sarvestani[b]

[a]School of Industrial Engineering, College of Eng, Tehran University, Tehran, Iran
[b]Department of Mathematics, Shahrood University of Technology, Shahrood, Iran

CHRONICLE	ABSTRACT
Keywords: Customer Relationship Management (CRM) SMEs Decision tree C&RT C4.5 ID3	Customer Relationship Management (CRM) has been an important part of enterprise decision-making and management. In this regard, Decision Tree (DT) models are the most common tools for investigating CRM and providing an appropriate support for the implementation of CRM systems. Yet, this method does not yield any estimate of the degree of separation of different subgroups involved in analysis. In this research, we compute three decision-making models in SMEs, analyzing different decision tree methods (C&RT, C4.5 and ID3). The methods are then used to compute ME and VoE for the models and they were then used to calculate the Mean Errors (ME) and Variance of Errors (VoE) estimates to investigate the predictive power of these methods. These decision tree methods were used to analyze small- and medium-sized enterprises (SME's) datasets. The paper proposes a powerful technical support for better directing market tends and mining in CRM. According to the findings, C&RT shows a better degree of separation. As a result, we recommend using decision tree methods together with ME and VoE to determine CRM factors.

1. Introduction

In recent decades, Customer Relationship Management (CRM) has specifically reflected the crucial role of the customer as a factor that helps a company's profitability and operation meet. The idea behind CRM is to learn the real requirements of the customer and to leverage this knowledge to increase the firm's profitability in the long term (Stringfellow et al., 2004). In the rapidly changing business culture, the economics of customer relationships is changing, and firms are facing the need to apply new solutions to address these changes (Ritter & Geersbro, 2011). In this context, the advent of information technology (IT) has transformed the way marketing is stated and how firms manage information about their customers (Stringfellow et al., 2004).

* Corresponding author.
E-mail address: hendalianpour@ut.ac.ir (A. Hendalianpour)

Customer Relationship Management (CRM) is an enterprise management strategy which concentrates on customers (Stringfellow et al., 2004). CRM applies modern IT to increase the capability of enterprises to maintain and recognize their customers through Business Process Reengineering (BPR), and to maximize the profitability. With the development of economy and competition among different organizations, there is an increase awareness of the fact that to acquire customers, only having good products and wide distribution networks are sufficient. In fact, enterprises could absorb faithful customers and be dominant in fierce market competitions only by considering customers' requirements, increasing the response speed, and providing customers with constant one-to-one services.

CRM can help enterprises better manage different activities concerning customers and render the business routines programmed and automated. In any small firm, to improve customer relationship process, a working group forms a committee to apply data mining algorithms to improve customer relationships, to increase process efficiency and to take necessary steps for organizational purposes.

Considering the increase in the complexity and accumulation of customer information, most organizations may succeed only by performing critical activities such as analyzing complex customer data, identifying customers' values, detecting the trend of customers' behaviors, appreciating the real value of customers, and analyzing customers from a lifecycle marketing perspective. However, all of these factors depend on data mining (DM), and the more the data are accumulated in a database, the more useful DM techniques are. On the other hand, DM is a process of gathering necessary information and knowledge hidden in a large reservoir of data which are incomplete, noisy, fuzzy, and random. DM is recognized by concepts, rules and patterns, etc. Compared with common database inquiry, the excellence of DM depends on how it could discover connections between businesses as well as the latent trends and patterns. For example, the problem of consumer attrition is sometimes out of control because of not having any early warnings, but DM can set up a model disclosing the rate of lost clients in advance. By using this model, enterprises could predict which clients they may lose in near future. Armed by this information, sellers, relying on dynamic marketing activities, could keep the clients who have the idea of leaving; even if clients are lost, the model assists sellers overcome their passivity that led to consumer attrition.

In general, through applying DM technology to analyze the data and determine the related knowledge and regulations, the whole CRM system may become a closed loop and work better. Customer data and information technology tools shape the foundation to build successful strategy (Ngai et al., 2009). With this trend, technologies such as data mining and data warehousing have changed CRM as a new area in which most organizations may gain competitive advantage. Data mining offers a sophisticated set of tools to excavate customer data in an analytical CRM framework. The data mining methods are indeed considered a leading CRM tool deeply influenced by IT.

There is no doubt, the upcoming advents in IT call for business organizations to shape the way CRM functions in their business culture. In the literature, many researchers have studied the potential advantages of data mining systems in managing customers (Ngai et al., 2009), but among them few have applied the principles of such strategic tools for small organizations. The interesting point here is that, although Small and Medium sized Enterprises (SMEs) have a strong focus on customers, suppliers, employees and other stakeholders, they are considered business enterprises which have not well-implemented the principals of e-business in their infrastructural marketing strategies. Data mining is one of those technology-driven tools of e-business that has gained less attention in smaller firms, compared to larger ones.

Considering prior research, one can argue that most of the studies did not propose a well-formulated technique to be used in SEMs. The present study applies three models (decision trees) and analyzes them to find the best model. Furthermore, the study tries to select the best method for SEMs in Fars province, Iran, by relying on a case study. The major contributions of the study is answering two critical questions: (a) how can use data mining algorithm for CRM in SMEs? and (b) which of the widely used decision tree methods is better to be used in SMEs?

The organization of this paper is as follows: section 2 is literature review. Section 3 describes the CRM in SMEs. Section 4 briefly introduces the decision trees methods (C&RT; C4.5; ID3). In Section 5, the statistics methods for validation is presented and the best method from C&RT; C4.5; ID3 is chosen. In section 6, we present how to use decision trees methods CRM with a case study in Small and Medium sized Enterprises in Fars Province. At the end, a concluding remark is given in section 7.

2. Literature review

Decision trees are produced by algorithms that identify various ways of splitting a data set into branch-like segments (Moon et al., 2012). These segments construct an inverted decision tree that originates with a root node at the top of the tree. The object of analysis is reflected in this root node as a simple, one-dimensional display in the decision tree interface (Nefeslioglu et al., 2010). The name of the field of data that is the object of analysis is usually displayed, along with the spread or distribution of the values that are contained in that field. A sample decision tree is illustrated in Fig 1, which shows that the decision tree can reflect both a continuous and categorical object of analysis. The display of this node reflects all the data set records, fields, and field values that are found in the object of analysis (Wu et al., 2009; Ture et al., 2009). The discovery of the decision rule to form the branches or segments underneath the root node is based on a method that extracts the relationship between the object of analysis (that serves as the target field in the data) and one or more fields that serve as input fields to create the branches or segments. The values in the input field are used to estimate the likely value in the target field. The target field is also called an outcome, response, or dependent field or variable (Nefeslioglu et al., 2010; Sindhu et al., 2010).

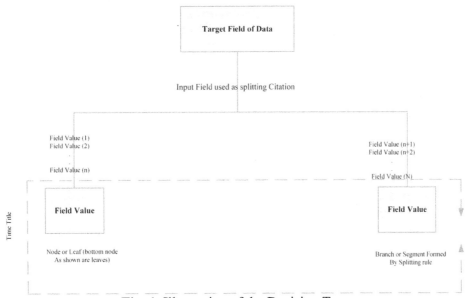

Fig. 1. Illustration of the Decision Tree

Many decision-tree algorithms have been developed. The most famous algorithms are C&RT, C4.5, ID3 that are simple decision tree learning algorithms developed by Ross Quinlan (T'sou et al., 2000, True et al., 2009), whose choice of split attribute is based on information entropy. The basic idea of ID3 algorithm is to build the decision tree by employing a top-down, greedy search through the given sets to test each attribute at every tree node. C4.5 is an extension of ID3 developed by Prather et al. in 1997 (Parther et al., 1997, Ture et al., 2009; Yıldız, 2011). It improves computing efficiency, deals with continuous values, handles attributes with missing values, avoids over-fitting, and performs other functions. To deal with continuous data, CART (classification and regression tree) algorithms have been proposed. CART is a data-exploration and prediction algorithm similar to C4.5, which is a tree construction algorithm developed by Martınez-Munoz and Suárez (2004). Breiman et al. (1984) summarized the classification and regression trees. Instead of information entropy, it introduces measures of node impurity. It relies on a variety of different problems, such as the detection of chlorine from the data contained in a mass spectrum, as proposed by Berson and Smith in 1997. CHAID (Chi-square automatic interaction detector) is similar to CART, but their difference lies in that it chooses a split node. It depends on a Chi-square test used in contingency tables to determine which categorical predictor is farthest from independence with the prediction values that proposed with Bittencourt and Clarke (2003). It also has an extended version, Exhausted-CHAID.

3. CRM in SMEs

Numerous researches have been carried out in the context of data mining in larger firms (Treacy & Wiersema, 1997), but the literature is underdeveloped in case of SMEs. The reason for this underdeveloped research trend is well justified: in many cases, smaller firms cannot afford the initial capital for the installation of a systematic data mining framework. In fact, data mining is used when there is a huge expanse of data with important implied information. Managing the information can help companies be successful in market competition.

Nowadays, in the competitive e-business environment, business organizations are switching from product-oriented business strategies to customer-oriented ones. Globalization, increasing competition, and advances in information and communication technology, have forced firms to concentrate on managing customer relationships to efficiently maximize revenues (Azad & Ahmadi, 2015). As a strategy to optimize the lifetime-value of the customers, CRM can help firms succeed in the world of e-business (Rygielski et al., 2002; Hsu, 2009), define CRM as a cross-functional procedure to attain a continuous exchange of ideas with customers, across all their contacts and access points, with a personalized treatment of the most valuable customers to increase customer retention and the effectiveness of marketing networks.

Both large and multinational enterprises and SMEs are rigorously seeking to deploy CRM to gain competitive advantage to build their long-term profitability. Particularly, customer retention is important to SMEs because of their limited resources (Özgener & İraz, 2006; Reddick, 2011). Skaates and Seppanen (2002) point out the major contribution of CRM to the competence development of small firms. Furthermore, SMEs are embracing CRM as a major element of business strategy, while technological applications allow for a precise segmentation, provide profiling and targeting of customers, and bring about a customer-centric culture due to competitive pressures (Day et al., 2002, Sulaiman, 2011; Skaates & Seppänen, 2002; Gurău et al., 2003).

4. Methods

4.1. Decision Tree

During the late 1970s and early 1980s, Quinlan, a researcher in machine learning, developed a decision tree algorithm known as ID3 (Iterative Dichotomiser). This work was expanded on earlier findings about concept learning systems described by others and Quinlan later presented C4.5 (a successor of ID3), which became a benchmark to which newer supervised learning algorithms are often compared. In 1984, a group of statisticians (Chang et al., 2012) published the book *Classification and Regression Trees* (CART), which described the generation of binary decision trees. ID3 and CART were invented independently of one another at around the same time, although they followed a similar approach to learning decision trees from training tuples. These two cornerstone algorithms spawned a flurry of work on decision tree induction (Gurău et al., 2003).

ID3, C4.5, and CART adopt a greedy (i.e., non-backtracking) approach in which decision trees are constructed in a top-down recursive divide-and-conquer manner. Most algorithms for decision tree induction also follow such a top-down approach, which starts with a training set of tuples and their associated class labels. The training set is recursively partitioned into smaller subsets as the tree is being built. In the following sections, we briefly introduce the C&RT, C4.5, ID3 methods.

3.1.1. Classification and regression tree

Classification and regression tree (C&RT) is a recursive partitioning technique implemented for both regression and classification. C&RT partitions the data into two subsets so that the records within each subset are more homogeneous than those in the previous subset. It is a recursive process through which each of those two subsets is then split again, and the process is repeated until the homogeneity criterion is reached or until some other stopping criterion is met (as in case of all of the tree-growing methods). The objective is to generate subsets of the data which are as homogeneous as possible with respect to the target variable (Breiman et al., 1984). In this study, measure of Gini impurity was used for categorical target variables.
Gini Impurity Measure:

The Gini index at node t, $g(t)$, is defined as:

$$g(t) = \sum_{j \neq 1} p(j|t) p(i|t), \qquad (1)$$

where i and j are categories of the target variable. The equation for the Gini index can also be written as:

$$g(t) = 1 - \sum_{j} p^2(j|t). \qquad (2)$$

Thus, when the cases in a node are evenly dispersed across the categories, the Gini index takes its maximum value of $1 - (1/k)$, where $\underline{k}$ is the number of categories for the target variable. When all cases in the node are found to be in the same category, the Gini index equals 0. If costs of misclassification are specified, the Gini index is computed via:

$$g(t) = \sum_{j \neq 1} c(i|j) p(j|t) p(i|t), \qquad (3)$$

where C (i-j) is the probability of misclassifying a category j case as category i. The Gini criterion function for split s at node t is defined as:

$$\phi(s,t) = g(t) - p_L g(t_L) - p_R g(t_R), \qquad (4)$$

where p_L, the proportion of cases in t, is sent to the left child node, and p_R is the proportion sent to the right child node. Split s is chosen to maximize the value of $\phi(s,t)$. This value is reported along with the progression in the tree (Breiman et al., 1984).

4.1.2. Commercial version 4.5

C4.5 is a kind of supervised learning classification algorithm which is used to build decision trees from the data (Treacy & Wiersema, 1997). Most empirical learning systems are given a set of pre-classified cases, each explained by a vector of attribute values and constructed from a mapping of attribute values to classes. C4.5 is such a system that learns decision tree classifiers. It applies a divide-and-conquer approach to growing decision trees (Azad & Ahmadi, 2015). The main difference between C4.5 and other similar decision tree building algorithms is in the test selection and evaluation process.

Let attributes be denoted $A = \{a_1, a_2, ..., a_m\}$, cases be denoted $D = \{d_1, d_2, ..., d_n\}$, and classes be denoted $C = \{c_1, c_2, ..., c_k\}$. For a set of cases D, a test Ti is a split of D derived from attribute at. It splits D into mutually exclusive subsets $D_1, D_2, ..., D_p$. These subsets of cases are single-class collections of cases. If a test T is chosen, the decision tree for D consists of a node identifying the test T, and one branch for each possible subset D_i. For each subset D_i, a new test is then chosen for further splits. If D_i satisfies a stopping criterion, the tree for D_i is a leaf associated with the most frequent class in D_i. One reason for stopping is that cases in D_i belong to one class.

C4.5 decision tree algorithm uses a modified splitting criterion called *gain ratio*. It uses *arg max (gain (D, T))* or *arg max (gain ratio (D, T))* to choose tests for split:

$$Info(D) = -\sum_{i=1}^{k} p(c_i, D) \log 2(p(c_i, D)), \tag{5}$$

$$Split(D, T) = -\sum_{i=1}^{p} \frac{|D_i|}{|D|} \log 2\left(\frac{|D_i|}{|D|}\right), \tag{6}$$

$$Gain(D, T) = Info(D) - \sum_{i=1}^{p} \frac{|D_i|}{|D|} Info(D_i), \tag{7}$$

$$GainRatio(D, T) = Gain(D, T) / Split(D, T), \tag{8}$$

where, $p(c_i, D)$ denotes the proportion of cases in D that belong to the i-th class. C4.5 selects the test that maximizes gain ratio value Quinlan (1996). Once the initial decision tree is constructed, a pruning procedure is initiated to decrease the overall tree size and decrease the estimated error rate of the tree (Bradley, 1998).

4.1.3. ID3 algorithm

In decision-tree analysis based approaches, the most influential analysis is represented by the ID3 algorithm which was proposed by Quinlan (1996). It uses the decreasing speed of entropy as the criterion of selecting the attribute to be studied. This method uses well-known sample categories to obtain the ordered testing attributes, until all of the known samples have been classified. In the process of forming a decision tree, a method of informatics is used which can provide the largest information increase at any time, i.e. the largest entropy decrease (Zhuge, 2011).

For N samples, they belong to classes $C_i (i = 1,2,...,C)$. There are N_i samples in class C_i; every sample has K attributes, and every attribute has J_k values. The process of forming decision involves:

(1) Computing the initial entropies.

$$entropy(I) = \sum_{i=1}^{c} -(N_i/N) \log_2(N_i/N) = \sum_{i=1}^{c} -p_i \log_2 p_i \tag{9}$$

For the given training sample aggregate, all the sample classes are known. So the sample aggregate constitutes the initial entropies of the system.

(2) Selecting an attribute as the root node of the decision tree.
- For attribute $A_k (i = 1,2,...,K)$ according to the J_k values (a_{kj}) of A_k, the initial samples are divided into the first grade sample aggregates. Although (a_{kj}) branch has (a_{kj}) samples, in general, the n_{kj} samples do not belong to the single class.

- For n_{kj} samples of the branch, assuming that the number of samples belonging to class C_i is $n_{kj}(i)$, we can use following formula to get the entropy of this branch.

$$entropy(I, A_k, j) = \sum_{i=1}^{c}\left[-n_{kj}(i)/n_{kj}\right]\log_2\left[n_{kj}(i)/n_{kj}\right] \quad (10)$$

$$entropy(I, A_k) = \sum_{j=1}^{J_k}\sum_{I=1}^{C}(n_{kj}/N)\times\left[-n_{kj}(i)/n_{kj}\right]\log_2\left[n_{kj}(i)/n_{kj}\right] \quad (11)$$

- Calculating the entropy decrease due to attribute A_k, i.e.

$$\Delta entropy(k) = entropy(I) - entropy(I, A_k) \quad (12)$$

- Selecting attribute A_{k0} which causes the maximum entropy decrease via:

$$\Delta entropy(A_{k0}) > \Delta entropy(A_k) \quad (K = 1,2,...,K; k \neq k_0) \quad (13)$$

- So, the attribute Ak0 is the root node of decision tree.

(3) Attribute A_{k0} has J_{k0} values and divides the sample into J_{k0} subsets. For every subset, we use the above method in turn and select an attribute A_k as the next lower grade node of the decision tree, in which the maximum entropy decrease is gained.

(4) Following step 3, we continuously construct the next lower grade nodes until all of subsets have only one class. Here, the entropies are zero and the decision tree has been accomplished.

5. Model Validation

Validating the model is a critical step in the process. It allows us to determine if we have successfully performed all the prior steps. If a model is not validated well, it can be due to data problems, poorly fitting variables, or problematic techniques. There are several methods for validating models. In this study, regarding recent studies of statistical methods for validation, we used two statistical methods: the first one is Mean Errors (ME) and the second one is Variance of Errors (VoE) (Montgomery & Runger, 2010). To make a statistical comparison of the two methods, mean errors (ME) and variance of errors (VoE) are adopted as defined by Eq. (14) and Eq. (15) respectively.

$$ME = \frac{1}{n}\sum_{h=1}^{n}\frac{\left|y_h^A - y_h^M\right|}{y_h^A}.100, \quad (14)$$

$$VoE = \frac{1}{n-1}(\sum_{h=1}^{n}\frac{\left|y_h^A - y_h^M\right|}{y_h^A}.100 - ME)^2, \quad (15)$$

where n is the total number of datasets y_h^A and y_h^M are the Actual values (from survey data) and the Model outputs (the proposed approach or statistical regression) for hth dataset respectively. It is noted that the smaller the ME and VoE values, the more accurate the model is. According to validation methods, a method is optimal if both mean errors and variance of errors have the minimum value On the other hand, if in special cases, both mean errors and variance of errors are not in minimum value for the same method, we consider variance of errors because computation of the mean errors is in the variance of errors. For more details regarding to ME and VoE a reader may see Montgomery and Runger's contribution (Montgomery & Runger, 2010)

6. Case Study

Considering the significance of decision tree and its application in unfolding relationships for managing communication with costumers, in the following sections three widely used decision tree algorithms, which were explained in the precious sections, are investigated in a case study. This study uses the algorithms to discover the internal relationships of data and to select the best method commonly used in SEMs.

The above-mentioned decision tree methods are used in this section for measuring the relationship of management regarding companies as well as customer opinions. Fig. 2 illustrates the implementation of three tree methods in a SMEs through a step-by-step flowchart.

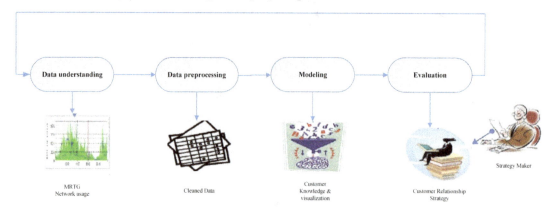

Fig. 2. Framework of tree methods

Fig. 2 shows the implementation process of the research through the data gathered from SEMs in Fars province, Iran. At the first stage of data understanding, considering experts' opinions, the main attributes of the research were extracted and, based on this primary structure, the data were collected. At the data preprocessing stage, statistical procedures were conducted on the collected data. Also, considering the possibility that some records might not involve any value in the effective attributes, decision-making, in such cases, is normally conducted by eliminating or substituting them; in this study we used the elimination technique. At the third stage called *modeling*, the collected data were computed using three decision tree models. Finally, given the outputs obtained from the three decision models, the defined criteria for selecting the best method in the SEMs were considered, and appropriate strategies were suggested. The effective specifications of the relationship between customers are shown in Table 1, in which Q11 is class attribute. In this data set, we try to predict who can find by this attribute the relationship of product quality and satisfaction, and then suggest a solution is to improve the problems with respect to output models.

Table 1
Set of all attributes

Attributes	Description	Type
Age	Between 15olds to above	Quantitative
Gender	Males or females	Binary
Education	Basic school, High school, University degree	Linguistic
Q1	Price compared to quality	Quantitative
Q2	Price compared to other companies	Quantitative
Q3	Price compared to expectations	Linguistic
Q4	Image of the store you deal with	Quantitative
Q5	Employees treated you politely and with respect when you complained	Linguistic
Q6	Services	Quantitative
Q7	Reliability of the products	Quantitative
Q8	Product variety	Binary
Q9	Product designing	Linguistic
Q10	Quality improvement	Linguistic
Q11	Overall satisfaction	Quantitative

Table 2
Statistical analysis of data set

Attribute	Statistical Methods		
	Mean	Standard deviation	Variance
Age	4.00	0.671	0.143
Gender	5.00	0.921	0.196
Education	3.82	0.853	0.182
Q1	3.36	0.727	0.155
Q2	4.09	0.811	0.173
Q3	3.23	1.020	0.218
Q4	4.09	0.684	0.146
Q5	3.59	0.734	0.157
Q6	3.18	0.853	0.182
Q7	3.86	0.889	0.190
Q8	3.82	0.795	0.169
Q9	3.36	1.002	0.214
Q10	3.41	1.008	0.215
Q11	4.55	0.671	0.143

This case study included 2000 individuals, as customers of SMEs in Fars Province, Iran (specific on food industrials). For this purpose, a questionnaire was designed which includes questions about product quality, price, services, and so on (a list of the questions are shown in Table 1). Next, through the above-mentioned decision tree methods, the customer relationship management of customers was evaluated. To do this, the decision tree (C&RT, C4.5 and ID3) methods were implemented in the C++ encoding language and after solving the proposed decision tree (C&RT, C4.5 and ID3) methods, the accuracy of the evaluation methods was calculated. Table 3 illustrates the values of statistics related to each of the attributes.

Table 3
Comparison of the error rates of models

Index	Models		
	C 4.5	CHAID	C&RT
Training-MAE	1425.057	1211.031	1415.059
Testing-MAE	1349.232	1190.404	1343.345
Training-Linear Correlation	0.246	0.515	0.335
Testing-Linear Correlation	0.165	0.462	0.187

In Table 3 we calculate the mean error for each of the four criteria for evaluating the algorithms employed in this study we have discussed. These criteria were used in both training and testing. These criteria indicate that the error rate for each of the algorithms used in the training set and the test is to what extent. Parameters for each algorithm, comparing the values specified in Table 6 is based on the method of least error. Regarding to output the C&RT is the maximum linear correlation.

According to validation method, from among C&RT, C4.5 and ID3, C&RT was found to be the best, because both ME and VoE showed the minimum value for this method. In this research, to justify the application of the appropriate method, we used a bar chart and scatter graphs. The result of each of these experiments is depicted in Fig. 3.

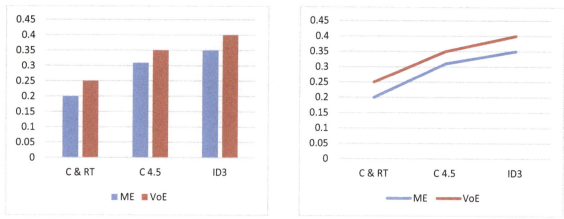

Fig. 3. Validation of decision tree methods with ME and VoE comparison

Table 4
Compared existing of decision tree methods

Index	Models		
	C&RT	C4.5	ID3
ME	0.2	0.31	0.35
VoE	0.25	0.35	0.4

Table 4 compares the outputs of the methods under study. Considering Table 4, one can observe that C&RT, compared to the two other methods, showed the minimum value of error in both of the statistical tests. Therefore, SMEs for costumer communication management is more appropriate than the two other methods.

Finally, from among the approaches to decision tree algorithms, certainly C4.5, compared to the other two algorithms, had a better performance in development model of CRM in SMEs. Therefore, C4.5 algorithm is useful for predicting the behavior of customers. Otherwise, respectively CRAT and ID3 algorithms can more appropriately predict behavior of customers in the long-term.

7. Conclusion

CRM involves important measures and necessary steps for enterprises to keep their competitiveness in market economy. The development and application of CRM, as a result, are taken seriously by enterprises. Presently, there are a number of well-established products of CRM. DM technology is the rapidly developing key technology which, through development and perfection, can help accomplish the aims of CRM. DM can completely activate CRM and lay a good foundation For CRM. Further development in DM technology will produce more extensive applications for the future and market values of CRM. Recently, decision tree models for this purpose have incorporated novel ideas and interpretations into the solution of such problems. In this study, we found that C&RT performed better than C4.5 and ID3 techniques. As a result, we recommend the application of decision tree methods altogether, especially C&RT with statistical comparisons (Mean Errors and Variance of errors) to select the best known approach for Small and Medium sized Enterprises.

Then, the proposed models were meticulously compared by using a real data set in order to provide helpful information on the general tendency of data, assess the effect of specific variables on survival in data sets, and help Small and Medium sized Enterprises to select the best method for solving CRM problems. There are limited data on the sufficiency of classification efforts by applying just one approach. Based on our observations, we suggest that data should be better explored and processed through high performance modeling procedures. Future studies can be conducted on applying hybrid robust models for this purpose.

References

Azad, N., & Ahmadi, F. (2015). The customer relationship management process: its measurement and impact on performance. *Uncertain Supply Chain Management, 3*(1), 43-50.

Bittencourt, H. R., & Clarke, R. T. (2003, July). Use of classification and regression trees (CART) to classify remotely-sensed digital images. In INTERNATIONAL GEOSCIENCE AND REMOTE SENSING SYMPOSIUM (Vol. 6, pp. VI-3751).

Breiman, L., Friedman, J. H., Olshen, R. A., & Stone, C. J. (1984). Classification and regression trees Belmont. CA: Wadsworth International Group.

Bradley, P. S., Fayyad, U. M., & Reina, C. (1998, August). Scaling Clustering Algorithms to Large Databases. In *KDD* (pp. 9-15).

Chang, S. H., Wang, K. Y., Chih, W. H., & Tsai, W. H. (2012). Building customer commitment in business-to-business markets. *Industrial Marketing Management, 41*(6), 940-950.

Day, G. S., & Van den Bulte, C. (2002). Superiority in customer relationship management: Consequences for competitive advantage and performance. Marketing Science Institute.

Gurău, C., Ranchhod, A., & Hackney, R. (2003). Customer-centric strategic planning: Integrating CRM in online business systems. *Information Technology and Management, 4*(2-3), 199-214.

Hsu, C. H. (2009). Data mining to improve industrial standards and enhance production and marketing: An empirical study in apparel industry. *Expert Systems with Applications, 36*(3), 4185-4191.

Moon, S. S., Kang, S. Y., Jitpitaklert, W., & Kim, S. B. (2012). Decision tree models for characterizing smoking patterns of older adults. *Expert Systems with Applications, 39*(1), 445-451.

Nefeslioglu, H. A., Sezer, E., Gokceoglu, C., Bozkir, A. S., & Duman, T. Y. (2010). Assessment of landslide susceptibility by decision trees in the metropolitan area of Istanbul, Turkey. *Mathematical Problems in Engineering, 2010*.

Martınez-Munoz, G., & Suárez, A. (2004). Aggregation ordering in bagging. In *Proc. of the IASTED International Conference on Artificial Intelligence and Applications* (pp. 258-263).

Montgomery, D. C., & Runger, G. C. (2010). *Applied statistics and probability for engineers*. John Wiley & Sons.

Ngai, E. W. (2005). Customer relationship management research (1992-2002) an academic literature review and classification. Marketing intelligence & planning, 23(6), 582-605.

Ngai, E. W., Xiu, L., & Chau, D. C. (2009). Application of data mining techniques in customer relationship management: A literature review and classification. *Expert systems with applications, 36*(2), 2592-2602.

Özgener, Ş., & İraz, R. (2006). Customer relationship management in small–medium enterprises: The case of Turkish tourism industry. *Tourism Management, 27*(6), 1356-1363.

Prather, J. C., Lobach, D. F., Goodwin, L. K., Hales, J. W., Hage, M. L., & Hammond, W. E. (1997). Medical data mining: knowledge discovery in a clinical data warehouse. In *Proceedings of the AMIA annual fall symposium*(p. 101). American Medical Informatics Association.

Quinlan, J. R. (1996, August). Bagging, boosting, and C4. 5. In AAAI/IAAI, Vol. 1 (pp. 725-730).

Reddick, C. G. (2011). Customer Relationship Management (CRM) technology and organizational change: Evidence for the bureaucratic and e-Government paradigms. *Government Information Quarterly, 28*(3), 346-353.

Ritter, T., & Geersbro, J. (2011). Organizational relationship termination competence: A conceptualization and an empirical test. *Industrial Marketing Management, 40*(6), 988-993.

Rygielski, C., Wang, J. C., & Yen, D. C. (2002). Data mining techniques for customer relationship management. *Technology in Society, 24*(4), 483-502.

Sulaiman, S., Ariffin, M. K. A., Esmaeilian, G. R., Faghihi, K., & Baharudin, B. T. H. T. (2011). Customer knowledge management application in Malaysian mobile service providers. *Procedia Engineering, 15*, 3891-3895.

Sindhu, S. S. S., Geetha, S., & Kannan, A. (2012). Decision tree based light weight intrusion detection using a wrapper approach. *Expert Systems with Applications, 39*(1), 129-141.

Skaates, M. A., & Seppänen, V. (2002). Managing relationship-driven competence dynamics in professional service organizations. *European Management Journal, 20*(4), 430-437.

Stringfellow, A., Nie, W., & Bowen, D. E. (2004). CRM: Profiting from understanding customer needs. *Business Horizons, 47*(5), 45-52.

T'sou, B. K., Lai, T. B., Chan, S. W., Gao, W., & Zhan, X. (2000, October). Enhancement of a Chinese discourse marker tagger with C4. 5. *In Proceedings of the second workshop on Chinese language processing: held in conjunction with the 38th Annual Meeting of the Association for Computational Linguistics-Volume 12 (pp. 38-45).* Association for Computational Linguistics.

Treacy, M., & Wiersema, F. D. (1997). *The discipline of market leaders: Choose your customers, narrow your focus, dominate your market.* Basic Books.

Ture, M., Tokatli, F., & Kurt, I. (2009). Using Kaplan–Meier analysis together with decision tree methods (C&RT, CHAID, QUEST, C4. 5 and ID3) in determining recurrence-free survival of breast cancer patients. *Expert Systems with Applications, 36*(2), 2017-2026.

Wu, D. (2009). Supplier selection: A hybrid model using DEA, decision tree and neural network. *Expert Systems with Applications, 36*(5), 9105-9112.

Yıldız, O. T. (2011). Model selection in omnivariate decision trees using Structural Risk Minimization. *Information Sciences, 181*(23), 5214-5226.

Zhuge, H. (2011). Semantic linking through spaces for cyber-physical-socio intelligence: A methodology. *Artificial Intelligence, 175*(5), 988-1019.

Evaluating impulse purchases generated by affections and advertisement effectiveness

Aakash Kamble[a*], Aatish Zagade[b] and Nayna Abhang[c]

[a]*Assistant Professor, Indira Global Business School, Pune – 410506, India*
[b]*Product Data Coordinator, Medline Industries Pvt. Ltd., Bhalerao Towers, Shivajinagar, Pune – 411005, India*

CHRONICLE	ABSTRACT
Keywords: Dual mediation hypothesis Celebrity endorsements Ad effectiveness Brand affections Consumer behavior	Impulse buying occurs when a consumer experiences a sudden, often powerful and persistent urge to buy something immediately. This on-going research considers the affections generated by consumers towards the chocolate brand which is endorsed by a celebrity. The Dual Mediation Hypothesis Model (DMH) is used to ascertain the ad effectiveness of the product/ brand, in this research advertisement featuring the celebrity. The affections generated by the ad leads to generation of affection towards the brand leading to purchase a product/ brand. The chocolate brand selected for the research has high market share and manufactures chocolate based products catering to all classes of consumers. The research primarily focuses on the significance of affections generated by the advertisement for the product. The purchase decision for such products is usually based on consumer impulses and attitudes towards the product/ brand. A convenience sample of 116 individuals was considered for the research and the survey was done using questionnaire method. The findings from the analysis revealed that the consumers purchased the products due to the impulses and affections generated by the ad and brand. There was no clear linkage between the celebrity and brand which lead to purchase intentions of the product/ brand. The Dual Mediation Model was found to be applicable as the affections towards the brand and the ad resulted in purchase intention.

1. Introduction

Over the years it has been presumed that endorsing products and services by celebrities yield better results in terms of increase in sales volume thus resulting in the better profits. Little or no thought is given to fact that the products or services endorsed by the celebrities are from various categories altogether. A celebrity who endorses varied products and services across different product lines and sectors usually ends up over-doing the act. Products and services with low investments are usually purchased on impulses of consumers, whereas the products and services having considerable high investment are subjected to rational buying behavior. There is a difference between the behaviors exhibited by the consumers in both these scenarios (Cohen & Areni, 1991).

The advertisements for the products which are purchased on consumer impulses play a role of generating awareness about the same. For the research, a renowned chocolate bar manufacturing company

---

* Corresponding author.
E-mail address: kamble.aakash@outlook.com (A. Kamble)

and their specific brand was considered. The advertisement of this brand of chocolate bars features a well-known celebrity from the Indian film industry. The brand has a high market share in Indian market and is also the market leader. With its neatly positioned advertising effort and the endorsements done by the celebrity, this product has been a leader for many years on a consecutive basis.

Dual Mediation Hypothesis Model (DMH) postulates that the affective attitudes towards the brand leads to Purchase Intention (PI) when the effort is low from consumer (Kamble, 2014). In this research, the DMH model is tested to find its applicability in the above mentioned situation. The research studied the samples who were exposed to the advert which was considered for the research and also were familiar with the celebrity in that advertisement. Based on the responses received from the sample the research ascertains the effectiveness of the advertisement and the purchases triggered by it. This research being a part of an on-going research, the findings from it are mentioned in the subsequent headings.

To summarize, the objective of this research is to evaluate the impulse purchases by consumers and the factors behind the same which primarily being the affections generated towards the advertisement and/or the celebrity and the overall effectiveness of the advertisement in communicating the message to the consumers. To ascertain this survey, 116 samples and the analysis of the same was done to substantiate the claim. Existing literature on impulse purchasing behavior and DMH model is reviewed in the research. In the subsequent sections, hypotheses are formulated and the evaluation impulse purchases tested and the implication of the research are discussed.

2. Literature review

For last half of the century, consumer researchers have invested their efforts to form a better definition of impulse buying. Early studies on impulse buying stemmed from managerial and retailer interests. Research here placed its emphasis on the taxonomic approach of classifying products into impulse and non-impulse items in order to facilitate marketing strategies such as point-of-purchase advertising, merchandising, or in-store promotions. However, local market conditions, systems of exchange and various cultural forces impact how consumers operate on impulse.

2.1 Impulse Buying Behavior

2.1.1 Nature of Impulse Buying

In impulse buying the purchase is made primarily without evaluating in great detail. Individuals buying impulse is less likely to consider the consequences or to think carefully before making the purchase (Rook, 1987). The person's attention is concentrated on the immediate gratification of responding to the urge to purchase rather than on solving a pre-existing problem or on finding an item to fill a predetermined need (Barratt, 1985; Rook, 1987). Finally, consistent with general impulsiveness, impulsive buying is immediate (Barratt, 1985; Rook, 1987).

2.1.2 Impulse Buying Behavior

Subsequent to 1982, when researchers started paying more attention to impulse buying behavior, researchers started to analyze the behavioral dimensions of impulse buying. Most recently, researchers appear to agree that impulse buying involves a hedonic or affective component (Cobb & Hoyer, 1986; Piron, 1991; Rook, 1987; Rook & Fisher, 1995; Weinberg & Gottwald, 1982). For instance, Rook (1987) reports accounts by consumers who felt the product 'calling' them, almost demanding they purchase it. This emphasis on the behavioral elements of impulse buying led to the definition of impulse as follows. Impulse buying happens when a consumer experiences a sudden, often powerful and persistent urge to buy something immediately (Kamble, 2014). The impulse to buy is hedonically complex and may stimulate emotional conflict. Also, impulse buying is prone to happen with diminished regard for its consequences (Rook, 1987, p. 191). Rook and Hock (1983) identified five crucial elements in impulse buying: the onset of psychological conflict and struggle, a reduction in cognitive evaluation, a sudden and spontaneous desire to act, a state of psychological disequilibrium, and a lack of regard for the consequences of impulse buying. Weinberg and Gottwald (1982), cited that, shopper with impulsive buying tendencies normally view an impulse purchase as negative and successfully resist the temptation, at other times they are also more likely to rationalize the negative feelings and make the purchase anyway. This indicates that, although impulsive shoppers may deliberate about the purchase on a cognitive level, at some point in the decision making process the shopper's affective state overcomes their cognitive willpower (Kamble, 2014). These findings support a study, which concluded that, although cognitive deliberation plays a part in the impulse buyer's decision, its influence is smaller than that of the affective state (Weinberg & Gottwald, 1982).

2.2 Dual Mediation Hypothesis Model

Fill (2006) defined marketing communications as a management process through which an organization seeks to engage with its various audiences, in order to (re)position the organization and its offerings in the minds of particular audiences, and in doing so encourage the development of relationships that are of mutual value. The amount of resources dedicated to communication initiatives has meant that companies and managers worry about how to assess whether outcomes coincide with results (Kamble, 2014). Several attempts, based on the relevance of communication effectiveness, have been made to describe how such communication activities work, leading to different frameworks (Vakratsas & Ambler, 1999) such as cognitive information models (Bharadwaj et al., 1993), pure affect models (Aaker et al., 1986; Blaney, 1986) and the Elaboration Likelihood Model (Petty & Cacioppo, 1981).

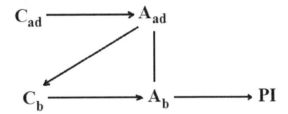

Fig. 1. Dual Mediation Hypothesis Model of Ad Processing

Here C_{ad}, A_{ad}, C_b, A_b and PI represent Advertising cognition, Attitude towards advertising, Brand cognition, Attitude towards brand and Purchase intention, respectively. In line with this, MacKenzie et al. (1986) published a seminal paper in which they explained and tested four alternative models of communication effectiveness. Their primary aim was to find out how attitude towards the ad (A_{ad}) mediates attitude towards the brand (A_b) and Purchase Intention (PI), with these three variables representing communication effectiveness. The four models thus analyzed were: the Affect Transfer Hypothesis, the Reciprocal Mediation Hypothesis, the Independent Influences Hypothesis and the Dual Mediation Hypothesis. In the research, the competing explanations share three common paths, namely, ad cognitions → A_{ad}, brand cognitions → A_b and A_b → PI. Cognitions are any thought that comes out during the elaboration of the information, measured using a written protocol known as thought elicitation (Meyers-Levy & Malaviya, 1999; Sicilia et al., 2005). The Affect Transfer Hypothesis (ATH) proposes a path from A_{ad} to A_b, which represents the peripheral route to persuasion in the Elaboration Likelihood Model (Petty & Cacioppo, 1996). The positive affect generated by the ad is transferred to the evaluation of the product/brand itself without further scrutiny of the information provided (Mitchell & Olson 1981). The Reciprocal Mediation Hypothesis (RMH) assumes a reciprocal causal relationship between A_{ad} and A_b. The idea that people attempt to maintain "balanced" cognitive relationships backs up this point of view (Heider, 1946). The Independent Influences Hypothesis (IIH) posits that A_{ad} and A_b exert an independent influence on PI. Finally, the Dual Mediation Hypothesis (DMH) specifies an indirect flow of causation from A_{ad} to A_b through brand cognitions (C_b), in addition to the direct influence that links both types of attitude. Compared with the other three alternative models, the

DMH (Fig. 1) turned out to be the one that best explained ad effectiveness. This implies that A_{ad} positively influences A_b, which lends further support to the idea that A_{ad} is an important mediator of brand attitude formation (Park & Young, 1984). Additionally, A_{ad} exerts a positive influence on brand cognitions, which means that not only the peripheral route plays a role in communication models but so does the central route of persuasion through its effect on cognitions (Petty & Cacioppo, 1981). The DMH is still considered one of the most widely accepted models of communication effects to date. Later research supported this perspective and confirmed the appropriateness of the DMH in analysing communication effectiveness (Brown & Stayman, 1992). The DMH remains to be considered the most widely accepted model of advertising effects hitherto.

Allen et al. (2005), although admitting that finding ways and means to incorporate emotional experience into consumer and market research has been an ongoing challenge for a long time, have carried out some research offline which features that emotional information may serve as a separate antecedent of attitude. That means that emotional reports will add to traditional cognitive information in explaining attitude's variance. However, the cognitive approach has dominated persuasion research whereas the affective processes have been given a relatively minor role in spite of the wide use of emotional appeals in advertising (Morris et al., 2002). Focusing only on cognitive processes and refusing to consider the role of emotions in communication could lead to a misunderstanding of various consumer behaviours.

3. Materials and methods

3.1 Hypothesis Development

Traditionally, most studies have treated product/brand attitude as a one-dimensional construct (Kamble, 2014). The assertion that attitudes are complex and multidimensional has led some researchers to try to integrate an experiential view of consumption with more traditional functional approaches (Mano & Oliver, 1993). The earliest exercise to measure the multiple dimensions of product/brand attitudes was that of Batra and Ahtola (1991), who stated that "consumers purchase goods and services and perform consumption behaviors for two basic reasons: (1) consummatory affective gratification (from sensory attributes) and (2) instrumental, utilitarian reasons". In short, consumption "involves experiential as well as instrumental outcomes" (Babin et al., 1994). The first is a *hedonic* dimension resulting from *sensations* derived from the experience of using products, and the second is a *utilitarian* dimension derived from *functions* performed by products (Voss et al., 2003). The domains, which evidence a fundamental presence across consumption literature, are meant to be neither exhaustive nor mutually exclusive (Babin et al., 1994). Capturing both dimensions with a reliable and valid scale turns out to be a difficult task (Kamble, 2014). Recently, Voss et al. (2003) developed a valid, reliable, and generalizable scale to measure the hedonic and utilitarian dimensions of consumers' attitude. They tested the scale for the central route of persuasion, using involvement as a proxy for cognitive elaboration. In the research, a global model is tested in which emotions and cognitions are used as antecedents of the hedonic and utilitarian dimensions of attitude towards the product/ brand, i.e., by testing the Dual Mediation Hypothesis model. Therefore, the same model is incorporated in the form of cognitive and emotional components that have traditionally been considered fundamental in communication effectiveness (Sicilia et al., 2005; Kempf & Smith, 1998; Burke & Edell, 1989).

H_0 – *Impulse purchases are not result of affections*

This is the null hypothesis which is presumed to be true. The impulse purchases made by the consumers of the product used for the research are not a result of the affections generated by the consumers towards the same due to its advertisement. This is the explanation for the null hypothesis which needs to be tested for its validity.

H_1 – *Affections towards the brand will result into purchase intention.*

Affections will be generated towards the brand and the same will result into purchase intention of the same. This will be caused due the sudden need or urge for the purchase of the product leading to impulse buying behavior.

H_2 – *Featuring celebrity in the ad leads to impulse purchases.*

This proposed hypothesis is that featuring a celebrity in the advertisement of the product will lead to impulse purchases and increase in sales volume.

1.3.2 Methodology

The research employed a convenience sample and was descriptive in design. The sample consisted of individual who were aware of the brand used for the research and the television advertisement for the same. We took individual from a pre-defined area as samples for the survey. Based upon the purpose of the study a total of 150 samples were surveyed and usable data was recovered from 116 questionnaires filled by the respondents. The rest of the data was discarded due to incomplete form of it. Therefore, the effective sample size used for this research was 116. Firstly, they answered questions related to their demographics which are described below in Fig. 2.

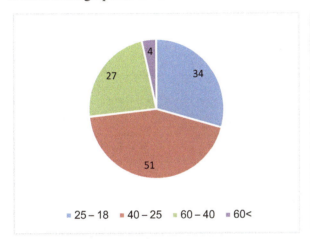

Age

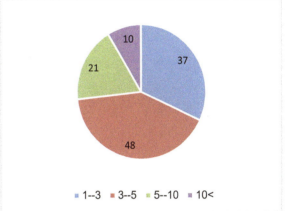

Income per annum (In million Indian Rupees)

Education

Fig. 2. Personal characteristics of the participants

At first the respondents' product involvement (Zaichkowsky, 1990) questions were asked followed by product knowledge (Smith & Park, 1992). Although, no previous hypotheses regarding these variables were present, it was decided to include them for controlling the external influences on the analysis.

Close ended questions related to affections towards the celebrity and purchase intentions and Likert Scale questions were asked to the respondents based on a 5-point Likert Scale. Firstly product involvement and product knowledge questions were asked followed by the affections generated towards the brand and celebrity resulting into impulse purchases. The personality and the image of brand and celebrity's image were then taken into consideration. The last set of questions were related to the Purchase Intention (PI) and the actual purchase of the product. The responses given by the samples were then analyzed and the following interpretations were made from the same.

4. Results

4.1 Hypothesis Testing

4.1.1. One Sample t-test

Based on the analysis we compute that the null hypothesis H_0 isn't true. This is further validated by the t- test carried out on the data. The null hypothesis was based on 2 variables 1. Brand Affections and 2. Preference of brand. Table 1 and Table 2 summarize the results of One-Sample t-test.

Table 1
One- Sample t-test Statistics

	N	Mean	Std. Deviation	Std. Error Mean
Brand Affections	116	1.2069	.40684	.03777
Preference	116	1.9828	.84424	.07839

Table 2
One-Sample t-test

Test Value = 1		Brand Affections	Preference
t		5.477	12.537
df		115	115
Sig. (2- tailed)		.000	.000
Mean Difference		.20690	.98276
95% Confidence Interval of the Difference	Lower	.1321	.8275
	Upper	.2817	1.1380

Here the test value was taken as 1, and from the One-sample Test we calculated the Significance (2-tailed) = 0.000. There is no method to calculate 1-tailed significance. Critical value tables were used to calculate 1- tailed significance for df = 115. From the results we can deduce that the Significance (1-tailed) is also less than test value. Hence we reject the null Hypothesis H_0.

4.1.2 Affections towards brand

A t- test failed to reveal a statistically reliable difference between the mean number of affections towards brand that the N = 116 has (M = 1.2069, s = 1.2069) and 1, t (115) = 5.477, p < 0.05, α = 0.05.

4.1.3 Brand preference

A t- test failed to reveal a statistically reliable difference between the mean number of brand preference that the N = 115 has (M = 1.9828, s = 1.9828) and 1, t (115) = 12.537, p < 0.05, α = 0.05.

Hence, based upon the above results, the significance < 0.05 in both the cases mentioned above. Hence the null hypothesis is discarded.

5. Discussions

50% of the respondents said that they purchased any brand of chocolate if their preferred brand isn't available. The sudden urge of consuming chocolate was so intense, that the brand preference was overlooked by the respondents. The notion of impulse purchases was reinforced by the fact that 67.24% of the respondents agreed to the statement that, they do not give much of a thought before purchasing chocolate bar. The preferred brand, if available, will be purchased else the respondents purchased any other brand of chocolate bar. The high market share of the chocolate bar was confirmed by the percentage of respondents purchasing it on impulses. Nearly 80% of the respondents preferred the brand of chocolate bar when they urged for a chocolate bar. Due to the affections towards the celebrity endorsing the brand, the respondents were inclined towards the affections generated by the ad towards the brand. 80% of the respondents agreed that, they had strong affections towards the celebrity in the advertisement. A contradicting view was given by the respondents when they were asked that, the affections towards the celebrity and his/ her influence in purchase decision. 80% of respondents did not agree to the statement. The respondents said that, the presence of celebrity did not influence their purchase decision, and the purchases were made purely on impulses. The respondents were insensitive towards the quantity, price and flavor of the chocolate bar. 54% of the respondents agreed that, they would purchase the chocolate bar of any quantity, price and flavor to satisfy their urge for the same. The ad effectiveness of the brand was mainly due to the affections towards the ad featuring the celebrity and due to the affections towards the brand. 64.65% of the respondents agreed that the ad was effective and helped them in finalizing the brand of chocolate bar.

From the analysis of the Likert Scale, few contradicting findings were deduced. The respondents showed strong affections towards the brand, but they overlooked the brand preference in case for strong urge for chocolate bar. Such erratic purchase pattern is usually seen in impulse purchases. Impulse buying behavior occurs when the consumers have strong persistent urge for a particular product, in this case chocolate bar. The linking of DMH to impulse purchases is justified by the purchases due to the ad effectiveness. But in this research, the celebrity endorsing the advertisements generated strong affections towards himself and the advertisement. But the purchase patterns were based on the urges of consumers. If the brand of chocolate bar wasn't available, the respondents purchased competitor's product. So it can be concluded that, the celebrity though creating strong affections, wasn't able to influence the purchase decision. The impulse buying behavior of the consumers was the prime reason for sales of the brand of chocolate.

6. Conclusion

The study was designed to evaluate the impulse purchases generated by the affections towards the product and the ad effectiveness of the same. The developments included the notions that the affections towards the brand and ad do result into purchase intention (PI) for the products/ brands. In the research it was found that affections towards the celebrity overshadowed the brand. The consumers would have purchased the product even if the ad did not feature any celebrity. The purchases were random in nature and were not fixed to the chocolate bar brand in the research. The consumers were ready to switch the brand in-case the preferred brand is not available. This was substantiated by the analysis of the survey. From all the above analysis it was found out that impulse buying behavior is not influenced by the celebrity, but the advertisements of such products are effective and lead to purchases.

References

Allen, C. T., Machleit, K. A., Kleine, S. S., & Notani, A. S. (2005). A place for emotion in attitude models. *Journal of Business Research*, *58*(4), 494-499.

Babin, B. J., Darden, W. R., & Griffin, M. (1994). Work and/or fun: measuring hedonic and utilitarian shopping value. *Journal of Consumer Research*, *20*(4), 644-656.

Batra, R., & Ahtola, O. T. (1991). Measuring the hedonic and utilitarian sources of consumer attitudes. *Marketing Letters*, *2*(2), 159-170.

Barratt, E. S. (1985). Impulsiveness subtraits: Arousal and information processing. *Motivation, Emotion, and Personality*, *5*, 137-146.

Bharadwaj, S. G., Varadarajan, P. R., & Fahy, J. (1993). Sustainable competitive advantage in service industries: a conceptual model and research propositions. *The Journal of Marketing*, 83-99.

Blaney, P. H. (1986). Affect and memory: a review. *Psychological Bulletin*, *99*(2), 229.

Brown, S. P., & Stayman, D. M. (1992). Antecedents and consequences of attitude toward the ad: A meta-analysis. *Journal of consumer research*, *19*(1), 34-51.

Burke, M. C., & Edell. J., (1989). The impact of feelings on ad-based affect and cognition. *Journal of Consumer Research*, *26*, 6-83.

Cobb, C. J., & Hoyer, W. D. (1986). Planned versus impulse purchase behavior. *Journal of retailing*.

Cohen, J.B., Areni, C. D., (1991). Affect and consumer behaviour, *Handbook of Consumer Behaviour*, A. Robertson y H. Kassarjian, Eds., Prentice Hall, Englewood Cliffs, NJ, 183- 240.

Fill, C. (2006). *Simply marketing communications*. Pearson Education.

Heider, F. (1946). Attitudes and cognitive organization. *The Journal of psychology*, *21*(1), 107-112.

Kamble, A. A. (2014). DMM Model in Celebrity: Brand Advertisements. *SCMS Journal of Indian Management*, *11*(4), 89.

Kempf, D. S., & Smith, R. E. (1998). Consumer processing of product trial and the influence of prior advertising: a structural modelling approach. *Journal of Marketing Research*, *35*(3), 325-338.

MacKenzie, S. B., Lutz, R. J., & Belch, G. E. (1986). The role of attitude toward the ad as a mediator of advertising effectiveness: A test of competing explanations. *Journal of Marketing Research*, *23*, 130-143.

Mano, H., & Oliver, R. L. (1993). Assessing the dimensionality and structure of the consumption experience: evaluation, feeling, and satisfaction. *Journal of Consumer Research*, *20*, 451-466.

Morris, J. D., Woo, C., Geason, J. A., & Kim, J. (2002). The power of affect: predicting intention. *Journal of Advertising Research*, *42*(3), 7- 17.

Meyers-Levy, J., & Malaviya, P. (1999). Consumers' processing of persuasive advertisements: An integrative framework of persuasion theories. *The Journal of Marketing*, 45-60.

Mitchell, A. A., & Jerry C. O. (1981). Are product attribute beliefs the only mediator of advertising effects on brand attitudes? *Journal of Marketing Research*, *18* (August), 318-31.

Park, C. W., & Young, S. M. (1984). *The effects of involvement and executional factors of a television commercial on brand attitude formation*. na.

Petty, R. E., & Cacioppo, J. T. (1981). *Attitudes and persuasion: classic and contemporary approaches*. Dubuque, IA: Wm C. Brown.

Petty, R. E., & Cacioppo, J. T. (1996). *Communication and persuasion: central and peripheral routes to attitude change*. Editorial Springer-Verlag, New York.

Piron, F. (1991). Defining impulse purchasing. *ACR North American Advances*.

Rook, D. W. (1987). The buying impulse. *Journal of consumer research*, *14*(2), 189-199.

Rook, D. W., & Fisher, R. J. (1995). Normative influences on impulsive buying behavior. *Journal of Consumer Research*, *22*(3), 305-313.

Rook, H., & Hock, A. (1983). Impulse Buying. *Advance in consumer Research*, 10, 562-567.

Sicilia, M., Ruiz, S., & Munuera, J. L. (2005). Effects of interactivity in a web site: The moderating effect of need for cognition. *Journal of Advertising*, *34*(3), 31-44.

Smith, D. C., & Park, C. W. (1992). The effects of brand extensions on market share and advertising efficiency. *Journal of Marketing Research*, *29*(3), 296-313.

Vakratsas, D., & Ambler, T. (1999). How advertising works: what do we really know?. *The Journal of Marketing*, 26-43.

Voss, K. E., Spangenberg, E. R., & Grohmann, B. (2003). Measuring the hedonic and utilitarian dimensions of consumer attitude. *Journal of Marking Research*, *40*, 310-320.

Weinberg, P., & Gottwald, W. (1982). Impulsive consumer buying as a result of emotions. *Journal of Business Research*, *10*(1), 43-57.

Zaichkowsky, J. L. (1990). Issues in Measuring Abstract-Constructs. *ACR North American Advances*.

The effect of corporate image on the formation of customer attraction

Reza Koohjani Gouji, Reza Taghvaei* and Hossein Soleimani

Department of Marketing, Malayer Branch, Islamic Azad University, Malayer, Iran

CHRONICLE	ABSTRACT
Keywords: Corporate Image Customer Attraction Irancell Telecommunications Services Company	This paper examines the relationship of corporate image with customer attraction in Irancell Telecommunications Services Company in city of Ahvaz, Iran. The study uses a sample of 384 randomly selected people who use the firm's services. Measuring tools for corporate image and customer attraction are an 18-item questionnaire of Rampersad (2001) [Rampersad, H. (2001). 75 painful questions about your customer satisfaction. *the TQM Magazine, 13*(5), 341-347.] and a 14-item questionnaire of Geib (2005) [Geib, M. (2005). Architecture for customer relationship management to attract and retain customers approaches in financial services, IEEE, *Proceedings of the 38th Hawaii International Conference on System Sciences*.], respectively. Results of regression analysis showed that there was a significant relationship between corporate image and attracting customers in Irancell firm. In addition, dimensions of corporate image including experience, character, competence, quality, differentiation, cost, technology, and culture and cognition increase customer attraction to the company. On the other hand, component of culture has the most effect on attracting customers in this firm.

1. Introduction

During the last ten years, researchers of public relations have focused on customer relationship management. Consequently, both experts and researchers of public relations have tried so much to find a key concept to prove the effectiveness of public relations on corporate levels. Therefore, in contemporary public relations researches, corporate image has been recognized as a central and essential concept to represent public relationship value in an organization (Gharibi et al., 2012). Corporate image helps organizations achieve credibility and popularity. Corporate image has had various meanings and interpretations for organizations and companies; therefore, there have been various definitions of corporate image (Bonenr, 2007). In service industry, corporate image is an invisible property of the organization that is the result of a common social judgment made by beneficiaries who are influenced by the ability of organization to meet the expectations and create value for stakeholders (Faircloth, 2005). In terms of economics, corporate image is a reflection of the past

---

* Corresponding author.
E-mail address: taghvaei_reza@yahoo.com (R. Taghvaei)

actions, which represent the company's actual attributes (Gregory, 1991). As it is mentioned, making a positive and influential corporate image is very important for organizations, so that they spent time, sources and efforts to advertise their goods or services to represent a positive image and reputation of themselves. Or, for example, they participate in charities and welfare affaires to look for a responsible organization in ideas of people, socially. Despite this fact, image of service organizations is of the areas that have been considered less (Chan-Olmsted, 2006). In addition, organizations have understood that in order to achieve their great purposes, they not only have to increase the image and the credibility of their organizations, but also this attempt must be aligned with attracting and maintaining the customers. Therefore, it must be confirmed that nowadays, markets are restricted and customers are scarce, so those organizations that look for new methods and ways to have leadership of market under their control will be successful. Leading market is one of the most important success factors for customer-oriented organizations and methods of attracting customers through improved corporate image to customers (Tahvildari, 2011).

Nowadays, in competitive condition of market, identifying factors that have long-term competitive privileges for the organization is very important. Of course, these factors are limited to tangible ones, but the provided services by the organization help to increase the value of organizations by making differentiation mode that leads to not only customer attraction and its faithfulness, but also, more importantly, increase of organization image in market. Additionally, organization's image is considered as one of the main elements of getting competitive advantage (Ranjbarian et al., 2011). Corporate image is a long-term investment and property to promote the ability of the planners, executives and employees in improving the delivery of effective services, according to the organization's service, in line with corporate goals (Venable et al., 2003). However, this depends on attempts and performance quality of staffs. Many communities, despite having rich natural resources, are not able to use them due to lack of qualified and competent human resource and pass the life by hardship. Other nations, despite the lack of natural resources, have welfare and comfort as a result of having trained and appropriate manpower and with firm strides, they track their progress over. This good manpower can act by his/her complete capability, if he/she is aware of the effect of his/her activity on image of the organization (Oh Mi, 2000). In service organizations, services are produced and consumed at the same time, therefore, service staffs are both providers of services and consumers of them. Also, their activities connect the organization to the customers and purpose of such activities is to attract and maintain customers through the realization of the promises that have been given (Berry, 1995). Therefore, examining effective factors on attracting and customer retention is essential and inevitable for non-profit organizations. Often, we have ignored the fundamental point that basically, not only must service provision be done for satisfaction of customer, but also it is suitable that all facilities and material and physical resources will be applied in order to provide complete customer satisfaction to attract and retain them (Tahvildari, 2011). Attracting and retaining customers is one of the primary concerns for companies providing mobile services. Technology development and growth in the number of mobile operators intrigue customers to use services of the other operators. Meanwhile, some of the subscribers tend to change their mobile operator or use one of them more than the other. As a result, income of operators will be changed. Therefore, attracting subscribers is very significant for mobile operators (Nazari, 2013). Increasing development of communication services, promotion of their quality and also attention to special services that help users in their daily activities cause neither of companies providing mobile services to be in secure margin. In such a climate, maintaining the available customers and increasing their numbers in a market that is very much competitive are hard jobs and increase costs of keeping the available customers and increasing their numbers. Therefore, despite the great importance of corporate image, its effect on development and success of telecommunication companies, intense competition between telecom companies in terms of customer acquisition and satisfaction and achieving their corporate goals, this subject has not been studied very much and it can be said that this subject has been somehow neglected. According to previous studies, a research vacancy for examining the relation between corporate images with customer attraction in Irancell communications Services Company seems urgent and profitable. Therefore, according to aforementioned explanations about corporate image and customer attraction in Irancell communications Services Company, here is the question: can corporate image be effective on attracting customers of Irancell communications Services Company in Ahvaz?

2. Literature Review

2.1. Concepts and Theories

2.1.1. Corporate Image

Corporate image, in the view of strategic management, is a collective vision and a collective image of the multiple beneficiaries of an organization or a company (Venable et al., 2003). Corporate image is a representation of past actions and perspectives of the future. Corporate image is one of the most important strategic and valuable properties that a company or an organization can have (Chan-Olmsted, 2006). It is, also, an evaluation of organization by beneficiaries during time (Oh Mi, 2000). Image of an organization means perceived confidence about the ability and the desire to constantly deliver what is promised and provides a great benefit for both customers and companies. In fact, purchasing a valid brand means that the efforts of merchants, due to extended probability of accepting the message, would be more affordable. As a result, sales of companies will increase following customer's referrals, and repeated purchase (Chan-Olmsted, 2006). In spite of increasing knowledge about the importance of credibility and image of organization as its specifics, a few studies have reviewed that how corporate image and credibility will affect customer's choice behavior. Understanding the combined mechanism of corporate credibility and image in formation of purchase tendency will be important and influential for advertisers and merchants, because it provides essential guide for development of brand positioning, through more appropriate advertising and brand-making strategies. Moreover, there is a restricted information about whether the available conditions in compound mechanism of credibility and corporate image are weaker or stronger or not in customer's decision-making among various groups of products (Martinson, 2007).

Components of corporate image: Despite numerous attempts to define the corporate image, a few researchers have tried to analyze principle and essence of the concept. Perhaps, Avenarius (1993) is one of the few people who has defined corporate image in accordance with its hidden components and elements. According to Lee (2004), corporate image is made of three components:

1: the rate of being known: that is requisite for each corporate image; it means that those organizations that are known can have effective roles.
2: fame: is a more active estimation and evaluation of society for which the base is history of organization or background of its performance.
3- (Brilliant and) special history and literature: by which each organization can be distinguished from its rival firms (that may have any equal fame)
There are five factors that have the ability and capability to affect customers' perceptions and interpretations of corporate reputation of service firms, including:
1: corporate identity, 2- fame, 3- form of servicing, 4- physical environment, 5 employees in contact (face to face) with customers.

2.1.2. Customer attraction

Customer attraction is a term to describe how to manage hyperactive communication with customers. Customer attraction is all the components within an organization that are intelligently associated with the customer. Customer management procedures connect all the components to each other with the support of operational roles and technical business. Due to the nature of business, attraction of customer can be complicated. Many of operations and daily activities of business must deal with customers; therefore, providing systems that can improve these tasks is vital for achieving success.

Customer attraction consists of business process, technology and required roles to manage customers in various steps of life cycles of organizations. It is beyond these departments and to a certain extent each separate corporate unit. A vendor using customer attraction in a corner of country does not need to access to all the information associated with the current position of selling of a customer in another corner of the country. However, they may need to access data related to customer or client's satisfaction to help to conclude a deal. The power to provide information at an accurate time is often the distinguishing key of a successful system (Cunningham, 2009).

Attracting customer means creating incentives to attract existing customers as well as the creation of a system for interacting with lost customers. Kotler (2984) believes losing profitable customers efficiently impacts on profitability of the organization. A group considers attraction of customers as strategy, some as a technology, some other as a process and some as information systems (Thompson, 2004). Here are a few of definitions of customer attraction:

"Attracting customer is a term for a collection of methodologies, processes, software packages and systems that help institutes and organizations in effective management and structured communication with customers" (Burnett, 1992). Attracting customers means creation and maintenance of a personalized relation with profitable customers through appropriate use of information technology and communications (Payne, 2000; Wilde et al., 2011). Attracting customers is a process consists of monitoring customer (e.g., collecting their suitable data), management and evaluation of the data, and finally creating a real advantage out of extracted information in the interaction with them (Hampe & Swatman, 2002). Attracting customer is a comprehensive strategy of business and marketing that integrates technology, processes and all business activities around customer (Feinberg & Romano, 2003).

2.1.2.1. Emergence fields of attracting customers

Patricia Siebold, an old fan of supporting systems and a fan of automatizing these systems, is one of the leaders in customer attraction. He has listed three following principles in his last book (Elahi & Heidari, 2012):

- Customers are under control
- Communication with customers is valuable and
- Customer's experience is an important topic

Siebold believes and strongly states that customers are under control. Referring to the revolution in the music industry, which led this industry to have a tendency toward customers, he states that power of customers and users, nowadays, is non-stoppable. Revolutions made by some companies such as Napster (provider of music or singing files) created a demand that could not be ignored in music industry. Today, these customers have made a completely new series of demands (such as recordable CDs, downloading mobile broadcast) that did not exist in the past.

Siebold believes the relationship between customer and provider must be at the top of the priority list of organization. Attracting customers requires costs and keeping these relations is even more costly. However, if these relationships are not kept, the cost of attracting customers or replacing new customers will be much more expensive. This capital is called customer. Changing customers to a valuable commodity must look as a clear duty to each person. But, even in the United States where services to customers are like high standards, many companies have faced with failure in this respect. Sometimes, the failures result from lack of attention, and sometimes they are due to lack of coordination in system of attracting customer. Comprehension of full experiences of customers is much more than making a good product or providing accurate information for people who are in relation with customers. However, experiences of customers, mentioned by Siebold in his book, are essential for success of an organization. Quality and services are able to change the brand by customers (Salarzehi & Amiri, 2011).

2.2.1.2. Principles of attracting customers

Applicable processes and programs for attracting customers are as the following according to basic principles:

Targeting individual customers: one the principles of attracting customers is the fact that customers have numerous choices and each client needs his/her own services. Attracting customers treats each customer individually because of being based on the philosophy of customization and personalization. Customization means that the content and services offered to the customer have to be designed according to their preferences and behaviors. This action makes comfort for customers and increased costs to the seller.

Attracting and retaining customer's loyalty through personal contact: when customization happens, organizations have to maintain this relationship. Continuous contacts with customer- especially when the contacts are designed to satisfy preferences- can lead to loyalty (Hamidizadeh et al., 2009). Customer's choice based on the concept of customer's lifetime value: this principle is considered that various customers have different values for the organization; therefore the most profitable customers must be attracted and maintained. Through differentiation, an organization can allocate its limited resources for better returns. To sum up, customization of products, customer loyalty and their selection based on the concept of lifetime value are the basic principles of customer relationship management (Wilde et al., 2011).

2.2. Research Background

Bagheri and Erfanifar (2010) reviewed the design of model of effective components on corporate image of University of Imam Sadeq (AS). Components such as identity and Culture of University, graduates, selectivity and other arrival factors, reputation and particular history, features and functionality of different parts, the physical environment and symbols, staff in contact with external audiences and media coverage of news and events have been identified as the most important effective factors on the image of this university.

Farahmand Sabet (2011) examined the relationship between corporate reputations with customers' behavioral intentions in the Novin Economy Bank. The results of the study indicated that first; the model had a good fitness. Second, corporate image and customer's behavioral intentions had a significant relation. Third, corporate image has relation with customer's behavioral intentions through the components of Customer's recognition, customer's commitment and customer's confidence. Shams Zaharias (2011) examined and determined the effective features of attraction and survival of customers. The findings showed that two variables of the use of the service and speed of service delivery had positive effects on the probability of attracting customers. The amount of customer's satisfaction cost of change and amount of service use have positive effect of the probability of customer's loyalty.

Haghighi et al. (2012) reviewed the effect of relational marketing tactics on attraction and loyalty of customers from the perspective of customers of Irancell Company. Data analysis showed that the company had been successful in implementing some of the tactics and at the significance level of 90 percent had been able to have the customers' satisfaction and trust; as a result, it could retain them and changed them into loyal customers.

Khajeh (2013) studied perspective of social identity of brand and its effect on attracting customers and developing loyalty to the brand in Irancell Company in Golestan province. The results were indicative of the fact that the identity of the brand, indirectly and through the variables of comprehended value, satisfaction and confidence, has positive effect on attracting customers and loyalty to the brand. In addition, this study concluded that when perspective of social identity of brand is compounded with other available perspectives can be useful it is possible to predict the mechanisms of loyalty to the brand.

Kandy (2007) examined the elements affecting on corporate image. The results indicated that two main elements show the image of the organization including emotional and functional elements. Functional element is associated with tangible features, which could be easily measured and emotional element is related to psychological aspects which are identified by emotions and attitudes about organization. These emotions are created because of various experiences with organization and processing the information on the features that are the functional indexes of the image.

Keropyan and Lafuente (2014) studied the programs affecting on attracting and retaining customers in the telecom market. The results of study were indicative of the importance of telecommunication (mobile) market in which tendency of customers to change the company is very high. Therefore, mobile telecommunication companies must provide special programs and services for their customers to satisfy them and prepare special services for each group of customers to increase number of attracted customers. Izogo (2015) examined the factors affecting on attracting and retaining customers in telecommunication market. In this study, 138 users of telecommunication services were used to gather data. The results showed that attracting and retaining customers was a process-based structure which starts from Service Assurance by the Organization and finally, leads to attracting and retaining customers.

2.3. Conceptual model of research

Conceptual model of study has been shown in Fig. 1:

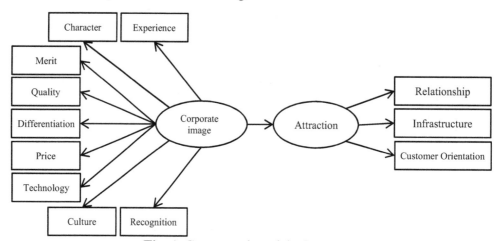

Fig. 1. Conceptual model of research

2.4. Research hypotheses

2.4.1. Main hypothesis

There is a significant relationship between corporate image and attraction of customers in Irancell Telecommunications Services Company in Ahvaz, Iran.

2.4.2. Secondary hypotheses

1- There is a significant relationship between experiences and attraction of customer in Irancell Telecommunications Services Company in Ahvaz, Iran.
2- There is a significant relationship between character and attraction of customer in Irancell Telecommunications Services Company in Ahvaz, Iran.
3- There is a significant relationship between merit and attraction of customer in Irancell Telecommunications Services Company in Ahvaz, Iran.
4- There is a significant relationship between quality and attraction of customer in Irancell Telecommunications Services Company in Ahvaz, Iran.
5- There is a significant relationship between differentiation and attraction of customer in Irancell Telecommunications Services Company in Ahvaz, Iran.
6- There is a significant relationship between price and attraction of customer in Irancell Telecommunications Services Company in Ahvaz, Iran.
7- There is a significant relationship between technology and attraction of customer in Irancell Telecommunications Services Company in Ahvaz, Iran.
8- There is a significant relationship between culture and attraction of customer in Irancell Telecommunications Services Company in Ahvaz, Iran.
9- There is a significant relationship between recognition and attraction of customer in Irancell Telecommunications Services Company in Ahvaz, Iran.

3. Methodology

The present study is applied respective to purpose; descriptive correlational regarding the method; and a quantitative study due to its method to gather data. Population of study includes entire customers of Irancell Telecommunications Services Company in Ahvaz, Iran. Because of lack of availability of all the customers, the population is considered unlimited. The sample was estimated to be 384 using sampling has been random sampling technique.

In the current study, data was gathered by questionnaire and field method. Measurement tool for corporate image is Rampersad (2001) corporate image questionnaire that has 18 fine-option questions. It is scored as 1= very little, 2= little, 3= fair, 4= high, 5= very high. The questionnaire has nine dimensions of "Experience, character, competence, quality, differentiation, cost, technology, culture and cognition" that each of them are marked with two questions. Validity and reliability of this questionnaire in other study (2001) were 0.81 and 0.89, respectively. Tool to measure attraction of customer is the 14- item questionnaire of Geib (2005). This questionnaire has three dimensions of: expanding customer relationships, infrastructure and customer orientation. Scoring in this questionnaire is as option 1 = very little, 2 = little, 3 = fair, 4= high, 5= very high. On the other hand, validity and reliability of the questionnaire has been 0.89 and 0.83, respectively. Due to being standard, and being applied in various researches as well as idea of experts, the validity of questionnaire is accepted. In addition, using Cronbach's Alpha on 30 people of sample, reliability for the questionnaires is measured in Table 1

Table 1
Cronbach's Alpha coefficients

Variables	Cronbach's Alpha coefficient	Variables	Cronbach's Alpha coefficient
Corporate image	0.81	Price	0.8
Attraction	0.78	Technology	0.75
Experiences	0.74	Culture	0.74
Character	0.72	Recognition	0.76
Merit	0.71	Relationship	0.75
Quality	0.73	Infrastructure	0.81
Differentiation	0.74	Customer orientation	0.77

The results of Table 1 show that Cronbach's alpha of the questionnaires and their dimensions are more than 0.7. Therefore, the questionnaires have acceptable reliability and therefore, they have the capability of generalizability in the population under study.

In inferential statistics and to estimate the results of assumptions, Kolmogorov-Smirnov (KS) Normal distribution of data and to study the normal distribution of data, Pearson correlation was used. The relationship between the two variables with small scale and multiple regression to predict the criterion variable based on the predictor variables was analyzed by SPSS software version 22.

4. Findings

4.1. Normality of variables

First, prior to examining the hypotheses of study, it is essential to evaluate normality of variables by Kolmogorov-Smirnov (KS) test. Therefore, Table 2 examines the normality of variables

Table 2
Variables normality

variables	Z Statistics	Level of significance	variables	Z Statistics	Level of significance
Corporate image	0.884	0.215	Differentiation	1.131	0.101
Attraction	0.316	0.627	Price	0.719	0.319
Experiences	0.614	0.423	Technology	1.136	0.099
Character	1.03	0.119	Culture	0.935	0.188
Merit	0.436	0.557	Recognition	0.812	0.27
Quality	1.153	0.092			

According to the results of Table 2, it can be concluded that the significance levels of all the variables is more than 0.05. Therefore, the hypothesis of H_0 is rejected and data of the above variables is normal. So, normality of the mentioned variables justifies using parametric tests to deduct the hypotheses of study.

4.2. A review of hypotheses of study

To examine the bilateral relation between variables of each hypothesis, correlation test is used. The results are stated in Table 3.

Table 3
Results of bilateral relation between hypotheses of study

Hypothesis	Independent variable	Dependent variable	Correlational coefficient	Level of significance	Result
Main	Corporate image	Attraction	0.507	0.001	H_0 Rejected
1	Experiences	Attraction	0.348	0.001	H_0 Rejected
2	Character	Attraction	0.353	0.001	H_0 Rejected
3	Merit	Attraction	0.323	0.001	H_0 Rejected
4	Quality	Attraction	0.257	0.001	H_0 Rejected
5	Differentiation	Attraction	0.267	0.001	H_0 Rejected
6	Price	Attraction	0.317	0.001	H_0 Rejected
7	Technology	Attraction	0.288	0.001	H_0 Rejected
8	Culture	Attraction	0.346	0.001	H_0 Rejected
9	Recognition	Attraction	0.315	0.001	H_0 Rejected

About all the variables, the level of significance attained from Pearson test is less than 0.01 which shows there was a significant relationship between two variables with 99% level of confidence. In addition, positive correlation coefficient indicates that the more independent variable is, the more the amount of customer's attraction is. Therefore, it can be claimed that the null hypothesis is rejected and the researcher's hypothesis can be replaced as a new hypothesis.

4.3. Prioritizing the influence of corporate reputation on customer attraction

To confirm prioritizing the influence of corporate reputation on customer attraction, Multiple Regression analysis in an Enter method is applied. To conduct this test, first, presupposition of regression analysis must be performed in order to make the results of regression analysis deductible.

1. Presuppositions of correlation between the criterion variable and independent variables (this presupposition is examined and confirmed in the first to ninth secondary hypotheses).
2. Presupposition of explanation of model: in this presupposition, it must be considered that whether independent variables have the ability to explain (the mean effect of independent variables on criterion variable) the criterion variable.
3. Presupposition of a review of linear relation between independent variables and criterion variables in which ANOVA test is applied.

4.3.1. Model explanation

Table 4 explains the amount of clarification of regression model in prioritizing the effects of corporate image dimensions.

Table 4
Regression model explanation

R	R square	Adjusted square of R	Durbin Watson
0.544	0.296	0.278	1.537

According to the results of Table 4, it is clearly seen that adjusted R-square is equal to 0.278, which means about 28% of changes in the variable of customer attraction is described by changes in dimensions of corporate image. In addition, as the amount of Durbin-Watson is between 1.5 and 2.5 so the supposition of independence between error terms is accepted.

4.3.2. Linear relation

Table 5 reviews linear relationship between criterion variable with predictor by ANOVA test.

Table 5
Linear relation between criterion and predictor variables

Model	Sum of squares	Freedom degree	Mean of squares	Statistic F	Level of significance
Regression	36.926	9	4.103	17.507	0.001
The remaining	87.651	374	0.234	-	-
Sum	124.577	383	-	-	-

4.3.3. Model Function

Since all three conditions for using multivariate regression were taken into consideration, a function must be provided to show the amount of prediction of the predictor variable in direction of criterion variable. Therefore, Table 6 represents regression coefficients. According to the results of Table 6, it can be mentioned that the level of significance of test is a fixed amount less than 0.05%. Therefore, the supposition of alpha being equal to zero is rejected and the fixed amount effects on criterion variable, so that it can participate in non-standard coefficients equation. In addition, in significance level of test, coefficient levels of dimensions of experience, character, price, culture and cognition are less than 0.05, therefore, they are suitable to enter to standard coefficient equation or in the other words, they can affect on criterion variable. While significance levels of competence, quality, differentiation and technology are higher than 0.05 and cannot be used in the equation. According to the above explanation, standard and non-standard coefficients function is as following:

According to above function, it can be concluded that due to the external factors, the dimensions of experience, personality, prices, culture and cognition can predict the rate of customer attraction. While the dimensions of competence, quality, differentiation and technology are not able to predict variable of attracting customers. Also, according to beta coefficient in the culture, it can be stated that culture has the greatest impact on customer attraction in Irancell Telecommunications Services Company in Ahvaz and then the dimensions of price, experience, knowledge and character are after culture.

Table 6
Regression coefficients

	Non-standard coefficients		Standard coefficient	statistic	Level of significance
	B	The standard error	Beta	t	
Constant	1.025	0.142	-	7.213	0.001
Experiences	0.077	0.032	0.128	2.39	0.017
Character	0.073	0.036	0.114	2.053	0.041
Merit	0.067	0.034	0.103	1.948	0.052
Quality	0.015	0.031	0.025	0.488	0.626
Differentiation	0.01	0.032	0.017	0.328	0.743
Price	0.116	0.031	0.176	3.785	0.001
Technology	0.001	0.031	0.00	0.025	0.98
Culture	0.148	0.033	0.209	4.509	0.001
Recognition	0.077	0.031	0.125	2.507	0.013

5. Conclusion and recommendations

5.1. Discussion and conclusion

In this study, the relationship between organizational image with customer attraction in Irancell Telecommunications Services Company was studied. The results showed that there was a positive and significant relationship between corporate image and customer attraction. In addition, according to comparison between the results of the present study and other conducted studies, it can be mentioned that there is an alignment between results of this study and results of studies of Alizadeh Zavarom et al. (2011), Ranjbarian (2011), Farahmand Sabet (2011), Shams Zahraei (2011), Ahmadzadeh (2011), Daneshfar (2012), Haghighi et al. (2012), Hassanzadeh Khatir (2014) and Keropyan and Gil-Lafuente (2014).

By the analogy of the main hypothesis of study with the results of previous studies, it can be concluded that corporate image will cause customer attraction including existence of incentives to attract potential customers, customer interaction system, bilateral interaction with the customer, a long-term relationship with the customer, a formal system for customer identification, senior managers' support of related activities to customer, remembering the names of customers by company members, the importance of the problem of customers for the company, attention to the changing needs and demands of customers, timely and accurate customer service, respond to the enterprise customer feedback and etc. to increase. In fact, better image the organization has among people, the more the level of confidence and trust of customers will be and makes the customers attracted to the services of company. Moreover, suitable image of organization makes the organization always be thinking about attracting customers and therefore, conducts some activities in this respect such as creating systems and accurate planning to pave the way of attracting customer by promoting the level of his satisfaction. Attracting customers can take place through channels like creating constant and effective relations with customers, managing relations with them, considering infrastructures in the organization for permanent relation of company with customers and also conducting tasks of company around the needs and demands of customers under the title of "customer- orientation".

By the analogy of the first secondary hypothesis of study with the results of previous research, it can be concluded that experience including the suitability of the company's employees work history, desirability of employment history of company, utilization of their experiences during responsiveness customer, customer greater use of the experience and knowledge of employees, etc. can increase attraction of customer. Because experience and learning from the previous experiences can be considered as an invisible but beneficial capital that makes the customer relies on the rich history of the company and makes use of the knowledge of company to meet his needs. On the other hand, experience of the company can create a good image and reputation for company that besides promoting level of knowledge of staffs can be considered as a credit making peace and comfort for customers while using the services.

By the analogy of the second secondary hypothesis of study with the results of previous research, it can be concluded that some characters including the appropriateness of public relations with customers, employees being patient toward customer's needs, persistence of staff to dealing with unforeseen issues, ability to solve conflicts among employees, etc. can increase attracting customers. Because the better and the longer relationship the company can make with its customers, the more constant the customers think about the company and the more attracted he/she will be. On the other hand, appropriate characteristics of the staffs of company can increase the level of dependence of customer to the company, because the more aligned behaviors of customers with social and cultural norms, the more relaxed the customer is. As a result the ground for his/her attraction will be provided. In the other word, characteristics associated with consistency of the staffs and their high abilities in unpredictable situations can attract customer's confidence in the company.

By the analogy of the third secondary hypothesis of study with the results of previous studies, it can be concluded that competence including high levels of professional skills and special abilities of employees, companies using modern methods, increasing knowledge and awareness of staffs through learning, high levels of employee's empowerment when dealing with issues and problems, their problem solving ability, etc. can grow customer's attraction. Because competence and ability of staffs regarding organizational issues cause the customer to rely on the company more in order to meet his/her needs, therefore, the level of his/her satisfaction and loyalty will increase. Specialized skills of staffs promise to provide better services to the customer by the company and so it will be able to attract and retain customers.

By the analogy of the forth secondary hypothesis of study with the results of previous studies, it can be concluded that quality including services provided to customers being up-to-date, optimized data services, high quality and quantity of provided services, the customer service standards being in line with his/her needs, etc. can enhance customer's attraction, because quality of services in the company is extracted from sufficient knowledge and experience in the form of importance of customers' needs for the company. When customer feels the provided services have a good quality, he/she will understand knowledge and awareness of the company and importance of his/her interests for the company, as a result, he/she will be more attracted to the services. Quality can lead to satisfaction of customer and satisfied customer always tries to get his/her previous experiences from the company and therefore, will be attracted to the services of the organization.

By the analogy of the fifth secondary hypothesis of study with the results of previous research, it can be concluded that differentiation including provision of differentiated services to customers from different social classes, provision of more and better services for customers, differentiation of customer service rather than the other competitors, difference in providing services for customers regarding quality and quantity in comparison with other competitors, etc. can increase customers' attraction; because differentiation can make a feeling for the customer that the company has acted better and more different than the others and so it can make a more desirable and better experience for the customer. Differentiation causes customer to have a modern and new service that has not earned any service like that in other companies. Therefore, customer will be attracted to the company for getting such a feeling. Differentiation makes the services to be better, in the other word, more qualified and cheaper for customer, so that customer always keeps this difference in his/her mind and will be loyal to the company, and finally will be attracted to the company.

By the analogy of the sixth secondary hypothesis of study with the results of previous research, it can be concluded that price including proportionality between payments of customer and received services, low cost of services compared to other competitors, reasonable prices for services of company, etc. can enhance customer's attraction; because the more provided services for customer and payments of customer have balance and alignment, the better customer can handle costs of received services and so will be attracted to the company. Customer must believe that costs that he/she pays for the received services will both meet his/her needs and costs are balanced with the received services. In this case, the customer can have tendency toward the company. Therefore, price plays in important role in this respect. An extremely high cost or an excessively low cost can make customer not to have a good idea about the received services and so he/she may decide to abandon the company and its services.

By the analogy of the seventh secondary hypothesis of study with the results of previous studies, it can be concluded that implementation of some technology features including using modern technologies in the company, appropriateness of processes of relation with customer, having modern and updated facilities and equipment in the company, etc. can increase customer attraction; because updated equipment and modern facilities in the company can be retrieved from high level of technology in the company and so it can cause processes within or outside the organization to be performed faster and with a better quality. Finally, useful effects will be provided for customer. Modern technology can minimize humans' errors and makes the services to be prepared for customers with the best accuracy and in the shortest time. Consequently, it can be transfer a sense of comfort and ease to the customer and intrigue him to use the services more.

By the analogy of the eighth secondary hypothesis of study with the results of previous studies, it can be concluded that culture including the constructive atmosphere in the company, an atmosphere of intimacy between employees and customers, respecting the rights of clients in the enterprise, the pursuit of customer problems to solve them by employees of the company, understanding the customer's demands by employees, etc. can increase attracting customers; because organizational culture makes the level of moral principles and professional behavior of staff to increase and the staffs allocate themselves to address the needs and problems of customers. High culture in company promises an effective and dynamic atmosphere in which customer feel calm and peace of mind and will be sure that staffs with high organizational culture are always trying to solve his/her problem, therefore, the customer will be attracted to the company.

By the analogy of the ninth secondary hypothesis of study with the results of previous studies, it can be concluded that cognition including staffs' high understanding of the client's actual needs, careful planning in order to meet customer needs, provision of useful information to customers, diversity in services, awareness of employees of their job status, etc. can improve customer attraction; because staffs' cognition gives a feeling to customer that company pays enough and essential attention to his/her needs and demands and issues of customers are considered very important to the company. Therefore, customer does not feel being alone and will be attracted to the company more than before. In the other word, staffs' accurate cognition of customer's needs cause the services to be compatible with customer's demands and so customer can be highly satisfied and it provides the ground for attracting customer to the company.

5.2. Recommendations

According to the main hypothesis of research and relationship between corporate reputation with attracting customer, it is recommended to all managers of Irancell Telecommunications Services Company in Ahvaz that for promoting the level of working character of staffs, they must increase the extent of their knowledge in the field of corporate reputation including special attention to the background of employees, increasing employee personality, organizational learning, paying attention to better quality services, comparing their services with other competitors, balanced price, taking advantage of the best equipment, raising the level of organizational constructive climate to involve employees in the organization's activities in order to know them better.

According to the first secondary hypothesis regarding research and experience with customers, it is recommended to all managers of Irancell Telecommunications Services Company in Ahvaz to increase the rate of attracting customer by hiring employees with a history of relevant work experience and utilization of employees during organizational decisions.

According to the second secondary hypothesis and the relationship of personality with attracting customers, it is recommended to all managers in Ahvaz Irancell Telecommunications Services Company to increase rate of customer attraction by creating good public relations with the customer and managing conflict in organizations.

According to the third secondary hypothesis and the relationship of competence with attracting customers, it is recommended to all managers in Ahvaz Irancell Telecommunications Services Company to increase rate of customer attraction by raising the level of specialized skills and abilities of staff and using modern methods.

According to the forth secondary hypothesis and the relationship of quality with attracting customers, it is recommended to all managers in Ahvaz Irancell Telecommunications Services Company to increase rate of customer attraction by updating provided services to customers and raising quality and quantity levels of provided services.

According to the fifth secondary hypothesis and the relationship of differentiation with attracting customers, it is recommended to all managers in Ahvaz Irancell Telecommunications Services Company to increase rate of customer attraction by providing more and more convenient services to customers and being different in the delivery of services to customers rather than other competitors.

According to the sixth secondary hypothesis and the relationship of price with attracting customers, it is recommended to all managers in Ahvaz Irancell Telecommunications Services Company to increase rate of customer attraction by the fitness between customer's payments and incoming services and reasonable prices for services companies.

According to the seventh secondary hypothesis and the relationship of technology with attracting customers, it is recommended to all managers in Ahvaz Irancell Telecommunications Services Company to increase rate of customer attraction by taking advantage of new technologies in the enterprise and use of new and up to date equipment and facilities in company.

According to the eighth secondary hypothesis and the relationship of culture with attracting customers, it is recommended to all managers in Ahvaz Irancell Telecommunications Services Company to increase rate of customer attraction by making a constructive atmosphere in the company and respecting the rights of customers and employees in the company.

According to the ninth secondary hypothesis and the relationship of cognition with attracting customers, it is recommended to all managers in Ahvaz Irancell Telecommunications Services Company to increase rate of customer attraction by careful planning in order to satisfy customer needs and raise the awareness of employees through in-service training,

References

Ahmadzadeh, S. (2011). The relationship between service quality, perceived value, customer satisfaction and loyalty in terms of subscribers MTN (Case Study: West Azerbaijan province). Master's thesis, Semnan: Semnan University.

Alizadeh Zavarem, A., Fallah, M. & Eslami, Gh. (2011). Injection study in brand image. *Management Journal, 5*(2), 88-65.

Avenarius, H. (1993). Introduction: Image and public relations practice. *Journal of public relations research, 5*(2), 65-70.

Bagheri, M.H. & Erfanifar, A. (2010). Factors affecting corporate image design of Imam Sadeq. *Journal of Management, 4*(2), 77-43.

Berry, L. L. (1995). Relationship marketing of services—growing interest, emerging perspectives. *Journal of the Academy of Marketing Science, 23*(4), 236-245.

Bonenr, C. (2007). Image is all: Deregulation, restructuring and reputation in the natural gas industry, American Gas.

Burnett, K. (1992). *Strategic Customer Alliances: How to win, manage, and develop key account business in the 1990s.* London, Pitman.

Chan-Olmsted, S. M. (2006). *Competitive strategy for media firms: Strategic and brand management in changing media markets.* Routledge.

Compdrsad, L. (2001). Corporate reputation: our role in sustaining and building a valuable asset. *Journal of Advertising Research, 45*(3), 5–29.

Cunningham, J. M. (2009). *Customer Relationship management: Wiley company.* Oxford United Kingdom. Available at: www.capstoneideas.com.

Daneshfar, Z. (2012). Celebrity organizational citizenship behavior from the perspective of the customer relationship with clients in Iran Insurance Company. *Master's Thesis, School of Accounting and Management, Tehran Allameh Tabatabai University.*

Elahi, Sh. & Heidari, B. (2012). Customer relation management. 3rd ed., Tehran: business publishing company (In Persian).

Izogo, E. E. (2015). Determinants of attitudinal loyalty in Nigerian telecom service sector: Does commitment play a mediating role?. *Journal of Retailing and Consumer Services, 23*, 107-117.

Faircloth, J. B. (2005). Factors influencing nonprofit resource provider support decisions: applying the brand equity concept to nonprofits. *Journal of Marketing Theory and Practice, 13*(3), 1-15.

Farahmand Sabet, M. (2011). The relationship between organizational reputation with customers' behavioral intentions in the New Economy Bank. *Master's Thesis, School of Accounting and Management, Tehran Allameh Tabatabai University.*

Feinberg, J., & Romano, C. (2003). Electronic customer relationship management revising the general principles of usability and resistance–an integrative implementation framework. *Business Process Management Journal, 9*(5), 340-359.

Fjermestad, J., & Romano Jr, N. C. (2003). Electronic customer relationship management: Revisiting the general principles of usability and resistance-an integrative implementation framework. *Business Process Management Journal, 9*(5), 572-591.

Geib, M. (2005). Architecture for Customer Relationship Management to Attract and Retain Customers Approaches in Financial Services, IEEE (*Proceedings of the 38th Hawaii International Conference on System Sciences*).

Gharibi, M.; Koushki, A.R; Taleghani, G.R. & Nargesian, A. (2012). The relationship between corporate image with that of Iran Khodro job. *Journal of Organizational Culture Management, 10*(1), 114-97.

Gray P., & Byun, J. (2010). Customer Relationship Management, University of California, Available at: www.crito.uci.edu.

Gregory, J. (1991). *Marketing Corporate Image. Chicago.* NTC Business Books.

Haghighi, M., Hosseini, S.H., Asgharieh Ahari, H., Arian, A., & Darikandeh, A. (2012). The effect of relationship marketing tactics to attract customers, customer loyalty from the perspective of Irancell. *Journal of Modern Marketing research, 2*(4), 62-45.

Hamidizadeh, M.R.; Hajikarimi, A.A. & Babaie Zagliki, M.A. (2009). Define and design the process model of customer loyalty (Case Study: private banks). *Exploration Journal of Business Management, 1* (2), 170-133.

Hampe, J. F., & Swatman, P. (2002). *Customer Relationship Management.* Institute Fur Wirschfs informatics.

Hassanzadeh Khatir, F. (2014). Telecommunications network service quality evaluation and satisfaction and attract citizens' case study: MTN Babylon area. *Master's thesis, Faculty of Literature and Human Sciences, Tehran, Islamic Azad University, Tehran.*

Kennedy, S. H. (1977). Nurturing corporate images. *European Journal of marketing, 11*(3), 119-164.

Keropyan, A., & Gil-Lafuente, A. M. (2012). Customer loyalty programs to sustain consumer fidelity in mobile telecommunication market. *Expert Systems with Applications, 39*(12), 11269-11275.

Khajeh, I. (2014). Check their social identity and their effect on attracting customers and the development of brand loyalty (case? Christmas in Golestan province). *Master's thesis, Faculty of Management and Accounting, Tehran Payam Noor University of Tehran.*

Khanlari, A. (2006). A Conceptual Model for Measuring the Maturity of customer relationship management in IT organizations. *Master's thesis, Tehran: Tehran University.*

Kotler, P. (2003). *Marketing Management.* 11th Edition. New Jersey; prentice Hall, 52.

Kotler, P., & Anderson, A. R. (1987). *Strategic Marketing foe Nonprofit Organizations* (3rd). Englewood Cliffs. NJ: prentice –Hall.

Lee, B. K. (2004). Corporate image examined in a Chinese-based context: A study of a young educated public in Hong Kong. *Journal of Public Relations Research, 16*(1), 1-34.

Lee, J. S., & Back, K. J. (2010). Reexamination of attendee-based brand equity. *Tourism Management, 31*(3), 395-401.

Martinsons, M. G. (2008). Relationship-based e-commerce: theory and evidence from China. *Information Systems Journal, 18*(4), 331-356.

Nazari, P. (2013). The effect of relationship quality and customer loyalty among subscribers of MTN in Mashhad barriers to change. *Master's thesis, Faculty of Economic and Administrative Affairs Management Group. Razavi Khorasan University of Mashhad.*

Oh Mi, Y. (2000). South Korean attitudes toward foreign Subsidiaries of Multinational Corporations (MNCS): The halfpence of corporate image and country of origin image and the presence of Halo effect. *Southern Illinois University.*

Payne, A. (2000). Customer Relationship Management. Paper from the inaugural meeting of the London based customer relationship foundation. Available at; www.crm-forum.com.

Rampersad, H. (2001). 75 painful questions about your customer satisfaction. *the TQM Magazine, 13*(5), 341-347.

Ranjbarian, B.; Khajeh, E. & Sadeghian, M. (2011). The role of corporate reputation on customer loyalty: A Case Study of four and five star hotels. *Tehran: Fourth International Conference of Marketing Management.*

Salarzehi, H. & Amir, Y. (2011). Factors affecting the deployment process of customer relationship management in private banks. *General Management Research, 4*(12), 144-131.

Shams Zahraei, M. (2011). Determine the characteristics affecting the uptake and survival of bank customers in the Sinai with analytical CRM approach using data mining techniques. *Master's Thesis, School of Management, Tehran, Islamic Azad University, Tehran.*

Tahvildari, M. (2011). Analysis of factors affecting customers in export development bank of Iran. *Banking and Economics,* 45-46.

Thompson, B. (2004). *What is CRM?.* Available at: www.Custhelp.com.

Venable, B, T, G., Rose, M., & Gilbert, W. (2003). Measuring the brand personality of nonprofit organizations. *Advance in Consumer Research, 30*(1), 77-89.

Investigating the impact of consumer values and advocacy behavior on buying decision satisfaction: A study through gender lens

Raja Ahmed Jamil[a]*, Syed Rameez ul Hassan[a], Asdaq Farid[b] and Naveed Ahmad[c]

[a]*Department of Management Sciences, University of Haripur, Pakistan*
[b]*College of Business Administration, Chonnam National University, South Korea*
[c]*COMSATS Institute of Information Technology, Abbottabad, Pakistan*

CHRONICLE	ABSTRACT
Keywords: Cultural values Emotional values Word of mouth Buying decision satisfaction Gender Millennial	Consumer's values, Cultural values, Emotional Values and Word of mouth expressiveness, are good predictors for their buying decision satisfaction. In current study sample of 500 was taken to assess the consumer's buying decision satisfaction in relation to the importance of their values associated with those decisions. This study also reveals how gender influences buying decision satisfaction. Consumer values have a positive and significant impact on buying decision satisfaction. While evaluation on the basis of gender and females have more emotional and word of mouth linkages than males, on the contrary to this, males are more concerned with cultural values, and are less expressive and have a tendency to suppress their emotions while making buying decisions.

1. Introduction

On the basis of different regional and religious distributions, every society has unique cultural norms and traditions that transform consumer preferences and thus influence buying behavior accordingly. Collectivists are more concerned about others in their decisions, while their social desirability is higher than individualists (Hui, 1988). Therefore in a collectivist society, people are more concerned with each other and care more about their emotional values attached to their families and their society for maximum satisfaction in their decision makings. Emotions and social values have strong influences in collectivist societies, thus having a positive relation with purchasing behavior and a higher satisfaction level in comparison to individualistic cultures (Xiao & Kim, 2009). Now, in collective cultures there are several pressures that are exerted by family, fellows, society, ideologies and other social norms on buying choices which are essence of decision satisfaction. With other consumption values, emotional

* Corresponding author.
E-mail address: raja.ahmed@uoh.edu.pk (R. A. Jamil)

and social values are the causes of consumer preferences (Sheth et al., 1991). The immediate family is the first social circle, while making any purchase decision is made with priority given to their family members, as well as social acceptance, for maximum approval and intrinsic satisfaction regarding buying decisions. Along with economic utility, other pleasures and intangible values (Transactional Utility Theory) are strongly supported in collectivist societies. (McNeill et al., 2014). Therefore, emotional attachment apart from utilitarian benefits is also much more important in buying decisions in order to tie the families and their approvals in society. A higher level of care is given in collectivist societies and their ties to their families (Pyke & Bengtson, 1996).

Purchase behavior is influenced by external factors such as cultural forces, economic forces and personal forces such as beliefs, attitudes, etc. (Grant & Stephen, 2006). Cultural values significantly affect behavior (Lam et al., 2009). Consumer behavior is strongly connected with one's culture; this separation of culture from consumer behavior is impossible (Lukosius, 2004). The decision making process is an important concern in consumer behavior and it is affected by gender, in addition to the gender composition within the nuclear family when making any buying decisions (Lee & Collins, 2000). Male dominancy was found in positive relation with cultural belongingness, while interaction also exists according to one's marital role in the process of decision making regarding purchase (Webster, 1994). Gender roles and cultural values observed in several studies have shown a strong influence on buying decisions (Bashir et al., 2013; Solka et al., 2011; Sun & Merritt, 2004; Mahmood, 2002; Lee & Robbins, 2000). A review of eighty six studies supports gender concern showing that males are effective in performing masculine roles and females in performing feminine roles (Eagly et al., 1995). In collectivist societies likes Pakistan where male dominancy rules, but a slight shift has been observed, and feminine involvement in the buying decision process has increased over the last few years. It has been remarked that females of this millennial group are accompanying their families in shopping or through individual shopping practices in urban areas. Due to the education younger females, interactions have increased in daily life matters and their role is changing in society in the area of family purchase decisions (Srivastava & Anderson, 2010). At this time, gender roles are changing from the previous generation due to income, improved education, and other family dynamics (Kraft & Weber, 2012). Women's actions are emotion oriented in purchase decisions, and we are interested to know why other women go for similar choices, as they made while males are interested to know the level of pleasure that others derives from similar purchases (Baker, 2012). As indicated in previous studies, gender has had a great influence on buying decisions with different feelings and satisfaction levels relating to their emotional and cultural values. In this study, we try to evaluate the role of gender in a male dominant culture like Pakistan, and how masculinity and femininity affect buying decision satisfaction, while the major role of emotional and cultural values of this millennial group are targeted. In collectivist cultures, strong interactions exists between people, and before decision making, people opt for suggestions, try to gain various benefits from the experiences of others, and listen to other's views in order to make the correct buying decisions. Word of mouth is another source for purchase decision satisfaction. Differences in referrals are noticed in a previous study on the base of national cultures like Japanese (collectivist) provide more referrals than Americans (Money et al., 1998). Thus due to strong connections and sharing in collectivist societies, word of mouth has a great impact on buying decision satisfaction. A referral group's influence is supported by the consumption decisions and thus results in changing preferences (Schiffman & Kanuk, 1997). This study will highlight whether millennial group people are more expressive and advocate more about their positive experiences with products and services.

2. Literature Review

2.1 Role of cultural values on buying decision

Culture is the impact of collectivity on human personality which shapes human personality (Hofstede, 1980). Normative powers have potential to control the behaviors (Moschis & Cox, 1989). Cultural Values play a vital role on influencing the human behaviors (Tybout & Artz, 1994). While studying Japanese and American cultures with regards to purchase decision making, it was found that decision making is strongly backed by their cultures (Knight & Calantone, 2000). In an impulse buying study of multi cultures it is supported that collectivism, individualism and other related factors have a great influence on buying behavior (Kacen & Lee, 2002). Another study supports the dominancy of social norms that has a significant positive impact on individual's personal norms (Ahn et al., 2012). Social values are in strong connection in collectivist societies having a positive relation with purchasing behavior and a higher satisfaction level in comparison with individualism (Xiao & Kim, 2009). Consumer decision making is different in varied cultures on behalf of their genders and cultural differences, so these aspects should be studied separately by marketers to satisfy their needs (Solka et al., 2011). Males are connected to social comparison while females are more connected to nurturance, care giving in relationships and physical closeness (Lee & Robbins, 2000). On the basis of a lifestyle survey of individualistic and collectivist cultures, these cultures opposed each other on the basis of family orientation and role of gender (Sun & Merritt, 2004). Cultural shifts have also been observed in a study which reveals that women of urban areas in Pakistan have almost equal participation in house hold matters, whereas women belonging to rural regions have their decision making dependent upon their husbands and other family members (Mahmood, 2002).Gender refers not only to biological characteristics but also qualities shaped by unique culture in men and women (DeMatteo, 1994). Gender role is an important variable of cultural values and the study noticed significant differences between male and female impulse buying behavior in Pakistan (Bashir et al., 2013).

2.2. Role of word of mouth in buying decision

Decisions regarding purchasing and information spread about commodities are guided by word of mouth (Soderlund & Rosengren, 2007). When selecting a brand, WOM plays a vital role. Negative WOM is more influential than positive word of mouth thus affecting purchase chances (East et al., 2008; Podnar & Javernik, 2012). Customer to customer communication and their communication quality has a significant impact on customer loyalty and satisfaction (Fakharyan et al., 2014). In online groups, buying intention and social factors are influenced by the media and personal referrals (Chen & Lu, 2015). Complaint handling is the source to create positive WOM that will leads to more chances of retaining the customers (Yuksel et al., 2006). In an online assessment of consumer reliance on others' reviews; personal standing, knowledge and message comprehensiveness of reviewers are the influential sources to rely upon (Jamil & Hasnu, 2013). WOM is more positive for self-relevant products than utilitarian products (Chung & Darke, 2006). Customer advocacy has a strong connection with commitment and purchase intention (Mosavi & Ghaedi, 2011). Family Members, fellows, and other close circles are the most reliable sources of word of mouth and have great control on the consumer's choices (Aslam et al., 2012). In an assessment of gender motivation, women have had a positive and significant relation with word of mouth and group affiliation (Swanson et al., 2003). Females are more expressive than males (Olsson & Walker, 2003). Word of mouth is an influential source of marketing where male and female gender has played a differential role to deliver one's perceptions and service experiences to others (Sun & Qu, 2011).

2.3 Role of emotional values in buying decision

In order to govern humans, the key variable is emotional influence (Andrade, 2014).In an automobile buying study of Asians and Europeans, it is revealed that exterior-interior designing, fragrances, color schemes, and seats coverings have a greater impact on emotions and these emotions have significant effects while purchasing cars (Wellings et al., 2010; Khalid & Helander, 2006). Consumer experiences have a strong influence on emotional values and customer satisfaction (Brunner-Sperdin & Peters, 2009). Another study related to tourism reveals that consumption emotions are associated with how fairly services are provided and affect customer satisfaction (Su & Hsu, 2013). Customer emotions are a better source for predicting their future behavior intention in contrast to customer satisfaction (Koenig-Lewis & Palmer, 2008). The correct judgment of customers' perceived emotions by the sales force will strengthen the buyer-seller relationship and enhance selling performances (Kidwell et al., 2007). In impulse buying, the emotional satisfaction of consumers has a significant positive relation with buying behavior and purchase in developing nations (Dhurup, 2014). A higher level of emotional intelligence controls the personal desires of middle class women and in link their emotions with other family stakeholder's benefits which are sought by impulse buying (Nair & Das, 2015). Women are reacting more emotionally to the outcomes of their preferences than men (Croson & Gneezy, 2009). Emotions plays key role in buying decisions for women and story linkages for creating emotional appealing is a successful strategy for their purchase decisions (Baker, 2012). In a study related to gender stereotypes, women have a higher level of sensitivity; they are much more expressive and exhibit greater emotions (Olsson & Walker, 2003).

2.4 Buying decision satisfaction

Decision and consumption pleasure is based on choice objectives and satisfaction, which are determined by individual preference, social norms, justification of purchases, built confidence of purchase and minimize the regret, cost related factors and any negative associated factor which will leads to more product recommendation and association with product (Heitmann et al., 2007).Interior decor and a customer oriented atmosphere provides good experience and positive emotions in service related products that will positively influence customer satisfaction (Brunner-Sperdin & Peters, 2009). Study of clothes designing disclose with economic factors socio-cultural forces also determines the individual's buying behavior thus marketers should highlights these aspects for more satisfaction designing clothes for varied markets (Lawan & Zanna, 2013). Consumer decision making is different in varied cultures on behalf of their genders and cultural differences, so these aspects should be studied separately by marketers to satisfy their needs (Solka et al., 2011). Gender role is changing in societies; younger and educated female contributions in daily life are increasing, so the marketer should examine such roles. Along with males, it is suitable to target females as well, for family purchase decisions (Srivastava & Anderson, 2010). Narratives are more influential in affecting the emotions of women, and these emotions leads to purchase decisions (Baker, 2012).

3. Research Methodology

3.1 Hypotheses

H1: Cultural values have significant effects on buying decision satisfaction.
H2: Emotional values have significant effects on buying decision satisfaction.
H3: Word of mouth has significant effects on buying decision satisfaction.
H4: Millennial Males and Females are associated with their cultural values and have significant effects on buying decision satisfaction.
H5: Millennial Females are more expressive than males and for both males/females have significant effects on buying decision satisfaction.
H6: Millennial Females are more emotional and have significant effects on buying decision satisfaction.

3.2 Conceptual framework

Conceptual framework for this study is shown in the Fig. 1. There are three independent variables i.e. emotional values, cultural values, and eWOM communication. The criterion variable is buying decision satisfaction. This study also checks for the influence of gender in overall relationship between predictor and criterion variables.

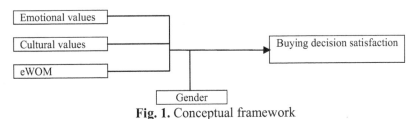

Fig. 1. Conceptual framework

3.3 Population and Sample

A total of 500 people were selected from several universities located in Pakistan. Respondents were approached using both online surveys and the physical distribution of questionnaires. The targeted population was selected because they were from the millennial age group as well as being currently more engaged in buying practices in comparison to previous decades. In order to access the true customer values of millennial, university students are the best fit for true representation. With both types of questionnaires (online survey/physical) distributed we ensured the equal participation of gender to achieve true outcomes for the study by their true representation to ensure the role of gender and its impact. Our area of targeted population is the millennial age group ranging between 18- 40 years.

3.4. Descriptive statistics

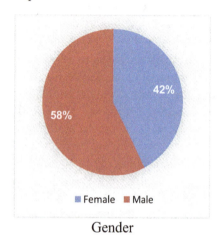
Gender

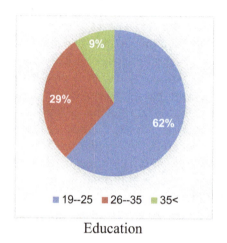
Education

Fig. 2. Descriptive statistics

A total number of 300 questionnaires were distributed physically from which were 280 were in useable condition. The remaining 200 hundred responses were collected through an online survey form with the help of different peers via Google docs. Thus, the sum of the total response was 480 with a response rate of (96%). The major reason for the high response rate is the use of personal linkages for data collection and on the spot filling of questionnaires at several universities, as well as students taking a keen interest in activities related to research work. The survey yielded that the usable responses were 42.4% were female and 57.6% were male. Where The majority of respondents (61.7%) were between the ages of 19 to 25 years, the second highest respondent group link aged 26-35 years with a percentage of (28.8%), and the rest of the respondents aged 36 or above with their percentage contribution of (9.5%).

3.5 Design

We made two segments of the said population, with half of the population having completed the online survey for their responses and half of population having filled out the physically distributed questionnaire for data collection. This technique enabled us to get online responses from educated people with higher education, and via the physically distributed questionnaire, we collected data from several households and students with lower education from the age of eighteen years or above. This was a generic study conducted without specifying any single product with the intention of attaining responses directed towards buying decision satisfaction. For data collection, we used convenience sampling.

3.6 Data analysis

SPSS version 21 was used to analyze the data. We performed linear regression to evaluate the impact of independent variables on dependent variables. To test the impact upon different genders, the data file was split and run for regression separately.

3.7 Scale or measured used

Instruments used for the collection of data were adapted from several studies on the five point Likert scale. For emotional values, questions are adapted from studies analyzing the relationship between consumption values and brand loyalty among young people. Scale was adopted from a study on personal care products (Candan et al., 2013) which was originally developed by (Sheth et al., 1991) to measure consumption values. To measure cultural values, we adapted a set of seven questions from the electronic thesis of a study conducted at The Florida State University DigiNole on Common Cultural Differences and Their Effect on Consumer Behavior by (Alkhalaf, 2008). A set of questions related to the dependent variable buying decision satisfaction are taken from study of Brand choice behavior as a function of information load (Jacoby, Speller & Kohn, 1974). In order to measure word of mouth, expressiveness items used are generated by Harrison-Walker (2001).

3.8 Regression analysis

As linear regression is performed during the analysis for all the independent variables for evaluating their impact on dependent variables we come to know several findings.

3.9 Cultural Values

Cultural values for millennial generation results have shown significant positive effect on their buying decision satisfaction (β = .145, P< .05) and support the H1 that buying decision is always influenced by the culture for satisfaction. This result is supported by earlier findings of (Knight & Calantone, 2000; Xiao & Kim, 2009; Solka et al., 2011; Ahn et al., 2012).

3.10 Regression Analyses

Table 1
Regression analysis (overall effect)

Independent Variables	B	Std. Error	T	Sig.
Cultural Values	.145	.119	1.216	.028
Emotional Values	.291	.155	1.874	.066
Word of Mouth	.371	.170	2.184	.033

Dependent Variable: Buying Decision Satisfaction

3.11 Emotional values

Targeting to emotions is also a great source that influences the decision satisfaction and we found positive significant linkage (β = .291, P< .010) thus emotional values have a significant impact on buying decision satisfaction (Nair & Das, 2015; Andrade, 2014; Dhurup, 2014; Wellings et al., 2010) which is also in line with our hypothesis number two.

3.12 Word of Mouth

People belonging to the millennial group express their emotions via word of mouth which has a positive and significant impact on buying decision satisfaction (β = .371, P< .05) results of the study are in direction to our H3 which is also supported by literature (Chung & Darke, 2006; Soderlund & Rosengren, 2007; Podnar & Javernik, 2012; Jamil & Hasnu 2013; Fakharyan et al., 2014)

3.13. Gender Role Assessment (Regression Analysis)

While assessing the influence of gender role for cultural values, results indicate males are more influenced by their culture values in buying decision than females (β = .218, P< .05) than females (β = .001, P< .10), Connection of males to socio-cultural values is stronger than females (Lee & Robbins, 2000). Overall, both genders have significant effect and are positively associated with their culture for decision satisfaction; therefore our hypothesis four is accepted. Gender role is an important variable of cultural values and the study noticed significant differences between male and female impulse buying behavior in Pakistan (Bashir, et.al 2013).

3.14 Role of Gender

Table 2

Regression analysis (Females)

	B	Std. Error	T	Sig.
Cultural Values	.001	.239	.006	.095
Emotional Values	.538	.210	2.562	.017
Word of Mouth	.726	.273	2.660	.013

Dependent Variable: Buying Decision Satisfaction

Table 3

Regression analysis (Males)

	B	Std. Error	T	Sig.
Cultural Values	.218	.136	1.604	.017
Emotional Values	-.008	.231	-.035	.072
Word of Mouth	.149	.234	.636	.029

Dependent Variable: Buying Decision Satisfaction

Females are more interactive and more expressive than males (Olsson & Walker, 2003), their buying decision satisfaction is more influenced by word of mouth in comparison to males ($\beta = .726$, $P < .05$) in comparison to males ($\beta = .149$, $P < .05$) The male and female gender have differential roles to deliver their perceptions and experiences to others (Sun & Qu, 2011).On the whole, our findings suggest that for both genders, buying decision is influenced by word of mouth or social group referrals , these results are also supportive of our H5.

As for emotional values, are concern females are more influenced by their emotions than males and their emotional values have a significant positive impact on buying decision satisfaction ($\beta = .538$, $P < .05$) and is in line with our H6. Thus, for women, emotional satisfaction is an important element to target for buying decision satisfaction (Croson & Gneezy, 2009; Baker, 2012; Nair & Das, 2015; Olsson & Walker, 2003). Women's emotional recognition power is far better than men's, enabling them to process negative emotions in a better way. Female emotions and sensitivity levels are hence proven higher than males, putting them at a higher risk averse of emotional threats pertaining to their children and family (Hampson, van Anders & Mullin, 2006). With regards to emotional values for males, there is a negative impact of emotional values on buying decision satisfaction ($\beta = -.008$, $P < .010$). As previous studies indicate, the relation that males are more connected to social comparisons while females made emotional comparisons ((Lee & Robbins, 2000). We also found social values for males are dominant over emotional values. Men are not only attached with the emotional value, but they also critically evaluate the several associations that they identify with. There are five truths about males. Men seek enlightenment, they seek experience, they seek success on their own terms, they happily define themselves as principle-driven and they identify themselves as family-centric (Moore, 2008).So their choices are not based on emotional decisions but on totality of benefit sought.

Consumer decision making is different in varied cultures on behalf of their genders and cultural differences, so these aspects should be studied separately by marketers to satisfy their needs (Solka et al., 2011). Males are connected to social comparison while females are connected more to nurturance, care giving, relationships and physical closeness (Lee & Robbins, 2000). On the basis of a lifestyle survey of individualistic and collectivist cultures, these cultures opposed each other on the basis of family orientation and role of gender (Sun & Merritt, 2004). A cultural shift is also observed in a study which reveals that women of urban areas in Pakistan have almost equal participation in house hold matters, whereas women belonging to rural regions have their decision making dependent upon their husbands and other family members (Mahmood, 2002).Gender refers not only biological characteristics but also qualities shaped by unique culture in men and women (DeMatteo, 1994). Gender role is an important variable of cultural values and the study noticed significant differences between male and female impulse buying behavior in Pakistan (Bashir et al., 2013).

4. Discussion

Cultural values, emotional values and word of mouth all independent variables that have a positive significant impact on dependent variable buying decision satisfaction. The consumer of any product or service is not only satisfied with the utilitarian benefits but also other associations (values) which are used as independent variables. In an aforementioned relationship, this study highlighted the importance of those values. Pre-purchase decision is properly assessed by the buyer from different angles like how much they got collective benefit they get from their purchase, their emotional satisfaction and what others think about their buying decision and are directly or indirectly effect by that decision.

In collectivist societies, the term "others" and "relationships with others" is a major cause that enforces any buyer to make a decision. An individual who is solely responsible for the whole family does not go for his/her personal choice. He must care for the emotions of others and the norms of society in order to minimize post purchase dissonance to get maximum satisfaction. Thus, all decisions taken by any individual must be backed by the social acceptability which might come from a close family circle or other normative pressures. Generation to generation several changes occurred in the values of society but in this study it is noticed that millennial strongly associated with their normative values and collectivism in making buying decisions. The results of this study in its entirety, and after splitting the data file on the basis of gender indicates that cultural values association, emotional effects and customer advocacy behavior all have their own importance in buying decision making. The intensity of these values may vary depending on the nature of a product like high involvement/low involvement or by the purpose of consumption. Both males and females stick to their cultural norms but the implementation of cultural values implementation is found higher in males. Males are dominant in asocial cultures like Pakistan and are usually the sole earning factor having decisional power. As a result, they have dominancy to direct the females towards their cultural association and care about cultural values while making buying decisions (Mahmood, 2002). Therefore their cultural orientation is higher than that of females.

Both genders suppressed their personal emotions over collective emotions to match socio-cultural values; their emotions are controlled by their close circle family members in order to satisfy their whole family by their buying decisions. Females are more concerned about their close family circle when making buying decisions, while males are more conscious about their dominancy and gender role to shape with cultural values rather than emotional values in buying decision. Another reason for the negative impact of emotions and buying decision satisfaction for males is their limited income. They have to think rationally rather than emotionally in purchase decision as they are considered the budget controller or main financer for the family. This assumption may not remain true in the case of unusual occurrences or in emergency situations.

Females are more highly expressive than males and narrate their positive association with buying decisions. Usually females have more time to interact with each other as they usually take part only in household matters. They not only provide information about their experience with the product or service but also the benefits, features and comparison of that product with other rivalry products. They tell more about the product they like and endorse it to others. In the case of branded or differentiated products they speak more in favor of their choice. On the other hand males are socially considered less talkative than females in Pakistan, and they usually provide information or suggestion at the time they are asked about or where it is necessary to tell or guide others in their buying decisions. WOM affects both genders but female's reliance on word of mouth is noticed higher than that of males. The reason behind this factor is they not only listen to other females but also seek suggestion from the family head like a husband, father etc. to gain maximum satisfaction from their buying decision.

5. Conclusion

Pakistan is a collectivist culture country where people live together in a family system and all the close circles of the family are influenced by the decisions of a man of authority. Therefore, every decision is taken after proper analysis of the situation. Sociocultural pressures influence people to make buying decisions according to the norms of the society rather than their own choice. Buying decision is very much influenced by the emotional values of customers which enforce them to react in a certain way in order to get the highest level of satisfaction. These emotional values tend to cause the decision maker to suppress their own emotions over the emotional care of others, especially the close family. In the area of emotional targeting, females are the most appropriate section rather than males. Females are more sensitive and they are more communicative about their sentiments, thus emotional appealing is a successful tool for influencing females in their buying decisions in Pakistan. Where advocacy behavior is concerned, females advocate more about their good or bad experiences with products or services in comparison to males. When decision making is solely on the part of females, they are more conscious and go for the suggestions of others, relying on experienced and trustworthy people according to their own perception.

5.1. Limitations

- Emergency situations may have different effects on buying decisions related to necessities, products or services.
- Increased sample size may give us a better picture for proper generalization.
- This is a cross-sectional study conducted in a limited time frame, and therefore might bring with new outcomes if the study is longitudinal.
- This study told about the consumer behavior of Pakistan. Results in other collectivist countries may differ.
- The tradeoff between the choices due to the limited income of the people in the underdeveloped country of Pakistan is another reason to think about collective benefits. Results may be totally different in developed collectivist countries where people have a higher level of disposable income.

5.2. Managerial implications

- Organizations should focus more on personal suggestions and recommendations of one customer to another or on the customer to customer information spread by their quality offering through the satisfied customer.
- Females are the more appropriate gender as communication is typically passed via positive word of mouth, but at the same time any negative experience will lead to much worse results. Therefore any buying decision in which there is involvement of females should be handled in careful manners to meet the promises thus providing a high level of satisfaction.
- Communication management is the essence of modern marketing. Managers should target the right person for emotional appealing, provide true information and make good experiences for the customers.
- Organization should increase personal interaction with customers to build more confidence.
- Managers should invest more on family incentive promotional activities.
- Managers should hire gatekeepers in profitable markets for high involvement products for the provision of maximum information, properly implementing complaint management cells in approachable market areas; they should chalk policy for complaint handling to minimize the effect of negative word of mouth.
- Contents of advertisement should be delivered in accordance with societal acceptability; information search process should be easier and simpler. It becomes more influential if the literature provided by the organization in both national and international languages.

5.3. Future research

Researchers can expand this study to make comparisons between developed and underdeveloped collectivist countries where huge disposable per capita income difference exists. This difference has ultimately effect on buying decisions both type of nations. Millennials can also be compared with Baby boomers in order to access the consumer values on the basis of generational differences within the same country. Longitudinal analysis with the same variables will generate more reliable results for drawing inferences.

References

Ahn, J. M., Koo, D. M., & Chang, H. S. (2012). Different impacts of normative influences on pro-environmental purchasing behavior explained by differences in individual characteristics. *Journal of Global Scholars of Marketing Science*, *22*(2), 163-182

Andrade, D. P. (2014). Governing 'emotional'life: passions, moral sentiments and emotions. *International Review of Sociology*, *24*(1), 110-129.

Alkhalaf, A. A. (2008). Cultural Differences and Their Effect on Consumer Behavior. *Electronic Theses, Treatises and Dissertations.* Paper 168.

Aslam, S., Jadoon, E., Zaman, K., & Gondal, S. (2012). Effect of word of mouth on consumer buying behavior. *MJSS*, *1*, 2.

Brunner-Sperdin, A., & Peters, M. (2009). What influences guests' emotions? The case of high-quality hotels. *International Journal of Tourism Research*, *11*(2), 171-183.

Baker, A. (2012).Gender Differences In Decision Making. Retrieved September 9, 2012, from http://www.decision-makingconfidence.com/gender-differences-in-decision-making.html

Bashir, S., Zeeshan, M. U. H. A. M. M. A. D., Sabbar, S. A. B. B. A. R. D. A. H. H. A. M., Hussain, R. I., & Sarki, I. H. (2013). Impact of cultural values and life style on impulse buying behavior: a case study of Pakistan. *International Review of Management and Business Research, 2*(1), 193-200.

Candan, B., Ünal, S., & Erciş, A. (2013). Analysing the relationship between consumption values and brand loyalty of young people: A study on personal care products. *Management*, *29*, 46.

Croson, R. & Gneezy, U. (2009). Gender differences in preferences. *Journal of Economic Literature* 47, 448– 474.

Chen, Y. F., & Lu, H. F. (2015). We-commerce: Exploring factors influencing online group-buying intention in Taiwan from a conformity perspective. *Asian Journal of Social Psychology*, *18*(1), 62-75.

Chung, C. M., & Darke, P. R. (2006). The consumer as advocate: Self-relevance, culture, and word-of-mouth. *Marketing Letters*, *17*(4), 269-279.

Dhurup, M. (2014). Impulsive Fashion Apparel Consumption: The Role of Hedonism, Fashion Involvement and Emotional Gratification in Fashion Apparel Impulsive Buying Behaviour in a Developing Country. *Mediterranean Journal of Social Sciences*, *5*(8), 168.

DeMatteo, L. A. (1994). From hierarchy to unity between men and women managers: towards an androgynous style of management. *Women in Management Review*, 9(7), 21-28.

East, R., Hammond, K., & Lomax, W. (2008). Measuring the impact of positive and negative word of mouth on brand purchase probability. *International Journal of Research in Marketing*, *25*(3), 215-224.

Eagly, A., Karau, S., & Makhijani, M. (1995). Gender and the effectiveness of leaders: A meta analysis. *Journal of Personality and Social Psychology*, 117, 125-145.

Fakharyan, M., Omidvar, S., Khodadadian, M. R., Jalilvand, M. R., & Nasrolahi Vosta, L. (2014). Examining the Effect of Customer-to-Customer Interactions on Satisfaction, Loyalty, and Word-of-Mouth Behaviors in the Hospitality Industry: The Mediating Role of Personal Interaction Quality and Service Atmospherics. *Journal of Travel & Tourism Marketing*, *31*(5), 610-626.

Grant, I. J., & Stephen, G. R. (2006). Communicating culture: an examination of the buying behaviour of 'tweenage'girls and the key societal communicating factors influencing the buying process of fashion clothing. *Journal of targeting, measurement and analysis for marketing*, *14*(2), 101-114.

Hampson, E., van Anders, S. M., & Mullin, L. I. (2006). A female advantage in the recognition of emotional facial expressions: Test of an evolutionary hypothesis. *Evolution and Human Behavior, 27*(6), 401-416.

Harrison-Walker, L. J. (2001). The measurement of word-of-mouth communication and an investigation of service quality and customer commitment as potential antecedents. *Journal of service research, 4*(1), 60-75.

Hui, C. H. (1988). Measurement of individualism-collectivism. *Journal of research in personality, 22*(1), 17-36.

Heitmann, M., Lehmann, D. R., & Herrmann, A. (2007). Choice goal attainment and decision and consumption satisfaction. *Journal of marketing research, 44*(2), 234-250.

Jacoby, J., Speller, D. E., & Kohn, C. A. (1974). Brand choice behavior as a function of information load. *Journal of Marketing Research*, 63-69.

Jamil, R. A., & Hasnu, S. A. F. (2013). Consumer's Reliance on Word of Mouse: Influence on Consumer's Decision in an Online Information Asymmetry Context. *Journal of Business & Economics, 5*(2), 171-205.

Kraft, H., & Weber, J. M. (2012). A look at gender differences and marketing implications. *International Journal of Business and Social Science, 3*(21), 247-253.

Kacen, J. J., & Lee, J. A. (2002). The influence of culture on consumer impulsive buying behavior. *Journal of consumer psychology, 12*(2), 163-176.

Knight, G. A., & Calantone, R. J. (2000). A flexible model of consumer country-of-origin perceptions: A cross-cultural investigation. *International Marketing Review, 17*(2), 127-145.

Khalid, H. M., & Helander, M. G. (2006). Customer emotional needs in product design. *Concurrent Engineering, 14*(3), 197-206.

Kidwell, B., McFarland, R. G., & Avila, R. A. (2007). Perceiving emotion in the buyer–seller interchange: The moderated impact on performance. *Journal of Personal Selling & Sales Management, 27*(2), 119-132.

Koenig-Lewis, N., & Palmer, A. (2008). Experiential values over time–a comparison of measures of satisfaction and emotion. *Journal of Marketing Management, 24*(1-2), 69-85.

Lee, C. K. C., & Collins, B. A. (2000). Family decision making and coalition patterns. *European Journal of Marketing, 34*(9/10), 1181-1198.

Lukosius, V. (2004). Consumer Behavior and Culture: Review Of Medium Being Reviewed Title Of Work Reviewed In Italics. *Journal of Consumer Marketing, 21*(6), 435-437.

Lam, D., Lee, A., & Mizerski, R. (2009). The effects of cultural values in word-of-mouth communication. *Journal of international marketing, 17*(3), 55-70.

Lee, R. M., & Robbins, S. B. (2000). Understanding social connectedness in college women and men. *Journal of Counseling & Development, 78*(4), 484-491.

Lawan, L. A., & Zanna, R. (2013). Evaluation of socio-cultural factors influencing consumer buying behaviour of clothes in Borno State, Nigeria. *Int. J. Basic Appl. Sci, 1*(3), 519-529.

McNeill, L. S., Fam, K. S., & Chung, K. (2014). Applying transaction utility theory to sales promotion–the impact of culture on consumer satisfaction. *The International Review of Retail, Distribution and Consumer Research, 24*(2), 166-185.

Moore, R. J. (2008). He Said, She Said: Marketing to the Sexes. Retrieved September 3, 2012, from Dynamic Graphics &

Create Magazine: http://dynamicgraphics.com/dgm/Article/28851/index.html

Money, R. B., Gilly, M. C., & Graham, J. L. (1998). Explorations of national culture and word-of-mouth referral behavior in the purchase of industrial services in the United States and Japan. *The Journal of Marketing*, 76-87.

Moschis, G. P., & Cox, D. (1989). Deviant consumer behavior. *Advances in Consumer Research, 16*(1), 732-737.

Mahmood, N. (2002). Women's Role in Domestic Decision-making in Pakistan: Implications for Reproductive Behaviour. *The Pakistan Development Review*, 121-148.

Mosavi, S. A., & Ghaedi, M. (2011, July). A survey on the relationships between perceived value and customer advocacy behavior. In *International Conference on Innovation, Management and Service IPEDR* (Vol. 14)., July).

Nair, D., & Das, S. (2015). Impact of Emotional Intelligence on Impulse Buying and Product Value Proposition. *European Journal of Business and Management*, 7(1), 165-172.

Olsson, S., & Walker, R. (2003). Through a gendered lens? Male and female executives 'representations of one another. *Leadership & Organization Development Journal*, 24(7), 387-96.

Olsson, S., & Walker, R. (2003). Through a gendered lens? Male and female executives' representations of one another. *Leadership & Organization Development Journal*, 24(7), 387-96.

Pyke, K. D., & Bengtson, V. L. (1996). Caring more or less: Individualistic and collectivist systems of family eldercare. *Journal of Marriage and the Family*, 379-392.

Podnar, K., & Javernik, P. (2012). The effect of word of mouth on consumers' attitudes toward products and their purchase probability. *Journal of Promotion Management*, 18(2), 145-168.

Swanson, S. R., Gwinner, K., Larson, B. V., & Janda, S. (2003). Motivations of college student game attendance and word-of-mouth behavior: the impact of gender differences. *Sport Marketing Quarterly*, 12(3), 151-162.

Sheth, J. N., Newman, B. I., & Gross, B. L. (1991). Why we buy what we buy: a theory of consumption values. *Journal of business research*, 22(2), 159-170.

Schiffman, L.G. & Kanuk L.L. (1997). *Consumer Behavior*. Prentice-Hall, 6th. Edition.

Sheth, J. N., Newman, B. I. & Gross, B. L. (1991a). *Consumption Values and Marketing Choices*. South-Western Pub.

Solka, A., Jackson, V. P., & Lee, M. Y. (2011). The influence of gender and culture on Generation Y consumer decision making styles. *The International Review of Retail, Distribution and Consumer Research*, 21(4), 391-409

Sun, T., Horn, M., & Merritt, D. (2004). Values and lifestyles of individualists and collectivists: a study on Chinese, Japanese, British and US consumers. *Journal of Consumer Marketing*, 21(5), 318-331.

Söderlund, M., & Rosengren, S. (2007). Receiving word-of-mouth from the service customer: An emotion-based effectiveness assessment. *Journal of retailing and consumer services*, 14(2), 123-136.

Sun, L. B., & Qu, H. (2011). Is there any gender effect on the relationship between service quality and word-of-mouth?. *Journal of Travel & Tourism Marketing*, 28(2), 210-224.

Srivastava, R. K., & Anderson, B. B. (2010). Gender roles and family decision making: a study of Indian automobile purchases. *International Journal of Services, Economics and Management*, 2(2), 109-120.

Su, L., & Hsu, M. K. (2013). Service fairness, consumption emotions, satisfaction, and behavioral intentions: The experience of Chinese heritage tourists. *Journal of Travel & Tourism Marketing*, 30(8), 786-805.

Tybout, A. M., & Artz, N. (1994). Consumer psychology. *Annual review of psychology*, 45(1), 131-169

Webster, C. (1994). Effects of Hispanic ethnic identification on marital roles in the purchase decision process. *Journal of Consumer Research*, 319-331.

Wellings, T., Williams, M., & Tennant, C. (2010). Understanding customers' holistic perception of switches in automotive human–machine interfaces. *Applied ergonomics*, 41(1), 8-17.

Xiao, G., & Kim, J. O. (2009). The investigation of Chinese consumer values, consumption values, life satisfaction, and consumption behaviors. *Psychology & marketing*, 26(7), 610-624.

Yuksel, A., Kilinc, U., & Yuksel, F. (2006). Cross-national analysis of hotel customers' attitudes toward complaining and their complaining behaviours. *Tourism Management*, 27(1), 11-24.

An empirical review of lean manufacturing and their strategies

Virender Chahal[a]* and M.S. Narwal[b]

[a]*Research Scholar Department of Mechanical Engineering, Deenbandhu Chhotu Ram University of Science and Technology, Sonipat, Haryana, India*
[b]*Associate professor, Department of Mechanical Engineering, Deenbandhu Chhotu Ram University of Science and Technology, Sonipat, Haryana, India*

CHRONICLE	ABSTRACT
Keywords: Lean Concept Lean strategies Lean waste Lean barriers and Lean implementation	The theory of lean manufacturing provides the quality of the products in minimum cost and provides customer satisfaction. Today, the competition level is very high and every industry tries to supply high quality products in nominal cost, so lean is the latest tool to achieve. The objective of this paper is to study different lean concepts under various lean strategies. This study helps to find out the status of lean manufacturing and its ways of implementation. Also in this paper, there is a discussion about lean manufacturing concept, lean waste, lean strategies, lean barriers and cycle of lean implementation. This paper presents a literature review to clear the status of lean manufacturing and their strategies with help of collection of relevant papers.

1. Introduction

Lean manufacturing is a discrepancy on the idea of efficiency based on optimizing flow. Lean manufacturing help to attract manufacturing operations and pick up the industrial jobs and customer satisfaction (Sing et al., 2010). When lean manufacturing is successfully followed, there is a good growth in the quality and the output productivity and also reduction in the completed wares inventory and work process (Seth & Gupta, 2005). The main goal of lean manufacturing is to help out the manufacturers who wish to progress the industry operations and best quality with good customer satisfactions in less amount. In manufacturing sector, there were new philosophies to produce maximum quantities by creating fewer unwanted activities. Proper implementation of different parameters profit will be much more (Delattre, 2002). Lean manufacturing lifts in overall production output and power up customer and the employee's job satisfaction (Soriano-Meier et al., 2002; Singh et al., 2010; Rose et al., 2013).

---

* Corresponding author.
E-mail address: vchahal68@gmail.com (V. Chahal)

After the finishing of World War 2, lean manufacturing was developed by Japanese manufacturers mainly in automotive industry. That time was a problem of shortage of materials, money and human resources. In Toyota motor company, Eiji toyoda and Taiichi ohno set a concept of "Toyota Production System", and today known as "Lean Manufacturing." The main concept after the system is to eliminate the wastage. After the quick success of lean manufacturing in Japan, other firms and industries, mainly in US, copied this amazing system. The expression "Lean" is defined as less utilization, in term of all inputs, to create the same outputs, as those shaped by a predictable mass production system, while contributory increased varieties for the end customer. The performance of smooth flow finds out quality problems that previously existed, and thus waste decline naturally happens as an end result. Lean Manufacturing (LM) has been widely recommended by different industries because LM eliminates waste without additional requirements of resources (Bhamu & Sangwan, 2012; Vamsi et al., 2014).

Current world is going from an era of disconnect national economies to the networked world economy. The beginning of liberalization, privatization and globalization has brought forth profound economic, social, environmental and technological pressures on the organizations. Competition has become more difficult, stronger and the customers are more demanding. Rivalry is severed in all aspects of production such as cost, quality of service product and technology (Poksinska, 2010; Pekuri et al., 2012).

1.1 Lean Manufacturing Strategies

When lean manufacturing concept was developed the main question was that which strategies will be more successive for this concept. After study literature, the result was in form of the number of strategies which can be used here. So this lean concept becomes a flexible system in which the strategies can be added, merged and be further explored as per requirement. Some lean strategies are:

- *5S*
- *Automation*
- *Continuous Flow*
- *Continuous Improvement*
- *Kan-Ban*
- *Kaizen*
- *Single Minute Exchange to Die (SMED)*
- *Cellular Manufacturing*
- *Six Sigma*
- *Team Development/Training*
- *Total Productive Maintenance*
- *Total Quality Management (TQM)*
- *Value Stream Mapping (VSM)*
- *Visual Management*
- *Work Standardization*
- *Flexible manufacturing System (FMS)*
- *Production leveling*
- *Inventory Management*
- *Zero Defect Concepts*
- *WIP (Work in Process)*
- *Lean Thinking*

In this paper, the main focus is on meaning of lean and its relative terms. There are also some benefits and barriers appear in lean implementation in industries. Some methods and principles are also discussed. Lean manufacturing is very necessary in today's market for manufacturers because this is only one strategy to survive in this competition. Lean manufacturing also focuses to achieve zero waste concept and provides better quality and benefits to customers as well as industry. That's why, this paper tries to give a good review of lean manufacturing for those industries that are following Lean manufacturing or wish to implement Lean in industry.

2. Methodology

This research paper is based on the literature review of lean manufacturing. The complete details were collected by following the number of journals worldwide, national and international conferences, internet and proceedings. In initial stage, there are so many innovation ideas through web and books which provided desirable recourses in research. The optimal solution has been identified by literature review. This paper will help to understand the concept of lean manufacturing, its enablers and barriers for implementation in industry. The solution is found by studying of numbers of papers on lean implementation, their effects with enabler and barriers. There are more than 25,000 research papers related to lean manufacturing. Then we select those research papers which are directly related to research work. The papers were selected from year 1997 to 2015 which are related to lean manufacturing, leanness, lean implementation, their strategies and lean wastes. All papers are directly collected from Google scholar and related searches. After that we select 102 papers which are related to research work in which lean manufacturing introduction and lean study papers are 28, lean manufacturing implementation papers are 19, lean strategies/tools & techniques papers are 26, lean relation with other strategies papers are 2, and leanness measurement papers are 29. The motive of this paper is to provide better understanding of lean and their strategies for research as well as industry.

3. Literature Review

The thought process of lean was thoroughly described in the book "The Machine That Changed the World" by James P. Womack, Daniel Roos and Daniel T. Jones in 1990.

In a subsequent volume, "Lean", by James P. Womack and Daniel T. Jones, in 1996. According these books, there are further divided lean principles:

- Specify the value desired by the customer
- Identify the value stream for each product providing that value and challenge all of generally nine out of ten) currently necessary to provide it
- Make the product flow continuously through the remaining value-added steps
- Introduce pull between all steps where continuous flow is possible
- Manage toward perfection so that the number of steps and the amount of time and information needed to serve the customer continually falls

Effective steps for lean manufacturing implementation

There are some effective steps:

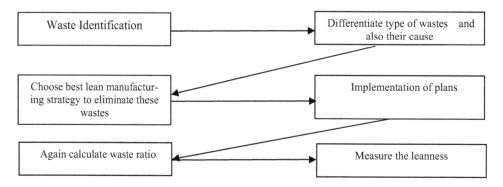

Fig. 1. Lean manufacturing implementation

Waste Identification: Every industry knows that there is some waste but not able to find out all types of hidden and unhidden wastes in industry.

Differentiate type of wastes and also their cause: This is very important to differentiate all types of waste and their causes. If the cause is eliminated then automatically waste will be reduced. There are so many techniques to eliminate different wastages.

Choose best lean manufacturing strategy to eliminate these wastes: In this step, we select a suitable lean manufacturing strategy for the identified wastes. There are many techniques which will give optimum solution for this plan. So we make appropriate plan for elimination.

Implementation of plans: After making plan, next step is implementation the plan.

Again calculate waste ratio: Compare the current waste status with past record.

Leanness measurement: Leanness can be measured with different lean measure techniques.

There are so many techniques which are used in Lean manufacturing. Many authors used different techniques to show the current status of developing countries. Bayou and Korvin (2008) presented the paper which shows the manufacturing leanness is a strategy used to achieve goals in less input to better output. The leanness measurement calculated by seven characteristics: relative, dynamic, long-term fuzzy logical, objective, integrative and comprehensive. Singh et al. (2010) presented a study of lean implementation and benefits in industry with the help of lean tool, value stream mapping (VSM). Paper presented to states of industry: current and future state. This presented the effect of VSM as very effective tool for Lean manufacturing.

3.1 Lean Manufacturing Cycle for Collected Literature Review

According to Karim and Arif-Uz-Zaman (2013), there are some effective methodologies and ways to implement lean manufacturing. But before implementation, we should know what way of implementation is. Lean manufacturing area is very vast but how and which data should be collected from literature, which types of barriers will be there and how solve these, why proper lean implementation is necessary etc., these are all questions which must be cleared in mind. The collection mode is written in below diagram and can implement lean according to this given cycle.

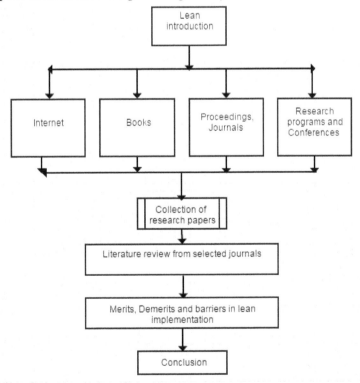

Fig. 2. Lean Manufacturing cycle for collected literature review

3.2 Seven Wastes of Industries

What is industrial waste and why they measures? It is very important question. In simple way," Any unnecessary action which produces unnecessary result called as waste". And lean manufacturing is also developed to eliminate these wastes. According to Hines and Rich (1997), there are basically seven lean industrial wastes which can be eliminated. They impact on industrial performance and reduce industrial output. Waste is nothing but its undesirable actions which are deeply studied below. Lean implementation can't be completed until all waste is removed. But before elimination, it should be know about all wastes which are:

The following are the seven wastes, as categorized by Taiichi Ohno:

- **Overproduction** - Manufacture of products in advance or in excess of demand wastes money, time and space. Overproduction happens when industry produces more than demanded product for future which affect total system. Mostly manufacturers have a reason to manufacture more but most of time it gives loss.
- **Waiting** - Processes are ineffective and time is wasted when one process waits to begin while another finishes. Instead, the flow of operations should be smooth and continuous. According to some estimates, as much as 99 percent of a product's time in manufacture is actually spent for waiting. Waiting for job plan, order, machine parts, e-mail etc., these all are the waiting waste.
- **Transportation** – It's a movement of tools, machine parts, product between workstations which are non-value added activities. It is costly and may be a cause of accident. Movement of material from one work place to another is a waste of time and money.
- **Inappropriate/over processing** – It is a type of waste in which extra processing happens to make it perfect which is expensive. Sometimes, it creates extra waste in form of labor, material, time and money. This processing occurs significant amount of time to take it in shape and, many times, whole system is disturbed.
- **Excessive inventory** - Wastes funds viva carrying costs of inventory storage and preservation. Main important thing to remember is that, inventory is not only in form of raw materials but also finished goods.
- **Unnecessary motion** - Resources are done in when workers have to twist, take an unnecessary motion from workstation distances to other place. Workplace ergonomics appraisal should be conducted to plan more capable surroundings. Other examples include the following:

    1. Re-assembling or arrangement of machine parts to get them into a new manner.
    2. Motion between work stations to get machine tools and parts.
    3. Placing all notes and files al right place.
    4. Placing tools nearby.

- **Defects** - Defects generally happen but not good when they repeat. They provide poor quality, bad customer satisfaction and loss to industry. They also affect sale and price of product. The market value and reliability also decreased. Lean manufacturing is based on a combination of different processes to make industry defect free.

3.3 Techniques used in Lean Manufacturing

According to Paez et al. (2005), Mahdiloo et al. (2014) Miller et al. (2010) and Anand and Kodali (2009), there are so many techniques available in literature but there are some important strategies discussed below which are mostly used. In Table 1, there are some techniques correlated with their requirements.

Table 1
The summary of lean manufacturing techniques and requirements

S. No	Lean Manufacturing Techniques	Requirements
1	5S	Reduce wasted time & motion.
2	Automation	Reduce human effort and provide accurate automatic system.
3	Continuous Flow	Ensuring the continuous flow throughout the value stream.
4	Continuous Improvement	Make sure that there is every little improvement every day and improve overall efficiency.
5	Kan-Ban	Schedule production and minimize work-in-process.
6	Kaizen	Change for better every day.
7	Single Minute Exchange to Die (SMED)	To minimize setup time and cost thereby freeing capacity and enabling the production of very small lots.
8	Cellular Manufacturing	Design cells to optimize process for better performance.
9	Six Sigma	Improve quality, operational performance, practices and systems.
10	Team Development/Training	Motivated team has better knowledge of work.
11	Total Productive Maintenance	Ensure uptime, Improve process capability and consistency
12	Total Quality Management (TQM)	Improve quality by preventing defects from occurring.
13	Value Stream Mapping (VSM)	Visualize of processes and their conformance to lean manufacturing principles.
14	Visual Management	To provide immediate, visual information that enables people to make correct decisions and manage their work and activities.
15	Work Standardization	To ensure that all workers execute their tasks in the same manner and thus reduce variation from differences in work method.
22	Flexible manufacturing System (FMS)	*To provide a systematic flexible change in manufacturing environment like layout, methods, machine etc.*
16	Production leveling	Reduce unevenness and waste in industry.
17	Inventory Management	Put all inventory products in a proper sequence to supply these items in proper network.
18	Zero Defect Concept	To eliminate all possibility which are responsible for wastage.
20	WIP (Work in Process)	WIP is the summation of all investment factors i.e. all types of costs puts during process.
21	Lean Thinking	Discover new ideas to deliver much comfort level and benefits to industry with eliminating waste.

3.4 Lean focused area

As per the study of literature review of lean we have used 102 research papers and the research found that there had been very few areas which focused on practical lean implementation. It was also found that almost lean manufacturing study is divided in basic three areas; Survey, Philosophy and case study. In Fig. 3, the results show that case study is most focused area. According to Gupta and Jain (2013), most of studies are done on case study of different lean manufacturing firms, then survey based study was done and at last not least lean philosophy study was done. But there is a lack of new and practical innovation about lean manufacturing strategies. The below diagram shows the status of lean manufacturing.

Fig. 3. Lean focused area

3.5 Technique highlights by Literature for different waste

There are many authors providing important information about lean and lean strategies. From literature study, it is clear that these lean strategies will eliminate different types of industrial waste and they are correlated. Here some papers are collected from literature review which is directly or indirectly related to lean manufacturing. The collections of these papers are based on only lean as master concept. There are also some individual techniques of lean in terms of the number of papers but they are specially related to eliminate respected waste which mention in literature of lean manufacturing. All data is differentiated in lean technique used by different authors. Some authors provide depth detail about used lean strategies and some gives only little introduction about used lean strategy. Main goal is to provide status of lean manufacturing between years, 1997-2015, by collecting some papers. These papers detail provides some interest of different authors also. And these all details are filled in Table 2 as follows,

Table 2
The literature review

	Lean Strategies	1	2	3	4	5	6	7	8	9	10	11	12	13	14	15
1	Hines and Rich (1997)								√							
2	Stewart & Adams (1998)				√											
3	Naylor et al. (1999)	√	√													
4	Hines et al. (1999)								√							
5	Vrijhoef and Koskela (2000)	√														
6	Bob Carroll (2001)					√										
7	Meier & Forrester (2001)	√				√										
8	Aitken et al. (2002)	√														
9	Fullerton et al. (2003)	√									√					
10	Shah and Ward (2003)	√				√		√								
11	Paez et al. (2004)					√		√	√							
12	Paez et al. (2005)					√	√									
13	Goldberg et al. (2006)								√							
14	Abdulmaleka and Rajgopalb (2007)								√							
15	Wan & Chen (2008)	√	√						√							
16	Sahoo et al. (2008)										√		√			
17	Gautam & Singh (2008)												√			
18	Pettersen (2009)					√										
19	Kodali (2009)	√				√		√						√		
20	Pattanaik & Sharma (2009)								√							
21	Nordin et al. (2010)	√				√		√								
22	Ramnath et al. (2010)			√												
23	Singh et al. (2010)	√		√							√					
24	Singh et al. (2010)				√					√					√	
25	Zanjirchi et al.(2010)	√				√		√	√							
26	Chauhan et al.(2010)										√	√				
27	Detty & Yingling (2010)	√	√		√											
28	Nordin et al.(2010)	√			√					√						
29	Behrouzi and wong (2010)	√	√													
30	Seyedhosseini et al. (2011)	√														
31	Vinodh &Balaji (2011)	√	√	√	√	√	√	√								
32	Yang et al.(2011)		√	√		√										
33	Schwarz et. al. (2011)					√		√	√							
34	Vinodh & Chintha (2011)	√	√	√	√	√	√						√			
35	Cuaa et al. (2011)	√				√		√								
36	Vinodh & Joy (2011)	√	√	√	√	√		√								
37	Kumar et al. (2011)		√	√												
38	Eswaramoorthi et al. (2011)	√		√							√					
39	Rajenthirakumar &Thyla (2011)											√				
40	Goriwondo et al. (2012)					√		√	√							
41	Gopinath & Freiheit (2012)		√	√	√	√									√	
42	Alaskari et al. (2012)	√	√	√				√			√					
43	Satao et al. (2012)	√	√						√							
44	Mohanraj & Sakthivel (2012)					√		√	√							
45	Ghosh (2012)	√	√	√	√	√	√	√			√					
46	Vinodh & Vimal (2012)	√	√	√	√	√	√	√			√					

Table 2
The literature review (Continued)

#	Author	1	2	3	4	5	6	7	8	9	10	11	12	13	14	15
47	Jainury et al. (2012)		√	√					√							
48	Gupta & Jain (2013)	√	√	√	√	√	√		√							
49	Karim and Zaman (2013)							√	√			√				
50	Krishnan, & Parveen (2013)	√	√	√		√		√								
51	Shabeena et al. (2013)											√				
52	Kumar et al. (2013)		√			√		√								
53	Chakraborty et al. (2013)				√											
54	Kumar & Pandey (2013)				√											
55	Thirunavukkarasu et al. (2013)				√			√								
56	Khadse, Sarode and Wasu (2013)	√	√	√	√	√	√	√			√					
57	Bhamu and Sangwan (2013)	√	√	√	√	√	√	√								
58	Gunasekharan et al. (2014)				√							√				
59	Jasti & Kodali (2014)	√	√	√	√	√	√	√								
60	Gupta & Jain (2014)	√	√	√	√	√	√	√								
61	Sundara et al. (2014)			√		√		√								√
62	Aikhuele & Azizi (2014)										√					√
63	Basu & Dan (2014)							√								
64	Zargun & Ashaab (2014)										√					
65	Jadhav et al. (2014)			√		√	√									
66	Obeidata et al. (2014)		√	√						√						
67	Modi & Thakkar (2014)				√							√				
68	Jadhav et al. (2014)	√			√		√									
69	Thanki & Thakkar (2014)	√	√	√	√	√	√	√								
70	Khanchanapong et al. (2014)	√	√	√	√	√	√	√								
71	Mostafa et al. (2015)				√			√	√							
72	Achanga et al. (2015)	√														
73	Wan & Chen (2015)		√								√					
74	Cottyn et al. (2015)	√	√	√	√											
75	Amin & Karim (2015)		√			√	√									
76	Hodge et al. (2015)			√		√			√							√
77	Mohammad et al. (2015)	√	√	√	√	√	√	√								
78	Jiménez et al. (2015)					√		√								
79	Vinodh & Chinth (2015)							√	√	√	√	√	√	√		
80	Parry & Turner (2015)			√				√								
81	Patel et al. (2015)							√								
82	Pakdil & Leonard (2015)			√	√			√	√							
83	Eswaramoorthi (2015)	√	√		√	√		√			√					
84	Jain et al. (2015)	√	√		√	√		√			√					
85	Susilawati et al. (2015)		√			√		√		√						
86	Virdi & Pandya (2015)	√			√			√								
87	Storch (1999)	√	√		√	√		√			√				√	
88	Isaksson & Seifert (2015)								√	√						
89	Ozelkan & Galambosi (2015)		√			√			√							
90	Panwar et al. (2015)	√	√		√	√					√				√	
91	Gollan et al. (2015)	√	√		√	√		√			√				√	
92	Panizzolo et al. (2015)		√			√	√									
93	Bamber & Dale (2015)			√		√	√	√								
94	Yang et al. (2015)			√					√							
95	Nithia et al. (2015)		√	√					√							
96	Yang et al. (2015), Yusup et al. (2015)	√	√	√	√	√	√	√	√	√	√					
97	Green et al. (2015); Ki & Park (2006)	√	√		√	√		√				√				
98	Brintrup et al. (2015)		√	√												
99	Bortolotti et al. (2015)		√			√		√								
100	Belekoukias et al. (2015)		√			√		√								
101	Hartinia & Ciptomulyonob (2015)	√	√	√	√	√			√							
102	Niall Piercy and Nick Rich (2015)		√			√			√							

Note: 1. 5'S 2. JIT 3. Kan-Ban 4. Kaizen 5. TQM 6. SMED 7. TPM 8. VSM 9. Cellular Manufacturing 10. Zero Defect Concept 11. Lean Thinking 12. WIP 13. FMS 14. Inventory Management 15. Production Leveling

3.5 Lean and its Strategies Implementation Barrier

According to Roslin et al. (2014), it is easy to say that lean can be easily implemented anywhere but in practical, it is not easy. Not a single industry will go to change its complete setup without any objection because nobody wants to change until it is highly needed. Workers also suffer when system environment and trend will change. There are some barriers:

1. The main work is to maintain industry on good running condition without any disturbance but it is not possible for management as well as workers. Every little change will shine that can be good or bad (Stanleigh, 2008).
2. Accepting and sudden implementation creates a difficulty to worker. These barriers can be in form of environment, trainings, layout change, responsibility and work output. Lean thinking creates a good skill level and communication that creates a good coordination level and mutual understanding to pass all information (Roslin et al., 2014).
3. Basically, these barriers exist which mostly come out when lean is implemented, i.e.

    - Lack of understanding between workers and managers or management to worker communication gap, and poor understanding of lean manufacturing concepts,
    - Ego factor also a big problem for industries which is vary state to state or area to area etc.,
    - Non motivated employees team with incentives and good targets etc.

3.6 Lean Manufacturing Advantages

According to Forza (1996) and Chahal et al. (2013), lean manufacturing have more advantages over traditional system. Some reasons are discussed below that why use lean manufacturing as primary system:

Table 3
Major differences between lean and traditional manufacturing approaches

S. No	Process	Lean Manufacturing	Tradition Manufacturing
1	Flexibility	High	Low
2	Inventories	As per demand	Excess demand
3	Production	Customer order	Stock
4	Layout	Product flow	Functional
5	Scheduling	Pull	Push
6	Lead time	Short	Long
7	Inspection	100%-by workers	Sampling
8	Empowerment	High	Low
9	Batch size	Small - continuous	High- batch & queue
10	Customer satisfaction	High	Low

Status of different lean strategies as per literature study

In this article, paper shows the status about lean and lean strategies. Different papers provide different status about lean. Here it is the collection of used 102 papers' data to show how papers focus on different lean strategies. It is possible that every lean strategy will not be highlighted every time for work but most of time a single strategy can be used. So in below figure, status shows about it. Vertical side shows the number of papers out of 102 and horizontal side shows the lean strategies.

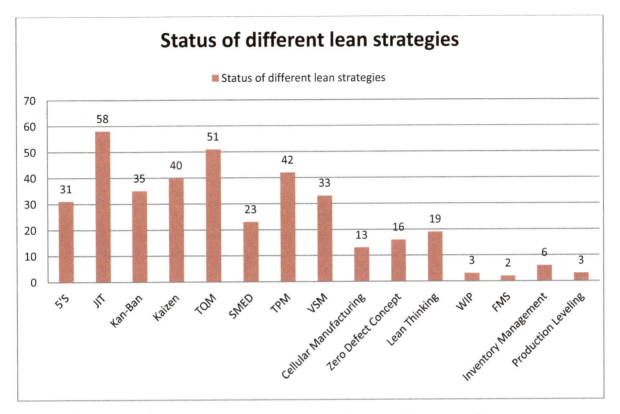

Fig. 5. Status of different lean strategies as per literature study

4. Discussion

Lean is a sea-depth concept in today industrial sector and also for research study. We have found that lean manufacturing concept was followed by industries as a roadmap philosophy. We have also experienced that in manufacturing sectors, lean provides a high impact theory. In this paper, different lean strategies were disused that can be implemented through providing lean training to all employees. This review paper has highlighted the status of lean and lean strategies by different author's interest. This paper is not the study of all literature review on lean strategies but it is just a try with collection of some lean papers. It's only a collection of some papers and results are based on different collecting parameters. It is just a try to give an overview on the bases of this literature. Here is also some comparison of author's interest about lean manufacturing in India and outside.

5. Conclusion

There is no depth of literature on lean manufacturing to give an in-depth details in actual practice and research area. It is accepted that lean manufacturing is the most profitable concept for both, manufacturing industries as well as customers so lean team prepared by different manufacturing industries (Jainury et al., 2012). All lean strategies are important at their own levels but these all are not used in all manufacturing environment. There are so many reasons like Purchasing cost, implementation time, worker training and layout change, etc. All types of industrial waste can be eliminated by these strategies (Belekoukias et al., 2014; Mabry & Morrison, 1996; Kisombe, 2012). Here, we have used literature papers in which lean strategy was used directly or indirectly. As the result of this research paper, lean manufacturing is very much important in every area of innovation which provided lean manufacturing strategies. But there is a lack of implementation in industry. Only few strategies were implemented thoroughly as shown in Fig. 5. These are some interested strategies which are selected by their own or by default with a reason of money and time to implement. Lean strategies and their effects can be shown by case study of industry and questionnaire study which will show the actual benefit of lean. Lean manufacturing is long lasting benefit system which reduces firm and customer all over tension (Singh et al., 2010). As per Abdollahi et al. (2015), benefits may be in terms of waste minimization or elimination, time and money benefits, controlled overproduction and inventory, zero delay, systematic arrangement, skilled worker, less work load and best customer satisfaction, etc. but here also some barriers that discussed earlier. They are: money and time to implement, worker behavior, now every industry wants to beneficial change with lean manufacturing due to its impact on production and quality (Behrouzi, & Wong, 2011; Begam et al, 2013; Chakraborttya & Paul, 2011; Diaz-Elsayed et al., 2013; Chiarini, 2013; Harris et al., 2014). Overall, lean is an efficient system to give a new achievement to industry and customers.

References

Abdollahi, M., Arvan, M., & Razmi, J. (2015). An integrated approach for supplier portfolio selection: Lean or agile? *Expert Systems with Applications, 42*(1), 679–690.

Abdulmalek, F. A., & Rajgopal, J. (2007). Analyzing the benefits of lean manufacturing and value stream mapping via simulation: A process sector case study. *International Journal of Production Economics, 107*(1), 223–236. http://doi.org/10.1016/j.ijpe.2006.09.009

Achanga, P., Shehab, E., Roy, R., & Nelder, G. (2012). A fuzzy-logic advisory system for lean manufacturing within SMEs. *International Journal of Computer Integrated Manufacturing, 25*(9), 839–852. http://doi.org/10.1080/0951192X.2012.665180

Aikhuele, D. O., & Souleman, F. S. (2014). Australian Journal of Basic and Applied Sciences Application of Fuzzy AHP for Ranking Critical Success Factors for the Successful Implementation of Lean Production Technique, *8*(December), 399–407.

Aitken, J., Christopher, M., & Towill, D. (2002). Understanding, Implementing and Exploiting Agility and Leanness. *International Journal of Logistics Research and Applications, 5*(1), 59–74.

Alaskari, O., M.M., A., Dhafr, N., & Pinedo-Cuenca., R. (2012). Critical Successful Factors (CSFs) for Successful Implementation of Lean Tools and ERP Systems. *Lecture Notes in Engineering and Computer Science, 2199*(1), 1627–1632.

Amin, M. Al, & Karim, M. a. (2012). A time-based quantitative approach for selecting lean strategies for manufacturing organisations. *International Journal of Production Research, 51*(May 2014), 1–22. http://doi.org/10.1080/00207543.2012.693639

Anand, G., & Kodali, R. (2009). Selection of lean manufacturing systems using the analytic network process - a case study. *Journal of Manufacturing Technology Management, 20*(2), 258–289.

Bamber, L., & Dale, B. G. (2000). Lean production: A study of application in a traditional manufacturing environment. *Production Planning & Control, 11*(3), 291–298.

Basu, P., & Dan, P. K. (2014). Capacity augmentation with VSM methodology for lean manufacturing. *International Journal of Lean Six Sigma, 5*(3), 279–292.

Begam, M., Swamynathan, R., & Sikkizhar, J. (2013). Current trends on lean management – A review. *International Journal of Lean Thinking, 4*(2), 1–7.

Behrouzi, F., & Wong, K. Y. (2011). Lean performance evaluation of manufacturing systems: A dynamic and innovative approach. *Procedia Computer Science, 3*, 388–395.

Belekoukias, I., Garza-Reyes, J. A., & Kumar, V. (2014). The impact of lean methods and tools on the operational performance of manufacturing organisations. *International Journal of Production Research, 7543*(July 2014), 1–21. http://doi.org/10.1080/00207543.2014.903348

Bhamu, J., & Sangwan, K. S. (2014). Lean manufacturing: literature review and research issues. *International Journal of Operations & Production Management, 34*(7), 876–940.

Bortolotti, T., Boscari, S., & Danese, P. (2015). Successful lean implementation: Organizational culture and soft lean practices. *International Journal of Production Economics, 160*, 182–201.

Brintrup, A., Ranasinghe, D., & McFarlane, D. (2010). RFID opportunity analysis for leaner manufacturing. *International Journal of Production Research, 48*(9), 2745–2764.

Chakraborttya, R., & Paul, S. (2011). Study and implementation of lean manufacturing in a garment manufacturing company: Bangladesh perspective. *Journal of Optimization in Industrial Engineering, 7*, 11–22.

Chakraborty, A., Bhattacharya, M., Ghosh, S., & Sarkar, G. (2013). Importance of kaizen concept in medium manufacturing enterprises. *International Journal of Management and Strategy*, 4(6).

Chauhan, G., & Sharma, T. P. S. S. K. (2010). Measuring the status of lean manufacturing using AHP. *Production*, 1(2), 115–120.

Chiarini, A. (2013). Waste savings in patient transportation inside large hospitals using lean thinking tools and logistic solutions. *Leadership in Health Services*, 26(4), 356–367.

Cottyn, J., Van Landeghem, H., Stockman, K., & Derammelaere, S. (2011). A method to align a manufacturing execution system with Lean objectives. *International Journal of Production Research*, 49(14), 4397–4413. http://doi.org/10.1080/00207543.2010.548409

Cua, K. O., McKone, K. E., & Schroeder, R. G. (2001). Relationships between implementation of TQM, JIT, and TPM and manufacturing performance. *Journal of Operations Management*, 19(6), 675–694. http://doi.org/10.1016/S0272-6963(01)00066-3

Detty, R., & Yingling, J. (2000). Quantifying benefits of conversion to lean manufacturing with discrete event simulation: A case study. *International Journal of Production Research*, 38(2), 429–445.

Diaz-Elsayed, N., Jondral, A., Greinacher, S., Dornfeld, D., & Lanza, G. (2013). Assessment of lean and green strategies by simulation of manufacturing systems in discrete production environments. *CIRP Annals - Manufacturing Technology*, 62(1), 475–478.

Eswaramoorthi, M., Kathiresan, G. R., Jayasudhan, T. J., Prasad, P. S. S., & Mohanram, P. V. (2012). Flow index based line balancing: a tool to improve the leanness of assembly line design. *International Journal of Production Research*, 50(12), 3345–3358.

Eswaramoorthi, M., Kathiresan, G. R., Prasad, P. S. S., & Mohanram, P. V. (2011). A survey on lean practices in Indian machine tool industries. *International Journal of Advanced Manufacturing Technology*, 52(9-12), 1091–1101. http://doi.org/10.1007/s00170-010-2788-y

Forza, C. (1996). Work organization in lean production and traditional plants: what are the differences?. *International Journal of Operations & Production Management*, 16(2), 42-62.

Fullerton, R. R., McWatters, C. S., & Fawson, C. (2003). An examination of the relationships between JIT and financial performance. *Journal of Operations Management*, 21(4), 383–404.

Garza-Reyes, J. A., Parkar, H. S., Oraifige, I., Soriano-Meier, H., & Harmanto, D. (2012). An empirical-exploratory study of the status of lean manufacturing in India. *International Journal of Business Excellence*, 5(4), 395–412. http://doi.org/10.1504/IJBEX.2012.047906

Gautam, N., & Singh, N. (2008). Lean product development: Maximizing the customer perceived value through design change (redesign). *International Journal of Production Economics*, 114(1), 313–332. http://doi.org/10.1016/j.ijpe.2006.12.070

Gautam, R., & Kumar, S. (2012). Kaizen Implementation in an Industry in India : A Case Study, 5762, 25–33.

Gollan, P. J., Kalfa, S., Agarwal, R., Green, R., Randhawa, K., Gollan, P. J., … Green, R. (2015). Lean manufacturing as a high-performance work system : the case of Cochlear. *International Journal of Production Research*, 7543(December), 6434–6447. http://doi.org/10.1080/00207543.2014.940430

Gopinath, S., & Freiheit, T. I. (2012). A waste relationship model and center point tracking metric for lean manufacturing systems. *IIE Transactions*, 44(2), 136–154.

Goriwondo, W. M., Mhlanga, S., & Marecha, A. (2011). Use O F the V Alue S Tream M Apping T Ool F or W Aste R Eduction I N M Anufacturing . C Ase S Tudy for Bread Manufacturing in Zimbabwe. *International Conference on Industrial Engineering and Operations Management Kuala Lumpur, Malaysia*, 236–241.

Green, J. C., Lee, J., & Kozman, T. A. (2010). Managing lean manufacturing in material handling operations. *International Journal of Production Research*, 48(10), 2975–2993.

Gunasekharan, S., Elangovan, D., & Parthiban, P. (2014). A Comprehensive Study to Evaluate the Critical Success Factors Affecting Lean Concept in Indian Manufacturing Industries. *Applied Mechanics and Materials*, 592-594, 2569–2576.

Gupta, S., & Jain, S. K. (2013). A literature review of lean manufacturing. *International Journal of Management Science and Engineering Management*, 8(4), 241–249.

Harris, G., Stone, K. B., Mayeshiba, T., Componation, P. J., & Farrington, P. A. (2014). Transitioning from teaching lean tools to teaching lean transformation. *Journal of Enterprise Transformation*,

4(3), 191–204.

Hartini, S., & Ciptomulyono, U. (2015). The Relationship between Lean and Sustainable Manufacturing on Performance: Literature Review. *Procedia Manufacturing*, *4*(Iess), 38–45.

Hines, P., Hines, P., Rich, N., Rich, N., Esain, A., Esain, A., ... Benchmarking, K. (1999). A distribution industry application. *International Journal*, *6*(1), 60–77.

Hines, P., Rich, N., Hines, P., & Rich, N. (1997). The seven value stream mapping tools. *International Journal of Operations & Production Management The*, *17*(1), 46–64.

Hodge, G. L., Goforth Ross, K., Joines, J. a., & Thoney, K. (2011). Adapting lean manufacturing principles to the textile industry. *Production Planning & Control*, *22*(3), 237–247.

Isaksson, O. H. D., & Seifert, R. W. (2013). Inventory leanness and the financial performance of firms. *Production Planning & Control*, *25*(12), 999–1014. http://doi.org/10.1080/09537287.2013.797123

Jadhav, J. R., Mantha, S. S., & Rane, S. B. (2014). Development of framework for sustainable Lean implementation: an ISM approach. *Journal of Industrial Engineering International*, *10*(3), 72.

Jadhav, J. R., Mantha, S. S., & Rane, S. B. (2015). Roadmap for Lean implementation in Indian automotive component manufacturing industry: comparative study of UNIDO Model and ISM Model. *Journal of Industrial Engineering International*, *11*(2), 179–198.

Jain, V., Benyoucef, L., & Deshmukh, S. G. (2008). What's the buzz about moving from "lean" to "agile" integrated supply chains? A fuzzy intelligent agent-based approach. *International Journal of Production Research*, *46*(23), 6649–6677. http://doi.org/10.1080/00207540802230462

Jainury, S. M., Ramli, R., & Rahman, M. N. a. (2012). Applying lean principles, tools and techniques in set parts supply implementation. *International Journal of Mechanical, Aerospace, Industrial and Mechatronics Engineering*, *6*(12), 76–80.

Jiménez, E., Tejeda, a., Pérez, M., Blanco, J., & Martínez, E. (2012). Applicability of lean production with VSM to the Rioja wine sector. *International Journal of Production Research*, *50*(7), 1890–1904. http://doi.org/10.1080/00207543.2011.561370

Karim, A., & Arif-Uz-Zaman, K. (2013). A methodology for effective implementation of lean strategies and its performance evaluation in manufacturing organizations. *Business Process Management Journal*, *19*(1), 169–196. http://doi.org/10.1108/14637151311294912

Khadse, P. B., Sarode, A. D., & Wasu, R. (2013). Lean Manufacturing in Indian Industries A Review, *3*(1), 175–181.

Khanchanapong, T., Prajogo, D., Sohal, A. S., Cooper, B. K., Yeung, A. C. L., & Cheng, T. C. E. (2014). The unique and complementary effects of manufacturing technologies and lean practices on manufacturing operational performance. *International Journal of Production Economics*, *153*, 191–203. http://doi.org/10.1016/j.ijpe.2014.02.021

Kim, D., & Park, H.-S. (2006). Innovative construction management method: Assessment of lean construction implementation. *KSCE Journal of Civil Engineering*, *10*(6), 381–388.

Kisombe, S. M. (2012). Lean manufacturing tools and techniques in industrial operations: A Survey of the sugar sector in Kenya. *Unpublished MBA Research Project). University of Nairobi, Nairobi*, 1–15.

Krishnan, V., & Parveen, C. M. (2013). Comparative studyof lean manufacturing tools used in manufacturing firms and service sector. *Lecture Notes in Engineering and Computer Science*, *1 LNECS*, 604–608.

Kumar, N., Kumar, S., Haleem, A., & Gahlot, P. (2013). Implementing lean manufacturing system: ISM approach. *Journal of Industrial Engineering and Management*, *6*(4), 996–1012.

Kumar, P., & Kajal, S. (2015). Implementation of Lean Manufacturing in a Small-Scale Industry. *IUP Journal of Operations Management*, *14*(2), 25–33.

Kumar, P., & Pandey, V. (2013). KAIZEN : A Case study in small scale organizations, *2*(May), 133–136.

Mabry, B. G., & Morrison, K. R. (1996). Transformation to lean manufacturing by an automotive component supplier. *Computers & Industrial Engineering*, *31*(1-2), 95-98.

Mahdiloo, M., Noorizadeh, A., & Farzipoor Saen, R. (2014). Benchmarking suppliers' performance when some factors play the role of both inputs and outputs: A new development to the slacks-based measure of efficiency. *Benchmarking: An International Journal, 21*(5), 792-813.

Miller, G., Pawloski, J., & Standridge, C. (2010). A case study of lean, sustainable manufacturing. *Journal of Industrial Engineering and Management, 3*(1), 11–32.

Modi, D. B., & Thakkar, H. (2014). Lean Thinking : Reduction of Waste , Lead Time , Cost through Lean Manufacturing Tools and Technique. *International Journal of Emerging Technologies and Advanced Engineering, 4*(3), 339–344.

Mohanraj, R., Sakthivel, M., & Vinodh, S. (2011). QFD integrated value stream mapping: an enabler of lean manufacturing. *International Journal of Productivity and Quality Management, 7*(4), 501–522. http://doi.org/10.1504/IJPQM.2011.040546

Mostafa, S., Dumrak, J., & Soltan, H. (2013). A framework for lean manufacturing implementation. *Production & Manufacturing Research, 1*(1), 44–64. http://doi.org/10.1080/21693277.2013.862159

Naylor, J. Ben, Naim, M., & Berry, D. (1999). Leagility: integrating the lean and agile manufacturing in the total supply chain. *International Journal of Production Economics, 62*, 107–118.

Nithia, K. ., Noordin, M. Y., & Saman, M. Z. M. (2015). Lean Production Weaknesses in Manufacturing Industry: A Review. *Applied Mechanics and Materials, 735*, 344–348.

Obeidat, M. S., & Pei, Z. J. (2012). Implementing Lean Manufacturing in the Sewing Industry. *Industrial Systems Engineering Research Conference, 8289*(November 2014), 1–8.

Ozelkan, E., & Galambosi, A. (2009). Lampshade Game for lean manufacturing. *Production Planning & Control, 20*(5), 385–402. http://doi.org/10.1080/09537280902875419

Paez, O., Dewees, J., Genaidy, A., Tuncel, S., Karwowski, W., & Zurada, J. (2004). The lean manufacturing enterprise: An emerging sociotechnological system integration. *Human Factors and Ergonomics In Manufacturing, 14*(3), 285–306. http://doi.org/10.1002/hfm.10067

Paez, O., Salem, S., Solomon, J., & Genaidy, A. (2005). Moving from lean manufacturing to lean construction: Toward a common sociotechnological framework. *Human Factors and Ergonomics In Manufacturing, 15*(2), 233–245. http://doi.org/10.1002/hfm.20023

Pakdil, F., & Leonard, K. M. (2014). Criteria for a lean organisation: development of a lean assessment tool. *International Journal of Production Research, 52*(15), 4587–4607.

Panizzolo, R., Garengo, P., Sharma, M. K., & Gore, A. (2012). Lean manufacturing in developing countries: evidence from Indian SMEs. *Production Planning & Control, 23*(10-11), 769–788.

Parry, G., & Turner, C. (2006). Application of lean visual process management tools. *Production Planning & Control, 17*(Janeiro 2006), 77–86. http://doi.org/10.1080/09537280500414991

Patel, N., Chauhan, N., & Trivedi, P. (2015). Benefits of Value Stream Mapping as A Lean Tool Implementation Manufacturing Industries: A Review. *IJIRST –International Journal for Innovative Research in Science & Technology, 1*(8), 53–57.

Pattanaik, L. N., & Sharma, B. P. (2009). Implementing lean manufacturing with cellular layout: A case study. *International Journal of Advanced Manufacturing Technology, 42*(7-8), 772–779.

Pekuri, A., Herrala, M., Aapaoja, A., & Haapasalo, H. (2012). Applying Lean in Construction – Cornerstones for Implementation. *Proceedings for the 20th Annual Conference of the International Group for Lean Construction*.

Pettersen, J. (2009). Defining lean production: some conceptual and practical issues. *The TQM Journal, 21*(2), 127–142. http://doi.org/10.1108/17542730910938137

Poksinska, B. (2010). The current state of Lean implementation in health care : literature review. *Quality Management in Health Care, 19*(4), 319–329.

Rajenthirakumar, D., & Thyla, P. (2011). Transformation to lean manufacturing by an automative component manufacturing company. *International Journal of Lean Thinking, 2(2)*, 1–13. Retrieved from http://www.ita.mx/files/gui-ingles-tecnico-nov-2012/ing-industrial-2-11-2012-1.pdf

Ramnath, B. V., Elanchezhian, C., & Kesavan, R. (2010). Application Of Kanban System For Implementing Lean Manufacturing (A Case Study). *Journal of Engineering Research and Studies, 1*(I), 13.

Rose, A. N. M., Md. Deros, B., & Ab. Rahman, M. N. (2013). A study on lean manufacturing implementation in Malaysian automotive component industry. *International Journal of Automotive and Mechanical Engineering, 8*(1), 1467–1476. http://doi.org/10.15282/ijame.8.2013.33.0121

Roslin, E. N., Shamsuddin, A., & Dawal, S. Z. M. (2014). Discovering Barriers of Lean Manufacturing System Implementation in Malaysian Automotive Industry. In *Advanced Materials Research* (Vol. 845, pp. 687-691). Trans Tech Publications.

Sahoo, A. K., Singh, N. K., Shankar, R., & Tiwari, M. K. (2008). Lean philosophy: Implementation in a forging company. *International Journal of Advanced Manufacturing Technology*, *36*(5-6), 451–462.

Satao, S. M., Thampi, D. G. T., Dalvi, S. d., Srinivas, B., & Patil, B. T. (2012). Enhancing Waste Reduction through Lean Manufacturing Tools and Techniques , a Methodical Step in the Territory of Green Manufacturing. *IRACST - International Journal of Research in Management & Technology (IJRMT)*, *2*(2), 253–257.

Schwarz, P., Pannes, K. D., Nathan, M., Reimer, H. J., Kleespies, A., Kuhn, N., ... Z??gel, N. P. (2011). Lean processes for optimizing or capacity utilization: Prospective analysis before and after implementation of value stream mapping (VSM). *Langenbeck's Archives of Surgery*, *396*(7), 1047–1053. http://doi.org/10.1007/s00423-011-0833-4

Seyedhosseini, S. M., Taleghani, A. E., Bakhsha, A., & Partovi, S. (2011). Extracting leanness criteria by employing the concept of Balanced Scorecard. *Expert Systems with Applications*, *38*(8), 10454–10461. http://doi.org/10.1016/j.eswa.2011.02.095

Shah, R., & Ward, P. T. (2003). Lean manufacturing: Context, practice bundles, and performance. *Journal of Operations Management*, *21*(2), 129–149.

Singh, B., Garg, S. K., & Sharma, S. K. (2010). Development of index for measuring leanness: study of an Indian auto component industry. *Measuring Business Excellence*, *14*(2), 46–53.

Singh, B., Garg, S. K., Sharma, S. K., & Grewal, C. (2010). Lean implementation and its benefits to production industry. *International Journal of Lean Six Sigma*, *1*(2), 157–168.

Soriano-Meier, H., & Forrester, P. L. (2002). A model for evaluating the degree of leanness of manufacturing firms. *Integrated Manufacturing Systems*, *13*(2), 104–109.

Stanleigh, M (2008). Effeting successful changemanagment initiatives, *Industrial and commercial training, 40, 34-37*

Stewart, S., & Adams, M. (1998). The lean manufacturing champion: reducing time and risk by encouraging risk-taking. *Strategic Change*, *7*(6), 357–366.

Storch, R. L. (1999). Improving flow to achieve lean manufacturing in shipbuilding. *Production Planning & Control*, *10*(February 2015), 127–137. http://doi.org/10.1080/095372899233280

Sundar, R., Balaji, A. N., & Satheesh Kumar, R. M. (2014). A review on lean manufacturing implementation techniques. *Procedia Engineering*, *97*, 1875–1885.

Susilawati, A., Tan, J., Bell, D., & Sarwar, M. (2015). Fuzzy logic based method to measure degree of lean activity in manufacturing industry. *Journal of Manufacturing Systems*, *34*(C), 1–11.

Thirunavukkarasu, S., Bheeman, B. V, Ashwin, R., Varadharajan, M., Devadasan, S. R., & Murugesh, R. (2013). Lean implementation through value stream mapping: A case study in an Indian pump manufacturing company. *International Journal of Services and Operations Management*, *16*(4), 506–524. http://doi.org/10.1504/IJSOM.2013.057511

Vamsi, N., Jasti, K., & Kodali, R. (2014). A literature review of empirical research methodology in lean manufacturing. *International Journal of Operations & Production Management*, *34*(10), 1080–1122. http://doi.org/10.1108/IJOPM-04-2012-0169

Vinodh, S., & Balaji, S. R. (2011). Fuzzy logic based leanness assessment and its decision support system. *International Journal of Production Research*, *49*(13), 4027–4041.

Vinodh, S., & Chintha, S. K. (2011a). Application of fuzzy QFD for enabling agility in a manufacturing organization: A case study. *The TQM Journal*, *23*(3), 343–357.

Vinodh, S., & Chintha, S. K. (2011b). Leanness assessment using multi-grade fuzzy approach. *International Journal of Production Research*, *49*(2), 431–445.

Vinodh, S., & Joy, D. (2012). Structural Equation Modelling of lean manufacturing practices. *International Journal of Production Research*, *50*(6), 1598–1607.

Vinodh, S., & Vimal, K. E. K. (2012). Thirty criteria based leanness assessment using fuzzy logic approach. *International Journal of Advanced Manufacturing Technology*, *60*(9-12), 1185–1195.

Vrijhoef, R., & Koskela, L. (2000). The four roles of supply chain management in construction. *European Journal of Purchasing & Supply Management, 6*(3-4), 169–178.

Wan, H.-D., & Chen, F. F. (2008). A leanness measure of manufacturing systems for quantifying impacts of lean initiatives. *International Journal of Production Research, 4623*(23), 6567–6584.

Wong, W. P., Ignatius, J., & Soh, K. L. (2012). What is the leanness level of your organisation in lean transformation implementation? An integrated lean index using ANP approach. *Production Planning & Control, 25*(4), 273–287. http://doi.org/10.1080/09537287.2012.674308

Yang, M. G., Hong, P., & Modi, S. B. (2011). Impact of lean manufacturing and environmental management on business performance: An empirical study of manufacturing firms. *International Journal of Production Economics, 129*(2), 251–261. http://doi.org/10.1016/j.ijpe.2010.10.017

Yang, T., Hsieh, C.-H., & Cheng, B.-Y. (2011). Lean-pull strategy in a re-entrant manufacturing environment: a pilot study for TFT-LCD array manufacturing. *International Journal of Production Research, 49*(6), 1511–1529. http://doi.org/10.1080/00207540903567333

Yang, T., Kuo, Y., Su, C. T., & Hou, C. L. (2015). Lean production system design for fishing net manufacturing using lean principles and simulation optimization. *Journal of Manufacturing Systems, 34*(1), 66–73. http://doi.org/10.1016/j.jmsy.2014.11.010

Yusup, M. Z., Mahmood, W. H. W., Salleh, M. R., & Yusof, A. S. M. (2015). Review the influence of Lean tools and its performance against the index of manufacturing sustainability. *International Journal of Agile Systems and Management, 8*(2), 116–131.

Zanjirchi, S. M., Tooranlo, H. S., & Nejad, L. Z. (2010). Measuring Organizational Leanness Using Fuzzy Approach. *Proceedings of the 2010 International Conference on Industrial Engineering and Operations Management*, 144–156.

Zargun, S., & Al-Ashaab, A. (2013). Critical Success Factors for Lean Manufacturing: A Systematic Literature Review an International Comparison between Developing and Developed Countries. *Advanced Materials Research, 845*, 668–681.

Analytic network process (ANP) approach for product mix planning in railway industry

Hadi Pazoki Toroudi[a]*, Mahsa Sadat Madani[b] and Fatemeh Sarlak[c]

[a]*Department of Industrial Engineering, Ghaemshahr Branch, Islamic Azad University, Ghaemshahr, Iran*
[b]*Department of Industrial Engineering, TaJan University, Ghaemshahr, Iran*
[c]*Department of Industrial Engineering, College of Engineering, University of Tehran, Tehran, Iran*

CHRONICLE	ABSTRACT
Keywords: *Product selection* *ANP* *Analytical Network Process*	Given the competitive environment in the global market in recent years, organizations need to plan for increased profitability and optimize their performance. Planning for an appropriate product mix plays essential role for the success of most production units. This paper applies analytical network process (ANP) approach for product mix planning for a part supplier in Iran. The proposed method uses four criteria including cost of production, sales figures, supply of raw materials and quality of products. In addition, the study proposes different set of products as alternatives for production planning. The preliminary results have indicated that that the proposed study of this paper could increase productivity, significantly.

1. Introduction

During the past years, there have been tremendous efforts on using multi criteria decision making techniques for production planning (Abedini et al., 2013; Paul et al., 2015). There is no doubt that profit maximization is not the only criterion for making strategic decision in today's marketing planning and other criteria including quality, political affairs, environmental issues, etc. influence planning decisions. Zarepour and Momeni (2014) performed an investigation to investigate various factors influencing on auto parts in Iran. The study requested some experts who worked for an auto parts supplier named SaipaYadak to express their opinions about the relative importance of factors affecting demand for auto parts in various regions of the Iran and their opinions were grouped into four groups of parts related issues, weather conditions, regional as well as cultural factors. They also used analytical network process (ANP) (Saaty, 1996) to rank various factors and their results indicated that regional factors were the most important items followed by cultural issues, auto parts and weather conditions. Kuan and Chen (2014) proposed a hybrid MCDM framework combined with DEMATEL-based ANP to make an assessment on enterprise technological innovation capabilities assessment.

* Corresponding author.
E-mail address: h.pazoki.ums@gmail.com (H. Pazoki Toroudi)

Atafar et al. (2013) presented a hybrid of balance score card (Kaplan, & Norton, 1992; Kaplan & Norton, 1996a; Kaplan & Norton, 1996b; Kaplan & Norton, 2000) with analytical network process to measure the relative performance of an educational unit in Iran. Fazli and Jafari (2002) applied a hybrid MCDM model, which presents the dependent relationships among criteria with DEMATEL method (Shen et al., 2011) to construct a relations-structure among criteria. They used ANP to determine the relative weights of each criterion with dependence and feedback, and the VIKOR (Opricovic, 1998; Opricovic & Tzeng, 2007) method was used to rank and select the best alternatives for investment.

2. The proposed study

2.1. Analytical network process (ANP)

Many multi criteria decision making (MCDM) techniques do not handle the interdependences among elements and to cope such problem, analytical network process (ANP) as an MCDM method was introduced by Saaty (1996). He demonstrated various types of ANP techniques, such as the Hamburger Model, the Car Purchase BCR model, and the National Missile Defense model (Saaty, 2004). The proposed model of this paper recommends a modified Feedback System model shown in Fig. 1, which takes into account inner dependences within the criteria.

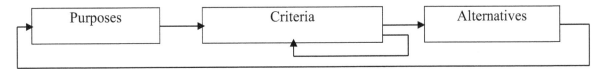

Fig.1. Feedback system model

To measure the relative importance among elements, 30 decision makers in this survey are requested to reply through a series of pair-wise comparisons based on the Saaty's nine-point scale 1-9. For evaluating the weights of elements, while analytical hierarchy process (AHP) (Saaty, 1988, 1990) uses the principal eigenvector of comparison matrix, the ANP implements the limiting process of the super-matrix (Sekitani & Takahashi, 2001). The case study of this paper is associated with an Iranian firm whose primary concern is to manufacture three groups of products, namely auto-part, railway-part and others. These products are compared in terms of four major criteria; namely cost, sales figures, supply of raw materials and quality. Fig. 2 shows the structure of the proposed study.

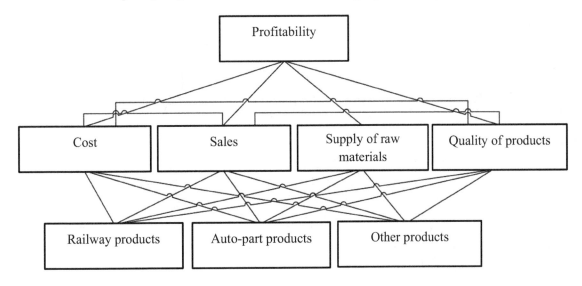

Fig. 2. The structure of the proposed study

To perform pairwise comparison, the study uses the insights of 30 managers who were working for the firm in different positions. Fig. 3 shows personal characteristics of the participants.

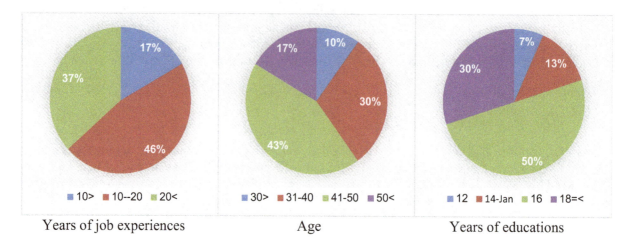

Years of job experiences   Age   Years of educations

Fig. 3. Personal characteristics of the participants

According to the results of Fig.3, 83% of the people who took part in this survey maintained at least 10 years of job experiences. In terms of their age, 10% of them aged less than 30 and the rest of them were mainly middle aged people and finally, most participants in our study hold good educational background. Table 1 shows the super matrix used for the proposed study.

Table 1

The results of super matrix used for the proposed study

	Objective	Cost	Sales	Raw materials	Quality	Railway	Auto-part	Others
Objective	-	-	-	-	-	-	-	-
Cost								
Sales								
Raw materials	A			B			C	
Quality								
Railway products	-					-	-	-
Auto-part products	-			D		-	-	-
Other products	-					-	-	-

3. The results

In this section, we present the results of the pairwise comparisons for different criteria and alternatives. Table 2 shows the results of the comparisons for different criteria.

Table 1

The results of pairwise comparison in section A

Criteria	Cost	Sales	Raw materials	Quality
Weight	0.409479	0.26369	0.213553	0.113278

As we can observe from the results of Table 1, cost of production is the most important criterion followed by sales figures, supply of raw material and quality. Table 2-4 present the results of pairwise comparison in section B, C and D.

Table 2
The results of pairwise comparison in section B

Criteria	Cost	Sales	Raw materials	Quality
Cost	0.564	0.093	0.291	0.118
Sales	0	0.422	0.085	0.263
Supply of raw materials	0.055	0.047	0.402	0.504
Quality	0	0	0	0

Table 3
The results of pairwise comparison in section C

Criteria	Railway products	Auto-part products	Other products
Cost	0.144	0.150	0.145
Sales	0.136	0.150	0.125
Supply of raw materials	0.136	0.112	0.188
Quality	0.136	0.168	0.089

Table 4
The results of pairwise comparison in section D

Criteria	Cost	Sales	Raw materials	Quality
Railway products	0.368	0.304	0.333	0.403
Auto-part products	0.368	0.391	0.238	0.376
Other products	0.263	0.323	0.429	0.198

Finally, Table 5 presents the results of super-matrix.

Table 5
The summary of the results of super matrix

	Objective	Cost	Sales	Quality	Supply	Railway	Auto	Others
Objective	-	-	-	-	-	-	-	-
Cost	0.40947	0.564	0.093	0.291	0	0.144	0.150	0.145
Sales	0.26369	0	0.422	0.085	0.118	0.136	0.150	0.125
Quality	0.21355	0.055	0.047	0.402	0.263	0.136	0.112	0.188
Supply of raw materials	0.11327	0	0	0	0.564	0.136	0.168	0.089
Railway-part	-	0.368	0.304	0.333	0.403	-	-	-
Auto-part	-	0.368	0.391	0.238	0.376	-	-	-
Others	-	0.263	0.323	0.429	0.198	-	-	-

Based on the results of the survey given in Table 5, we are now able to present the results of ranking in Table 6 as follows,

Table 6
The results of ranking of different products

Products	Railway-part	Auto-part	Others
Weight	0.0984	0.1181	0.0689

4. Conclusion

In this paper, we have presented an empirical investigation to prioritize different groups of products according to various criteria. The proposed study has implemented analytical network process to consider the interrelationships among various criteria. The results have indicated that it is possible to reach better profitability by concentrating on auto-part production. The results are consistent with recent development of auto-industry in Iran since this sector was under an embargo until recent years and the recent political change in Iran may create better opportunities for auto part makers to expand their operations.

Acknowledgement

The authors would like to thank the anonymous referees for constructive comments on earlier version of this paper.

References

Abedini, E., Naami, A & Modiri, M. (2013). A study on ranking ethical factors influencing customer loyalty. *Management Science Letters, 3*(10), 2597-2602.

Atafar, A., Shahrabi, M & Esfahani, M. (2013). Evaluation of university performance using BSC and ANP. *Decision Science Letters, 2*(4), 305-311.

Fazli, S., & Jafari, H. (2002). Developing a hybrid multi-criteria model for investment in stock exchange. *Management Science Letters, 2*(2), 457-468.

Kuan, M & Chen, Y. (2014). A hybrid MCDM framework combined with DEMATEL-based ANP to evaluate enterprise technological innovation capabilities assessment. *Decision Science Letters, 3*(4), 491-502.

Kaplan, R. S., & Norton, D. (1992). The balanced scorecard measures that drive performance. *Harvard Business Review, 70*(1), 71–79.

Kaplan, R.S., & Norton, D. (1996a). Using the balanced scorecard as a strategic management system. *Harvard Business Review, 74*(1), 75-85.

Kaplan, R.S., & Norton, D.P. (1996b). *The Balanced Scorecard: Translating Strategy into Action*. Harvard Business School Press.

Kaplan, R.S., & Norton, D.P. (2000). *The strategy-focused organization: How balanced scorecard companies thrive in the new business environment*. Harvard Business Press.

Opricovic, S. (1998). *Multicriteria optimization of civil engineering systems*. Belgrade: Faculty of Civil Engineering.

Opricovic, S., & Tzeng, G. H. (2007). Extended VIKOR method in comparison with outranking methods. *European Journal of Operational Research, 178*(2), 514–529.

Paul, D., Agarwal, P., Mondal, G & Banerjee, D. (2015). A comparative analysis of different hybrid MCDM techniques considering a case of selection of 3D printers. *Management Science Letters, 5*(7), 695-708.

Saaty, T. L. (1988). What is the analytic hierarchy process?. In *Mathematical models for decision support* (pp. 109-121). Springer Berlin Heidelberg.

Saaty, T. L. (1990). How to make a decision: the analytic hierarchy process.*European journal of operational research*, *48*(1), 9-26.

Saaty, T. L. (1996). *The analytic network process-decision making with dependence and feedback*. Pittsburgh, PA: RWS Publications.

Saaty, T. L. (2004). Decision making—the analytic hierarchy and network processes (AHP/ANP). *Journal of systems science and systems engineering*, 13(1), 1-35.

Sekitani, K., & Takahashi, I. (2001). A unified model and analysis for AHP and ANP. *Journal of the Operations Research Society of Japan*, 44(1), 67–89.

Shen, Y.-C., Lin, G. T. R., & Tzeng, G.-H. (2011). Combined DEMATEL techniques with novel MCDM for the organic light emitting diode technology selection. *Expert Systems with Applications, 38*(3), 1468-1481.

Zarepour, A & Momeni, H. (2014). An application of ANP for ranking different factors influencing on demand for auto parts. *Management Science Letters, 4*(4), 631-634.

Predicting customer's intentions to use internet banking: the role of technology acceptance model (TAM) in e-banking

Samar Rahi[a]*, Mazuri Abd. Ghani[b] and Feras MI Alnaser[a]

[a]*PhD scholar, University Sultan Zainal Abidin, Terengganu, Malaysia*
[b]*Senior Lecturer, University Sultan Zainal Abidin, Terengganu, Malaysia*

CHRONICLE	ABSTRACT
Keywords: Internet banking Perceived usefulness Perceived ease of use Attitude Intention Technology acceptance model (TAM)	Information and communication technology (ICT) developments and trends in recent years have had great impacts on banking sector worldwide. Therefore, the disruptive innovative technology has accelerated changes in the way of banking business. The purpose of this paper is to explore the factors that influence on Pakistani customer's intentions to adopt internet banking. The sample used in this empirical study includes 265 responses of internet banking users collected through structured questionnaire. For statistical analysis, structural equation model (SEM) approach was used. The present study suggests that internet banking use increases as long as customer perceives it as useful tool. Findings confirmed that perceived usefulness, perceived ease of use and attitude were the key constructs for promoting internet banking usage in Pakistan. Furthermore, the importance performance matrix analysis has shown that attitude was the most important factor. Thus, banks can focus on cultivation of positive attitudinal beliefs about internet banking among prospect customers.

1. Introduction

Since 1995, Internet banking has allowed consumers to utilize the internet as a platform to interact with their banks (O'Reilly & Finnegan, 2003). The use of disruptive innovative technologies has accelerated changes in the way banking business is conducted and consumers are swept with such changes. Thus, in today's competitive market, it is necessary to provide fast services for customers. Internet banking allows customers to use their banks' websites to perform common banking transactions such as paying bills, transferring funds inquiring about account balances, etc. (Lee, 2009). According to Rahi et al.(2017), internet banking involves a process where users get access to their own bank accounts and perform transaction directly such as payment of utility bills, transfer of funds, etc. Furthermore, Martins et al. (2014) explained that internet banking is the delivery of banking services through an open access computer network (the Internet) to offer a wider range of potential benefits to financial institutions due to more accessible and user friendly use of the technology.

* Corresponding author.
E-mail address: sr_adroit@yahoo.com (S. Rahi)

Internet banking provides a very convenient and effective method of managing personal finances because it is flexible (Lee, 2009). Additionally, the convenience offered by internet banking is making it popular, which, in turn, encourages banks to provide a safe and efficient banking system for their customers (Lee, 2009). The use of internet is not limited to banking sector. It could be used for non-commercial activities like paying the tax or entertainment. According to Rahi (2015) e-commerce is defined as an applications that facilitate two or more than two parties for the purpose of business exchanges. Internet technology plays essential role in banking system and performs different types of transactions with minimum risk. Soon people will give priority to internet banking for all types of transactions (Rahi, 2016). Furthermore, the technology is playing a key role in every type of business and it is impossible to get competitive advantages without having the access to technology (Zhuang & Lederer, 2004). Jayawardhena and Foley (2000) argue that internet banking will change the way of services and interaction between mangers and customers. Although several studies have examined the banking industry, however most of these focused on traditional banking services such as evaluation the quality, marketing and development of new services (Rahi, 2015; Rahi, 2016a; Rahi, 2016b; Rahi & Ghani, 2016a; Rahi & Ghani, 2016b; Suleiman Awwad & Mohammad Agti, 2011). Several studies have focused on positive aspects of internet banking for instance related benefits, trust worthiness and innovation (Han & Baek, 2004). One study conducted by Chong et al. (2010) empirically examined that the factors such as perceived ease of use, trust and government support influence on adoption of internet banking. In line with Chong et al. (2010) the present study scrutinized the technology acceptance model to investigate the internet banking adoption issues in Pakistan.

2. Literature Review

2.1 Theoretical background

Earlier studies related to adoption of technology were conducted which sought to understand how different factors affect individuals' technology adoption behavior. During the last two decades, technology acceptance model has been extensively evolved in technology adoption studies. Technology acceptance model has gone through three phases of development: adoption, validation and extension. At adoption level TAM was tested with several information system applications; for instance communication technologies and internet related applications. In validation phase, it was tested to prove causal links among TAM constructs whilst extension phase presents the extension of the two main constructs perceived usefulness and perceived ease of use (Han, 2003). In views of Wixom and Todd (2005), the TAM model includes three types of extension approaches. The first approach suggests an extension with related factors involved in models; for instance subjective norms or perceived behavioral control. The second approach recommends involving alternative beliefs for instance compatibility, visibility or demonstrability whilst, the third approach is directed to extension with external variables.

2.2 Behavioral Intention

Behavioral intention has been observed as an indicator of system success (Venkatesh et al., 2003). According to Zeithaml et al. (1996) behavioral intention is relevant to customers' decision and their desires to stay or switch from company services. Zhang and Prybutok (2005) suggested that customer experience is more related to behavioral intention. It is said that the more positive customer's experience, the more likely that the customers will show the intention to buy or use the services.

2.3 Perceived Usefulness

According to Wang et al. (2003) perceived usefulness is defined as the extent to which a person believes that using a particular system will enhance his or her job performance. In internet banking context, perceived usefulness could be in transactions such as request for cheque/demand draft, sending monthly e-statements, online payments, that improves performance, save time and increase effectiveness of the services (Kesharwani & Singh Bisht, 2012). Moreover, these benefits also are expected to be further enhancing over a period of time through technological advancement or break through. The more useful the system is seen, the more likely intention towards the use of internet banking (Lee, 2009). The literature shows that perceived usefulness has significant effect on behavioral intention concerning technology use and has been tested and validated by different researchers (Kesharwani & Singh Bisht, 2012; Lee, 2009; Venkatesh & Davis, 2000). Thus, the following hypothesis is formulated:

H1: Perceived Usefulness positively influences on attitude.

2.4 Perceived Ease of Use

According to Venkatesh and Davis (2000) technology will be more useful if it is easier to use. If an internet service is found to be very difficult to use, customers will choose another way to make transaction (Venkatesh & Davis, 2000). The more difficult the system is to use, the less likely the customer uses. Venkatesh and Davis (2000) revealed several determinants of perceived ease of use by integrating computer self-efficacy and facilitation condition into technology acceptance model. In internet banking context researchers show that perceived ease of use had a positive and significant influence on perceived usefulness (Bashir & Madhavaiah, 2015; Rahi, 2016a,b; Wang et al., 2003). Thus, following hypothesis is formulated;

H2: Perceived Ease of Use influences positively on perceived usefulness.

H3: Perceived Ease of Use influences positively on attitude.

2.5 Attitude

In previous studies, Attitude is defined as " the degree to which a person has a favorable evaluation or appraisal of the behaviors in question" (Ajzen & Fishbein, 1980). Several studies have confirmed that in technology field attitude has a significant influence on behavioral intention (Al-Ajam & Md Nor, 2015; Kesharwani & Singh Bisht, 2012). In technology related studies, Wu (2006) found significant relationship between attitude and intention in online bookstore. The effect of attitude on intention has been also supported in internet banking domain (AbuShanab et al., 2010; Al-Ajam & Md Nor, 2015; Rahi, 2016a,b). Thus, it can be concluded that attitude played a significant role on individual intention for adoption of internet banking. Therefore, the following hypothesis is generated;

H4: Attitude influences positively on intention to use internet banking.

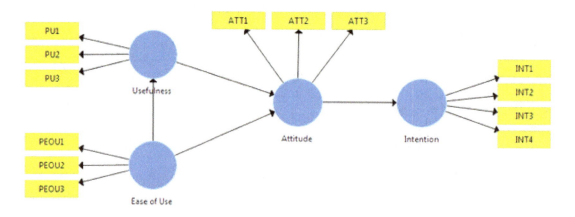

Fig. 1. Theoretical Framework

3. Methods

3.1 Survey Design and Sampling

This study is conducted under positivist paradigm. Becker et al. (2012) postulated that positivists believe in employing quantitative approaches for data analysis and support objectivity to define their ontological statements. Thus quantitative approach was used to verify the influence of technology acceptance model on intention to adopt internet banking. A questionnaire was developed for measuring the respondent's observation. Survey was directed towards customers of commercial Banks in Lahore city of Pakistan. The data was collected between the months of October 2015 and November 2015 from Lahore city of Punjab, Pakistan. Convenience sampling method was used in this study. Convenience sampling is defined as a process of data collection from population that is close at hand and easily accessible to researcher (Rahi, 2017). Hair (2003) illustrated that convenience sampling allows researcher to complete interviews or get responses in a cost effective way. Comrey and Lee (1992) stated that sample size of 50 is very poor, while 100 is poor, 200 is reasonable, 300 is good, 500 is very good and 1000 is brilliant for structural equation modeling. Thus, for this study the required sample size was 265. However, researcher set out to collect data which was slightly larger than the required number. A set of 400 structured questionnaires were distributed out of 265 useable response received from internet banking users.

3.2 Instrument Development

The survey instrument was consisted on two parts. First part asked about demographic characteristics like region, age, gender, qualification while, second part included four latent constructs namely; perceived usefulness, perceived ease of use, attitude and intention to adopt internet banking. All the constructs items were adopted from previous research works. Items of intention was adopted from Rahi et al. (2017) while perceived usefulness, perceived ease of use and attitude were adapted from Davis (1989). The items anchored on a 7-point Likert scale (1= strongly disagree to 7 strongly agree)

3.3 Respondent's Profile

The demographics of 265 respondents are tabulated in Table 1. Males were (53.2%) slightly more than females (46.8%). The age of the respondents 26.8% was for less than 25 years old, 35.8% that counts at age between 26 to 35 years, 26.7% for 36 to 45years and about 9.4% respondents were above 46. Overall a good mixture of age was directed in this study of internet banking adoption. Data was further analyzed with demographic characteristics such as education. Education of the respondents were asked where only 1.9% respondents were considered below high school education, 4.2% from those who attended high school, 8.3% respondents who attended college, the maximum share was graduate respondents with 56.2% and finally 29.4% respondents were post graduated and participated in internet banking adoption study.

Table 1
Demographic profile of the respondents

Demographic Characteristics	Frequency	Percentage (%)
Gender		
Male	141	53.2
Female	124	46.8
Age		
Less than 25 years	71	26.8
26-35 years	95	35.8
36-45 years	74	27.7
46 years and above	25	9.4
Education		
Below high School	5	1.9
Attended High School	11	4.2
Attended College	22	8.3
Graduate	149	56.2
Post Graduate	78	29.4

4. Data Analysis

To analyze the research model Partial Least Square (PLS) analysis technique was employed by using the SmartPLS3.0 software (Ringle et al., 2015). Following two-stage analytical procedure, researchers tested the measurement model (validity and reliability of the measures) and structural model (Hypothesis testing) recommended by Hair Jr et al. (2014).

4.1 Measurement Model

Prior to structural modelling assessment, the study has to evaluate the measurement model of latent construct for their dimensionality, validity, and reliability by going through the process named as confirmatory factor analysis (CFA). As the study is quantitative in nature, usually Cronbach's (α) is recommended to ensure reliability. Therefore, Composite Reliability (CR) is also preferred (Henseler et al., 2009). Two types of validity approached: Convergent and discriminate validity.

4.2 Convergent Validity

Convergent validity of measurement model is usually ascertained by examining the factor loading, average variance extracted and compost reliability (Hair et al., 2010). Fig. 2 depicted the result where, factor loading values was supported by Chin (1998) by recommended threshold level of 0.6. All the values were above than 0.6 that indicates the convergent validity.

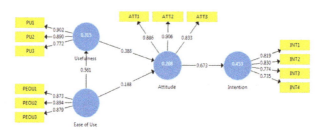

Fig. 2. Measurement Model

The convergent validity was also confirmed through estimation of average variance extracted (AVE) by recommended values of Fornell and Larcker (1981) as it must be greater than 0.5. The average variance extracted that reflects the overall amount of variance in the indicators was accounted for latent construct.

Table 2
Results of Measurement Model

Constructs	Loading	(α)	CR	AVE
Perceived Usefulness	PU	0.816	0.892	0.734
I think internet banking makes it easier for me to do my banking activities.	0.902			
I think internet banking enables me to complete my banking activities more quickly.	0.89			
I think internet banking allows me to manage my banking activities more efficiently.	0.772			
Perceived Ease of Use	PEOU	0.857	0.913	0.778
I think it is easy to learn how to use internet banking.	0.873			
I believe that it is easy to get internet banking to do what I want it to do.	0.894			
I think it is easy to remember how to use internet banking.	0.879			
Attitude	ATT	0.847	0.908	0.766
In my opinion, it is desirable to use the banks Website.	0.886			
Using bank's Website is a pleasant experience.	0.906			
Using bank's Website is a wise idea.	0.833			
Intention to adopt internet Banking	INT	0.803	0.869	0.625
I expect to use internet banking in the future.	0.819			
I plan to use internet banking in the next months.	0.83			
I intend to consult the balance of my account on the platform of Internet banking.	0.774			
I intend to perform a transfer on the platform of Internet banking.	0.735			

Further to this measurement, model needs to assess the composite reliability. Table 2 depicts composite reliability (CR) degree where the construct indicator represents the latent construct, values exceeded 0.7 recommended by Hair et al. (2010).

4.3 Discriminate Validity

The discriminate validity of the measures was examined by Fornell and Larcker (1981). Discriminate validity is the degree where items are differentiated among constructs and measures distinct concepts (Fornell & Larcker, 1981). It is measured by examining the correlation between the measures of the potential overlapping constructs (Fornell & Larcker, 1981). According to Compeau et al. (1999) the average variance shared between each construct and its measure should be greater than the variance shared between the constructs and other constructs. Table 3 shows that the square root of the AVE as shown in bold values on the diagonals were greater than the corresponding row and column values that indicates the measures were discriminate.

Table 3
Discriminate validity of Measurement Model

Constructs	Attitude	Ease of Use	Intention	Usefulness
Attitude	0.875			
Ease of Use	0.406	0.882		
Intention	0.673	0.463	0.79	
Usefulness	0.494	0.561	0.542	0.857

Note: Bold values indicate the square root of AVE of each construct

Discriminate validity can be measured by examining the cross loading of the indicators (Hair Jr et al., 2016). It can be performed by comparing an indicator's outer loadings on the associated constructs and it should be greater than all of its loading on the other constructs (Ngah et al., 2015). Table 4 depicts that all the items measuring a particular constructs loaded higher on that construct and loaded lower on the other constructs that confirms the discriminate validity of the constructs.

Table 4
Loading and Cross Loadings

Items	Attitude	Intention	Ease of Use	Usefulness
ATT1	**0.886**	0.568	0.325	0.444
ATT2	**0.906**	0.614	0.391	0.476
ATT3	**0.833**	0.585	0.348	0.373
INT1	0.618	**0.819**	0.295	0.393
INT2	0.585	**0.830**	0.413	0.407
INT3	0.454	**0.774**	0.359	0.468
INT4	0.435	**0.735**	0.422	0.476
PEOU1	0.365	0.387	**0.873**	0.471
PEOU2	0.302	0.393	**0.894**	0.51
PEOU3	0.403	0.443	**0.879**	0.504
PU1	0.442	0.486	0.536	**0.902**
PU2	0.407	0.496	0.475	**0.890**
PU3	0.421	0.406	0.425	**0.772**

4.3.1 Heterotrait-Monotrait Ratio (HTMT)

There is another approach to assess the discriminant validity suggested by Henseler et al. (2015) through multitrait and multimethod matrix, namely the Heterotrait-Monotrait Ratio (HTMT). There are two ways of using the HTMT approach to assess the discriminant validity. At first, when using it as a criterion, if HTMT value is greater than 0.85, then there is a problem with discriminant validity. Secondly, by using statistical test for HTMT inference when the confidence interval of HTMT values for the structural paths contains the value if 1, it indicates a lack of discriminant validity. If the value of 1 falls outside the interval's range, it suggests that the constructs are empirically distinct. HTMT results can be seen in following Table 5.

Table 5
Heterotrait-Monotrait Ratio (HTMT)

Constructs	Attitude	Ease of Use	Intention	Usefulness
Attitude	--------			
Ease of Use	0.474 CI.90 (0.361, 0.575)			
Intention	0.800 CI.90 (0.703, 0.879)	0.564 CI.90 (0.454, 0.654)		
Usefulness	0.594 CI.90 (0.502, 0.676)	0.669 CI.90 (0.582, 0.747)	0.679 CI.90 (0.595, 0.762)	----------

Note: Heterotrait-Monotrait Ratio (HTMT) discriminate at (HTMT <0.9/ HTMT <0.85)

Based on the results of Table 5, all HTMT values are lower than the required threshold value of HTMT.85 by Kline (2011) and HTMT of .90 by Gold and Arvind Malhotra (2001), indicating that discriminate validity is valid for this study. Furthermore, the result shows that neither lower nor upper confidence interval (CI) includes a value of 1. To sum up, both convergent and discriminant validity of the measure were developed.

4.4 Structural Model Evaluation

Measurement model was achieved after conducting validity and reliability analysis. Moving further with Smart PLS3.0 software (Ringle et al., 2015) structural equation model (SEM) was performed to assess the strength of the of the proposed model for this study. In order to assess the structural model lateral collinearity test (VIF), R^2 values and corresponding t-values were evaluated as suggested by Hair Jr et al. (2016). The proposed hypothesis were tested by running a bootstrapping procedure with a resample of 5000, as suggested by Hair Jr et al. (2014).

4.5. Lateral Collinearity Assessment

At first stage of structural equation model, lateral collinearity was assessed with collinearity statistics VIF. According to Kock and Lynn (2012) although vertical collinearity are met, lateral collinearity (predictor- criterion collinearity) may sometimes be misleading the findings. This type of collinearity is occurred when two variables that are hypothesized to be causally related measure the same construct. This type of collinearity is assessed with VIF values, where the values of VIF 3.3 or higher, indicate a potential collinearity (Diamantopoulos & Siguaw, 2006). Table 6 shows the results of VIF values.

Table 6
Results of Lateral Collinearity Assessment

Constructs	Attitude	Ease of Use	Intention	Usefulness
Attitude			1.000	
Ease of Use	1.460			1.000
Intention				
Usefulness	1.460			

As presented in Table 6 the inner VIF values of the independent variables (Ease of use and Usefulness) that needs to be examined for multicollinearity are less than 5 and 3.3, indicating lateral multicollinearity is not a concern in this study Hair Jr et al. (2014).

4.6. Hypothesis Testing

The hypothesis developed for this study were tested by running a bootstrapping procedure with a resample of 5000, as suggested by Hair Jr et al. (2014). The results of Table 7 depict path coefficients of respective constructs with their level of significance.

Table 7
Results of Structural Model Analysis (Hypothesis Testing)

#	Constructs	B	S.E	t-values	P-Values	Results
H1	Usefulness → Attitude	0.388	0.057	6.875	***	Supported
H2	Ease of Use → Usefulness	0.561	0.045	12.447	***	Supported
H3	Ease of Use → Attitude	0.188	0.066	2.851	***	Supported
H4	Attitude → Intention	0.673	0.038	17.557	***	Supported

Note: Significance level where, $*p < 0.05$, $**p < 0.01$, $***p < 0.001$.

The results reveal that all four hypotheses had significance relationship with their respective endogenous variables. Table 7 depicts that the relationship between usefulness to attitude is supported by H1: ($\beta = 0.388$, $p < 0.001$). Next, the relationship between perceived ease of use to usefulness is supported by H2: ($\beta = 0.561$, $p < 0.001$). H3 showed that perceived ease of use is positively related with attitude by ($\beta = 0.188$, $p < 0.001$). Finally, the results of H5, where the relationship between attitude to intention is supported by ($\beta = 0.673$, $p < 0.001$).

4.7 Evaluating Effect Size

The R^2 for attitude, perceived usefulness and intention to adopt internet banking were 0.268, 0.315 and 0.453, respectively which are acceptable based on the cut-off suggested by Cohen (1988). Researchers also assessed the effect size of (f^2). As suggested by Cohen (1988) P value can show the effect exists however it does not reveal the size of the effect. In Table 8 the effect of the size of (f^2) can be seen where hypothesis H2 and H4 depicted large effect size, whereas H1 has small effect size and H3 presented medium effect size as suggested by Cohen (1988). Further to this, researchers also assessed predictive relevance of the model by using the blindfolding procedure. Blindfolding procedure should only be applied to endogenous constructs that have a reflective measurement (Hair Jr et al., 2016). If the Q^2 values are greater than 0 it shows that the model had predictive relevance for a certain endogenous construct (Cohen, 1988; Hair Jr et al., 2016). Table 8 shows that the value of Q^2 is greater than 0 that depicts the proposed model had significant predictive relevance.

Table 8
Evaluating Effect Size

Path	Constructs	R^2	Q^2	f^2	Decision
	Attitude	0.268	0.191		
	Intention	0.453	0.260		
	Perceived Usefulness	0.315	0.216		
H1	PU → ATT			0.141	Small
H2	PEOU → PU			0.460	Large
H3	PEOU → ATT			0.033	Medium
H4	ATT → INT			0.830	Large

Note: f^2: 0.02, small; 0.15, medium; 0.35, large

4.7 Importance performance matrix analysis (IPMA)

A post-hoc importance performance matrix analysis (IPMA) was performed by using intention to adopt internet banking as target construct. The IPMA builds on the PLS estimates of the structural equation model relationship and includes an additional dimension to the analysis of that latent constructs (Hair Jr et al., 2016). The importance scores were carried from the total effects of outcome variable in structural equation model. While performance score or index were derived by rescaling the latent variables score ranges from 0 for the lowest to 100 for the highest (Hair Jr et al., 2016). Table 9 presents the total effects (importance) and index values (performance) used for the importance performance matrix analysis.

Table 9
Index Values and Total Effects

Latent Variables	Total effect of the latent variable Intention to adopt Internet Banking (Importance)	Index values (Performance)
Attitude	0.689	67.74
Ease of Use	0.276	63.485
Usefulness	0.261	60.401

Table 9 shows the index values and total effect scores. It can be seen that attitude is the most important factor in order to determine the intention to adopt internet banking due to higher importance values compared to other latent variables. Ease of use is at intermediate level, while perceived usefulness has the lowest importance level after perceived ease of use. The level of importance and performance can be seen in Fig. 3.

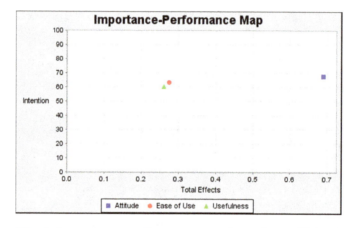

Fig. 3. Importance performance matrix analyses (IPMA)

Importance performance matrix map shows that, attitude has the highest importance level to influence on customers intentions to adopt internet banking. With respect to predecessor of attitude, the constructs perceived ease of use depicted intermediate importance while perceived usefulness showed the lowest importance. To sum up, for managerial activities to achieve customer intention towards adoption of internet banking we should focus on improving the performance of attitude and perceived ease of use.

5 Discussion and Conclusion

Drawing upon the technology acceptance factors, this paper has investigated the interrelationship among proposed variables and examined their effects on customer's intentions to use the internet banking. Internet banking is becoming prevalent (Jayawardhena & Foley, 2000). Improvements in service can only be achieved when it is measured in its first place (Rahi, 2015). Furst et al. (2002) stated that the profitability of the banks by using internet banking was higher than nonusers of internet banking. Furthermore, internet banking is creating new marketing opportunities and improving customer loyalty (Rahi, 2016). In Pakistani banking sector there is a great need to identify the factors that affect adoption of internet banking (Rahi, 2015). The present model provides core factors of technology acceptance that would helpful for new internet banking users. Customers intentions of internet banking was measured with perceived usefulness, perceived ease of use and attitude and findings also supported with previous studies (Al-Bakri & Katsioloudes, 2015; Bashir & Madhavaiah, 2015; Kesharwani & Singh Bisht, 2012; Kumar Sharma & Madhumohan Govindaluri, 2014; Marakarkandy et al., 2017; Shanmugam et al., 2015).

6 Research Contribution

This study has contributed significantly to research on consumer behavioral intention to adopt internet technology. The contribution of this study is in threefold; theoretical, methodological, and managerial contribution, which are discussed below.

6.1 Theoretical contribution

In theory perspective, this study suggests a new direction for academic and researcher by presenting the technology acceptance model factors. It is worthy to note that in measuring adoption behaviors of internet banking users, the proposed technology acceptance model is compatible. The findings of this study suggest that perceived ease of use was the most influential factor after attitude in prediction of customer's intentions. Furthermore, the proposed model makes important contribution to the emerging literature on e-commerce especially in internet banking context.

6.2 Managerial Implication

The results of this study revealed that the willingness to adopt internet banking will increase if customers believe that perceived ease of use and perceived usefulness are correctly managed. Perceived ease of use plays a major role on usefulness of internet banking websites. Therefore, banks can focus on website development process and how they can bring easiness in use of internet banking websites. Furthermore, in importance performance matrix analysis attitude has seen the most important factor. Thus, banks can focus on cultivation of positive attitudinal beliefs about internet banking among prospect customers.

6.3 Methodological Contribution

This study used structural equation modelling (SEM) approach, respectively, to validate the measurements and test the causal relationships and empirically examined the determinants of customer intention to adopt internet banking. Furthermore, this study collects the actual internet banking customer's responses from one of commercial bank in Lahore city of Pakistan.

6.4 Limitations and directions for Future Research

Future research can apply this model in other developing countries to contrast and compare the factors that affect the internet banking adoption. Second, the variables selected in this study may not include all the variables that affect internet banking adoption. Using other variables derived from technology acceptance theory or theory of planned behaviors researchers can observe the behavioral intention of internet banking users. This study is cross-sectional in its nature and measures the internet banking user's behavior at one point in time that may be less significant as compare to longitudinal study.

References

AbuShanab, E., Pearson, J. M., & Setterstrom, A. J. (2010). Internet banking and customers' acceptance in Jordan: the unified model's perspective. *Communications of the Association for Information Systems, 26*(1), 23.

Ajzen, I., & Fishbein, M. (1980). Understanding attitudes and predicting social behaviour.

Al-Ajam, A. S., & Md Nor, K. (2015). Challenges of adoption of internet banking service in Yemen. *International Journal of Bank Marketing, 33*(2), 178-194.

Al-Bakri, A. A., & Katsioloudes, M. I. (2015). The factors affecting e-commerce adoption by Jordanian SMEs. *Management Research Review, 38*(7), 726-749.

Bashir, I., & Madhavaiah, C. (2015). Consumer attitude and behavioural intention towards Internet banking adoption in India. *Journal of Indian Business Research, 7*(1), 67-102.

Becker, S., Bryman, A., & Ferguson, H. (2012). *Understanding research for social policy and social work: themes, methods and approaches*: Policy Press.

Chin, W. W. (1998). Commentary: Issues and opinion on structural equation modeling: JSTOR.

Cohen, J. (1988). Statistical power analysis for the behavioural sciences. Hillside. *NJ: Lawrence Earlbaum Associates*.

Compeau, D., Higgins, C. A., & Huff, S. (1999). Social cognitive theory and individual reactions to computing technology: A longitudinal study. *MIS quarterly*, 145-158.

Comrey, A., & Lee, H. (1992). Afirst course infactor analysis. *Hillsdale, NJ: Erlbaum*.

Davis, F. D. (1989). Perceived usefulness, perceived ease of use, and user acceptance of information technology. *MIS quarterly*, 319-340.

Diamantopoulos, A., & Siguaw, J. A. (2006). Formative versus reflective indicators in organizational measure development: A comparison and empirical illustration. *British Journal of Management, 17*(4), 263-282.

F. Hair Jr, J., Sarstedt, M., Hopkins, L., & G. Kuppelwieser, V. (2014). Partial least squares structural equation modeling (PLS-SEM) An emerging tool in business research. *European Business Review, 26*(2), 106-121.

Fornell, C., & Larcker, D. F. (1981). Structural equation models with unobservable variables and measurement error: Algebra and statistics. *Journal of Marketing Research*, 382-388.

Furst, K., Lang, W. W., & Nolle, D. E. (2002). Internet banking. *Journal of Financial Services Research, 22*(1-2), 95-117.

Gold, A. H., & Arvind Malhotra, A. H. S. (2001). Knowledge management: An organizational capabilities perspective. *Journal of Management Information Systems, 18*(1), 185-214.

Hair, J. F. (2003). *Essentials of Business Research Methods*: Wiley.

Hair, J. F., Black, W. C., Babin, B. J., Anderson, R. E. & Tatham, R. L. . (2010). Multivariate Data Analysis 7.

Hair Jr, J. F., Hult, G. T. M., Ringle, C., & Sarstedt, M. (2016). *A primer on partial least squares structural equation modeling (PLS-SEM)*: Sage Publications.

Han, S.-L., & Baek, S. (2004). Antecedents and consequences of service quality in online banking: An application of the SERVQUAL instrument. *ACR North American Advances, 31*, 208-214.

Han, S. (2003). Individual adoption of information systems in organizations: A literature review of technology acceptance model. *Turku Centre for Computer Science (TUCS)*.

Henseler, J., Ringle, C. M., & Sarstedt, M. (2015). A new criterion for assessing discriminant validity in variance-based structural equation modeling. *Academy of Marketing Science. Journal, 43*(1), 115.

Henseler, J., Ringle, C. M., & Sinkovics, R. R. (2009). The use of partial least squares path modeling in international marketing. *Advances in International Marketing, 20*(1), 277-319.

Jayawardhena, C., & Foley, P. (2000). Changes in the banking sector–the case of Internet banking in the UK. *Internet Research, 10*(1), 19-31.

Kesharwani, A., & Singh Bisht, S. (2012). The impact of trust and perceived risk on internet banking adoption in India: An extension of technology acceptance model. *International Journal of Bank Marketing, 30*(4), 303-322.

Kline, R. (2011). Principles and Practice of Structural Equation Modeling, 3rd edn Guilford Press. *New York*.

Kock, N., & Lynn, G. (2012). Lateral collinearity and misleading results in variance-based SEM: An illustration and recommendations.

Kumar Sharma, S., & Madhumohan Govindaluri, S. (2014). Internet banking adoption in India: structural equation modeling approach. *Journal of Indian Business Research, 6*(2), 155-169.

Lee, M.-C. (2009). Factors influencing the adoption of internet banking: An integration of TAM and TPB with perceived risk and perceived benefit. *Electronic Commerce Research and Applications, 8*(3), 130-141.

Marakarkandy, B., Yajnik, N., & Dasgupta, C. (2017). Enabling internet banking adoption: An empirical examination with an augmented technology acceptance model (TAM). *Journal of Enterprise Information Management, 30*(2), 263-294.

Martins, C., Oliveira, T., & Popovič, A. (2014). Understanding the Internet banking adoption: A unified theory of acceptance and use of technology and perceived risk application. *International Journal of Information Management, 34*(1), 1-13.

Ngah, A. H., Zainuddin, Y., & Thurasamy, R. (2015). Barriers and enablers in adopting of Halal warehousing. *Journal of Islamic Marketing, 6*(3), 354-376.

o'Reilly, P., & Finnegan, P. (2003). Internet banking systems: An exploration of contemporary issues. *Journal of systems and information technology, 7*(1/2), 93-110.

Rahi, S. (2015). Moderating role of brand image with relation to internet banking and customer loyalty: A case of branchless banking. *The Journal of Internet Banking and Commerce, 20*(3).

Rahi, S. (2016a). Impact of customer perceived value and customer's perception of public relation on customer loyalty with moderating role of brand image. *Journal of Internet Banking and Commerce, 21*(2).

Rahi, S. (2016b). Impact of customer value, public relations perception and brand image on customer loyalty in services sector of Pakistan. *Arabian Journal of Bussiness Management Review, S, 2,* 2.

Rahi, S., & Ghani, M. (2016a). Internet banking, customer perceived value and loyalty: The role of switching costs. *Journal of Accounting and Marketing, 5*(2), 188.

Rahi, S., & Ghani, M. A. (2016b). Customers' perception of public relation in e-commerce and its impact on e-loyalty with brand image and switching cost. *Journal of Internet Banking and Commerce, 21*(3).

Rahi, S. (2017). Research design and methods: A systematic review of research paradigms, sampling issues and instruments development. *International Journal of Economics & Management Sciences, 6*(2).

Rahi, S., Yasin, N. M., & Alnaser, F. M. (2017). Measuring the role of website design, assurance, customer service and brand image towards customer loyalty and intention to adopt interent banking. *The Journal of Internet Banking and Commerce, 22*(S8).

Ringle, C. M., Wende, S., & Becker, J.-M. (2015). SmartPLS 3. Boenningstedt: SmartPLS GmbH.

Shanmugam, M., Wang, Y.-Y., Bugshan, H., & Hajli, N. (2015). Understanding customer perceptions of internet banking: the case of the UK. *Journal of Enterprise Information Management, 28*(5), 622-636.

Suleiman Awwad, M., & Mohammad Agti, D. A. (2011). The impact of internal marketing on commercial banks' market orientation. *International Journal of Bank Marketing, 29*(4), 308-332.

Venkatesh, V., & Davis, F. D. (2000). A theoretical extension of the technology acceptance model: Four longitudinal field studies. *Management science, 46*(2), 186-204.

Venkatesh, V., Morris, M. G., Davis, G. B., & Davis, F. D. (2003). User acceptance of information technology: Toward a unified view. *MIS Quarterly, 27*(3), 425-478.

Wang, Y.-S., Wang, Y.-M., Lin, H.-H., & Tang, T.-I. (2003). Determinants of user acceptance of Internet banking: an empirical study. *International Journal of Service Industry Management, 14*(5), 501-519.

Wixom, B. H., & Todd, P. A. (2005). A theoretical integration of user satisfaction and technology acceptance. *Information systems research, 16*(1), 85-102.

Wu, S.-I. (2006). A comparison of the behavior of different customer clusters towards Internet bookstores. *Information & Management, 43*(8), 986-1001.

Yee-Loong Chong, A., Ooi, K.-B., Lin, B., & Tan, B.-I. (2010). Online banking adoption: an empirical analysis. *International Journal of Bank Marketing, 28*(4), 267-287.

Zeithaml, V. A., Berry, L. L., & Parasuraman, A. (1996). The behavioral consequences of service quality. *the Journal of Marketing, 60*(2), 31-46.

Zhang, X., & Prybutok, V. R. (2005). A consumer perspective of e-service quality. *IEEE transactions on Engineering Management, 52*(4), 461-477.

Zhuang, Y., & Lederer, A. L. (2004). The impact of top management commitment, business process redesign, and IT planning on the business-to-consumer e-commerce site. *Electronic Commerce Research, 4*(4), 315-333.

Systematic model for lean product development implementation in an automotive related company

Daniel Osezua Aikhuele[a]

[a]*Faculty of Manufacturing Engineering, Universiti Malaysia Pahang, 26600 Pekan, Malaysia*

CHRONICLE	ABSTRACT
Keywords: Lean product development practices Fuzzy Shannon's entropy Modified Technique for Order Preference by Similarity to the Ideal Solution Systematic model Implementation limitations	Lean product development is a major innovative business strategy that employs sets of practices to achieve an efficient, innovative and a sustainable product development. Despite the many benefits and high hopes in the lean strategy, many companies are still struggling, and unable to either achieve or sustain substantial positive results with their lean implementation efforts. However, as the first step towards addressing this issue, this paper seeks to propose a systematic model that considers the administrative and implementation limitations of lean thinking practices in the product development process. The model which is based on the integration of fuzzy Shannon's entropy and Modified Technique for Order Preference by Similarity to the Ideal Solution (M-TOPSIS) model for the lean product development practices implementation with respective to different criteria including management and leadership, financial capabilities, skills and expertise and organization culture, provides a guide or roadmap for product development managers on the lean implementation route.

1. Introduction

The increasing demands for customized and hybrid products are gradually moving new product development from being a competitive advantage to a necessity in today's fast-growing global market (Carulli et al. 2013). For product development companies to stay competitive in the market they are being pressured to address their product development challenges innovatively, and one way of doing that is through the integration of lean thinking practices in their product development process (Aikhuele & Turan 2016d). Lean which is an improvement philosophy was first developed by the Toyota Motor Company, primarily to eliminate waste from the production system. However, in recent years, these thinking have been extended to other areas including the product development process. According to John et al. (2014), applying lean thinking practices in new product development can help save the huge resources normally spent fighting sudden quality and reliability issues, and can lead to faster product

* Corresponding author.
E-mail address: danbishop_22@yahoo.co.uk (D. O. Aikhuele)

development time, reduction in warranty costs, easier and cheaper manufacturing processes, high-quality suppliers products since the supply chain are involved in the development process of the product and finally the creation of an atmosphere and culture of doing things right the first time.

Despite the many benefits and high hopes in the lean strategy, many companies are still struggling, and unable to neither achieve nor sustain substantial positive results with their lean implementation efforts (Stenius 2011; Azizi & Aikhuele 2015). In the work of León and Farris (2011), they suggested that, one of the major issue affecting the efficient administration and implementation of lean product development practices in companies lies in the absent of a unified and holistic model for assessing the performance of lean product development practices and in tracking their progress as they seek to achieve efficient and effective lean product development process executions. Letens et al. (2011), claim that the poor implementation of lean product development practices is due to the lack of clear understanding of lean thinking and their characteristic practices. While Stenius (2011) suggest that, the lack of lean thinking when implementing lean is the main issue affecting the efficient administration and implementation of lean product development practices, and proposed a framework for the prioritization of lean development actions.

As the first step towards addressing this issue, this paper, however, seeks to propose a systematic model that considers the administrative and implementation limitations of lean thinking practices in the product development process. The model which is based on fuzzy Shannon's entropy and the Modified Technique for Order Preference by Similarity to the Ideal Solution (M-TOPSIS) model originally proposed in (Ren et al. 2007; Aikhuele & Turan 2016a;b) is applied to the lean product development practices with respective to the criteria; management and leadership, financial capabilities, skills and expertise and organization culture which was initially introduced in (Shah and Ward 2003) for lean manufacturing, which the author believe could provide a guide or roadmap for product development managers on lean implementation route and in the adoption of lean practices in the product development process.

Most of the proposed methods, models and frameworks for implementing lean practices in the lean product development literature have all been conceptual and based on the experience of implementing lean. Extensive literature review shows that there are no systematic methods or model for implementing lean thinking practices in the product development process or models that consider the vulnerabilities, limitations and implementation risk of the practices.

The implementation of the proposed methodology in this study stands as a pioneer multi-criteria approach for assessing lean practices in the product development environment. It is hoped that it will assist product development managers to lead their department as well as the entire organization to leanness. This study technically contributes to process improvement of decision making, modeling, analysis of lean product development practices and the identification and analyzing of administrative and implementation limitations in lean product development process.

The rest of the paper is organized as follows. The following section presents the literature review, preliminaries, research methodology, application of the proposed model and finally discussion, comparison of the result, limitations of the study and conclusion.

2. Literature Review

2.1. Lean product development framework

Over the last two decades, several papers including the theoretical and practical aspects of the lean product development practices have been published, where some have focused on defining the lean product development (Hoppmann et al., 2011), other concentrated on the development of implementation and support models and frameworks which include steps and tools for the implementation of lean product development practices. The focal point of some models and frameworks are reviewed below.

Furuhjelm, et al. (2011), provide input to a generic Lean Product Development framework by defining an explanatory model for effective knowledge enhancement and execution of development projects. The model which consist of a two by two matrix, with value streams, Product Value Stream and the Knowledge Value Stream at one hand, product and the Concept phase and Implementation phase on the other hand serves as a basis for discussing how the Lean principles, Flow, Visualization, Standardization, and Continuous Improvement could be implemented. Wasim et al. (2013) develop a cost modeling system for lean product and process to support a proactive decision-making process as well as in the elimination of mistake in the design stage using lean enablers like the set-based concurrent engineering, mistake proofing (Poka-yoke) and knowledge-based engineering.

Nepal, et al. (2011), through a reflective case study of a lean product development presented a lean transformation framework which was based on 13 lean principles of the Toyota Product Development System and it was implemented in a manufacturing firm in the US, using design structure and cause and effect matrixes for the analysis of the lean transformation and to determine the root causes of wasteful reworks in the company. Hines, et al. (2006) propose a six-step theoretical framework that they hope could serve as a reference point for academic discussion on the development of systemic approaches to the lean product development process, as well as for industry searching for a framework in their new product development process.

Letens, et al. (2011), propose a multilevel framework which captures key lean product development principles at the functional, project, and portfolio levels; tools and practices for implementing the lean product development practices at each level; and also discuss the approaches for managing the interactions between levels. Saad et al. (2013), presents a new approach, A3 thinking approach for solving problems in the product design process. Narayanamurthy (2014), presents the 7A process selection model for guiding the identification and selection of a suitable process for lean implementation. Parry and Turner (2006), develop a lean visual process management tools which serve as communication aids and are used to drive operations and processes in real time. Wang et al. (2012), presents a step-by-step implementation framework for lean product development starting from the marketing research on the product development process, product design through to the launch of the final product, where the framework was aimed at overcoming the weaknesses in the existing framework in terms of reliability and feasibility.

Even with a large number of proposed models and frameworks for implementing lean in the product development process, none of these models and frameworks accounts for the administrative constraint, risk and other limiting factors associated with the lean implementation. The models and frameworks all rely on output from lean assessment to define and design their implementation sequence, route, and startup point regardless of the implementation constraints and limitations. This study intends however, to address this issue by integrating the outcome of the lean assessment with the systematic model that involves all the lean implementation constraints as evaluating criteria for possible implementation strategy (lean practices), thus selecting the optimal lean practice that suits the situation of the organization.

2.2. Lean product development assessment

The lean product development assessment which represents the first step of all proposed lean implementation models and frameworks is aimed at defining the current leanness level of the lean practicing organization (Wang et al. 2012). Upon reviewing the lean product development assessment literature and case studies, different assessment models and tools have been found for conducting the lean assessment including (Haque & Moore, 2004; Al-Ashaab et al., 2015; Mohammadi, 2010; Chase, 2000;

Sopelana et al., 2012). However, no unique assessment model or tool identified can be said to fit all product development company.

The models and tools which are based on observation, survey and questionnaire, uses sets of typical questions which are arranged in clusters, with each one of them relating to a particular aspect of the assessment. The main different between them however includes; the lean practices assessed, the different metrics and evaluating criteria, the level of details included in them, cost, general implementation approaches and the answering form of the questionnaire questions. For example, some of the models and tools assigned numerical score on a customized scale, between one and five for each of the questions (Al-Ashaab et al., 2015), while other used the value stream mapping approach to determine the current state and then design a future state for series of events (Chase, 2000).

3. Research methodology

In this paper, the proposed systematic model which is used to determine the optimal lean practices that suit the organization situation is carried out in two phases that are the lean product development assessment by experts (E) and then the implementation of the M-TOPSIS and fuzzy Shannon entropy model using information obtain from the experts. Each the phase is accomplished following the steps as shown in the flowchart in Fig. 1.

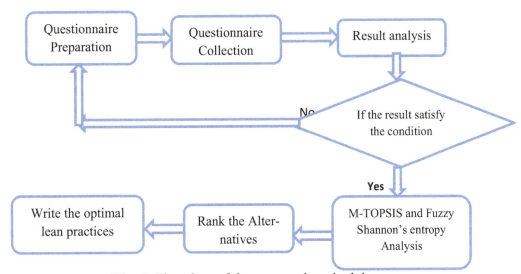

Fig. 1. Flowchart of the proposed methodology

The lean product development assessment by experts is used to determine the current situation of the company, as it relates to the application of lean practices in the product development department, how far it is from full leanness level with special considerations of all the implementation constraints. This phase starts by preparing a questionnaire survey that contains all the implemented lean practices in the company as shown in Table 1, follows the collection and analysis of the questionnaire answers.

The outcome of the analysis is then transferred to the final phase, where the weight of the evaluating criteria are determined by the fuzzy Shannon's entropy method using $\alpha = 0.5$ for the sensitivity analysis while the final optimal lean practices that suit the organization situation is determined with the M-TOPSIS model with special considerations of the vagueness and uncertainty of the results of the questionnaire. In implementing the M-TOPSIS model, the study will be exploring the application of the Normalized-Hamming distances metric functions for the Fuzzy Positive Ideal Solution (FPIS) and Fuzzy negative Positive Ideal Solution (FNIS).

Table 1
Extended lean product development framework

	Lean product development practices	Literature support
(A_1)	Set-based concurrent engineering	(Khan et al. 2011; Aikhuele and Turan 2016c)
(A_2)	Chief Engineer technical leadership	(Aikhuele and Turan 2016d; Al-Ashaab, Shehab, and Alam 2010)
(A_3)	Cross-functional teams	(Kim and Kang 2008; Sethi and Al. 2001)
(A_4)	Continuous improvement	(Berger 1997; Yan and Makinde 2011; Kano and Shimizu 2001)
(A_5)	Supplier integration	(Petersen, et al. 2005a; Ragatz, et al. 2002)
(A_6)	Rapid prototyping, simulation, and testing	(Azeem and Gondal 2011; Marvel and Standridge 2013)
(A_7)	A3 Reports Thinking	(Mohd Saad et al. 2013; Lind 2009; Aikhuele and Turan 2016c)
(A_8)	Value stream mapping in product development (VSM-PD)	(Gershenson and Pavnaskar 2003; McManus 2005)
(A_9)	Knowledge-based engineering,	(Rodriguez and Ashaab 2007; Maksimovic et al. 2012)
(A_{10})	Standardization	(Krichbaum 2008) (Aikhuele and Turan 2016d)
(A_{11})	Modularity	(Pugh 1996; Chen and Tan 1994; Harland and Uddin 2014)
(A_{12})	Visual management	(Carulli, Bordegoni, and Cugini 2013; Jurado 2012; Parry and Turner 2006)

3.1. Preliminaries

Fuzzy Set Theory

Fuzzy set theory was introduced by Zadeh in 1965. Its concept is based on the fact that, the range of truth value of membership function (relations) are the closed interval [0,1] of real numbers (Zadeh 1965). The FST is designed in such a way that it can deal with problems in which source of vagueness and uncertainties are involved. The concept has been successfully utilized in modeling and incorporating imprecise and vague information into decision framework and judgments of decision makers.

Mathematically fuzzy set (e.g. fuzzy set $\tilde{A}$) are defined by means of membership function $\mu_A(x)$, which associates with each element x in the universe of discourse X a real number in the interval [0, 1]. A triangular fuzzy number $\tilde{A}$ which can be defined by the triplet (l_1, m_1, u_1), their membership function are express as;

$$\mu_A(x) = \begin{cases} \frac{x-1}{m-1} & \text{for } l \leq x \leq m, \\ \frac{u-x}{x-m} & \text{for } m \leq x \leq u, \\ 0 & \text{for } x > u, \end{cases} \quad (1)$$

where **l**, **m** and **u** are real numbers and **l** < **m** < **u**. Outside the interval [**l**, **u**], the pertinence degree is null, and **m** represents the point in which the pertinence degree is maximum. Basic arithmetic operations on the triangular fuzzy numbers are shown below;

Definition 1: Given any real number **K** and two fuzzy triangular numbers $\tilde{A} = (l_1, m_1, u_1)$ and $\tilde{B} = (l_2, m_2, u_2)$, the main algebraic operations are expressed as follows:

(1) Addition of two triangular fuzzy numbers

$$\tilde{A}(+)\tilde{B} = (l_1 + l_2, m_1 + m_2, u_1 + u_2), \quad l_1 \geq 0, l_2 \geq 0 \quad (2)$$

(2) Multiplication of two triangular fuzzy numbers

$$\tilde{A}(\times)\tilde{B} = (l_1 \times l_2, m_1 \times m_2, u_1 \times u_2), \quad l_1 \geq 0, l_2 \geq 0 \quad (3)$$

(3) Subtraction of two triangular fuzzy numbers

$$\tilde{A}(-)\tilde{B} = (l_1 - l_2, m_1 - m_2, u_1 - u_2), \quad l_1 \geq 0, l_2 \geq 0 \tag{4}$$

(4) Division of two triangular fuzzy numbers

$$\tilde{A}(\div)\tilde{B} = (l_1 \div l_2, m_1 \div m_2, u_1 \div u_2), \quad l_1 \geq 0, l_2 \geq 0 \tag{5}$$

(5) Inverse of a triangular fuzzy number

$$\tilde{A}^{-1} = \left(\frac{1}{u_1}, \frac{1}{m_1}, \frac{1}{l_1}\right) \geq 0 \tag{6}$$

(6) Multiplication of a triangular fuzzy number by a constant

$$k \times \tilde{A} = (k \times l_1, k \times m_1, k \times u_1) \; l_1 \geq 0, k \geq 0 \tag{7}$$

(7) Division of a triangular fuzzy number by a constant

$$\frac{\tilde{A}}{k} = \left(\frac{l_1}{k}, \frac{m_1}{k}, \frac{u_1}{k}\right) \; l_1 \geq 0, k \geq 0 \tag{8}$$

3.2. M-TOPSIS and fuzzy Shannon's entropy

TOPSIS which is an abbreviation of Technique for Order Preference by Similarity to the Ideal Solution was first proposed by Hwang and Yoon. (1981) and ever since it has remained one of the most widely used MCDM method with so many literatures published and in several different field of study including, Chemical science (Soufi et al., 2015), Design (Yang & Wu, 2008), Engineering (Zhu et al., 2012), Health and medicine (Chou et al., 2012) etc. However, due to some of its limitation, many different improvement and modifications have been proposed, prominently among such improvement is the M-TOPSIS model by Ren et al. (2007).

The M-TOPSIS method which was presented to meet the need for a better and simpler method creates an understanding of the inherent relationship between the R value and alternative evaluation. The M-TOPSIS method is "described as a process of calculating the distance between the alternatives and the reference points in the D+D−-plane and constructing the R value to evaluate the quality of alternative" (Ren et al., 2007; Aikhuele & Turan, 2016a). The M-TOPSIS method is unique for its ability to solve ranking reversals issues in TOPSIS and to evaluate failure when alternatives are symmetrical. This study intends to explore the application of the M-TOPSIS method in a fuzzy environment and to apply the Normalized-Hamming distance method in the analysis, instead of the traditional Euclidean distance method. From the best of our knowledge, this is the first study to apply the M-TOPSIS method and the Normalized-Hamming distance methods for its lean product development analysis.

The M-TOPSIS under a fuzzy environment can be expressed concisely using the following steps:

Step 1. Construct the fuzzy decision matrix $(\tilde{D})$ of the alternatives (A_i) with respect to the criteria (C_i):

$$\tilde{D} = \begin{matrix} & C_1 & C_2 & \cdots & C_m \\ A_1 \\ A_1 \\ \vdots \\ A_n \end{matrix} \begin{bmatrix} \tilde{x}_{11} & \tilde{x}_{12} & \cdots & \tilde{x}_{1m} \\ \tilde{x}_{21} & \tilde{x}_{22} & \cdots & \tilde{x}_{2m} \\ \vdots & \vdots & \ddots & \vdots \\ \tilde{x}_{n1} & \tilde{x}_{n2} & \cdots & \tilde{x}_{nm} \end{bmatrix} \tag{9}$$

Step 2. Normalize the fuzzy decision matrix of the alternatives $(\widetilde{D})$ using linear scale transformation. The normalized decision matrix $\widetilde{R}$ is given by:

$$\widetilde{R} = [\tilde{r}_{ij}]_{m \times n} \qquad (10)$$

where $\tilde{r}_{ij} = \left(\frac{l_{ij}}{u_j^+}, \frac{m_{ij}}{u_j^+}, \frac{u_{ij}}{u_j^+}\right)$ and $u_j^+ = \max_i u_{ij}$ (benefit criteria) or, $\tilde{r}_{ij} = \left(\frac{l_j^-}{u_{ij}}, \frac{l_j^-}{m_{ij}}, \frac{l_j^-}{l_{ij}}\right)$ and $l_j^- = \max_i l_{ij}$ (cost criteria)

Step 3. Determine the weight of each of the evaluating criteria. Then compute the weighted normalized decision matrix, $\widetilde{V}$, by multiplying the weights of the evaluation criteria, $\widetilde{w}_j$, by the elements $\tilde{r}_{ij}$ of the normalized fuzzy decision matrix. The weights of the criteria are determined using the fuzzy Shannon entropy method. But first, data are collected about the alternatives according to the criteria using the linguistic terms as shown in the Table 2 below.

Table 2
Fuzzy numbers for approximating the linguistic variable

Linguistic terms	Triangular Fuzzy Numbers (TFN)
Very low (VL)	(0.1, 0.25, 0.3)
Low (L)	(0.2, 0.3, 0.55)
Good (G)	(0.3, 0.45, 0.6)
High (H)	(0.5, 0.6, 0.7)
Excellent (EX)	(0.6, 0.75, 0.9)

$$\widetilde{V} = [\tilde{v}_{ij}]_{m \times n} \qquad (11)$$

where $\tilde{v}_{ij}$ is given by $\tilde{v}_{ij} = \tilde{r}_{ij} \times \widetilde{w}_j$ and $\widetilde{w}_j$ is the entropy weight.

Fuzzy Shannon's entropy method based on $\propto$-level

In computing the criteria weight using the $\propto$-cut of TFN, first a decision matrix is formed for the criteria which express the level of importance of each of the criterion using linguistic terms, which are later converted to the TFN $a_{ij} = (l_{ij}, m_{ij}, u_{ij})$ and then to crisp value using Eq. (12)

$$x_{ij} = \frac{l_{ij} + m_{ij+}, u_{ij}}{3} \qquad (12)$$

- Normalized each of the criteria to obtain the projection value $\widetilde{P}_{ij}$;

$$\widetilde{P}_{ij} = \frac{x_{ij}}{\sum_{i=0}^{m} x_{ij}}, \text{ where } i=1,\dots, m, j=1,\dots, n. \qquad (13)$$

Thus, the projective matrix which represents the relative weight of each of criterion from the expert's assessment is expressed as;

- Compute the entropy values Ep_j;

$$Ep_j = -k \sum_{i=0}^{m} \widetilde{P}_{ij} \ln \widetilde{P}_{ij}, \quad j = 1, \dots, n \qquad (14)$$

where k is constant and is defined as $k = (\ln m)^{-1}$, if $\widetilde{P}_{ij} = 0$, then $\widetilde{P}_{ij} \ln \widetilde{P}_{ij} = 0$

- Compute the degree of diversification, d_j and finally the criteria weight w_j;

$$d_j = 1 - Ep_j, \quad w_j = \frac{d_j}{\sum_{k=1}^{n} d_k}, \quad (j = 1, \dots, n) \qquad (15)$$

Step 4. Define the fuzzy positive ideal solution (FPIS, A^+) and the fuzzy negative ideal solution (FNIS, A^-)

$$A^+ = \{\tilde{v}_l^+, \tilde{v}_j^+, \cdots, \tilde{v}_m^+\} \qquad (16)$$
$$A^- = \{\tilde{v}_l^-, \tilde{v}_j^-, \cdots, \tilde{v}_m^-\} \qquad (17)$$

Step 5. Compute the distances d_j^+ and d_j^- of each alternative from FPIS, A^+ and from FNIS, A^- using $\tilde{v}_j^+$ and $\tilde{v}_j^-$ respectively

Let $d(\tilde{A}, \tilde{B})_{L2_i}$ represents the distance point between two fuzzy numbers $(\tilde{A}, \tilde{B})$. According to the Normalized-Hamming distance method, the distance for the two fuzzy numbers in a fuzzy environment is shown respectively in the equations below (Li, 2013).

- Normalized-Hamming distance method (L_2)

$$d(\tilde{A}, \tilde{B})_{L2_{i+}} = \sqrt{\sum_{i=1}^{n} \frac{1}{6}\left[\left(l_{ij} - \tilde{v}_j^+\right)^2 + 4\left(m_{ij} - \tilde{v}_j^+\right)^2 + \left(u_{ij} - \tilde{v}_j^+\right)^2\right]} \qquad (18)$$

Similarly,

$$d(\tilde{A}, \tilde{B})_{L2_{i-}} = \sqrt{\sum_{i=1}^{n} \frac{1}{6}\left[\left(l_{ij} - \tilde{v}_j^-\right)^2 + 4\left(m_{ij} - \tilde{v}_j^-\right)^2 + \left(u_{ij} - \tilde{v}_j^-\right)^2\right]} \qquad (19)$$

Step 6. Set a point to say A as the optimized ideal references point for (A, B), for each of the distance method such that;

$$A\left(\min d(\tilde{A}, \tilde{B})^+_{L2_i}, \max d(\tilde{A}, \tilde{B})^-_{L2_i}\right)$$

Then calculate the distances from each alternative. The relative closeness R_i to the ideal solution is calculated for the distances method as shown below;

$$R_i = \sqrt{\left[\left(d(\tilde{A}, \tilde{B})^+_{L2_i} - \min d(\tilde{A}, \tilde{B})^+_{L2_i}\right)^2 + \left(d(\tilde{A}, \tilde{B})^-_{L2_i} - \max d(\tilde{A}, \tilde{B})^-_{L2_i}\right)^2\right]} \qquad (20)$$

Step 7. Rank the preference order. For ranking of alternative, R_i should be ranked in increasing order. However if there are two alternatives A_1 and A_2, $R_1 = R_2$ where $1 \neq 2$, then R_i is calculated using equation (20) then choose the better one with the smaller R_i value for all three method.

$$R_i = d(\tilde{A}, \tilde{B})^+_{l2_i} - \min d(\tilde{A}, \tilde{B})^+_{l2_i} \qquad (21)$$

Step 8. Rank the preference order of the alternatives according to their relative closeness to the ideal solution. The greater value of relative closeness represents a higher-ranking order among alternatives and will be chosen as a recommended alternative.

4. Numerical Case study of an automotive related company

In this section, we put the proposed systematic model into practice at a dedicated company that specialized in designing, developing and manufacturing automotive related parts in Pekan Malaysia. We intend to demonstrate how the model can be used in selecting optimal or the most appropriate lean practices for the company while considering their lean implementation challenges. The authors believe the starting point of achieving leanness in the company should be through the adoption of a systematic approach, thinking lean while implementing lean (Stenius, 2011), that is prioritizing the lean product development practices while considering the identified lean challenges and limitations in the past. As stated above the administrative and lean implementation limitations which serve as the criteria are described below.

- Management and leadership (C_1): According to Karlsson and Ahlström (Karlsson & Ahlström, 2013) the managerial overemphasis on R&D in development projects hampers efforts to achieve cross-functional integration, which is at the center of the lean product development initiative. A Cross-functional team cannot perform effectively in the present of sequential view on the development process rather on iterative view.
- Financial capabilities (C_2): The initial resources for introducing and implementing the different lean practices can hamper its implementation as most companies are faced with restricted resources in terms of finance and manpower. Most especially small and medium enterprise (SME) like our case company.
- Skills and expertise (C_3): Product development teams often develop specialized knowledge and skills, which often make them wanting to resist any changes away from existing specialized knowledge since they've invested so much in such knowledge.
- Organization culture (C_4): According to Liker (Liker, 2004) one of the biggest challenge when becoming Lean is "how to create an aligned organization of individuals who each have the DNA of the organization and are continually learning together to add value to the customer"

The implementation of the proposed systematic model is summarized as follows;

Step 1: The research uses the linguistic variables and then TFN to express the ratings of the lean practices A_i with respect to each of the criterion C_j to form the decision matrix ($\tilde{D}$) as shown in Tables (3-4).

Table 3
Experts ratings with Linguistic terms

C_i	E_1	E_2	E_3	E_1	E_2	E_3	E_1	E_2	E_3	E_1	E_2	E_3
	C1			C2			C3			C4		
A_1	L	G	VL	H	L	H	VL	H	G	G	L	VL
A_2	H	H	VL	EX	G	EX	L	EX	H	VL	G	L
A_3	EX	EX	L	VL	H	H	G	H	EX	L	H	G
A_4	H	H	G	L	G	G	L	L	VL	G	L	VL
A_5	H	G	L	G	H	G	H	G	L	L	G	L
A_6	VL	G	H	H	EX	H	EX	L	VL	G	H	G
A_7	L	H	VL	EX	H	H	L	G	L	H	G	H
A_8	H	EX	L	VL	EX	EX	G	H	G	G	H	L
A_9	VL	H	H	VL	H	H	VL	G	VL	G	VL	G
A_{10}	L	VL	EX	L	EX	EX	L	L	L	H	L	H
A_{11}	G	L	H	VL	H	H	G	G	G	EX	G	H
A_{12}	VL	H	G	H	H	G	VL	H	H	L	EX	G

Table 4
Decision matrix for the proposed fuzzy model

	C1	C2	C3	C4
A_1	(0.20, 0.33, 0.48)	(0.40, 0.50, 0.65)	(0.30, 0.43, 0.53)	(0.20, 0.33, 0.48)
A_2	(0.37, 0.48, 0.57)	(0.47, 0.65, 0.80)	(0.43, 0.55, 0.72)	(0.20, 0.33, 0.48)
A_3	(0.43, 0.55, 0.67)	(0.27, 0.40, 0.58)	(0.17, 0.28, 0.47)	(0.20, 0.33, 0.48)
A_4	(0.33, 0.45, 0.62)	(0.37, 0.50, 0.63)	(0.33, 0.45, 0.62)	(0.23, 0.35, 0.57)
A_5	(0.30, 0.43, 0.53)	(0.53, 0.65, 0.77)	(0.30, 0.43, 0.58)	(0.37, 0.50, 0.63)
A_6	(0.27, 0.38, 0.52)	(0.53, 0.65, 0.77)	(0.23, 0.35, 0.57)	(0.43, 0.55, 0.67)
A_7	(0.43, 0.55, 0.72)	(0.43, 0.58, 0.70)	(0.37, 0.50, 0.63)	(0.33, 0.45, 0.62)
A_8	(0.37, 0.48, 0.57)	(0.37, 0.48, 0.57)	(0.17, 0.32, 0.40)	(0.23, 0.38, 0.50)
A_9	(0.30, 0.43, 0.58)	(0.47, 0.60, 0.78)	(0.20, 0.30, 0.55)	(0.40, 0.50, 0.65)
A_{10}	(0.33, 0.45, 0.62)	(0.37, 0.48, 0.57)	(0.30, 0.45, 0.60)	(0.47, 0.60, 0.73)
A_{11}	(0.30, 0.43, 0.58)	(0.10, 0.25, 0.30)	(0.23, 0.37, 0.43)	(0.43, 0.55, 0.67)
A_{12}	(0.40, 0.50, 0.65)	(0.27, 0.40, 0.58)	(0.33, 0.45, 0.62)	(0.37, 0.50, 0.68)

Step 2: Same as Step 1, decision matrix for the criteria are constructed, using linguistic variables, TFN, and then crisp values to express the level of importance of each of the criterion. Thereafter the criteria weight is calculated using Eqs. (12-15), the result of the evaluations are shown in Tables (5-7).

Table 5
Aggregated decision matrix for fuzzy Shannon's Entropy

	C_1	C_2	C_3	C_4	C_1	C_2	C_3	C_4
E_1	VL	H	EX	H	(0.1, 0.25, 0.3)	(0.5, 0.6, 0.7)	(0.6, 0.75, 0.9)	(0.5, 0.6, 0.7)
E_2	L	EX	H	H	(0.2, 0.3, 0.55)	(0.6, 0.75, 0.9)	(0.5, 0.6, 0.7)	(0.5, 0.6, 0.7)
E_3	G	VL	EX	L	(0.3, 0.45, 0.6)	(0.1, 0.25, 0.3)	(0.6, 0.75, 0.9)	(0.2, 0.3, 0.55)
E_4	L	G	EX	G	(0.2, 0.3, 0.55)	(0.3, 0.45, 0.6)	(0.1, 0.25, 0.3)	(0.2, 0.3, 0.55)

Table 6
Crisp values and criterion projection value

	C_1	C_2	C_3	C_4	$\tilde{P}_{C_1}$	$\tilde{P}_{C_2}$	$\tilde{P}_{C_3}$	$\tilde{P}_{C_4}$
E_1	(0.217)	(0.600)	(0.750)	(0.600)	0.100	0.277	0.346	0.277
E_2	(0.350)	(0.750)	(0.600)	(0.600)	0.152	0.326	0.261	0.261
E_3	(0.450)	(0.217)	(0.750)	(0.350)	0.255	0.123	0.424	0.198
E_4	(0.350)	(0.450)	(0.217)	(0.350)	0.256	0.329	0.159	0.256

Table 7
Shannon's Entropy weight

	Ep_j	d_j	w_j
C_1	0.876	0.124	0.725
C_2	0.970	0.030	0.175
C_3	0.991	0.009	0.053
C_4	0.992	0.008	0.047

In following the other implementation steps as stated above (i.e. Steps 4-8), the optimal lean practices with respects to the evaluating criteria are calculated. The results for M-TOPSIS model for the alternatives and the rankings are shown in Table 8.

Table 8
The M-TOPSIS result

	$d(\tilde{A}, \tilde{B})_{L2_{i+}}$	$d(\tilde{A}, \tilde{B})_{L2_{i-}}$	R_i	Ranking	Fuzzy TOPSIS	Ranking
A_1	1.826	0.266	0.205	11	0.127	11
A_2	1.769	0.368	0.090	4	0.172	4
A_3	1.779	0.409	0.056	2	0.187	2
A_4	1.789	0.351	0.113	6	0.164	6
A_5	1.782	0.334	0.126	8	0.158	8
A_6	1.794	0.308	0.155	10	0.147	10
A_7	1.753	0.423	0.033	1	0.194	1
A_8	1.790	0.359	0.105	5	0.167	5
A_9	1.786	0.339	0.123	7	0.159	7
A_{10}	1.785	0.350	0.112	6	0.164	6
A_{11}	1.818	0.324	0.149	9	0.151	9
A_{12}	1.780	0.381	0.081	3	0.176	3

4.1. Discussion

The determination of the optimal lean practices with respect to administrative and lean implementation limitations; management and leadership, financial capabilities, skills and expertise and organization culture, has been realized. According to the relative closeness R_i to the ideal solution calculated, the ranking of the lean practice are in the order $A_1 > A_7 > A_{13} > A_{12} > A_6 > A_{10} > A_5 > A_{11} > A_9 > A_2 > A_{14} > A_4 > A_8 > A_3$.

The main advantage of the proposed systematic model is that it makes the decision to implement a particular lean practice over another within the product development environment with respect to the identified administrative and lean implementation limitations more reliable and more objective.

The results from the systematic model are compared with that of fuzzy TOPSIS under the same condition with the same weight values, the comparison which is based on the ranking of the methods found that the ranking for the fuzzy TOPSIS method shows that the M-TOPSIS method is quite better intense of ranking of the lean practices. The results are shown in Table 8 above. According to the fuzzy TOPSIS method, A_7 outperformed other lean practices with A_4 and A_{10} having the same rank, unlike the M-TOPSIS where the ranks for are the alternatives are quite clear.

4.2. Limitations and future scope of the research work

The results from the proposed systematic model are limited to the experiences and assessment from the case company. The values used for the evaluation in the analysis are based on the knowledge and assessment from the engaged experts and company. The scores for the relationship among the alternatives were all obtained from the experts. Hence, the accuracy of the result depends on the expert's opinion. To further improve the result, more research is certainly called for within the context of the study with more companies involved and more experts interviewed and the method can be applied in other industries.

5. Conclusion

In this paper, we proposed a systematic model based on the integration of fuzzy Shannon's Entropy method and M-TOPSIS model under a fuzzy environment, using Normalized-Hamming distance method for the lean product development practice.

The study contributes to the lean product development literature by identifying some core lean practices that have found applications in the lean product development process in companies which hitherto have not been reported in the lean product development literature. Also, it provides a guide or roadmap for product development managers on the lean implementation route, intense of, the adoption of lean practices in the product development process with respect to the identified administrative and lean implementation limitations.

In handling the subjectivity and vagueness in the data provided by the experts and the case company, a set of fuzzy numbers for approximating linguistic variable values was developed and was used in collecting the evaluation data. The importance of the Fuzzy number concept in this work lies in the fact that it helps in accounting for the degree of inherent uncertainty in the evaluation which was never considered in the previous assessment in the literature. Also, it serves as a means of incorporating uncertainty into parameters, properties, geometry or initial conditions of the evaluating method.

The result from the analysis shows that set-based concurrent engineering is ranked as the most effective lean practice, follow by rapid prototyping, simulation and testing and Modularity etc. The result from this study will serve as an advisory system and a guide for product development managers planning to evaluate their current practices, in the allocation of reasonable resources and in the implementation of lean practices in the product development with special consideration of uncertainties, administrative and lean implementations limitations.

Reference

Aikhuele, D. O., & Turan, F. B. M. (2016a). An improved methodology for multi-criteria evaluations in the shipping industry. *Brodogradnja, 67*(3), 59-72.

Aikhuele, D. O., & Faiz, M. T. (2016b). An interval fuzzy-valued M-TOPSIS model for design concept selection. *The National Conference for Postgraduate Research 2016, Universiti Malaysia Pahang*, 374-84.

Aikhuele, D. O., & Turan, F. M. (2016c). A Hybrid Fuzzy Model for Lean Product Development Performance Measurement. In *IOP Conference Series: Materials Science and Engineering* (Vol. 114, No. 1, p. 012048). IOP Publishing.

Aikhuele, D. O., & Turan, F. M. (2016d). Proposal for a Conceptual Model for Evaluating Lean Product Development Performance: A Study of LPD Enablers in Manufacturing Companies. In *IOP Conference Series: Materials Science and Engineering* (Vol. 114, No. 1, p. 012047). IOP Publishing.

Al-Ashaab, A., Golob, M., Urrutia, U. A., Gourdin, M., Petritsch, C., Summers, M., & El-Nounu, A. (2016). Development and application of lean product development performance measurement tool. *International Journal of Computer Integrated Manufacturing, 29*(3), 342-354.

Al-Ashaab, A., Shehab, E., Alam, R., Sopelana, A., Sorli, M., Flores, M., ... & James-Moore, M. (2010). The conceptual leanPPD model. In *New World Situation: New Directions in Concurrent Engineering* (pp. 339-346). Springer London.

Azeem, M., & Gondal, M. B. (2011). Prototype framework: prototypes, prototyping and piloting in terms of quality insurance. *Academic Research International 1*(2), 301–307.

Azizi, A., & Aikhuele, D. O. (2015, March). An integrated model of Kano and quality function deployment for evaluation of lean production tools in assembly environment. In *Industrial Engineering and Operations Management (IEOM), 2015 International Conference on* (pp. 1-6). IEEE.

Berger, A. (1997). Continuous improvement and kaizen: standardization and organizational designs. *Integrated manufacturing systems, 8*(2), 110-117.

Carulli, M., Bordegoni, M., & Cugini, U. (2013). An approach for capturing the voice of the customer based on virtual prototyping. *Journal of Intelligent Manufacturing, 24*(5), 887-903.

Chase, J. P. (2000). Measuring value in product development. *Massachusetts Institute of Technology*.

Chen, S. M., & Tan, J. M. (1994). Handling multicriteria fuzzy decision-making problems based on vague set theory. *Fuzzy sets and systems, 67*(2), 163-172.

Chou, S. Y., Vincent, F. Y., Dewabharata, A., & Dat, L. Q. (2012, November). A fuzzy TOPSIS approach for medical provider selection and evaluation. In *Fuzzy Theory and it's Applications (iFUZZY), 2012 International Conference on* (pp. 322-326). IEEE.

Furuhjelm, J., Swan, H., & Tingström, J. (2011, August). Creating value through lean product development: applying lean principles. In *Proceedings of the 18th International Conference on Engineering Design (ICED 11)(8 pp.) Copenhagen: The Design Society*.

Gershenson, J. K., & Pavnaskar, S. J. (2003). Eight Basic Lean Product Development Tools. In *DS 31: Proceedings of ICED 03, the 14th International Conference on Engineering Design, Stockholm*.

Haque, B., & Moore, M. J. (2004). Measures of performance for lean product introduction in the aerospace industry. *Proceedings of the Institution of Mechanical Engineers, Part B: Journal of Engineering Manufacture, 218*(10), 1387-1398.

Harland, P. E., & Uddin, Z. (2014). Effects of product platform development: fostering lean product development and production. *International Journal of Product Development 18, 19*(5-6), 259-285.

Hines, P., Francis, M., & Found, P. (2006). Towards lean product lifecycle management: a framework for new product development. *Journal of Manufacturing Technology Management, 17*(7), 866-887.

Hoppmann, J., Rebentisch, E., Dombrowski, U., & Zahn, T. (2011). A framework for organizing lean product development. *Engineering Management Journal, 23*(1), 3-15.

Hwang, C. L., & Yoon, K. (1981). *Multiple Attribute Decision Making Methods and Applications*. Berlin: Springer.

Paschkewitz, J. J. (2014, January). Risk management in Lean Product Development. In *Reliability and Maintainability Symposium (RAMS), 2014 Annual* (pp. 1-6). IEEE.

Jurado, M. C. (2012). Visual Planning in Lean Product Development. *KTH Royal Institute of Technology*.

Kano, Shigeto, and Hirokazu Shimizu. 2001. "A Guide to GD3 Activities and DRBFM Technique to Prevent Trouble." *Vehicle Technology Dept No. 1, Toyota Motor Corporation*. Vol. Version 5.

Karlsson, C., & Ahlström, P. (1996). The difficult path to lean product development. *Journal of product innovation management*, *13*(4), 283-295.

Khan, M., Al-Ashaab, A., Doultsinou, A., Shehab, E., Ewers, P., & Sulowski, R. (2011). Set-based concurrent engineering process within the LeanPPD environment. In *Improving Complex Systems Today* (pp. 433-440). Springer London.

Bo-Young, K. (2008). Cross-functional cooperation with design teams in new product development. *International Journal of Design*, *2*(3), 43–54.

Krichbaum, B. D. (2008). Standardized work : The power of consistency standardized work : The power of consistency standardized work : The Principles.

Li, L., & Fan, G. (2014). Fuzzy MADM with triangular numbers for project investment model based on left and right scores. *Research Journal of Applied Sciences, Engineering, and Technology*, 7(13), 2793–97.

León, H. C. M., & Farris, J. A. (2011). Lean product development research: Current state and future directions. *Engineering Management Journal*, *23*(1), 29-51.

Letens, G., Farris, J. A., & Van Aken, E. M. (2011). A multilevel framework for lean product development system design. *Engineering Management Journal*, *23*(1), 69-85.

Li, M. (2013). A multi-criteria group decision making model for knowledge management system selection based on TOPSIS with multiple distances in fuzzy environment. *Kybernetes*, *42*(8), 1218-1234.

Liker, J.K. (2004). *The Toyota Way, 14 Management Principles from the World's Greatest Manufacturer*. New York: McGraw-Hill.

Lind, M. (2009). Lean Product Development and PLM's Supporting Role. *Aras Corporate*.

Maksimovic, M., Al-Ashaab, A., Sulowski, R., & Shehab, E. (2012, December). Knowledge visualization in product development using trade-off curves. In *Industrial Engineering and Engineering Management (IEEM), 2012 IEEE International Conference on* (pp. 708-711). IEEE.

Marvel, J. H., & Standridge, C. R. (2009). Simulation-enhanced lean design process. *Journal of Industrial Engineering and Management*, *2*(1), 90-113.

McManus, H. L. (2005). Product Development Value Stream Mapping (PDVSM) Manual Release 1.0. *Massachusetts Institute of Technology*, no. September.

Mohammadi, A. (2010). Lean Product Development -Performance Measurement System. *Gothenburg: Gothenburg University*, 1–64.

Saad, N. M., Al-Ashaab, A., Maksimovic, M., Zhu, L., Shehab, E., Ewers, P., & Kassam, A. (2013). A3 thinking approach to support knowledge-driven design. *The International Journal of Advanced Manufacturing Technology*, *68*(5-8), 1371-1386.

Narayanamurthy, G. (2014). 7A model - A process selection guide for lean implementation. In *Proceedings of the Twenty-Fifth Annual Conference Production and Operations Management Society (POM 2014), 9-12 May 2014, Atlanta, USA.*, 1–13.

Nepal, B. P., Yadav, O. P., & Solanki, R. (2011). Improving the NPD process by applying lean principles: A case study. *Engineering Management Journal*, *23*(1), 52-68.

Parry, G. C., & Turner, C. E. (2006). Application of lean visual process management tools. *Production Planning & Control*, *17*(1), 77-86.

Petersen, K. J., Handfield, R. B., & Ragatz, G. L. (2005). Supplier integration into new product development: coordinating product, process and supply chain design. *Journal of operations management*, *23*(3), 371-388.

Pugh, S. (1996). *Creating Innovative Products Using Total Design: The Living Legacy of Stuart Pugh*. Reading, MA: Addison-Wesley.

Ragatz, G. L., Handfield, R. B., & Petersen, K. J. (2002). Benefits associated with supplier integration into new product development under conditions of technology uncertainty. *Journal of business research*, *55*(5), 389-400.

Ren, L., Zhang, Y., Wang, Y., & Sun, Z. (2007). Comparative analysis of a novel M-TOPSIS method and TOPSIS. *Applied Mathematics Research eXpress*, *2007*, abm005.

Rodriguez, K., & Al-Ashaab, A. (2007). Knowledge web-based system to support e-manufacturing of injection moulded products. *International journal of manufacturing technology and management*, *10*(4), 400-418.

Sethi, R., Smith, D. C., & Park, C. W. (2001). Cross-functional product development teams, creativity, and the innovativeness of new consumer products. *Journal of marketing research*, *38*(1), 73-85.

Shah, R., & Ward, P. T. (2003). Lean manufacturing: context, practice bundles, and performance. *Journal of operations management*, *21*(2), 129-149.

Sopelana, A., Flores, M., Martinez, L., Flores, K., & Sorli, M. (2012, June). The application of an assessment tool for lean product development: an exploratory study in Spanish Companies. In *Engineering, Technology and Innovation (ICE), 2012 18th International ICE Conference on* (pp. 1-10). IEEE.

Dehghani Soufi, M., Ghobadian, B., Najafi, G., Sabzimaleki, M. R., & Yusaf, T. (2015). TOPSIS multi-criteria decision modeling approach for biolubricant selection for two-stroke petrol engines. *Energies*, *8*(12), 13960-13970.

Stenius, P. (2011). Making Lean Work Leaner by Prioritizing Actions and Moving Promptly into Implementation. *Reddal-BusinessDeveloperNewsletter*.

Wang, L., Ming, X. G., Kong, F. B., Li, D., & Wang, P. P. (2011). Focus on implementation: a framework for lean product development. *Journal of Manufacturing Technology Management*, *23*(1), 4-24.

Wasim, A., Shehab, E., Abdalla, H., Al-Ashaab, A., Sulowski, R., & Alam, R. (2013). An innovative cost modelling system to support lean product and process development. *The International Journal of Advanced Manufacturing Technology*, *65*(1-4), 165-181.

Yan, B., & Makinde, O. D. (2011). Impact of continuous improvement on new product development within SMEs in the Western Cape, South Africa. *African Journal of Business Management*, *5*(6), 2220.

Yang, C., & Wu, Q. (2008, October). Decision model for product design based on fuzzy TOPSIS method. In *Computational Intelligence and Design, 2008. ISCID'08. International Symposium on* (Vol. 2, pp. 342-345). IEEE.

Zadeh, L.A. (1965). Fuzzy sets. *Information and Control, 8*, 338–53.

Zhu, X., Wang, F., Liang, C., Li, J., & Sun, X. (2012). Quality credit evaluation based on TOPSIS: Evidence from air-conditioning market in China. *Procedia Computer Science*, *9*, 1256-1262.

Critical success factors model developing for sustainable Kaizen implementation in manufacturing industry in Ethiopia

Haftu Hailu[a,b*], Abdelkadir Kedir[b], Getachew Bassa[b] and Kassu Jilcha[c]

[a]*Public Service and Human Resource Development Ministry: Ethiopia Kaizen Institute, Addis ababa, Ethiopia*
[b]*Ethiopian Institute of Technology Mekelle, Mekelle University, Tigray, Ethiopia*
[c]*Addis Ababa University, Addis Ababa Institute of Technology, Addis Ababa, Ethiopia*

CHRONICLE	ABSTRACT
Keywords: Kaizen Critical Success Factor Success Indicator Factor analysis Peacock	The purpose of the research is to identify critical success factors and model developing for sustaining kaizen implementation. Peacock shoe is one of the manufacturing industries in Ethiopia facing challenges on sustaining. The methodology followed is factor analysis and empirically testing hypothesis. A database was designed using SPSS version 20. The survey was validated using statistical validation using the Cronbach alpha index; the result is 0.908. The KMO index value was obtained for the 32 items and had a value of 0.642 with Bartlett's Test of Sphericity Approx. Chi-Square 4503.007, degree of freedom 496 and significance value 0.000. A factor analysis by principal components and varimax rotation was applied for finding the critical success factors. Finding designates that 32 items were merged into eight critical success factors. All the eight factors together explain for 76.941 % of the variance. Multiple regression model analysis has indicated that some of the critical success factors had relationship with success indicators. Due to constraint of time, the researcher focused only at peacock shoe manufacturing industry. Other limitation also includes the absence of any local research that shows the critical success factors at the moment.

1. Introduction

Now a days manufacturing industries are facing challenges due to the fastest changes of pace in technology and market demands. In recent years, manufacturing industries have also experienced unprecedented degrees of change in management, process technology, customer expectations, supplier attitudes and competitive behavior. This elaborates that industries which have manufacturing systems, with great trustworthiness, have implemented superlative manufacturing approaches such as Kaizen philosophy. Change is now a permanent feature of the business environment and organizations, which adapt to this new environment, are more likely to gain a significant competitive advantage (Mfowabo, 2006). In 1970 Japan's export was better than its import, the main reason for this achievement was Japan's manufacturing industries successfully implemented kaizen (Bisht, 2013) following the success of Japan's firms, Japan takes initiative to support Africa under Yokohama action plan. Ethiopia has experienced

* Corresponding author.
E-mail address: hhea192741@gmail.com (H. Hailu)

a fast economic growth in recent years with the annual GDP growth rate average 11%. The industry sector also shows growth at an alarming rate for the past four years in the local share of production quantity ranging from 10.30 % to 14.3 %. The GDP share of the manufacturing sector ranging from 4.4 % to 4.6 % which is less than those of other countries with the similar income level (MOI: GTP - II, 2015).

In Ethiopia manufacturing sector, the slow development of the private sector, the poor quality control, and the low productivity have been major obstacles for promoting exports and domestic and foreign investments. For sustainable economic growth and poverty reduction in Ethiopia, it is essential to develop the private sector or to strengthen the competitiveness of its economy through improving the quality control and productivity. Therefore, Peacock shoes manufacturing industry is one of the export oriented industry which have implemented the Kaizen philosophy to enhance its competitiveness. At the time of implementation, company was achieving substantial tangible and intangible improvements with attractive physical changes. However, the company is facing challenges on sustaining Kaizen implementation and substantial improvements. This research addresses on identifying critical success factors that enables to sustain the implementation. The research is done by listing factors that affect Kaizen implementation from previous researchers reported from different companies and countries. According to (García et al., 2013). Critical success factor (CSFs) were proposed by Daniel in 1961, and this idea was popularized by Rock arts in 1979. Study of information systems, over the past two decades has demonstrated that the CSFs method has been widely adopted and used in a variety of fields of study to determine the most critical factors influencing enterprise success. However, there is no one particular definition of success, as the definition of success is different from one person to another, depending on the perspective of the person who defines it.

There are different definitions for CSF. According to Rockmart, critical success factors are defined as inadequate number of duties and responsibilities which enables to confirm successful competitive performance for any manufacturing industry are critical success factors. Leidecker's definition of critical success factors is those items that, when appropriately standardized, maintained, improved, sustained or managed, can have a substantial impact on the success of an organization rival in particular industry (Leidecker & Bruno, 1984). According to Boynton and Zmud (1984), critical success factors are defined as those insufficient items which confirms success for any manufacturing industry. The researcher also defines critical success factors as those few or many key main activities (depends on the wing of the industry) which are driving forces for successful completion of any strategy by achieving qualitative and quantitative results. Based on this, When manufacturing industries want to improve their existing gaps on implementation or working processes, they need to focus on some specific areas in order to identify critical success factors. This also allowed them to see their capability to meet any requirements related to critical success factors. Furthermore, the CSFs concept is the most important for overall organizational objectives, mission and strategies. The researcher wants to ask an important question based on the above CSF concept: what companies are doing in other countries for successful implementation of their continuous improvement activities? And what should peacock manufacturing industry do to sustain kaizen implementation activities? Regarding to react the questions shown above, the researcher found in a literature review that there are adequate components that contribute to the successful implementation of Kaizen. 20 authors and 41 factors sorted according to their numbers of references. Some factors that were cited only once, which are associated with effective internal processes, 5s implementation (Leidecker & Bruno, 1984) workplace safety (Farris, 2003), focus on customers (Romero et al., 2009), application of methodologies to understand customer's voice, resistance to change, consistent approach to improvement activities and development of structures to stop the bugs, make operating practices, establishment of long-term goals, and shaping a learning organization and focus on development of critical processes and quality management systems (Landa, 2009). Other factors that were cited at least two times from literature are: commitment and motivation of staff (Tapias et al., 2010); support from senior management (Cooney & Sohal, 2004); allocated resources (time, economic, spaces) (Bisgaard, 2007); leadership (Leidecker & Bruno, 1984); developing a culture of continuous improvement

(Prajogo & Sohal, 2004); set goals for improvement programs (Jørgensen et al., 2004); using an appropriate methodology (Bisgaard, 2007); standardization and process measurement (Farris, 2003); organization of support teams, presence of a facilitator to support the program (Prajogo & Sohal, 2004); interdepartmental communication (Tapias et al., 2010); differences between the focus of improvement and the existing culture, Employee attitude (Landa, 2009); Interdepartmental cooperation, follow the PDCA cycle (Bisgaard, 2007); training and education (García et al., 2013); heterogeneity of improvement teams, assessment system (Readman, 2003); skills and experience,; establish policies, objectives and structure (Tapias et al., 2010); clarify goals and common ideas, documentation and evaluation; workers integration and award; customer focus (García et al., 2013). Besides, many view Kaizen as a long term journey, Kaizen champions, financial capabilities, involve and value employees at all levels of the organization, problem solving by involving people, realistic timescales for changes, standardization, views and understand kaizen as a philosophy rather than another strategy are factors affecting the successful kaizen implementation (Alaskari et al., 2012).

The researcher criticizes different authors for only identifying critical factors; they are not developing any model which enables sustainable Kaizen implementation. Even Vermaak (2008) focused only on people and process. These two only did not enable for successful completion. Rather during implementation people should solve problems faced on each process by creating new improvement ideas in good management. Based on this reason this research gave high focus for the 4p's of people, philosophy, process and problem solving for successful completion and sustainable kaizen implementation.

There have been several studies on the reasons on why companies implement Kaizen, the benefits to be derived from Kaizen, as well as the tools and techniques of Kaizen have been well researched and documented. However, little is known about the reasons for failed kaizen implementation, how to avoid the pitfalls and what to do to ensure the success of kaizen in Ethiopia manufacturing context. It is clear that despite the popularity and growth Kaizen philosophy takes in Ethiopia. Most of the manufacturing industries are not successful and even the few successful manufacturing industries like peacock are backfiring and suffering a lot of challenges on sustaining the Kaizen implementation and substantial improvements. Most of the problems are internal like high machine breakdowns, high concentration of wastes, lower employee involvement, high defects and reworks are few due mentioned. With this in mind, the researcher has, therefore, focused on Peacock shoes manufacturing with a view to determine the questions: what are the critical success factors for sustainable Kaizen implementation in Peacock manufacturing industry? What are the main critical success factors of kaizen reported in the previous researchers? Which model should be used at peacock? What kind of model was developed for sustainable kaizen implementation? Therefore, the researcher believed that identifying and developing model of few critical success factors in the company would lead them on sustaining kaizen activities, competitive globally and leading line of existing companies in the country.

2. Experimental Procedure

The research was done using different materials and methods. 32 main items affecting the implementation, 19 success indicators, theoretical model and 10 hypotheses are used on the research. Since the population size of the company is known, so to decide the required sample size, the following proven formula was used as shown in Eq. (1) (Krejcie & Morgan, 1970).

$$S = x^2 NP(1-P) / (d^2(N-1) + x^2 P(1-P). \tag{1}$$

where, s = required sample size; = the table value of chi-square for 1 DOF at the desired confidence level (3.841); N = the population size (for the case of peacock N = 256); P = the population proportion (assumed to be 0.50 since this would provide the maximum sample size); d = the degree of accuracy expressed as a proportion (0.05). After applying the survey, a database was designed using Statistical Package for Social Sciences, version 20. The statistical analysis included several phases.

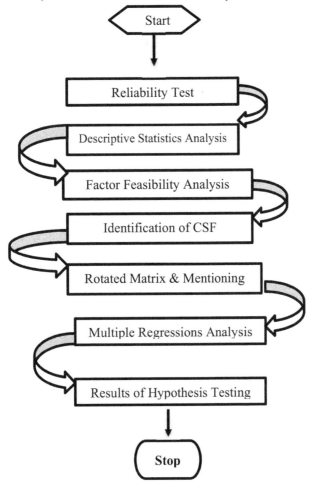

Fig.1. Flow chart of methodology

The potential influence of critical success factors on success indicators are described in Fig. 2. The following hypotheses were formulated for each linkage. These are theories that will be empirically tested. The researcher tried to modify, propose the theoretical model and go through (Vermaak, 2008).
H1: Providing comprehensive training and education to all levels of the company starting from shop-floor employees to top managements will result in increased employees performance, customer satisfaction and decreasing manufacturing costs.
H2: Having ownership towards the philosophy will result in increased employees performance, customer satisfaction and decreased manufacturing cost.
H3: when employees working in team will result in increased employee's performance, customer satisfaction and decreased manufacturing cost.
H4: Having effective vertical and horizontal communication in providing frame work of strategic improvement plan will result in increased employees performance, customer satisfaction and decreasing in manufacturing cost.
H5: All levels of company employee's participation in the Kaizen implementation will result in increased employees performance, customer satisfaction and decreasing in manufacturing cost.
H6: Using process control and improvement techniques will result in increased employee's performance, customer satisfaction and decreasing manufacturing cost.

H7: Continual evaluation of the implementation and the performance of all levels of employees will result in increased employee's performance, customer satisfaction and decreased manufacturing cost.
H8: Establishing recognition and reward system in the company will result in increased employee's performance, customer satisfaction and decreased manufacturing cost.
H9: Knowledgeable and committed effective Kaizen leadership will result in increased employee's performance, customer satisfaction and decreased manufacturing cost.
H10: Employee's attitude will result in increased employee's performance, customer satisfaction and decreased manufacturing cost.

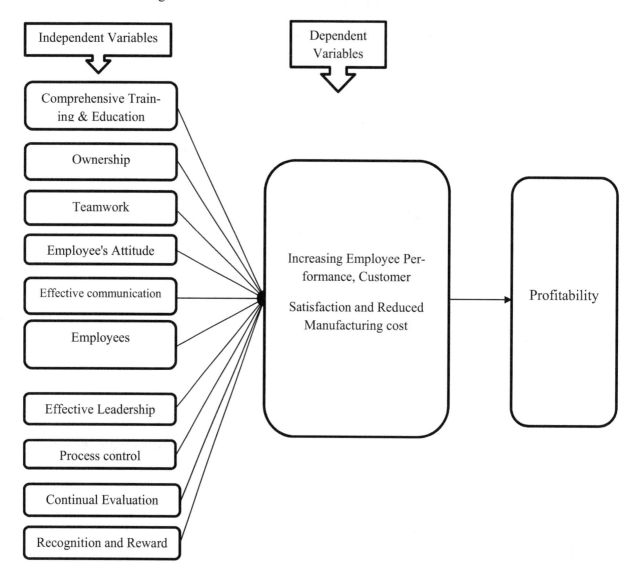

Fig. 2. Conceptual model before emperically testing

3. Results and Discussion

3.1. Statistical Analysis of Questionnaire

3.1.1. Reliability Test Result

Different authors accept different values of this test in order to achieve internal reliability, according to Asedesach (2014), the minimum required value is 0.7. The CAI was obtained for the 32 initial items that is 0.908. Different authors agree that removing some items from the questionnaire results on improving the CAI value (Bisgaard, 2007). The researcher found that not important eliminating the variables since the existing variables internal consistency was maintained. The Cronbach's coefficient alpha was calculated for each item of the questionnaire with minimum 0.901, maximum 0.913 and the 32 items as a whole scored CAI value 0.908 that is excellent. Therefore, based on the test, the results for the items are reliable and acceptable.

3.1.2. Descriptive Statistics Analysis

Descriptive analysis is done first to know the level of importance of factors. With 5 point Likert scales, the interval for breaking range in measuring each variable is calculated by Eq. (2):

$$R = (N - 1)/N \tag{2}$$

where R is the interval for breaking the range; N is the maximum applied Likert scale. According to the analysis, 32 items recorded minimum 3.94 and maximum 4.68 that is 31 items falling on the interval breaking range 4.20 to 5.00 most important items and one item on the interval breaking range 3.40 to 4.19 high important. This result is excellent and shows that all the respondents agree on the importance of all variables for successful Kaizen implementation.

3.1.3. Factor Feasibility Analysis

The following criteria are used to assess and describe the sampling adequacy: 0.90 = excellent; 0.80 = very good; 0.70 = good; 0.60 = fair; 0.50 = poor and below 0.50 = unacceptable. If KMOs < 0.5, it is a good idea not to do factor analysis. The Bartlett's Test of Sphericity is the test for null hypothesis that the correlation matrix has an identity. Very small values of significance (below 0.05) indicate a high probability that there are significant relationships between the variables, whereas higher values (above 0.05) indicate the data is inappropriate for factor analysis.

Table 1
KMO and Bartlett's Test Measure of Sampling Adequacy as a whole

KMO and Bartlett's Test		
Kaiser-Meyer-Olkin Measure of Sampling Adequacy.		0.642
Bartlett's Test of Sphericity	Approx. Chi-Square	4503.007
	Df	496
	Sig.	0.000

Table 1 illustrates the KMO index value obtained for the 32 items and had a value of 0.642 which is above 0.6 average and acceptable. The Bartlett's Sphericity test gave a chi-square value of 4503.007 with 496 degrees of freedom that represents a p – value (significance) of 0.000 which is less than a 95% level of Significance, = 0.05. The determinant value of the correlation matrix was estimated in 0.000. With this feasibility indexes, the conclusion was that the factor analysis could be applied. Factor analysis is a statistical technique that is used to identify a relatively small number of factors in order to represent the relationship among a set of interrelated variables (Blanche et al., 2006). The researcher applied three steps for factor analysis: Computing inter correlations between variables (correlation matrix); Extracting initial factors, and Rotate in the factors to obtain a clearer picture of the factor content. The researcher tried to know the inter correlation between variables. The result illustrates that after extraction, the 32 items have KMO index value: 1 item score above 0.9 Excellent, 10 items score above 0.8 Very good, 15 items score above 0.7 Good, 5 items score above 0.6 Faire, 1 item score above 0.5 poor but acceptable. These items are with allowable SAM value. In factor analysis, only those factors with an eigenvalue greater than unity were considered], and only eight factors meet that requirement, which together accounts for 76.941 % of all eigenvalues. Therefore, eigenvalue of component

1,2,3,4,5,6,7,8 are 9.206 , 3.472 , 3.141 , 2.748 , 1.940 , 1.624 , 1.260 , 1.230 respectively. Table 3.2.below describes the total variance explained extraction sums of squared loadings. The researcher therefore wants the items to be loading properly on the factors. Different authors agreed that, the greater the loading, the more the variable is a pure measure of the factor. Loadings in excess of: 0 .71 are considered excellent, 0.63 are considered very good, 0.55 are considered good, 0.45 are considered fair, and 0.32 are considered poor. Choice of the cutoff for size of loading to be interpreted is a matter of researcher preference]. Eight factors have been extracted based on their eigenvalues greater than one. Besides, each factor is constituted of all those variables that have factor loadings greater than the maximum limit 0.7 as shown in Table 2 which is excellent. 32 variables were clubbed into eight factors.

Table 2
Total variance explained extraction sums of squared loadings

Component	Extraction Sum of Square Loading		
	Total	% of Variance	Cumulative %
1	9.206	28.768	28.768
2	3.472	10.850	39.618
3	3.141	9.817	49.434
4	2.748	8.589	58.023
5	1.940	6.063	64.086
6	1.624	5.075	69.160
7	1.260	3.938	73.098
8	1.230	3.843	**76.941**

Table 2 illustrates, the eight extracted factors explained 76.941 % of the variability factors for successful Kaizen implementation. This explains above three-fourth of the variability.

The researcher tried to use the scree plot for showing the relationship between eigenvalues and factors: Fig. 3 illustrates the scree plot graphs the eigenvalues against each factor. We can see that from the graph that after factor eight there is a sharp change in the curvature of the scree plot. This shows that after factor eight the total variance accounts for smaller and smaller amounts. Factors are interpreted through their factor loadings.

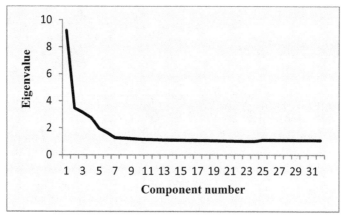

Fig. 3. Scree plot

3.1.4. Identification of Critical Factors

The researcher here wants rotating the factors to obtain a clearer picture of the factor content. The factor matrix was than rotated to simple structure by means of Varimax Rotation with Kaiser Normalization (Vermaak, 2008).

Table 3 illustrates the total variance explained – rotation sum of square loadings after rotation. Thus, after rotation, Factor 1 accounts for 16.056 % of the variance; Factor 2 accounts for 10.286 % of the variance; Factor 3 accounts for 9.996 % of the variance; Factor 4 accounts for 9.157 % of the variance; Factor 5 accounts for 8.525 % of the variance; Factor 6 accounts for 8.253 % of the variances; Factor 7 accounts for 7.369 % of the variance; Factor 8 accounts for 7.298 %. All the eight factors together explain for 76.941 % of the variance in successful kaizen implementation.

Table 3
Total variance explained – rotation sum of square loadings

Factors	Rotation Sums of Squared Loadings		
	Total	% of Variance	Cumulative %
1	5.138	16.056	16.056
2	3.291	10.286	26.342
3	3.199	9.996	36.338
4	2.930	9.157	45.496
5	2.728	8.525	54.021
6	2.641	8.253	62.274
7	2.358	7.369	69.643
8	2.335	7.298	**76.941**

3.1.5. Rotated Matrix and Mentioning CSF

The researcher mentions critical success factors after examines the rotated factor matrix as shown in table 4 below. This table illustrates the rotated factor matrix correlation of the variables with each of the extracted factors. Usually, each of the variables is highly loaded in one factor and less loaded towards to the other factors. To identify the variables, included in each factor, the variable with the value maximum in each row is selected to be part of the respective factor. The values greater than and equal to 0.494 have been highlighted in each of the rows to group the 32 variables in to 8 critical factors.

Table 4
After rotated matrix mentioning eight critical success factors

Factor	Code	Factor load	Name of the factor
1.	PII23	0.628	
	PII24	0.795	
	PII27	0.788	Preparation (Ownership; Training & Education) 16.056 %
	PII29	0.715	
	PII31	0.576	
	PII32	0.795	
2.	PII2	0.740	
	PII3	0.771	Process control & improvement 10.286 %
	PII4	0.646	
	PII8	0.549	
3.	PII7	0.666	
	PII11	0.854	Planning (Effective communication) 9.996 %
	PII12	0.751	
	PII22	0.600	
4.	PII6	0.885	
	PII13	0.901	Implementation (teamwork and Employee participation) 9.157%
	PII16	0.538	
	PII20	0.565	
5.	PII10	0.925	
	PII14	0.494	
	PII15	0.585	Effective leadership 8.525 %
	PII18	0.624	
	PII19	0.541	
6.	PII5	0.794	Continual evaluation 8.253 %
	PII9	0.579	
	PII30	0.799	
7.	PII1	0.761	Recognition & rewarding 7.369 %
	PII17	0.636	
	PII25	0.595	
8.	PII21	0.648	
	PII26	0.577	Employee's attitude 7.298 %
	PII28	0.589	

Six items loaded on Factor 1, four items on Factor 2, four items on Factor 3, four items on Factor 4, five items on Factor 5, three items on Factor 6, three items on Factor 7, three items on Factor 8. All factors consist of at least three items, which is in line with Thurstone's recommendation of at least three variables per factor for exploratory analysis.

3.1.6. Multiple Regression Analysis

In order to empirically evaluate the various relationships in success indicators and critical success factors, a multiple regression analyses is needed to be applied. As such the influence of each of the eight critical success factors or independent variables on each of the three success indicators or dependent variables needed to be assessed. Multiple regression analysis is one of the most commonly used multivariate procedures and is used to build models for predicting scores on one variable, the dependent variable, from scores on a number of other variables, the independent variables (Terre et al., 2006). The researcher tried to predict successful kaizen implementation in terms of staff performance, customer satisfaction and manufacturing cost reduction variable from independent variables of preparation (ownership, education & training), process control and improvement, planning (effective communication), implementation (employee's participation and teamwork), effective leadership, continual evaluation, recognition and reward, employee's attitude.

Table 5
Summary result from regression model (Customer satisfaction)

Code	R square	Coefficients (Beta)	t	Sig
PII29	0.244	.385	3.815	0.000
PII24	0.244	.327	2.491	0.014
PII12	0.194	0.214	2.031	0.044
PII11	0.194	-0.353	-3.274	0.001
PII22	0.194	0.282	2.967	0.004
PII10	0.304	-0.234	-2.721	0.007
PII14	0.304	0.295	3.294	0.001
PII18	0.304	0.432	4.545	0.000
PII19	0.304	-0.238	-3.068	0.003
PII25	0.106	0.257	2.367	0.019
PII28	0.153	.410	4.581	0.000

Note: Significance value of 0.05 or less

Table 5 above describes significant value, t-test and coefficients of independent variables that indicate the relationship between independent and dependent variables.

Table 6
Summary result from regression model (employee's performance)

Code	R square	Coefficient (Beta)	t	Sig
PII23	0.404	.232	2.347	0.020
PII29	0.404	.409	4.565	0.000
PII8	0.205	-.223	-2.462	0.015
PII2	0.205	.324	3.472	0.001
PII7	0.264	.551	5.688	0.000
PII11	0.264	-.331	-3.212	0.002
PII10	0.275	-.334	-3.810	0.000
PII14	0.275	.407	4.444	0.000
PII18	0.275	.243	2.500	0.014
PII5	0.271	-.441	-4.357	0.000
PII30	0.271	.599	7.185	0.000
PII17	0.403	.329	3.688	0.000
PII25	0.403	.335	3.775	0.000
PII28	0.162	.400	4.493	0.000

Note: Significance value of 0.05 or less

Since the significance value is 0.05 or less, there are several non- significant coefficients, indicating that independent variables are not related with customer satisfaction. They are: Process control and improvement, Implementation, Continual evaluation. There are 11 variables that are significant. It means that the predictor CSF have relation with customer satisfaction. They are: preparation; planning; effective leader ship; recognition and reward; employee's attitude. Table 6 describes significant value, t-test and coefficients of independent variables that indicate the relationship between independent and dependent variables. Since the significance value is 0.05 or less, there are non-significant coefficients, indicating that critical success factors are not related with staff performance like implementation (employee's participation). There are 14 variables that are significant. It means that the predictor (critical success factors) have relation with staff performance. They are: preparation, process control & improvement, planning, effective leadership, continual evaluation, recognition & reward, employee's attitude.

Table 7
Summary result from regression model (Cost reduction)

Code	R square	Coefficients (Beta)	t	Sig
PII29	0.207	.249	2.412	0.017
PII32	0.207	.311	2.814	0.006
PII8	0.040	.203	2.044	0.043
PII7	0.155	.206	1.983	0.049
PII11	0.155	-.304	-2.753	0.007
PII22	0.155	.310	3.183	0.002
PII20	0.057	.224	2.583	0.011
PII18	0.260	.358	3.649	0.000
PII5	0.037	-.247	-2.128	0.035
PII17	0.179	.219	2.097	0.038
PII25	0.179	.270	2.597	0.010
PII28	0.097	.246	2.668	0.008

Note: Significance value of 0.05 or less

Table 7 above describes significant value, t-test and coefficients of independent variables that indicate the relationship between independent and dependent variables. Since the significance value is 0.05 or less, there are significant coefficients, indicating that critical success factors are related with manufacturing cost reduction: They are: preparation, process control & improvement, planning, implementation, effective leadership, continual evaluation, recognition & reward, employee's attitude.

3.1.7. Results of Hypothesis Testing

Theoretical hypotheses are empirically tested. Independent variables with significant values less than 0.05 are accepted. The result is shown below.

H1: Providing comprehensive training and education to all levels of the company starting from front line workers to top managements will result in increased employee performance, customer satisfaction and decreasing manufacturing costs. This result is accepted. Since the significance value of the predictor training and education in comparison with employee performance, customer satisfaction and cost reduction are 0.00, 0.00 and 0.017 respectively. These results are less than the upper limit significant value of 0.05.

H2: Having ownership towards the philosophy will result in increased employee performance, customer satisfaction and decreased manufacturing cost. This result is rejected. Since the significance value of the predictor ownership with employee performance, customer satisfaction and cost reduction are 0.647, 0.504 and 0.130 respectively. These results are greater than the upper limit significant value of 0.05.

H3: when employees working in team results in increased employee performance, customer satisfaction and decreased manufacturing cost. This result is rejected. Since the significance value of the predictor teamwork with employee performance, customer satisfaction and cost reduction are 0.972, 0.296, and 0.191 respectively. These results are greater than the upper limit significant value of 0.05.

H4: Having effective vertical and horizontal communication in providing frame work of strategic improvement plan will result in increased employee performance, customer satisfaction and decreasing in manufacturing cost. This result is accepted. Since the significance value of the predictor planning or effective communication in comparison with employee performance, customer satisfaction and cost reduction are 0.02, 0.01 and 0.007 respectively. These results are less than the upper limit significant value of 0.05.

H5: All levels of company employee's participation in the Kaizen implementation will result in increased employee performance, customer satisfaction and decreasing in manufacturing cost. This result is accepted only for comparison with cost reduction. Since the significance value of the predictor employee's participation in comparison with cost reduction is 0.011. But in comparison with employee performance and customer satisfaction, the significant value is 0.162 and 0.481 respectively. These results are greater than the upper limit significant value of 0.05.

H6: Using process control and improvement techniques will result in increased employee performance, customer satisfaction and decreasing manufacturing cost. This result is accepted only for comparison with staff performance and cost reduction. Since the significance value of the predictor process control and improvement in comparison with employee performance and cost reduction is 0.01and 0.043 respectively. But in comparison with customer satisfaction, the significant value is 0.812. This result is greater than the upper limit significant value of 0.05.

H7: Continual evaluation of the implementation and the performance of all levels of employees will result in increased employee performance, customer satisfaction and decreased manufacturing cost. This result is accepted only for comparison with employee performance and cost reduction. Since the significance value of the predictor continual evaluation in comparison with employee performance and cost reduction is 0.00and 0.035 respectively. But in comparison with customer satisfaction, the significant value is 0.665. This result is greater than the upper limit significant value of 0.05.

H8: Establishing recognition and reward system in the company will result in increased employee performance, customer satisfaction and decreased manufacturing cost. This result is accepted. Since the significance value of the predictor recognition and reward in comparison with employee performance, customer satisfaction and cost reduction are 0.00, 0.019 and 0.01 respectively. These results are less than the upper limit significant value of 0.05.

H9: Knowledgeable and committed effective Kaizen leadership will result in increased employee performance, customer satisfaction and decreased manufacturing cost. This result is accepted. Since the significance value of the predictor effective leadership in comparison with employee performance, customer satisfaction and cost reduction are 0.014, 0.00 and 0.00 respectively. These results are less than the upper limit significant value of 0.05.

H10: Employee's attitude will result in increased employee performance, customer satisfaction and decreased manufacturing cost. This result is accepted. Since the significance value of the predictor employee's attitude in comparison with employee performance, customer satisfaction and cost reduction is 0.00, 0.019 and 0.008 respectively. These results are less than the upper limit significant value of 0.00. These results are less than the upper limit significant value of 0.05.Based on this multiple regression analysis, the new developed model is shown as in Fig. 4.

The above empirically tested model elaborates that even though the factorial analysis, as shown in the conceptual model, ownership and training & education; teamwork and employee participation were independently 4 success factors, but, factorial analytical output merges them to 2 critical factor categories of preparation and implementation respectively as shown in Table 4. The multiple regression analysis output also shown that significant values of code items PII27, PII31, PII1, PII21, PII26, PII15, PII9, PII3, PII4, PII16, PII6 and PII13 are above the recommended 0.05 significant value. So, these items are rejected. Based on this, from 32 items only 20 items have high contribution for sustainable kaizen implementation in manufacturing industry, peacock. Besides to this, peacock should also focus on the 4p's of people, philosophy, process and problem solving to attain sustainable substantial improvements. In the conceptual model, there were 10 independent variables, after empirically testing these success factors were reduced to eight critical factors as shown in Fig. 3. Finally, the identified 8 critical factors in relation to their respective listed items have a big role on successful and sustainable kaizen implementation.

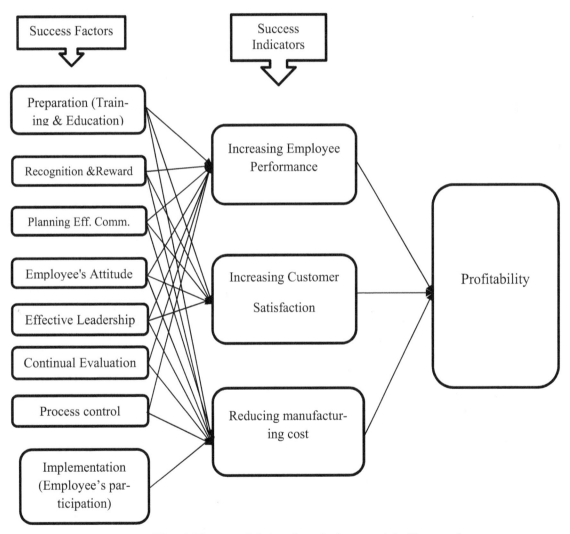

Fig. 4. New model developed after empirically tested

4. Conclusion

The following specific conclusions have been compiled from the surveys administered during the research process. The critical success factors for sustainable Kaizen implementation in Peacock shoes manufacturing industry are: Preparation - 16.056 %, Process control - 10.286%, Planning - 9.996%,

Implementation – 9.157%, Effective leadership-8.525%, Continual evaluation - 8.253%, Recognition & reward - 7.369%, 8) Employee's attitude- 7.298%. Preparation associated with education and training is key. This CSF is linked to people and related with employee performance, customer satisfaction and manufacturing cost. Process control is key. This factor is linked to process and related with employee performance and manufacturing cost. Planning associated with effective communication is key. This factor is linked to people and related with employee performance, customer satisfaction and manufacturing cost. Implementation associated with employee's participation is key. This factor is linked to problem solving and related with only manufacturing cost. Effective leadership on kaizen philosophy is key. This factor is linked to philosophy and people and related with employee performance, customer satisfaction and manufacturing cost. Continual evaluation is key. This factor is linked to process and related with staff performance and manufacturing cost. Recognition and reward is key. This factor is linked to people and related with employee performance, customer satisfaction and manufacturing cost. Employee's attitude is key. This factor is linked to people and related with employee performance, customer satisfaction and manufacturing cost. The peacock shoes manufacturing industry have, to an extent, made varying degrees of improvement with critical success factors. The researcher tried to show the hypothesis that is empirically tested. It indicates the identified 8 critical factors have high contribution on success indicators. The company top management should give focus on training and education during preparation time to develop employee's kaizen knowledge. The facilitators should control the process by applying improvement activities. There should be good planning that deploys to employees with effective horizontal and vertical communication. Peacock should implement kaizen activities with 100 % employee's participation. The top management, facilitators and team leaders should have real leadership style in order to be role model and successfully completion of the implementation. There should be continual evaluation of activities on peacock by Ethiopian Kaizen Institute, Peacock Kaizen office and companies stakeholders like leather Industry Development Institute. The company should encourage best performer employees and teams by introducing recognition & rewarding system continuously. The front line workers should also have positive attitude on implementing and accepting constructive feedbacks from their leaders. So, Peacock should implement 8 critical success factors and use the developed model for enabling sustainable kaizen implementation in order to achieve more qualitative, & quantitative results and sustain these substantial improvements. Due to constraint of time, the research is limited to one company, and the study was undertaken in view of peacock shoes manufacturing industry. The identified critical factors and model developed also works only for the company. Other limitations include the absence of any local studies that shows the critical success factors for sustainable Kaizen implementation at the moment. Due to this fact the factors affecting for sustainable Kaizen implementation for successful completion of the research were taken from out of the country. For the future, the researcher will do on identifying and developing critical success factors model for selected textile, garment, leather, chemical, metal and agro processing industries in Ethiopia. At the end, the researcher believed that all findings on this research can be implemented in any shoe manufacturing industries in Ethiopia.

Acknowledgments

First of all, I would like to thank the Almighty GOD for giving me the inspiration to start and patience to finalize this article. Secondly, an article cannot be successfully done without the assistance, detractors, motivation and partnership of many individuals who have supported in different ways with the completion of the article. I would like to thank all those who have encouraged, enthused and abetted me in completing this article. Particularly, my deepest and heartfelt thanks to Dr. Kassu Jilcha assisstance professor and researcher for his unlimited support, creative suggestions, direction, advice, and patience with me during the preparation of this article. Last, but not least, I would like to thank my dearly loved wife for her darling, encouragement, patience and support throughout the preparation.

References

Alaskari, O., Ahmad, M. M., Dhafr, N., & Pinedo-Cuenca, R. (2013). Critical successful factors (CSFs) for successful implementation of lean tools and ERP systems.

Asedesach, A.(2014). A Thesis on Effects of kaizen Implementation, p. 41.

Bateman, N. (2005). Sustainability: the elusive element of process improvement. *International Journal of Operations & Production Management, 25*(3), 261-276.

Bisgaard, S. (2007). Quality management and Juran's legacy. *Quality and Reliability Engineering International, 23*(6), 665-677.

Bisht, D. S. (2013). The Japanese Wow: Kaizen. *VSRD International Journal of Business and Management Research,* 167-172.

Blanche, M. T., Blanche, M. J. T., Durrheim, K., & Painter, D. (Eds.). (2006). *Research in practice: Applied methods for the social sciences.* Juta and Company Ltd.

Boynton, A. C., & Zmud, R. W. (1984). An assessment of critical success factors. *Sloan management review, 25*(4), 17-27.

Cooney, R., & Sohal, A. (2004). Teamwork and total quality management: a durable partnership. *Total Quality Management & Business Excellence, 15*(8), 1131-1142.

Farris, J.A. (2003). A standard frame work for sustaining Kaizen events. Master's Thesis, Department of Industrial and Manufacturing. Wichita, KS, USA.

García, J., Rivera, D., & Iniesta, A. (2013). Critical success factors for Kaizen implementation in manufacturing industries in Mexico. *International Journal of Advanced Manufacturing Technology, 68,* 1-4.

Jørgensen, F., Boer, H., & Gertsen, F. (2004). Development of a team-based framework for conducting self-assessment of continuous improvement. *Journal of Manufacturing Technology Management, 15*(4), 343-349.

Landa, Am (2009). Critical success factors and permanence for Kaizen events. Sinnco, 1–20 (In Spanish).

Leidecker, J. K., & Bruno, A. V. (1984). Identifying and using critical success factors. *Long range planning, 17*(1), 23-32.

Mfowabo, N. (2006). The impact of Total productive maintenance on manufacturing performance, 6(31), 5–14 (In Spanish).

Prajogo, D. I., & Sohal, A. S. (2004). Transitioning from total quality management to total innovation management: an Australian case. *International journal of quality & reliability management, 21*(8), 861-875.

Readman, J., & Bessant, J. (2007). What challenges lie ahead for improvement programmes in the UK? Lessons from the CINet Continuous Improvement Survey 2003. *International Journal of Technology Management, 37*(3-4), 290-305.

Krejcie, R. V., & Morgan, D. W. (1970). Determining sample size for research activities. *Educational and psychological measurement, 30*(3), 607-610.

Romero, R., Noriega, S., Escobar, C., & Avila, D. (2009). Critical success factors: A competitiveness strategy. *CULCYT, 6*(31), 5-14.

Tapias A, Yeison A, Correa R & Hernan J (2010). Kaizen: a case study. Redalyc, *16*(45), 59–64 (In Spanish).

Vermaak, T. D. (2008). Critical success factors for the implementation of lean thinking in South African manufacturing organisations.

Vichea, S. (2005). *Key Factors Affecting the Performance of foreign Direct Investment in Cambodia* (Doctoral dissertation, a thesis submitted in partial fulfillment of Masters of Business Administrations, university of the Tai chamber of commerce).

Appendix

The 32 items and respected code is presented as:

PII1: A salary promotion system to encourage employee participation in Kaizen

PII2: Standardization and designing "foolproof" implementation processes to minimize errors

PII3: Using idea generation soft techniques by following PDCA cycle extensively for process control and improvement

PII4: Well maintaining production equipment's according to the maintenance plan.

PII5: Regularly top management and relatives auditing the implementation

PII6: All employees recording Kaizen related data during implementation

PII7: Establish policy for Kaizen and cross functional goals realize through policy deployment and audits

PII8: Discussion of all employees Kaizen - related issues in meetings

PII9: Establishing evaluation systems to measure the performance of all employees

PII10: Focusing on bench marking activities for best practicing

PII1: Providing frame work of strategic improvement plan for achieving the objectives broadly defined by managements

PII12: Clarifying the organization's goals and objectives formulated

PII13: Working in team for fixing problems and scale up employee's capability

PII14: Top management's pledging to the development of the entire workforce and encourage participation, learning, innovation, and creativity throughout the organization to get shop floor commitment and employee trust

PII15: Aligning of short & long term plans with a company's vision

PII16: Applying generated new ideas from employees for process modifications and change layouts

PII17: Financially rewarding for excellent suggestions to get shop floor commitment and employee trust

PII18: Testing the organization's mission and vision statements against the principles implicit in Kaizen

PII19: Top managements participation in formation of realistic time scale for change and Kaizen organizational structure

PII20: The company implements various inspections effectively (incoming, process, and final products).

PII21: The company employees openness for accepting feedbacks

PII22: Organizing KPT from members of same disciplines

PII23: Views and understand Kaizen as a philosophy and a corporate strategy rather than another strategy

PII24: Provide support and direction for Kaizen by allocating resources

PII25: Value employees as long term resources at all levels of the organization

PII26: Having positive attitude to actively involved employees in problem solving, quality & productivity improvement

PII27: Change in organizational culture by build systems, procedures, and structures conducive to Kaizen

PII28: All employees of the willingness to accept the philosophy

PII29: Providing training and education for all personnel in Kaizen - related concepts and skills

PII30: Continually providing feedback to employees concerning the implementation

PII31: Maximizing ownership with management and employees commitment

PII32: Providing specific work-skills training to all employees

Pay-What-You-Want pricing: An integrative review of the empirical research literature

Torsten J. Gerpott[*]

Chair of Strategic and Telecommunications Management, Mercator School of Management, University of Duisburg-Essen, Lotharstr. 65, D-47057 Duisburg, Germany

CHRONICLE	ABSTRACT
Keywords: Pay What You Want pricing Price setting Empirical pricing research Voluntary customer payments Customer integration	In a Pay What You Want (PWYW) setting companies empower their customers to fix the prices buyers voluntarily pay for a delivered product or service. The seller agrees to any price (including zero) customers are paying. For about ten years researchers empirically investigate customer reactions to and economic outcomes of this pricing method. The present paper distinguishes PWYW from other voluntary payment mechanisms and reviews 72 English- or German-speaking PWYW publications, which appeared between January 2006 and September 2016 and contain 97 independent empirical data sets. Prior PWYW research is structured with the help of a conceptual framework which incorporates payment procedure design, buyer, seller, focal sales object and market context characteristics as factors potentially influencing customer perceptions of the PWYW scheme and their behavioral reactions to PWYW offers. The review discusses both consistent key findings as well as contradictory results and derives recommendations for future empirical PWYW research efforts.

1. Introduction

In the recent past various types of customer-centered pricing procedures have attracted substantial attention among management researchers and practitioners. The common feature of the various "participative" price setting approaches is that they do not rely on one fixed price, which the seller unilaterally determines as valid for any buyer of a product. Rather the schemes invite customers to actively influence the prices they pay which in turn results in additional price differentiation and individualization (Gahler, 2016; Kim et al., 2009; Stegemann, 2014). One such procedure is "Pay-What-You-Want" (PWYW) pricing. It involves the complete delegation of the power to set prices to buyers in transactions that do not cover several sellers or buyers competing for the same order or offering, respectively, but concern exactly one vendor and one customer. The buyers solely decide whether, and where appropriate, how much they pay to sellers for the goods consumed. The supplier consciously agrees to accept any price set by the buyer. Consequently, the provider is not entitled to withdraw from a sale even if the customer pays nothing (i.e., a price of zero) or an amount that falls below a minimal threshold value of the seller (unknown to the customer) as in the case of the "Name-Your-Own-Price" procedure (Fay,

---

[*] Corresponding author.
E-mail address: Torsten.Gerpott@uni-due.de (T. J. Gerpott).

2004). The English-speaking literature also uses the terms "Pay What You Think It Is Worth" (El Harbi et al., 2014), "Pay What You Believe Is Fair" (Sleesman & Conlon, 2016), "Pay As You Wish" (Bertini & Koenigsberg, 2014), "Pay What You Like" (Fernandez & Nahata, 2009), "Pay What You Can" (Saccardo et al., 2015) and "Pick Your Own Price" (Bourreau et al., 2015) as synonyms for the PWYW pricing method.

The PWYW procedure is a variant of "voluntary market payment mechanisms" (Natter & Kaufmann, 2015, p. 149) that additionally encompass tipping, donations, gift giving and trust-based billing methods ("honor systems"). Five attributes listed in Figure 1 are pivotal in distinguishing the PWYW approach from the four other payment methods where buyers also independently decide on the size of their payments to suppliers. Accordingly, the PWYW method differs from the remaining mechanisms mentioned in Figure 1 through its focus on representing a financial compensation for the core instead of an ancillary product of the vendor. Furthermore, in the PWYW case customers are paying for themselves, not for others (cf. Jung et al., 2014a) and not primarily for pro-social or ethical purposes (e.g., charity). Finally, in a PWYW setting sellers do not appeal to buyers to pay a (fixed) price named beforehand in situations in which vendors do not monitor the extent to which buyers actually pay the posted "official" price (e.g., trust- or honesty-based payments for flowers, fruit, sweets or newspapers provided at unmanned points of sales; see Schlüter & Vollan, 2015).

Attribute	Payment Approach				
	Tipping	Donation	Gift Giving	Honor System	PWYW
1. Payment in direct exchange for core product/service	–	–	–	✓	✓
2. Payment in direct exchange for ancillary service	✓	–	–	–	–
3. Payment related to charitable purpose	–	✓	–	–	–
4. Quotation of a aspired fixed price/amount by recipient	–	–	–	✓	–
5. Strong emphasis on honesty/ ethic integrity of payer	(✓)	✓	–	✓	–

Legend: ✓ = Yes   (✓) = Partially yes   – = No

Fig. 1. Profile of voluntary payment mechanisms in commercial transactions on moral markets

The literature is rather mixed in assessing the degree of novelty of the PWYW idea and its dissemination in management practice. The majority of the authors claim that the method is "innovative" (Schons et al., 2014, p. 26). In contrast, a few contributions take the opposite view that PWYW pricing is "neither novel nor uncommon in practice" (Stegemann, 2014, p. 3) because cultural institutions (e.g., museums) and street artists have resorted to this approach for a long time and because the authors believe that a considerable number of firms from a broad range of industries is already using the PWYW method (Mak et al., 2015; Natter & Kaufmann, 2015; Stegemann, 2014).

At first glance, the supply of goods under PWYW conditions is inconsistent with classical economic theory because according to its predictions purely selfish buyers would always take products without paying any money with the outcome that sellers inevitably suffer losses. However, noting that customers do not only incur monetary but also social, psychological or moral transaction costs on markets (e.g. perceived lack of fairness, social or self-image concerns) it may be "rational" or "profit maximizing" for buyers to pay prices > 0 when facing PWYW offerings (Gneezy et al., 2012; Lee et al., 2015; Natter & Kaufmann, 2015; Santana & Morwitz, 2013). In a similar vein, suppliers may rate an introduction of the PWYW method as being commercially advantageous for them because they expect that its use will improve the awareness for their offerings and their overall image among potential customers. These effects in turn, may increase the sales volume or the average unit price for goods sold under PWYW conditions or other products offered at conventional fixed prices (Kim et al., 2010b; Riener & Traxler, 2012).

Against the background of such potential benefits of PWYW pricing plans it should not come as a surprise that meanwhile, there is a considerable number of scholarly empirical PWYW studies mainly authored by economists and psychologists. In the face of the significant and quickly growing volume of research on PWYW pricing several authors have already tried to summarize the available evidence (Greiff & Egbert, 2016; Natter & Kaufmann, 2015; Pöyry, 2015; Stegemann, 2014). Unfortunately, the previous reviews consider much less than half of the relevant publications and omit important subject areas of empirical work on PWYW pricing. Hence, a full review of the empirical PWYW literature is still missing. Therefore, the present paper's objective is to provide a comprehensive conceptual framework for structuring the main thematic areas covered in empirical PWYW studies and to use the framework to organize and discuss the relevant findings, to identify research gaps and derive overall implications for PWYW applications in practice. For researchers in the fields of consumer behavior and pricing such a review ought to be valuable because it provides them with a quick to read overview of the state of empirical knowledge on the PWYW approach. In addition, management practitioners should benefit from a research summary, which derives clues for a better design of PWYW pricing in corporations and other types of organizations.

The article is structured as follows. Firstly, section 2.1 explains the procedures to identify and select empirical PWYW contributions for the present review. Then, section 2.2 reports descriptive statistics with regard to method characteristics of the investigations which are pivotal to the summary. Section 2.3 develops a conceptual framework organizing the subject fields addressed in PWYW studies. In section 3 we use this framework to summarize the empirical evidence on factors significantly influencing the acceptance of PWYW offerings and voluntary payment amounts at the level of the individual consumer. Section 4 discusses findings concerning customer perceptions of PWYW price plans. Section 5 analyzes empirical work containing evaluations of the business effects of PWYW pricing at the organizational level. Finally, in section 6, we conclude with general implications for future PWYW research and overarching notes regarding conductive conditions and design principles for practical PWYW applications.

2. Identification, method profile and systematization of empirical PWYW evidence

2.1 Study identification and selection procedures

To identify empirical PWYW work published either in English or in German as comprehensively as possible, we supplemented an initial Google scholar search by scanning the following online (meta-)databases of commercial and non-profit publishers and information brokers: EBSCOhost (including EconLit, PsycINFO, Sociological Collections), Elsevier (Science Direct, Scopus), Emerald, Inderscience, JSTOR, ProQuest (inter alia Sociological Abstracts), PubMed, Sage, Springer, Web of Science and Wiley. The keywords "pay what you want/can/like/think it is worth/wish", "innovative/participative pricing" and "voluntary payment" served as starting points. Identified publications were checked for potentially relevant, previously unknown references. We concluded our search on 30th September 2016.

Then we refined the selection to leave only papers that contain empirical PWYW pricing analyses based on self-collected data. In doing so, we classified three research streams as not being directly relevant and excluded each of them from the in-depth analysis. Firstly, all contributions developing microeconomic models mainly to work out preconditions for generating seller profits from PWYW offers were eliminated if they did not contain tests of the validity of their model with empirical primary data. Accordingly, our review does not count, for instance, the articles of Chao et al. (2015), Greif et al. (2014), Isaac et al. (2015), Kahsay & Samahita (2015) or Tudón (2015) as empirical contributions. Secondly, empirical work on tipping, donations, customer gifts and trust-/honor-based billing variants was not included, because these four voluntary market payment mechanisms differ in terms of important attributes from the PWYW price setting approach (see Figure 1). Apart from that, excellent research reviews for these participative, voluntary payment procedures are already available (Azar, 2007; Bekkers & Wiepking, 2011; Natter & Kaufmann, 2015; Schlüter & Vollan, 2015). Thirdly, we excluded laboratory studies of so-called "dictator games" in which individuals act as payers or recipients of money (see the reviews of Engel, 2011; Mousazadeh & Izadkhah, 2015). The reason for this elimination is that the payment situations artificially created in this type of experimental research differ fundamentally from PWYW pricing, because payments in such games are not linked to the purchase and sale of any good.

As a result, the present synopsis focuses on academic empirical primary studies, which each look at a larger number of PWYW transactions and *either* explore correlates of the level of prices determined independently by buyers *or* compare behavioral reactions of customers confronted with the PWYW method with those observed in case that other pricing setting mechanisms are in place. Hence, the limited set of studies that merely report distributions of PWYW prices in a sample of transactions (e.g., Chen & Liang, 2014; Lynn, 1990; Steiner, 1997) is only of marginal importance for this review. The application of the criteria described above resulted in the inclusion of 72 empirical PWYW studies, which contain 97 independent data sets and were published between 2006 and 2016, in our substantive detailed analysis. The reference list of the present paper marks these 72 sources by an asterisk.

2.2 Profile of the methods of the reviewed studies

This section profiles the methodological design of the 97 data sets under review in terms of the following five attributes: (1) sample size, (2) type of study subjects/buyers (student or non-student customers), (3) type of transaction situation and of payment measures associated with the situation (field study of real payment behaviors or fictitious/hypothetical intentions to pay according to questionnaire responses), (4) temporal structure of the data collection and analysis and (5) category of goods sold under PWYW conditions.

The total number of PWYW transactions covered in those 96 studies reporting sample size statistics amounts to 30,634,507. Of this total, 98.7 % are attributable to the two investigations of Bourreau et al. (2015), who studied sales data of music albums, and of Gneezy et al. (2010), who gathered PWYW data of roller coaster customers offered a photo taken during their ride. Leaving these two studies aside, the overall number of PWYW transactions in the remaining 94 data sets is 407,131. The number of transactions underlying an analysis varies between 22 and 81,641. 16.0 % of the datasets include less than 100 purchases, 46.8 % between 100 and 499 cases, 16.0 % between 500 and 999 transactions, 11.7 % between 1,000 and 9,999 purchases and 9.5 % at least 10,000. The median of the number of transactions per data set is 355.

46.4 % (53.6 %) of the 97 data sets use samples in which the majority of the subjects are students (no students). 96 studies indicate whether they investigate (a) a fictitious/hypothetical purchase and therefore captured payment amounts as *intentions* to pay stated in a questionnaire or (b) a *real* transaction in the field and consequently captured payment amounts in the form of actual *behaviors* observed by technical systems or documented in retrospective reports from the buyers. 36.5 % (63.5 %) of the data sets analyze hypothetical (real) purchases/payments. In the subset of 44 investigations reporting payment amount statistics and using mainly students the share of studies based on fictitious purchase scenarios and claimed *intentions* to pay is 45.5 %. This proportion is marginally higher than the corresponding share of 28.8 % found in 52 PWYW data sets, which include real transactions in buyer samples not primarily composed of students (($\chi^2 = 2.84$; df = 1; p < 0.09). 20.8 % of the total of 96 studies, which provide information on the two aforementioned method attributes can be classified as very problematic in terms of their methodology because they analyze hypothetical buys of students. The first reason for this evaluation is that they are limited to a buyer group for which the extent to which they allow to derive valid conclusions with regard to "normal consumers" is highly controversial. The second reason is that they rely on hypothetical prices and intentions to pay, respectively, which are highly likely to exceed the corresponding amounts in case of real transactions (Gahler, 2016; Jung et al., 2016; Kim et al., 2014a; Kunter & Braun, 2013).

94.8 % of the 97 studies refer to one point in time and are therefore cross-sectional. Reversely, 5.2 % of the investigations are truly longitudinal and capture developments of the level of PWYW prices for a category of goods over time at the overall sample level or intraindividual changes in voluntary payments under PWYW conditions. In addition, two cross-sectional analyses report supplementary qualitative evidence on variations in the mean PWYW amounts over time.

The most frequently studied categories of goods are food and beverages offered by service providers (e.g., restaurants, bars) for immediate consumption. This category is covered in 42 data sets. Various other service categories (e.g., museum, concert, cinema, sport event, flight, hotel overnight, fitness studio) are the focus of 24 investigations and therefore make up the second most studied category of goods. 20 investigations deal with a broad variety of physical goods mostly sold at low absolute prices (e.g., printed book, photo, music CD, DVD, mobile phone, wet razor, coffee mug, grocery bag). Finally, 19 studies are concerned with goods offered in digitized form (e.g., newspapers, books, games, music albums, software). Overall, the survey of the product and service categories covered so far in PWYW investigations suggests that researchers tacitly assume the following: PWYW pricing primarily comes into question to sell (gastronomical) services or digitized products for which free production capacities are at hand, which generate low absolute variable costs and where – from the perspective of an average consumer – purchases at a standard (fixed) market price do not require a considerable willingness to make financial sacrifices.

2.3 Conceptual framework for structuring key themes covered in the reviewed studies

The various research topics addressed in the reviewed 72 PWYW publications/97 PWYW data sets can be organized with the help of the conceptual framework shown in Figure 2. Roughly, the thematic fields of empirical PWYW studies incorporate three main streams. Firstly, a large number of studies are concerned with variables that are interpreted as factors potentially influencing the level of the prices paid voluntarily by customers or other significant economic effects of the PWYW price setting method (e.g., take-up/purchase rate of offers, seller image). These "success factors of PWYW pricing" (Stegemann, 2014, p. 19) can again be subdivided into five classes, namely characteristics of (1) the design of PWYW procedure, (2) the buyers, (3) the sellers, (4) the focal sales objects and (5) the market context. Investigations within the first main stream implicitly apply the "stimulus–response–paradigm" as they do not directly consider buyer perceptions of the PWYW pricing method. Secondly, a much less voluminous stream of studies follows the "stimulus–organism–response–paradigm" by exploring correlations between each of the five five classes of factors listed above and buyer perceptions of various features of the PWYW method applied as well as between such perceptions and criteria reflecting effects of the use of the PWYW price setting approach at the level of the individual consumer (e.g., prices paid, (re-)purchase rates). Within the third research stream, the particular emphasis is on evaluations of the success or outcomes of PWYW pricing applications. The assessments especially include criteria measured at the company level and thereby surpass individual customer/micro level investigations.

The subsequent sections 3 to 5 discuss the findings, which can be derived from each of these three streams of empirical PWYW research.

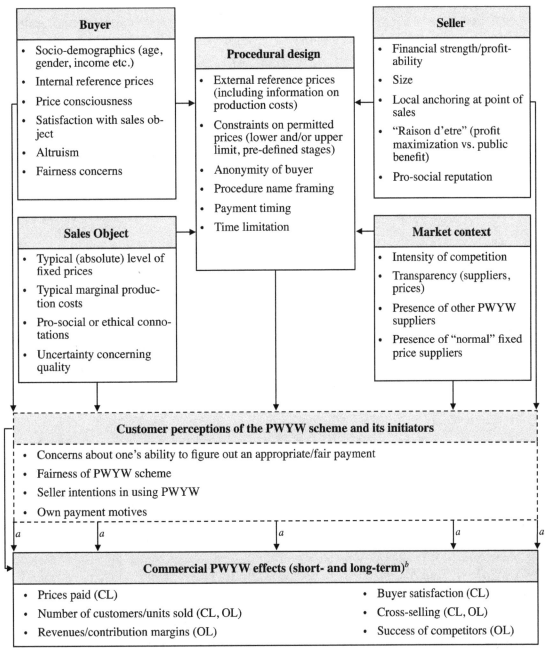

a) Direct success effects of variable blocks procedural design, buyer, seller, sales object and market context according to stimulus–response paradigm.
b) Impact criteria can be measured at the micro/customer level (CL), the macro/organizational level (OL) or both at the CL and OL.

Fig. 2. Conceptual framework of the most important variable categories and interconnections in the PWYW research field

3. Factors influencing individual-level outcomes of PWYW pricing

3.1 Design characteristics of the PWYW procedure

As can be seen from Figure 2, we extracted six features of the PWYW method itself, which suppliers can deliberately shape and which were taken up in past investigations. According to Table 1, by far the most frequently researched design characteristic is the use and construction of information on *reference prices* (*RP*). This feature is about price nominations made by suppliers (*external RP*) or recalls from buyers' memories with regard to prices that they have observed or paid for similar goods in the past (*internal RP*) (cf. Mazumdar et al., 2005). As internal RP are not directly malleable by suppliers, they do not constitute a PWYW design feature but a buyer characteristic, which is discussed in section 3.2.

3.1.1 External reference prices

External RP can be introduced by sellers in the form of an obligatory minimum price, which buyers are not allowed to undercut (Thomas & Gierl, 2014). Furthermore, suppliers have the option to provide customers with a small number of predetermined tiered prices and to ask them to select the price level they want to pay (Lynn, 1990). Finally, sellers can not only quote lower but also upper price limits, which customers are not entitled to overbid (Johnson & Cui, 2013; Jung et al., 2016; Regner, 2015; Regner & Barria, 2009; Regner & Riener, 2012). A commonality underlying the three variants of binding external RP is that they consistently imply a considerable dilution of the central idea of the PWYW method according to which seller price recommendations or pressures are undesired to ensure that buyers are really free in their decision on which amount they pay.

Instead of binding external RP, suppliers can revert to various types of less restrictive price nominations. Such prices can have a normative frame ("we recommend that you pay <...>"). Alternatively, sellers have the option to provide descriptive information on their fixed prices in the recent past or amounts that other buyers have paid for the same good under PWYW conditions (Armstrong Soule & Madrigal, 2015; Johnson & Cui, 2013; Jung et al., 2016; Krawczyk et al., 2015). The violation of the aforementioned fundamental PWYW principle of an unrestricted freedom of consumer price choice is less serious in cases, where sellers use non-binding external RP compared to situations in which binding external RP are quoted.

The bulk of the literature emphasizes that external RP act as anchor points reducing consumer uncertainty with respect to an "appropriate" or "fair" price, because buyers can use them to calibrate their PWYW price setting decisions. Accordingly, higher levels of external RP provided by sellers should lead to higher payment amounts. Similarly, PWYW sales accompanied by external RP should result in higher payments relative to offers that are not supplemented by external RP nominations. The majority of the empirical PWYW studies, which analyze external RP, support these suppositions (Armstrong Soule & Madrigal, 2015; Gautier & Van der Klaauw, 2012 (in case of incidental customer encounters with PWYW offers); Jang & Chu, 2012; Jung et al., 2016 (in case of hypothetical payments); Kim et al., 2014a; Krawczyk et al., 2015; Lee et al., 2011, 2015; León et al., 2012; Parvinen et al., 2013; Perfecto et al., 2013; Perfecto et al., Pöyry & Parvinen, 2014; Pöyry et al., 2013; Regner & Barria, 2009; Riener, 2008). Furthermore, several PWYW studies, in which customers were provided with information on the variable production costs of the goods offered, find significantly positive correlations between the level of the stated direct costs – which can be regarded as a special variant of external RP – and the level of voluntary customer payments (Jang & Chu, 2012; Kim et al., 2014a; Krämer et al., 2015; Schmidt et al., 2015; for an insightful theoretical analysis of this association see Greiff et al., 2014). In light of these results, it is not surprising that earlier reviews of the empirical PWYW literature summarize the state of the evidence as follows: "the provision of external reference prices in the form of a regular or suggested price usually has a positive impact on the prices paid [voluntarily]" (Stegemann, 2014, p. 33; for similar summaries see Gahler, 2016, p. 31; Pöyry,

Table 1
Significance and direction of variable associations in PWYW studies[a]

	Significance and direction			
	Significant		Insignificant/	
Type of association	Positive	Negative	zero	Sum
• Procedural design characteristics				
– External RP → PWYW amount	18	6	5	29
– Buyer anonymity → PWYW amount	1	11	8	20
– Buyer anonymity → Exploitation of buyer potential	0	3	0	3
– Procedure name framing → PWYW amount (1 = emphasis on value; 0 = emphasis on savings)	9	0	0	9
– Payment timing → PWYW amount (1 = after consumption; 0 = before consumption)	4	0	0	4
– Temporary offering[b] → PWYW amount	0	0	2	2
• Buyer characteristics				
– Age → PWYW amount	5	1	3[c]	9
– Female gender[b] → PWYW amount	2	4	10	16
– Income → PWYW amount	5	0	3	8
– Internal RP → PWYW amount	11	0	0	11
– Price consciousness → PWYW amount	0	6	2	8
– Satisfaction → PWYW amount	9	0	2	11
– Altruism → PWYW amount	6	0	3	9
– Fairness concerns → PWYW amount	15	0	2	17
• Seller characteristics				
– Pro-social connotation[b] → PWYW amount	9	1	0	10
• Characteristics of the goods offered				
– Absolute posted price → PWYW amount	10	0	0	10
– Absolute posted price → PWYW amount relative to posted price	0	8	0	8
• Market context characteristics				
– Competition from posted price suppliers[b] → PWYW amount	0	2	0	2
– Competition from PWYW suppliers[b] → Market share of posted price supplier	0	2	0	2

a) The table contains the absolute number of independent data sets with a respective result.
b) 1 = yes; 0 = no.
c) Insignificant linear, but significant curvilinear association (inverted U-shape).

2015, p. L-28). However, there are strong empirical and conceptual reasons to suggest that this conclusion is immature.

Firstly, the cited conclusion neglects the results of several PWYW studies, which detect no significant associations between the level or the use of external RP and prices paid (Gautier & Van der Klaauw, 2012 (in case of self-selected PWYW participation of customers); Gneezy et al., 2012; Hildenbrand et al., 2016; Jung et al., 2016 (in case of field studies on actual prices paid); Weisstein et al., 2016) or even find significantly negative correlations, particularly if the external RP was displayed as a minimal threshold value (Johnson & Cui, 2013; Jung et al., 2016 (study 12a); Kunter & Braun, 2013; Racherl et al., 2011; Roy et al., 2016a; Thomas & Gierl, 2014). Secondly, it ignores that significantly positive effects of external RP are mainly observed in studies which are highly problematic in terms of their methodology, because they focus on hypothetical payments of students, whereas field studies of real purchases almost never report such effects (Jung et al., 2016, p. 356). Thirdly, it does not take note of conceptual arguments according to which buyers may perceive the addition of external RP to PWYW offers as an illegitimate attempt to influence their payment as well as an undesired limitation of their discretion in setting their own prices and who therefore may react negative to such cues (Racherla et al., 2011).

In conclusion, the overall present state of the empirical evidence suggests that external RP effects on the level of PWYW prices paid are *not* consistently positive but depend on additional situational constraints (see also Greiff & Egbert, 2016, p. 6). Therefore, future PWYW research should concentrate less on exploring bivariate associations between the use or the level of external RP on the one hand and voluntary payment amounts on the other. Rather, as similarly proposed by Natter & Kaufmann (2015), a more seminal approach would be to analyze how external RP effects are moderated by other features of the PWYW design (e.g., anonymity of buyers), the goods sold (e.g., novelty), the buyers (e.g., price knowledge) and the seller (e.g., pro-social reputation). Three such potential moderators have already received some attention in the PWYW literature:

– *Anonymity of buyers*: This variable may moderate external RP effects in the following way: In circumstances where buyers do not pay anonymously, they experience heavier social pressure as a result of which they should be more inclined to put a greater weight on external RP in choosing a voluntary payment amount. Conversely, if buyers remain unobserved or anonymous during the payment process, they should be less guided by external RP and more by other considerations or constraints (e.g., fairness concerns) in setting their level of payment (Gahler, 2016; Gneezy et al., 2012; Pöyry et al., 2013; Riener, 2008; Roy et al., 2016a).

– *Availability of internal RP among buyers*: If buyers are able to memorize an internal RP, it should be easier for them to develop a sense of an "adequate" level of payment on their own. Consequently, effects of external RP are likely to be stronger if buyers lack internal RP, for instance, because the offered goods are new to them or do not trigger a high personal involvement (Kunter & Braun, 2013; Schröder et al., 2015).

– *Fairness of external RP*: If customers are convinced that the external RP quoted by sellers are fair, credible or plausible in the sense that they reflect standard fixed prices currently charged for the focal good in the relevant market or average PWYW amounts paid by other buyers or the good's direct production costs with sufficient precision, then the external RP level should have positive impacts on offer acceptance rates and voluntary payment amounts. However, in a situation, in which buyers perceive external RP as being unfair, implausible, extreme outliers and not cost-oriented, such external RP effects should be absent or even become negative (Gautier & Van der Klaauw, 2012; Greiff & Egbert, 2016; Johnson & Cui, 2013; Jung et al., 2016; Kim et al., 2014a; Krawczyk et al., 2015; León et al., 2012; Weisstein et al., 2016). Fairness perceptions of external RP under PWYW conditions should, in turn, to a large extent depend on the image of sellers from the perspective of buyers (see below section 3.3).

Apart from the very limited analysis of factors potentially moderating the impacts of external RP on the level of prices paid voluntarily, the present review reveals a second research gap in connection with external RP in a PWYW context: Past studies have focused on external RP effects on voluntary payment levels. For this reason, there is a dearth of research on external RP effects on *other* equally important business outcomes. However, empirical findings of Jung et al. (2016; study 2) and microeconomic modelling results of Kahsay & Samahita (2015) suggest that as external RP provided by suppliers rise, an increasing share of consumers avoid buying from them and instead either purchase the product concerned from competitors who sell it at (lower) market standard fixed prices or completely refrain from buying it. Therefore, future research in the PWYW field should extend its outcome measures in the direction of additional business-relevant criteria, such as the number of customers or the ratio of persons who buy a product under PWYW conditions to all persons who have the possibility to accept a PWYW offering or the seller's image in the eyes of buyers (cf. Natter & Kaufmann, 2015, p. 152).

In terms of implications for price setting in practice, the review results indicate that suppliers should *not* name lower PWYW payment boundaries which are well below standard market prices for the relevant product or which define minimal mandatory payment amounts. Such lower thresholds incentivize buyers to deemphasize their own internal RP if it falls above the sellers' external RP, and to give more weight to the (low) external RP communicated by the supplier in choosing the price they wish to pay. Furthermore, the provision of external RP in a PWYW process should, at best, be financially advantageous for sellers if they offer goods which are quite unknown to potential buyers and for which the latter have no clear ideas with regard to currently charged market prices or variable production costs and if they place a high level of trust in prices named by their supplier (e.g., because of a long business relationship). If these three situation characteristics are absent, then the state of research suggests that the sellers' cost-benefit-balance of providing external RP is likely to be negative because the PWYW scheme deters potential customers from buying at all. Consequently, under these circumstances suppliers are probably well-advised to make PWYW offers without the provision of external RP.

3.1.2 Buyer anonymity

This PWYW feature reflects whether supplier representatives or other persons, who are more or less personally acquainted with the buyers, are physically present when and therefore are in a position to note the amounts customers are paying. If other human beings are around and observe the payments of buyers, then the PWYW design is *non-anonymous*, otherwise the process is *anonymous*. The vast majority of PWYW studies argue that a non-anonymous PWYW procedure increases the "normative influence of social environments (Stegemann, 2014, p. 34) on customers to pay a "fair" price (e.g., Armstrong Soule & Madrigal, 2015; Dorn & Suessmair, 2016; Machado & Sinha, 2012). Consequently, the average PWYW price paid should be higher, if buyers are not anonymous compared to situations in which buyers' personal identity remains undisclosed. In contrast to this, a smaller number of authors emphasize that the average prices paid are unlikely to differ as a function of buyer anonymity. The explanation given for a missing anonymity effect is that anonymous customers also strive to keep a positive self-image by not treating a supplier unfair. This has the consequence that anonymous buyers do not pay lower prices than their non-anonymous counterparts (Gneezy et al., 2012; Jang & Chu, 2012).

The empirical results obtained to date (see Table 1) predominantly indicate that buyer anonymity decreases the average amount paid in PWYW settings (Bondos & Lipowski, 2016; Dorn & Suessmair, 2016; Hilbert & Suessmair, 2015; Kim et al., 2014a (study 1); Lee et al., 2015; Machado & Sinha, 2012; Pöyry & Parvinen, 2014; Riener & Traxler, 2012; Santana & Morwitz, 2011, 2013; Veit & Ammermann, 2013). However, the negative effects are primarily reported in studies of hypothetical intentions to pay in student samples whose validity is highly questionable. Furthermore, some researchers find no or even significantly positive effects of buyer anonymity on the mean of the prices paid under PWYW conditions (Gahler, 2016; Gneezy et al., 2012; Kim et al., 2014a (study 2); Park et al., 2016; Parvinen et al., 2013; Regner & Riener, 2012; Riener, 2008; Roy et al., 2016a; Saccardo et al., 2015).

Moreover, the analysis of Regner & Riener (2012) provides strong evidence suggesting that many potential customers perceive a non-anonymous PWYW process as unpleasant, restrictive and disconcerting. The result of this negative evaluation is that in non-anonymous contexts a much larger share of prospective customers is completely deterred from buying from PWYW suppliers than in situations in which buyers remain anonymous. This "deterrence proposition" also receives support in field studies of actual non-anonymous PWYW purchases conducted by Gneezy et al. (2012) and Jung et al. (2014b).

The studies according to which non-anonymous PWYW procedures come along with strong customer self-selection effects also suggest that future research should no longer look only at anonymity effects on the prices paid in samples of consumers who did not deliberately opt for or against purchases in a PWYW setting but who were simply unable to circumvent them because the researchers' data generation set-ups forced them into such transactions. Instead, the distribution of voluntarily paid prices should be specifically examined in subgroups of consumers, who completely voluntarily decided to enter into a PWYW context. In this regard the results of Gautier & Van der Klaauw (2012) and León et al. (2012) reveal that even in the case of self-selected participants a non-anonymous PWYW design leads to significantly lower payments than an anonymous approach. These studies argue that a non-anonymous process mainly attracts consumers who look for a bargain relative to standard fixed prices (Kunter, 2015) and therefore are even prepared to disclose their identity. Furthermore, it is desirable to improve the explanatory power of studies on effects of buyer anonymity in PWYW settings by including additional moderators in the analysis. Two such potential key moderators are the degree to which (1) (non-)anonymous payments for the specific category of goods under study are customary under "normal" fixed price conditions and (2) PWYW buyers accept an offering because they value the high level of participation in setting prices or because of the possibility to obtain a good at a low price (type of PWYW motivation).

In practice, the current state of evidence implies that PWYW processes are more acceptable for consumers when buyers can pay without being directly observed by the supplier or other persons. In case of a non-anonymous PWYW procedure with a high visibility of the amount paid to other parties, there is a high probability that many prospective buyers are dissuaded from a transaction and that the remaining customers are characterized by a low willingness to pay.

3.1.3 Other design features

Apart from the two PWYW design features discussed above, there are three other procedural PWYW attributes that have been repeatedly included in the relevant empirical literature.

Firstly, researchers have explored framing effects, which are caused by the procedure name chosen to introduce PWYW offerings, on the prices paid (see Table 1). Atlas (2015) finds higher voluntary payments if consumers are asked to choose a rebate on the fixed price compared to the standard PWYW framing. Machado & Sinha (2012) detect significantly higher average payment amounts if the procedure was called "Pay What It Is Worth To You" compared to a presentation under the name PWYW. Saccardo & Gneezy (2014) and Saccardo et al. (2015) observe that the levels of voluntary payments were significantly higher if the price setting approach was addressed with the heading "Pay What You Can" or "Donate What You Want" than if it was labeled as PWYW. Schröder et al. (2015) find that naming the procedure as "Reduce The Price As Much As You Can" resulted in significantly lower payments than presenting it as PWYW. Sleesman & Conlon (2016) report significantly higher payments if the name framing is "Pay What You Believe/s Fair" instead of PWYW. Taken together the six studies and their nine data sets point in the direction that the prices paid in PWYW contexts can be positively influenced by presenting name frames that emphasize the value of the goods offered or the financial standing of the buyers instead of saving opportunities triggered by this price setting approach.

The second other design feature relates to the "timing" of the voluntary payment before or after the consumption of the goods purchased (see Table 1). Four pieces of research contain indications that voluntary prices paid are higher in situations where buyers pay *after* they have already consumed or tried out the goods offered in a PWYW context than in cases where buyers first decide about their payment amount and then consume a service or receive the product they purchased (Drevs, 2013; Kim et al., 2014a; Machado & Sinha, 2012; Regner, 2015). An explanation for these differences in the amounts paid is that paying after service consumption or product trials reduces information asymmetries favoring sellers over buyers particularly in case of experience goods (Greiff et al., 2014). Of course, the positive effects of ex-post payments compared to paying in advance are the larger, the more customers are satisfied with the services or products they purchase (see section 3.2.4). Consequently, practitioners would be well-advised to prefer an ex-post price setting approach over an ex-ante timing if it is very likely that customers positively evaluate the goods which they buy.

The third design characteristics analyzed is whether a PWYW offering is temporary or not (see Table 1). Kim et al. (2014a) and Parvinen et al. (2013) both find that the level of prices paid is not significantly affected by whether sellers communicate to prospective buyers that their PWYW offer is a temporary sales promotion measure or a pricing approach of indefinite duration.

3.2 Buyer characteristics

Figure 2 and Table 1 reveal that the following attribute classes of buyers have attracted greater attention in the empirical literature: (1) Socio-demographic variables, (2) internal RP, (3) price consciousness, (4) satisfaction with the purchased goods and (5) general social preferences. Subsequently, we summarize pertinent empirical results for each of the variable categories.

3.2.1 Socio-demographic variables

Age, gender and income are the most frequently studied socio-demographic correlates of payment amounts for PWYW goods. Investigations on *age* effects contain mixed results. Five studies identify significantly positive interrelations between age and PWYW prices (Borck et al., 2006; Kim et al., 2014a; León et al., 2012; Racherla et al., 2011; Waskow et al., 2016). Regner (2015) finds a negative association, whereas research of Gautier & Van der Klaauw (2012), Gneezy et al. (2012) and Riener (2008) suggests an inverted U-shaped pattern.

Research results with regard to *gender* differences in voluntarily paid prices are also heterogeneous. Borck et al. (2006) and Saccardo & Gneezy (2014) discover that females pay more than males. Four other analyses contain opposite results (Gautier & Van der Klaauw, 2012 (in case of self-selected PWYW participants); Kim et al., 2014a (study 1); Schröder et al., 2015; Waskow et al., 2016). Ten publications report no significant gender impact on prices paid (Gahler, 2016; Gautier & Van der Klaauw, 2012 (in case of incidental encounter with PWYW offering); Gneezy et al., 2012; Kim et al., 2014a (study 2); Rachelor et al., 2011; Regner, 2015; Regner & Barria, 2009; Riener, 2008; Roy, 2015; Roy et al., 2016a).

Empirical evidence on effects of buyer *income* on voluntarily paid amounts in PWYW settings is a little less diverging. Five studies indicate that the association between the two variables is significantly positive (Kim et al., 2009, 2014; Mills, 2013; Regner, 2015; Riener & Traxler, 2012). Three investigations observe an insignificant correlation (Borck et al., 2006; Roy, 2015; Roy et al., 2016a), but the validity of two of the three null-result-publications is low because they examine student samples with restricted income variances.

Faced with the inconclusive evidence with respect to associations between socio-demographic buyer characteristics and prices paid in a PWYW context, one may be tempted to argue that additional studies with a focus on this class of variables are required to better understand the reasons behind the mixed findings. However, such research endeavors will only achieve greater scholarly importance if they more extensively draw on theoretical frameworks explaining socio-demographic effects by explicitly dealing with the psychological and economic phenomena for which socio-demographic variables are just proxies. In practice, the results summarized in this section imply that managers should refrain from trying to target PWYW offerings to consumer subgroups defined by means of a specific socio-demographic profile because such an approach is unlikely to increase the average amount paid voluntarily per customer.

3.2.2 Internal reference prices

Internal RP are price benchmarks retrieved from buyers' memories which customers rate as adequately reflecting normal market prices or which they have already paid in the past for a similar offering or for which they assume that such prices have already been paid by other individuals in the focal PWYW setting (Roy, 2015). The PWYW literature takes the view that internal RP help buyers to derive the amount they want to pay voluntarily. Thus, the correlation between the two variables should be positive (Stegemann, 2014). Without exception, the available empirical evidence is in line with this hypothesis (see Table 1). Results are affirmative regardless of whether internal RP are measured as a memorized amount which buyers had paid for comparable offerings under fixed price conditions (Mills, 2011, 2013; Roy, 2015; Roy et al., 2016a, 2016b; Schons et al., 2014) or as the presumptions of buyers with respect to the typical amount paid by other persons for a similar good (Borck et al., 2006; Gneezy et al., 2012; Kunter & Braun, 2013; Machado & Sinha, 2012). The clarity of the internal RP findings combined with the ambiguity of the pertinent results for external RP (see section 3.1.1) suggest the following proposition to be tested in future research: Due to the higher credibility of internal compared to external RP, internal RP have a positive impact on voluntary payments in PWYW settings, which is significantly stronger than the effect of external RP.

The internal RP results also have important implications for setting PWYW prices in practice. They indicate that an identification of buyer groups characterized by high internal RP should be an effective lever to increase the amounts paid. However, the positive financial consequences of such a strategy are limited by the boundary condition that positive internal RP effects on prices paid become the smaller, the larger the absolute values of standard market prices of the PWYW goods are (see section 3.4 below).

3.2.3 Price consciousness

This buyer characteristic refers to the weight consumers assign to low prices when making purchasing decisions (Kim et al., 2009). The general notion is that buyers' price consciousness significantly negatively affects PWYW prices paid. Six studies contain indications supporting this position (Kim et al., 2009; Kunter, 2013; Marrett et al., 2012; Mills, 2013; Roy et al., 2016b; Schons et al., 2014). According to findings of Roy (2015), the effects of price consciousness are moderated by the internal RP of buyers: Price consciousness has the expected negative effect on the amount paid if buyers' internal RP is high, but not in case of low internal RP. Finally, Drevs (2013) and Kim et al. (2014a) observe insignificant correlations between price consciousness and PWYW prices paid. On balance, the empirical results are more in line with the proposition that highly price-conscious buyers make lower voluntary payments than consumers who are not so keen on low purchase prices. Hence, in practice, managers should reflect upon the degree to which their PWYW offerings primarily attract highly price-conscious buyers. If price strategists expect such a strong self-selection of bargain hunters, then it is usually economically better to operate with (regular) fixed prices instead of a PWYW approach.

3.2.4 Satisfaction

Service or product satisfaction captures the extent to which buyers believe that their quality expectations are met by the good sold. The literature typically posits: "Satisfaction plays a distinct role in PWYW pricing, as this mechanism allows consumers to immediately express their satisfaction or dissatisfaction with the product/service in terms of the amount they pay for it" (Stegemann, 2014, p. 30). However, an unmentioned prerequisite for significant impacts of satisfaction on the level of voluntary payments in PWYW settings is that consumers need to have already had the opportunity to experience the nature of the goods sold and pay for them *after* this experience. Otherwise, in contexts where customers pay *before* consumption satisfaction is likely to exert a clear influence on prices paid *only* if buyers are already very familiar with the peculiarities of the purchased service or product and have therefore formed a stable evaluation of the offering and/or its supplier. A total of nine studies find that buyer satisfaction is significantly positively correlated with prices paid voluntarily *after* consumption (see Table 1: Borck et al., 2006; Gautier & Van der Klaauw, 2012; Kim et al., 2009, 2014a; León et al., 2012; Machado & Sinha, 2012; Racherla et al., 2011; Riener, 2008; Schmidt et al., 2015). Solely, Drevs (2013) and Schons et al. (2014) observe no significant association between the two variables. Hence, overall it can be concluded that the link between buyer satisfaction with the products or services offered by a PWYW seller and the amounts paid after being served is sizable and significantly positive.

3.2.5 General social preferences

The key buyer attitudes related to beliefs about the way in which other persons should be treated in general and PWYW sellers in particular and which the PWYW literature often addresses as "social preferences" (Stegemann, 2014, p. 24), "underlying motives" (Natter & Kaufmann, 2015, p. 154) or "payment motivation" (Kunter, 2015, p. 2355) of buyers are altruism, fairness concerns, desire to keep sellers in business and strategic intention to motivate suppliers in such a manner that they perform well in future sales encounters. Out of these constructs, altruism and fairness concerns have attracted the most attention.

Altruism deals with the general tendency of persons to help other individuals without expecting one-to-one compensatory returns from them (Huber et al., 2016). Six studies include evidence according to which altruism of buyers has significantly positive impacts on the magnitude of their voluntary payment (Gahler, 2016; Huber et al., 2013; Huber et al., 2014; Kim et al., 2009; Roy et al., 2016b; Santana & Morwitz, 2011, 2013). Two analyses of Kim et al. (2009), who examine PWYW food sales in a restaurant and ticket sales in a cinema, as well as a study of Drevs (2013), who also looks at the sale of cinema tickets in a PWYW setting, report insignificant correlations between buyer altruism and PWYW prices paid. With the exception of the work of Kim et al. (2009) the studies which report significant correlations share the methodological weakness that they capture both altruistic attitudes as well as PWYW prices paid in a cross-sectional survey. Therefore, it may well be assumed that the detection of associations between the focal variables is mainly an artefact of the data collection approach, namely so-called "common method biases" (Podsakoff et al., 2009, p. 879): Survey participants who claim to be strongly altruistically motivated are likely to respond consistently in the same questionnaire by stating that they would also pay higher prices in fictitious PWYW sale contexts. However, in case of a real PWYW purchase they would actually pay a considerably lower amount.

Fairness concerns reflect attitudes of buyers according to which they are convinced that customers should respond to the goods they get from sellers by allocating a proportional return in the form of an "adequate" voluntary payment to the seller (Kim et al., 2009; Natter & Kaufmann, 2015; Roy et al., 2016b). Nine publications using a total of 15 data sets report significantly positive associations between buyers' "preference for fairness" (Pöyry, 2015, p. L-26) and the level of PWYW prices paid (see Table 1; Drevs, 2013; Gahler, 2016; Kim et al., 2009, 2014 (study 2); Kunter, 2015; Lee et al., 2015; Santana & Morwitz, 2015, 2016; Schons et al., 2014). Two data sets suggest insignificant associations (Kim et al., 2014a (study 1); Regner, 2015). With regard to the fairness construct it should also be taken into account that "common method biases" present in the relevant studies are likely to lead to inflated estimates of the size of correlations between fairness norms and voluntary payment amounts. In line with this proposition Regner (2015, p. 212) similarly concludes as follows: "There seems to be a discrepancy between the ex post reasoning for generous decisions and the actual motivations as customers expect fairness concerns to lead to generous payments, although there is no evidence in the data that these drive behavior."

3.2.6 Interim conclusions

Work exploring buyer characteristics as correlates of the magnitude of voluntary payments in PWYW contexts has so far yielded no consistent results with regard to the socio-demographic variables age, gender and income. Internal RP, price consciousness, satisfaction, altruism and fairness motives nearly always correlate significantly positively with the level of prices paid, but many investigations presumably contain inflated estimates of these associations because they are plagued with common method problems. In addition, the effects of the five last-mentioned factors on PWYW price levels can be qualified as being intuitively plausible, if not even as trivial. Finally, the accumulated knowledge concerning associations between the aforementioned psychographic buyer characteristics and the magnitude of voluntary payments in PWYW settings is not particularly useful in designing PWYW offerings in practice because sellers are simply unable to capture these attributes with reasonable effort.

Against this background, we conclude that additional research on buyer characteristics as potential drivers of the level of PWYW prices paid is not urgently needed. If researchers wish to further examine buyer characteristics in PWYW settings, then it is more promising to investigate associations between this class of variables and buyer decisions on whether to prefer a PWYW transaction to a fixed price purchase or not. So far such studies are entirely lacking.

3.3 Seller characteristics

The pertinent literature discusses the five characteristics of PWYW sellers shown in Figure 2 primarily in a qualitative manner as potential determinants of the amounts customers pay and seller decisions in favor of making PWYW offerings instead of a conventional fixed price sales strategy. In comparison, quantitative statistical results are rare to find. Accordingly, Regner & Barria (209, p. 405), León et al. (2012, p. 411) and Schmidt et al. (2015, p. 1232) similarly argue that higher PWYW prices paid can be expected for sellers, who customers perceive as financially less strong and less profitable and not as a faceless large-scale corporation but rather as a locally rooted small- or at best medium-size trustworthy supplier/family business. Moreover, some authors stress that suppliers, who do not solely strive to maximize their profits but visibly operate in a pro-social and ethically exemplary way (e.g., through donating for charitable organizations) receive higher PWYW amounts than sellers, who do not possess such characteristics (Jung et al., 2014b; cf. section 3.4 below). The investigations of Gneezy et al. (2010), Kim et al. (2014a, study 2), Lee et al. (2015), Machado & Sinha (2012), Marrett al. al. (2012), Roy et al. (2016b) and Santana & Morwitz (2011, 2013) contain empirical results supporting this position. Similarly, Schlüter & Vollan (2015) detect that in an honesty-based payment situation with fixed target prices (unobserved payments for flowers where the money is put into an honor box) buyers pay significantly higher prices if the seller is described as a small family business compared to a seller profile as a large corporate business. In contrast, Park et al. (2016) find that a rate schedule including PWYW and a charity donation results in significantly lower payments per customer than a fixed price scheme.

All in all, the empirical evidence thus confirms the proposition that in PWYW contexts buyers unconsciously take into their (mental) calculation whom they support or harm by paying a high or low price, respectively (see Table 1). Moral concerns against a low price are put aside or reversely gain behavioral relevance if sellers are qualified as financially robust and, more generally, as unlikable or as financially weak and as likable, respectively. With a view to using the PWYW approach in practice, the results concerning PWYW seller characteristics imply the following: This price setting procedure is especially worth to be considered by smaller companies with strong social ties at their business locations and long-term business relationships to a loyal customer base than by organizations with the opposite attributes. From a scholarly perspective, it is vital that future research provides more fine-grained analyses of the effects of precisely defined supplier characteristics (e.g., corporate size, age, profitability and credibility) on the probability that PWYW offerings are taken up at all by prospective customers and on the prices paid in the subgroup of all buyers, who do not avoid a PWYW offering.

3.4 Characteristics of the goods offered

Effects of characteristics of the goods offered under PWYW conditions on customer take-up rates and the magnitude of voluntarily paid prices are also scarcely examined in PWYW research and, if at all, primarily in qualitative terms. Out of the sales object-related attributes listed in Figure 2, the absolute fixed prices, which are generally charged for a certain category of goods in the market and frequently labeled as "product value" (Pöyry, 2015, p. L-27; Stegemann, 2014, p. 27), the variable unit costs and the total unit costs still have achieved the most attention of PWYW researchers. The research results quite consistently suggest that normal absolute fixed prices of products or services significantly positively correlate with the absolute amount paid under PWYW conditions and are significantly negatively correlated with the relative PWYW price paid, which is the ratio of voluntary payments amounts to standard fixed market prices of the goods studied (see Table 1; Gahler, 2016; Gautier & Van der Klaauw, 2012; Jang & Chu, 2012; Kim et al., 2014a; León et al., 2012; Machado & Sinha, 2012; Mak et al., 2015; Mills, 2013). In a similar vein, the (absolute) magnitude of voluntarily paid prices increases with the variable and average unit costs of the goods sold in a PWYW context in case that buyers are informed about these costs in advance of their price setting choice (Greiff et al., 2014; Krämer et al., 2015; Riener, 2008; Schmidt et al., 2015).

The explanatory power of these results should, however, be put into perspective due to the fact that they were almost without exception generated in samples of customers who were expectedly confronted with PWYW offerings. Therefore, a deliberate self-selection of buyers in favor of a PWYW setting was impossible. Gautier & Van der Klaauw (2012) are the only researchers who compared a subsample of buyers who consciously opted for a PWYW offering (hotel-stay) with customers who were unexpectedly involved in a PWYW sales situation. They observe a significantly positive correlation between the normal fixed market price of the service customers received and the voluntary payment level only in the subsample of participants for whom the PWYW offer was unforeseen but not in the subsample of buyers who specifically selected the PWYW setting.

Overall, the evidence on PWYW prices paid as a function of the common "market value" or the variable production costs of the goods sold corroborate the following theoretical explanation: In cases of goods that are normally sold at low absolute (fixed) prices and that generate low costs, buyers are inclined to make voluntary payments which are relatively high compared to the standard market value of the goods offered. Buyers do this because a generous or at least fair payment level improves their self-image so clearly that the resulting subjective incremental benefit exceeds the subjective costs which result from the insight to have not minimized payouts by setting a (moderately unfair) low price. On the other hand, in cases of goods with high absolute fixed prices/costs the image benefit of buyers resulting from a high voluntary payment to market value/price ratio tends to be smaller than their subjectively perceived costs resulting from not having minimized their payouts by setting the voluntary payment at a low (and unfair) level. In other words, the functional relationship between a good's fixed price/market value/costs on the one hand and the image benefits or, respectively, costs of overpayment of a high ratio between the voluntarily paid price and the fixed price/market value/costs of goods on the other hand should be concave or convex, respectively (cf. Jang & Chu, 2012; Kahsay & Samahita, 2015; Machado & Sinha, 2012). In practice, the empirical results and the respective theoretical explanations mean that from the view of sellers it is for the most part profit-wise preferable to limit PWYW offerings to products and services normally sold at low absolute (fixed) prices and produced at low costs. It is exactly this type of goods that is without exception analyzed in empirical PWYW field studies of real (and not just hypothetical) purchases (see section 2.2 above).

Apart from customary (fixed) market prices and production costs of PWYW goods, effects of a "prosocial" or "ethical" connotation of the products or services offered on prices paid voluntarily are explored in a few investigations. The issue here is whether donations of parts of the sales prices of goods for charitable purposes or production and marketing of goods under morally acceptable conditions furnish products or services with an additional value component, which reaches beyond their pure functional utility (Newholm & Shaw, 2007; Small & Cryder, 2016). The main result of studies on PWYW offerings with pro-social or ethical elements is that the share of potential customers voting in favor of such products and services is smaller than the corresponding share for strictly commercial offerings.

At the same time, however, in the subsample of people, who opted for the "special" offerings, voluntarily paid prices are significantly higher than the amounts paid for "normal" products and services in PWYW settings (Gneezy et al., 2010, 2012; Jung et al., 2014b; Perfecto et al., 2013, 2014; Roy et al., 2016a; Santana & Morwitz, 2011, 2013; Thomas & Gierl, 2014; Ven, 2012).

To sum up, to date empirical PWYW studies have devoted little attention to effects of the characteristics of the goods sold under PWYW conditions on various outcomes of this price setting method. Therefore, a considerable number of questions important for extending pricing theories and improving price setting in practice have not yet been addressed. For instance, from a theoretical viewpoint, it is to be expected that new products or services, for which consumers experience considerable difficulties in assessing their quality and which are sold under PWYW conditions, are purchased by a lower share of potential customers and are characterized by a larger variance of the prices paid voluntarily for them than established goods whose quality is well know to prospective buyers. The PWYW studies of Sleesman & Conlon (2016) and Weisstein et al. (2016) contain some support for this proposition. The expected differences can be explained by information gaps and resulting uncertainty of consumers, who are heavily influenced by characteristics of the goods sold in a PWYW setting (Greiff et al., 2014). Consequently, more empirical tests of this proposition and other hypotheses related to the characteristics of PWYW goods are highly desirable.

3.5 Market context characteristics

Corporations, which sell goods under "true" PWYW conditions, typically operate in a market environment, in which competitors also offer comparable products or services at traditional (fixed) prices or based on other pricing methods which promote consumer participation in price setting (e.g., Name Your Own Price, auctions, see section 1 above). In free markets, consumer switching from PWYW suppliers to offers of competitors is the easier, the larger the number of competitors present in the same relevant geographical area and the higher the similarity between the goods sold by competitors and PWYW providers (Greiff & Egbert, 2016; Stegemann, 2014). Such external conditions including, in particular, the intensity of competition or consumer transparency with regard to the availability of other sellers and their pricing policies can be subsumed under the generic label "market context" (see Figure 2).

Market context characteristics are largely ignored in the empirical PWYW literature. Exceptions are the laboratory experiments of Krämer et al. (2015) and Schmidt et al. (2015). They show that the presence of competitors using conventional fixed prices has a negative effect on the level of price that PWYW buyers pay. Furthermore, they find the PWYW suppliers can push fixed price competitors completely out of a market.

In light of the neglect of market context conditions in prior PWYW research, future studies should take a much closer look at the effects of such factors on sales volumes and prices paid in PWYW contexts. In practice, the sparsely available evidence on the role of market context characteristics in PWYW settings already now implies that a general economic principle according to which sales and profit prospects of a company deteriorate with more intense competition, still remains fully in force even if sellers resort to the PWYW method in setting their prices.

4. Customer perceptions of PWYW schemes

By far the largest part of empirical work on PWYW follows the stimulus–response paradigm. This means that researchers explore how the (blocks of) variables discussed in the preceding sections 3.1 to 3.5 directly affect individual level outcome criteria such as offer acceptance rates or the magnitude of voluntarily paid amounts. Customer perceptions of PWYW schemes are hardly ever addressed. An explanation for this approach is that investigations assume consistently positive customer perceptions and preferences in favor of the innovative PWYW price setting method in spite of its low use frequency in practice. In line with this presumption Kim et al. (2009) find that 87 % of the customers of a restaurant selling meals under PWYW conditions stated in a survey that they prefer the PWYW approach over binding price specifications imposed by sellers. Nevertheless, the neglect of customer perceptions and preferences concerning the PWYW method is regrettable because it makes it more difficult to understand and predict behavioral customer reactions to PWYW offerings in general and to various design characteristics of this price setting approach in particular. Thus, Figure 2 includes a block of variables titled "customer perceptions of PWYW schemes and their initiators", even though such perceptual facets are rarely covered in earlier research.

An exception is the work of Kim et al. (2014b). They gave product samples (razor blades) to one group of consumers and asked the people to voluntarily pay for them as much as they wanted (including 0). Another group of consumers received the sample for free. The PWYW group rated the sales promotion measure significantly better in terms of its entertainment value and innovativeness and significantly worse with regard to its saving potential and personal effort caused by the measure than the consumer group with the free of charge sample. A second field study, which was also conducted by Kim et al. (2014b) and focused on a professionally produced portrait photo, reveals similar results: Fixed discounts or free sample price settings outperformed the PWYW approach in terms of the personal effort of participating in the promotion as perceived by customers.

The studies of Gneezy et al. (2010), Machado & Sinha (2012), Riener (2008), Santana & Morwitz (2011, 2013) and Schmidt et al. (2015) contain additional mainly casuistic and qualitative evidence regarding the higher "cognitive effort" (Mendoza-Abarca & Mellema, 2016, p. 120) triggered by the PWYW method in comparison with fixed prices. The reason for the higher effort imposed on consumers in a PWYW setting is that buyers have to think more for themselves about a price which fairly factors in currently charged market prices as well as the costs and interests of sellers. Taken together, the six publications just cited suggest that the extra cognitive effort combined with consumer uncertainties regarding the "appropriate" voluntary payment level and the seller motives underlying their PWYW offerings jointly decrease the attractiveness of PWYW price setting in the eyes of consumers. Hence, it is quite likely that in many PWYW application cases a significant share of consumers likes the established fixed price approach more than the PWYW method and therefore abstains from entering into a PWYW sales situation.

The few empirical results with respect to perceptions of PWYW schemes by consumers and the effects of an introduction of the PWYW method on consumer perceptions of the seller (= image) are contradictory. On the one hand, Stegemann (2014) observes that consumers evaluate sellers (restaurants, hair salons) significantly more positive if they use PWYW schemes instead of the fixed price approach. This is in contrast to results of Reese (2012, 2013), who finds no difference in perceived price fairness between consumers, who buy an entry ticket for a sports event under PWYW conditions and their counterparts, who receive a fixed price offering. Jostrup & Salic (2015) report that customer attitudes towards a product (pear juice) do not vary depending on whether the product is offered under PWYW conditions or is given away for free. Finally, Mills (2013) detects that consumers with a positive attitude towards the PWYW method are significantly less likely to pay nothing for the download of a computer game than buyers with a negative attitude towards PWYW price setting.

So far, Gahler (2016) is the only researcher who analyzed how customer perceptions of PWYW schemes are influenced by attributes of their design and characteristics of the goods sold in a PWYW context. According to his data buyers rate the fairness of PWYW offerings as being better if sellers present external RP to help buyers in choosing appropriate prices and if the good offered has low variable production costs and therefore has a typical market price which is low in absolute terms.

Within the research stream addressing perceptions of PWYW customers, studies on customer self-assessments of the importance of various "motivation-related payment factors" (Kunter, 2015, p. 2347) cover a special niche. According to such examinations, buyers name fairness considerations, attempts to avoid feelings of guilt or shame, product or service satisfaction, constrained financial resources, desires to make a bargain and external RP as factors that they believe to have the strongest impacts on their decisions regarding the prices paid voluntarily (Dorn & Suessmair, 2016; Kunter, 2015; Regner, 2015). The work of Regner (2015), however, contains strong indications in support of the position that customer self-ratings of the importance of various payment motives in determining PWYW prices are correlated only very weakly with the amounts effectively paid.

In summary, research on customer perceptions of PWYW schemes with regard to various dimensions such as psychological costs of price choices under time pressure and uncertainties or presumed seller motives for using the PWYW method is still in its infancy. The number of already existing relevant investigations is not only small. Rather, their focus on hypothetical purchases of students gives strong reasons to question the external validity of this stream of research. Accordingly, at present, it is very difficult to derive sound statements with regard to the value distributions for various dimensions reflecting customer perceptions of PWYW schemes. Similarly, it is impossible to make empirically substantiated recommendations for practitioners on how to influence customer perceptions of PWYW schemes as a prerequisite for improving the economic success prospects of such schemes. This means that customer perceptions of PWYW schemes should play a very prominent role in future empirical work.

5. Evaluation of economic outcomes of PWYW pricing

The criteria for assessing direct economic outcomes of an implementation of PWYW pricing for sellers used most frequently by PWYW researchers are (1) the prices paid voluntarily, (2) the number of units sold or customers served and (3) the resulting revenues generated in the PWYW application period (see Figure 2). Values of these three criteria captured for periods during which prices are exclusively fixed by sellers are normally called on as yardsticks required to derive a comprehensive evaluation of the economic success level of PWYW pricing. In general, "one-shot" analyses that merely examine a single and narrow time window by far outweigh work covering the development of economic success measures over longer periods.

The evaluation results of field studies, which contain behavioral data on PWYW prices paid voluntarily for real purchases and compare them with common fixed market prices, yield the following overall picture (Bourreau et al., 2015; Drevs, 2013; Gautier & Van der Klaauw, 2012; Gneezy et al., 2010, 2012; Kim et al., 2009, 2010a, 2010b, 2014a, 2014b; León et al., 2012; Machado & Sinha, 2012 (study 3); Regner, 2015; Riener & Traxler, 2012):

- Only a very small portion of buyers pays nothing or more than the standard fixed price for the good, respectively.
- The majority of buyers pays less than the standard fixed price so that the average payment per unit/ customer in a PWYW setting is lower than the regular fixed market price for the good.
- Notwithstanding that PWYW price averages are often found to be below the standard fixed prices for various categories of goods, the likelihood is quite substantial that PWYW pricing may result in revenue increases in comparison to periods during which sellers charged fixed prices. This implies that the PWYW method deters few customers and attracts many new accounts which in turn leads to raises in the number of customer that are so large that they more than offset the negative revenue effect of lower payments per customer or purchase.

Overall, empirical evaluations of the economic outcomes of PWYW pricing draw a cautiously optimistic picture with regard to the immediate financial advantages of this price setting method in comparison with standard fixed prices. A significant exception is the work of León et al. (2012), according to which customers of a Spanish holiday tour operator on average merely paid 7.9 % of the regular prices for holiday trip packages offered under PWYW conditions. However, the tour operator designed the PWYW offers as a time-limited sales promotion measure. This way, increases in the number of packages sold were impossible and customers were encouraged to classify the offers as a temporary marketing action in the course of which very low payments would not seriously harm the seller. However, even empirical investigations, which rate certain PWYW application cases as being economically successful, consistently emphasize that a customized design of the method adapted to the individual use situation combined with a careful selection of the targeted consumer group and of the goods offered are crucial for ensuring that the economic outcomes of PWYW pricing are favorable relative to the results of a fixed price setting approach.

The long-term development of the amounts paid voluntarily in PWYW applications is an important driver of the sustainability of economic PWYW advantages relative to a situation, in which sellers set fixed prices. Research results with regard to such changes over time are contradictory. Based on intra-individual comparisons of PWYW prices paid at subsequent purchase events Gravert (2014), Regner & Barria (2015) and Schons et al. (2014) observe significant decreases in voluntary payment amounts over the course of time. In contrast to that, Jung et al. (2014b) report that the magnitude of voluntary payments, which customers make at consecutive purchases of the same type of goods, remains constant. Looking at price averages measured at various points in time, Riener & Traxler (2012) and Schons et al. (2014) find that the monthly means of the voluntary payments sellers record over 24 or two months, respectively, drop. On the other hand, Kim et al. (2010b) and Mills (2011, 2013) note that the prices buyers pay on average grow during 12 months or 14 days, respectively. Finally, Regner & Barria (2009) detect no significant differences between the monthly mean PWYW amounts which an online seller of music tracks receives over an 18-months period.

Considering the mixed empirical evidence generalizing reliable conclusions, with regard to the intertemporal stability of the amount of voluntary payments at the within and between customer level, are currently impossible. Therefore, additional research is sorely needed which details the factors causing significant within and between individual changes in the prices buyers voluntarily pay over time.

A few authors point out that evaluations of the economic outcomes of PWYW pricing should include criteria which measure less immediate financial and non-financial effects of the method as a supplement to variables reflecting its direct economic results (Stegemann, 2014; Natter & Kaufmann, 2015). The most prominent "indirect" financial outcomes of PWYW pricing are additional revenues that a supplier generates through stimulating demand for other and potentially more expensive products or services which typically complement the goods sold at PWYW (e.g., drinks served with a meal in a restaurant). The empirical literature occasionally mentions such cross- and up-selling effects of the PWYW method (Gneezy et al., 2010; Kim et al., 2009, 2010b, 2014a, 2014b; Schmidt et al., 2015; Steiner, 1997). However, these effects have not yet been the focus of systematic empirical investigation.

Behavioral and attitudinal customer reactions, which are captured *after* an isolated PWYW purchase or a series of transactions and which go beyond the choice of a payment amount, can be considered as prime *non-financial* PWYW outcomes. For instance, it is plausible that deliberate or incidental customer encounters with PWYW may influence buyer satisfaction with a good *after* its purchase, seller image in the eyes of the buyers, follow-up purchases and seller recommendations communicated by buyers to other consumers (Kim et al., 2009, 2014a, 2014b; Natter & Kaufmann, 2015; see also Figure 2). This class of criteria has also been almost never taken into account in earlier empirical PWYW research. Finally, hardly any empirical study has yet addressed effects that the use of PWYW by one specific supplier has on financial and non-financial outcomes of its competitors (cf. Figure 2).

In conclusion, the literature review reveals that research systematically evaluating economic outcomes of PWYW pricing is scarce and mostly limited to short-term effects on the seller's number of units sold or customers served and revenues. On balance, economic evaluations of economic PWYW outcomes in comparison to those of fixed prices or free give-aways are more often positive than negative. One reason for this may be that unsuccessful PWYW trials do not find their way into the published literature. In any event, future PWYW evaluation studies are required that include additional economic outcome criteria supplementing established unit sales and revenue measures and that track the development of success variables over long time periods.

6. Perspectives

The present article reviews the results of 72 PWYW research contributions published between January 2006 and September 2016 which contain a total of 97 independent empirical data sets. A comprehensive conceptual framework is used to organize the analysis of the literature. Detailed findings of the review do not have to be repeated in this concluding section. Instead, we highlight more general implications of the current state of empirical PWYW studies which are of fundamental importance for future scholarly research in the PWYW field and practical applications of this price setting approach in corporations.

In terms of future research, content-related and methodological perspectives need to be differentiated. According to our review, the most promising *content-related* improvement of empirical PWYW work is likely to be achieved by extending the stimulus–response paradigm currently underlying most research in the direction of the stimulus–organism–response approach. Future investigations should not only explore how specific characteristics of the procedural PWYW design, suppliers, buyers, goods sold and the market context affect the acceptance rate of PWYW offers among prospective customers and the magnitude of the price paid. Instead, they should additionally integrate perceptions of the PWYW approach and its initiator as potential drivers of economic PWYW outcomes both in the group of consumers, who purchase under PWYW and of their counterparts, who reject this pricing method (see section 4).

As far as *methodology* is concerned, when choosing statistical analytical techniques, earlier PWYW investigations have not sufficiently taken into account that their techniques actually ought to be able to model two distinct consumer choices, namely: (1) binary fundamental decision about whether to purchase the PWYW good or not (yes or no) and (2) selection of the amount paid voluntarily (Regner, 2014, p. 197). Thus, a two-step analysis is desirable. In a first step, researchers should, for example with the help of binary Probit or Logit regression techniques, explore which variables significantly contribute to discriminating PWYW buyers from avoiders. Second, within the subgroup of PWYW buyers variables significantly contributing to explaining variance in the prices paid voluntarily should be identified, for instance by means of Ordinary Least Squares or "truncated" regression techniques (cf. Green, 2013, chapter 19). As part of the second step, it would be interesting to additionally work out to what extent variables, which significantly contribute to distinguishing buyers who pay nothing from consumers who pay a price > 0, are also suited to predict the voluntary payment amounts in the subgroup of buyers paying more than zero.

With a view to implementing the PWYW approach in *practice*, the preceding literature review allows to derive a number of propositions on constraints whose fulfillment increases the likelihood that sales under PWYW become economically viable to suppliers. Accordingly, from a seller perspective, PWYW offers seem to be particularly suitable in case that

- the goods sold cause low variable/direct costs and are otherwise marketed at low absolute standard fixed prices;

- the supplier has, at least temporarily, significant quantities of unused production capacities;
- the supplier is a small business which is socially rooted at its sales locations;
- the supplier targets less price-conscious consumers who are convinced that the seller has fair intentions in reverting to PWYW, place great emphasis on acting fairly towards their suppliers and are satisfied with the purchased good;
- external RP are quoted only if it is highly likely that addressed consumers qualify them as being credible or reasonable, respectively;
- the anonymity of buyers or their personal encounter with seller representatives or other people are not artificially reduced or increased, respectively, compared with sales contexts in which the focal category of goods is available at fixed prices.

The present review of the empirical PWYW literature already allowed to draw a number of significant, albeit preliminary conclusions for future investigations and applications of this price setting method in corporations. Nevertheless, noting the large number of research gaps identified above, it is evident that there are many different promising starting points for theory-grounded empirical PWYW studies. Hopefully, the present analysis of the state of evidence is helpful in inspiring such additional work.

References[1]

Armstrong Soule, C.A., & Madrigal, R. (2015)*. Anchors and norms in anonymous pay-what-you-want pricing contexts. In: *Journal of Behavioral and Experimental Economics, 57*, 167-175.

Atlas, S. (2015)*. Rebate what you want. In: *Advances in Consumer Research, 43*, 10.

Azar, O.H. (2007). The social norm of tipping: A review. In: *Journal of Applied Social Psychology, 37*, 380-402.

Bekkers, R., & Wiepking, P. (2011). A literature review of empirical studies of philanthropy: Eight mechanisms that drive charitable giving. In: *Nonprofit and Voluntary Sector Quarterly, 40*, 924-973.

Bertini, M., & Koenigsberg, O. (2014). When customers help set prices. In: *MIT Sloan* Management *Review, 55*(4), 57-64.

Bondos, I., & Lipowski, M. (2016)*. Effectiveness of PWYW – Are there interchannel differences? In: *Proceedings of the Joint International Conference 2016 Management, Knowledge and Learning*, May 25-27, Timisoara. Available at http://www.toknowpress.net/ISBN/978-961-6914-16-1/papers/ML16-033.pdf (accessed November 16, 2016).

Borck, R., Frank, B., & Robledo J.R. (2006)*. An empirical analysis of voluntary payments for information goods on the Internet. In: *Information Economics and Policy, 18*, 229-239.

Bourreau, M., Dogan, P., & Hong, S. (2015)*. Making money by giving it for free: Radiohead's pre-release strategy for In Rainbows. *Information Economics and Policy, 37*, 77-93.

Chao, Y., Fernandez, J., & Nahata, B. (2015). Pay-what-you-want pricing: Can it be profitable? In: *Journal of Behavioral and Experimental Economics, 57*, 176-185.

Chen, Z., & Liang, X. (2014). The performance of pay-as-you-wish pricing with relational and forward-looking customers. In: *Proceedings of the 11th International Conference on Service Systems and Service Management (ICSSSM)*, June 25-27, Beijing. Available at http://ieeexplore.ieee.org/stamp/stamp.jsp?tp=&arnumber=6943418 (accessed November 16, 2016).

---

[1] Entries marked with an asterisk behind their year of publication are the (72) empirical contributions whose analysis lies at the heart of the present article. A table with a brief profile of each of these papers is available on request from the author.

Dorn, T., & Suessmair, A. (2016)*. Is it really worth it? A test of pay-what-you-want pricing strategies in a German consumer behavior context. In: *Global Business and Economics Review*, *18*, 82-100.

Drevs, F. (2013)*. The challenge of the unknown – The effect of pay-what-you-want on the market success of publicly subsidized films. In: *Zeitschrift für öffentliche und gemeinwirtschaftliche Unternehmen*, *36*, 255-270.

El Harbi, S., Grolleau, G., & Bekir, I. (2014). Substituting piracy with a pay-what-you-want option: Does it make sense? In: *European Journal of Law and Economics*, *37*, 277-297.

Engel, C. (2011). Dictator games: A meta study. In: *Experimental Economics*, *14*, 583-610.

Fay, S. (2004). Partial-repeat-bidding in the name-your-own-price channel. In: *Marketing Science*, *23*, 407-418.

Fernandez, J., & Nahata, B. (2009). Pay what you like. Louisville University: MPRA Paper No. 16265. Available at http://mpra.ub.uni-muenchen.de/16265/ (accessed November 16, 2016).

Gahler, M. (2016)*. *Pay-What-You-Want im Internet*. Wiesbaden: Springer Gabler.

Gautier, P.A., & Van der Klaauw, B. (2012)*. Selection in a field experiment with voluntary participation. In: *Journal of Applied Econometrics*, *27*, 63-84.

Gneezy, A., Gneezy, U., Nelson, L.D., & Brown, A. (2010)*. Shared social responsibility: A field experiment in pay-what-you-want pricing and charitable giving. In: *Science*, *329*, 325-327.

Gneezy, A., Gneezy, U., Riener, G., & Nelson, L.D. (2012)*. Pay-what-you-want, identity, and self-signaling in markets. In: *Proceedings of the National Academy of Sciences*, *109*, 7236-7240.

Gravert, C. (2014)*. *Pride and patronage – The effect of identity on pay-what-you-want prices at a charitable bookstore*. Aarhus University: Economics Working Papers 2014-04. Available at http://pure.au.dk/portal/files/68738741/wp14_04.pdf (accessed November 16, 2016).

Greene, W.H. (2013). *Econometric analysis* (7th ed.). New York: Pearson.

Greiff, M., & Egbert, H. (2016). A survey of the empirical evidence on PWYW pricing. Justus-Liebig University Giessen and Anhalt University of Applied Sciences: MPRA Paper No. 68693. Available at http://mpra.ub.uni-muenchen.de/68693/ (accessed November 16, 2016).

Greiff, M., Egbert, H., & Xhangolli, K. (2014). Pay what you want – But pay enough! Information asymmetries and PWYW pricing. In: *Management & Marketing*, *9*, 193-204.

Hilbert, L.P., & Suessmair, A. (2015)*. The effects of social interaction and social norm compliance in pay-what-you-want situations. In: *American Journal of Industrial and Business Management*, *5*, 548-556.

Hildenbrand, A., Pabst, E., Schilling, U., Bitsch, L., & Hanf, J.H. (2016)*. Der Pay-What-You-Want-Mechanismus als Preissetzungsmechanismus für Weinverkostungen. *Paper presented at the Annual Meeting of the Austrian Society of Agricultural Economics*, September 15–16, Vienna.

Huber, F., Appelmann, E., & Lenzen, M. (2016). *Pay-What-You-Want*. Lohmar: Eul.

Huber, F., Lenzen, M., Meyer, F., & Appelmann, E. (2013)*. The role of altruistic and egoistic motivations in pay what you want situations. In: Kubacki, K. (Ed.), *Ideas in Marketing: Finding the New and Polishing the Old – Proceedings of the 2013 Academy of Marketing Science (AMS) annual conference*, New York: Springer, 28-31.

Huber, F., Meyer, F., & Appelmann, E. (2014)*. The moderating role of loyalty and satisfaction on the effectiveness of altruistic and egoistic motivation in pay what you want situations. Beitrag zur *Association of Consumer Research European Conference*.

Isaac, R.M., Lightle, J.P., & Norton, D.A. (2015). The pay-what-you-want business model: Warm glow revenues and endogenous price discrimination. In: *Journal of Behavioral and Experimental Economics*, *57*, 215-223.

Jang, H., & Chu, W. (2012)*. Are consumers acting fairly toward companies? An examination of pay-what-you-want pricing. In: *Journal of Macromarketing*, *32*, 348-360.

Johnson, J.W., & Cui, A.P. (2013)*. To influence or not to influence: External reference price strategies in pay-what-you-want pricing. In: *Journal of Business Research*, 66, 275-281.

Jostrup, E., & Salic, E. (2015)*. *Pay for it and love it more: A comparative study in marketing psychology between the two campaign methods pay what you want and free*. Bachelor psychology course student paper, Lund University, Department of Psychology. Available at http://lup.lub.lu.se/luur/download?func=downloadFile&recordOId=7365833&fileOId=7365971 (accessed November 16, 2016).

Jung, M.H., Nelson, L.D., Gneezy, A., & Gneezy, U. (2014a). Paying more when paying for others. In: *Journal of Personality and Social Psychology*, 107, 414-431.

Jung, M.H., Nelson, L.D., Gneezy, A., & Gneezy, U. (2014b)*. Signaling virtue: Charitable behavior under consumer elective pricing. SSRN paper 2447960. Available at http://papers.ssrn.com/sol3/papers.cfm?abstract_id=2447960&download=yes (accessed November 16, 2016).

Jung, M.H., Perfecto, H., & Nelson, L.D. (2016)*. Anchoring in payment: Evaluating a judgmental heuristic in field experimental settings. In: *Journal of Marketing Research*, 53, 354-368.

Kahsay, G.A., & Samahita, M. (2015). Pay-what-you-want pricing schemes: A self-image perspective. In: *Journal of Behavioral and Experimental Finance*, 7, 17-28.

Kim, J.-Y., Kaufmann, K., & Stegemann, M. (2014a)*. The impact of buyer-seller relationships and reference prices on the effectiveness of the pay what you want pricing mechanism. In: *Marketing Letters*, 25, 409-423.

Kim, J.-Y., Natter, M., & Spann, M. (2009)*. Pay what you want: A new participative pricing mechanism. In: *Journal of Marketing*, 73 (*1*), 44-58.

Kim, J.-Y., Natter, M., & Spann, M. (2010a)*. Pay-what-you-want – Praxisrelevanz und Konsumentenverhalten. In: *Zeitschrift für Betriebswirtschaft*, 80, 147-169.

Kim, J.-Y., Natter, M., & Spann, M. (2010b)*. Kish: Where customers pay as they wish. In: *Review of Marketing Science*, 8 (*article 3*), 1-12.

Kim, J.-Y., Natter, M., & Spann, M. (2014b)*. Sampling, discounts or pay-what-you-want: Two field experiments. In: *International Journal of Research in Marketing*, 31, 327-334.

Krämer, F., Schmidt, K.M., Spann, M., & Stich, L. (2015)*. *Delegating pricing power to customers: Pay what you want or name your own price*. Centre for Economic Policy Research London: Discussion Paper No. 10605. Available at http://www.cepr.org/active/publications/discussion_papers/dp.php?dpno=10605 (accessed November 16, 2016).

Krawczyk, M., Kukla-Gryz, A., & Tyrowicz, J. (2015)*. *Pushed by the crowd or pulled by the leaders? Peer effects in pay-what-you-want*. University of Warsaw: Faculty of Economic Sciences Working Papers No. 25/2015 (173). Available at http://www.wne.uw.edu.pl/files/1514/3872/2613/WNE_WP173.pdf (accessed November 16, 2016).

Kunter, M. (2015)*. Exploring the Pay-What-You-Want payment motivation. In: *Journal of Business Research*, 68, 2347-2357.

Kunter, M., & Braun, D. (2013)*. "The price is up to you!" – "Oh no! What am I gonna do?" Customers' product category inexperience and belief about other customers' payments under pay-what-you-want conditions. In: *European Journal of Management*, 13 (*2*), 15-21.

Lee, S.R., Baumgartner, H., & Pieters, R. (2011)*. Are you really paying what you wish? Interpersonal influences on price decisions. In: *Advances in Consumer Research*, 39, 540-541.

Lee, S.R., Baumgartner, H., & Pieters, R. (2015)*. *Are you really paying as little as possible? Constraints on consumers' self-interest seeking in participative pricing*. Unpublished manuscript.

León, F.J., Noguera, J.A., & Tena-Sánchez, J. (2012)*. How much would you like to pay? Trust, reciprocity and prosocial motivations in *El trato*. In: *Social Science Information*, 51, 389-417.

Lynn, M. (1990). Choose your own price: An exploratory study requiring an expanded view of price's functions. In: *Advances in Consumer Research, 17,* 710-714.

Lynn, M., Flynn, S.M., & Helion, C. (2013)*. Do consumers prefer round prices? Evidence from pay-what-you-want decisions and self-pumped gasoline purchases. In: *Journal of Economic Psychology, 36,* 96-102.

Machado, F., & Sinha, R.K. (2012)*. The viability of pay what you want pricing. Manuscript submitted to *Management Science*. Available at http://ebape.fgv.br/sites/ebape.fgv.br/files/Working-Paper-Fernando-Machado-Viability-of-Pay-What-you-Want-Pricing.pdf (accessed November 16, 2016).

Mak, V., Zwick, R., Rao, A.R., & Pattaratanakun, J.A. (2015)*. "Pay what you want" as threshold public good provision. In: *Organizational Behavior and Human Decision Processes, 127,* 30-43.

Marett, K., Pearson, R., & Moore, R.S. (2012)*. Pay what you want: An exploratory study of social exchange and buyer-determined prices of iProducts. In: *Communications of the Association for Information Systems, 30* (article 10), 1-14.

Mazumdar, T., Raj, S.P., & Sinha, I. (2005). Reference price research: Review and propositions. In: *Journal of Marketing, 69* (4), 84-102.

Mendoza-Abarca, K.I., & Mellema, H.N. (2016). Aligning economic and social value creation through pay-what-you-want pricing. In: *Journal of Social Entrepreneurship, 7,* 101-125.

Mills, P. (2011)*. Economic and financial insights from a cross-cultural pay-what-you-want study. In: *Proceedings of the 2011 Annual Meeting of the Academy of Behavioral Finance and Economics,* September 21-23, Los Angeles. Available at https://p11.secure.hostingprod.com/@www.aobf.org/ssl/attachments/2011/ABF_2011_Proceedings_Book.pdf (accessed November 16, 2016).

Mills, P. (2013)*. Trust, reciprocity and fairness in a large scale pay what you wish experiment. In: *Competitive Paper Session, Society for the Advancement of Behavioral Economics, SABE/IAREP/ICABEEP conference,* Atlanta. Available at http://apps.clayton.edu/SABE-IAREP-ICABEEP-Conference/Papers/Download/26 (accessed November 16, 2016).

Mousazadeh, M., & Izadkhah, M. (2015). The ultimatum game: A comprehensive literature review. In: *Applied Mathematics in Engineering, Management and Technology, 3,* 158-165.

Natter, M., & Kaufmann, K. (2015). Voluntary market payments: Underlying motives, success drivers and success potentials. In: *Journal of Behavioral and Experimental Economics, 57,* 149-157.

Newholm, T., & Shaw, D. (2007). Studying the ethical consumer: A review of research. In: *Journal of Consumer Behaviour, 6,* 253-270.

Park, S., Nam, S., & Lee, J. (2016)*. Charitable giving, suggestion, and learning from others: Pay-What-You-Want experiments at a coffee shop. In: *Journal of Behavioral and Experimental Economics,* in press, DOI: http://dx.doi.org/10.1016/j.socec.2016.04.010.

Parvinen, P., Pöyry, E., & Kaptein, M. (2013)*. Pay-what-you-want pricing – The impact of framing. Paper presented at the *American Marketing Association Winter Marketing Educator Conference,* February 15-17, Las Vegas, 110-121. Available at http://connection.ebscohost.com/c/articles/86740067/pay-what-you-want-pricing-impact-framing (accessed November 16, 2016).

Perfecto, H., Jung, M.H., & Nelson, L.D., (2014)*. Precision aversion in pay-what-you-want pricing. In: *Proceedings of the Annual Conference of the Society of Consumer Research,* March 6-8, Miami. Available at http://www.myscp.org/pdf/conference%20documents/SCP2014_Proceedings_04282014.pdf (accessed November 16, 2016).

Perfecto, H., Jung, M.H., Nelson, L.D., Gneezy, A., & Gneezy, U. (2013)*. Default effects under pay-what-you-want: Evidence from the field. In: *Advances in Consumer Research, 41,* 265-266.

Podsakoff, P.M., MacKenzie, S.B., Lee, J.-Y., & Podsakoff, N.P. (2003). Common method biases in behavioral research: A critical review of the literature and recommended remedies. In: *Journal of Applied Psychology, 88,* 879-903.

Pöyry, E. (2015). Pay-what-you-want pricing research: Review and propositions. In: Ahearne, M., & Hughes, D.E. (Eds.), *2015 AMA Marketing Summer Educators' Conference "Improving Business Practice Through Marketing Insight"*, August 14-16, Chicago, Vol. 26, L-23-L-31.

Pöyry, E., & Parvinen, P. (2014)*. Pay-what-you-want – A field experiment on anonymity and reference price cues. In: Grewal, D., Roggeveen, A.L., & Nordfält, J. (Eds.), *Proceedings of the "Shopper Marketing & Pricing Conference"*, May 8-10, Stockholm, 18-19.

Pöyry, E., Parvinen, P., & Kaptein, M. (2013)*. Using pay-what-you-want in new product pricing. In: *Proceedings of the 2013 Aalto University-GAMMA Joint Symposium*, April 26, Helsinki, 54-57.

Racherla, P., Babb, J.S., & Keith, M.J. (2011)*. Pay-what-you-want pricing for mobile applications: The effect of privacy assurances and social information. In: *Proceedings of the 4th Information Systems Applied Research Conference*, November 3-6, Wilmington. Available at http://proc.conisar.org/2011/pdf/1833.pdf (accessed November 16, 2016).

Reese, J.D. (2012)*. *Participatory pricing in sport: An examination of name-your-own-price and pay-what-you-want*. Dissertation Texas A&M University.

Reese, J.D. (2013)*. *Participatory pricing in sport: An examination of name-your-own-price and pay-what-you-want*. Stephen F. Austin State University at Nacogdoches, Texas, Faculty Publications Paper 12. Available at http://scholarworks.sfasu.edu/cgi/viewcontent.cgi?article=1011&context=management_facultypubs (accessed November 16, 2016).

Regner, T. (2014). Social preferences? Google Answers! In: *Games and Economic Behavior, 85*, 188-209.

Regner, T. (2015)*. Why consumers pay voluntarily: Evidence from online music. In: *Journal of Behavioral and Experimental Economics, 57*, 205-214.

Regner, T., & Barria, J.A. (2009)*. Do consumers pay voluntarily? The case of online music. In: *Journal of Economic Behavior & Organization, 71*, 395-406.

Regner, T., & Riener, G. (2012)*. *Voluntary payments, privacy and social pressure on the Internet: A natural field experiment*. University of Dusseldorf: Institute for Competition Economics Discussion Paper No. 82. Available at https://www.econstor.eu/dspace/bitstream/10419/68231/1/734357842.pdf (accessed November 16, 2016).

Riener, G. (2008)*. *How free is your lunch: Evidence from an "Eat-as-you-want-pay-as-you-wish" restaurant*. University of Essex. Available at http://deewan.at/wp-content/uploads/2012/02/Riener.pdf (accessed November 16, 2016).

Riener, G., & Traxler, C. (2012)*. Norms, moods, and free lunch: Longitudinal evidence on payments from a pay-what-you-want restaurant. In: *Journal of Socio-Economics, 41*, 476-483.

Roy, R. (2015)*. An insight into pay-what-you-want pricing. In: *Marketing Intelligence & Planning, 33*, 733-748.

Roy, R., Rabbanee, F.K., & Sharma, P. (2016a)*. Exploring the interactions among external reference price, social visibility and purchase motivation in pay-what-you-want pricing. In: *European Journal of Marketing, 50*, 816-837.

Roy, R., Rabbanee, F.K., & Sharma, P. (2016b)*. Antecedents, outcomes, and mediating role of internal reference prices in pay-what-you-want pricing. In: *Marketing Intelligence & Planning, 34*, 117-136.

Saccardo, S., & Gneezy, A. (2014)*. Want vs. can: Self-signaling via participative price appeals. In: *Proceedings of the Annual Conference of the Society of Consumer Research*, March 6-8, Miami. Available at http://www.myscp.org/pdf/conference%20documents/SCP2014_Proceedings_04282014.pdf (accessed November 16, 2016).

Saccardo, S., Li, C., Samek, A., & Gneezy, A. (2015)*. Shifting mindset in consumer elective pricing. In: *Advances in Consumer Research, 43*, 7-8.

Santana, S., & Morwitz, V.G. (2011)*. Buying what you can get for free: How self-presentation motives influence payment decisions in pay-what-you-want contexts. In: *Advances in Consumer Research*, *39*, 253.

Santana, S., & Morwitz, V.G. (2013)*. We're in this together: How sellers, social values, and relationship norms influence consumer payments in pay-what-you-want contexts. Manuscript submitted to *Journal of Marketing*. Available at http://www8.gsb.columbia.edu/programs/sites/programs/files/marketing/seminar_papers/paper_santana_fa13.pdf (accessed November 16, 2016).

Santana, S., & Morwitz, V.G. (2015)*. Because we're partners: How social values and relationship norms influence consumer payments in pay-what-you-want contexts. In: *Advances in Consumer Research*, *43*, 8-9.

Santana, S., & Morwitz, V.G. (2016)*. Because we're partners: How social values and relationship norms influence consumer payments in pay-what-you-want contexts. Unpublished manuscript submitted to *Journal of Marketing Research*.

Schlüter, A., & Vollan, B. (2015). Flowers and an honour box: Evidence on framing effects. In: *Journal of Behavioral and Experimental Economics*, *57*, 186-199.

Schmidt, K.M., Spann, M., & Zeithammer, R. (2015)*. Pay what you want as a marketing strategy in monopolistic and competitive markets. In: *Management Science*, *61*, 1217-1236.

Schons, L.M., Rese, M., Wieseke, J., Rasmussen, W., Weber, D., & Strotmann, W.-C. (2014)*. There is nothing permanent except change – Analyzing individual price dynamics in "pay-what-you-want" situations. In: *Marketing Letters*, *25*, 25-36.

Schröder, M., Lüer, A., & Sadrieh, A. (2015)*. Pay-what-you-want or mark-off-your-own-price – A framing effect in customer-selected pricing. In: *Journal of Behavioral and Experimental Economics*, *57*, 200-204.

Sleesman, D.J., & Conlon, D.E. (2016))*. Encouraging prosocial decisions: The role of fairness salience and uncertainty. In: *Journal of Behavioral Decision Making*, in Press, DOI: 10.1002/bdm.1970.

Small, D.A., & Cryder, C. (2016). Prosocial consumer behavior. In: *Current Opinion in Psychology*, *10*, 107-111.

Stegemann, M. (2014)*. *Success factors of pay what you want pricing*. Dissertation University of Muenster.

Steiner, F. (1997). Optimal pricing of museum admission. In: *Journal of Cultural Economics*, *21*, 307-333.

Thomas, S., & Gierl, H. (2014)*. Pay what you want: How to affect the price consumers are willing to pay. In: *Proceedings of the 13th International Conference on Research in Advertising*, June 26-28, Amsterdam.

Tudón, J.F. (2015). Pay what you want because I don't know how much to charge you. *Economic Letters*, *137*, 41-44.

Veit, K., & Ammermann, S. (2013)*. *Why would you pay? An exploratory study in pay-what-you-want pricing*. Masters Thesis, Lund University, School of Economics and Management. Available at http://lup.lub.lu.se/luur/download?func=downloadFile&recordOId=3799386&fileOId=3799387 (accessed November 16, 2016).

Ven, L. van de (2012)*. *Fair play via fair pay: A PWYW pricing strategy for fairtrade*. Master Thesis, Erasmus University, Rotterdam School of Management. Available at http://www.rsm.nl/fileadmin/Images_NEW/Events/Sustainability_Forum/Thesis_Laura_van_de_Ven_RSM_2012_2013.pdf (accessed November 16, 2016).

Waskow, S., Markett, S., Montag, C., Weber, B., Trautner, P., Kramarz, V., & Reuter, M. (2016)*. Pay what you want! A pilot study on neural correlates of voluntary payments for music. In: *Frontiers in Psychology*, *7*, in press, DOI: http://dx.doi.org/10.3389/fpsyg.2016.01023.

Analyzing the effect of customer loyalty on virtual marketing adoption based on theory of technology acceptance model

Peyman Ghafari Ashtiani[a], Atefeh Parsayan[b*] and Moein Mohajerani[b]

[a]Department of Management, Arak Branch, Islamic Azad University, Arak, Iran
[b]Master of EMBA, Department of Management, Arak Branch, Islamic Azad University, Arak, Iran

CHRONICLE	ABSTRACT
Keywords: Customer loyalty Viral marketing Theory of technology acceptance model TAM	One of the most advantages of the internet and its expansion is probably due to its easy and low cost access to unlimited information and easy and fast information exchange. The accession of communication technology for marketing area and emergence of the Internet leads to creation and development of new marketing models such as viral marketing. In fact, unlike other marketing methods, the most powerful tool for selling products and ideas are not done by a marketer to a customer but from a customer to another one. The purpose of this research is to analyze the relationship between customers' loyalty and the acceptance of viral marketing based on the theory of technology acceptance model (TAM) model among the civil engineers and architects who are the members of Engineering Council in Isfahan (ECI). The research method is descriptive–survey and it is applicable in target. The statistical population includes civil engineers and architects who are the members of Engineering Council in Isfahan including 14400 members. The sample size was determined 762 members based on Cochran sampling formula, the sample was selected as accessible. The data was collected by field method. Analyzing the data and recent research hypothesis, the data was extracted from the questionnaires. Then, all the data was analyzed by computer and SPSS and LISREL software. According to the results of the data, the loyalty of the civil engineers and architects members of ECI was associated with the acceptance and practical involvement of viral marketing.

1. Introduction

The easy and low cost access to unlimited data and easy exchange of information can probably be the most advantages of the Internet and its surprising expansion. The accession of information technology to marketing and the emergence of Internet can lead to creation and expansion of new marketing models such as viral marketing. Information exchange is the leaven of viral marketing (Masouleh et al., 2012). There are several methods and tools for realization of viral marketing. One type of viral marketing is based on email communication (Hubona & Burton, 2003), which is more examined in this research.

* Corresponding author.
E-mail address: parsayanatefeh@yahoo.com (A. Parsayan)

There are several factors involved in the decision of the applicants for sending or not sending of these email messages and as the result involvement or dis-involvement in viral marketing. The target of this research is to investigate the role of loyalty in this case (Day, 1969; Ho & Dempsey, 2010). This paper analyzes the effect of customer loyalty on virtual marketing adoption based on theory of technology acceptance model. The selected statistical population of this research includes civil engineers and architects of Engineering Council of Isfahan. The findings of this research can directly be used for improvement of viral marketing systems especially in construction industry.

2. The proposed study

The entrance of information technology in marketing and revelation of the internet resulted to creation and development of new models of marketing such as viral marketing. One of the most common methods of viral marketing is based on resending the received email messages by applicants. These email messages can be made by users or designed by a company but the whole or part of these emails contains advertising messages directly or indirectly.

In this paper, Technology Acceptance Model (TAM) is selected as the basic model of this research to develop and reflect the reaction and viral features. The structure of the proposed model is called loyalty, which increases acceptance of customers. One of the aspects of loyalty is recommendation of previous customers of organizations to potential customers for using the products of organization. Also, designing messages can decrease or increase the loyalty of customers to a brand (Jacoby & Chestnut, 1978) and plays a key role in sending this message to others. This type of application can also reduce or increase the loyalty. Thus, it seems that loyalty is one of the effective factors for the success of viral marketing strategies. In this research, we analyze the effects of customer loyalty on the acceptance of viral marketing based on TAM model among the civil engineers and architects of the members of Engineering Council of Isfahan (ECI).

2.1 Research Objectives

Primary Objectives: To determining the relationship between customer loyalties with the acceptance of Viral Marketing based on TAM model among the civil engineers and architects of the members of Engineering Council of Isfahan.

Secondary objectives:

The secondary objective of this study is to

1. To determine the relationship between perceived usefulness of customer with his/her loyalty in involving in viral marketing among the ECI civil engineers and architectures members.
2. To determine the relation of loyalty of customers with their attitudes for involving in viral marketing among the ECI civil engineers and architectures members.
3. To determine the relation of loyalty of customers with their intention (Fishbein & Ajzen, 1975) for involving in viral marketing among the ECI civil engineers and architectures members.
4. To determine the relationship between the clients perceived ease of use and their perceived usefulness for involving in viral marketing among the ECI civil engineers and architectures members.
5. To determine the relationship between the clients perceived usefulness with their attitudes for involving in viral marketing among the ECI civil engineers and architectures members.
6. To determine the relationship between the clients perceived ease of use and their attitudes for involving in viral marketing among the ECI civil engineers and architectures members.
7. To determine the relationship between the clients perceived usefulness with their intentions for involving in viral marketing among the ECI civil engineers and architectures members.

8. To determine the relationship between the clients perceived ease of use and their intentions for involving in viral marketing among the ECI civil engineers and architectures members.

9. To determine the relationship between the customer's intention with their actual use (acceptance) in viral marketing among the ECI civil engineers and architectures members.

2.2 Research Application

1. The findings of this research can be used for expansion of viral marketing system specifically in construction industry. According to the strong competition between the providers of construction industry and due to the necessary cost and time for developing of viral marketing system, ensuring that the addressed people use it is so essential.

2. The findings of this research can contain practical suggestions and recommendations for the providers of construction industry on how to involve customers in the process of viral marketing based on the cultural and social parameters of the country and the features of professional market and the customers of construction industry.

3. In this research, the main focus is on customer satisfaction for introducing the product to others for developing viral marketing culture and for decreasing the costs of advertising of companies.

The main advantage of viral marketing is that marketers can create customers by almost zero cost, and the mode is changed from "marketer-consumer" to "consumer-consumer" (Jan Nesar Ahmadi & Ghafari, 2007). In fact, on the contrary with other marketing methods, the most influence in selling products and ideas is not through a marketer to a customer but from a customer to another customer. On the other hand, social networks have moved towards the web. Thus, there is a suitable field for applying viral marketing. The innovation of this research is that the subject is analyzed from the perspective of a customer. The aim of this research is to analyze the relationship of loyalty with viral marketing among the civil engineers and architects of Engineering Council of Isfahan in city of Isfahan, Iran.

3. Theoretical framework and conceptual model of research

During the recent decades, the perceived usefulness and facility in usage are considered as determining factors in the acceptance of information systems and information technology and communication among customers exclusively. These organizations are the foundations of acceptance of technology. Technology Acceptance Model (TAM) is one of the models which is widely welcomed by users and customers for explaining the effective factors on the acceptance of information systems and information technology and communication. Several researches have confirmed the validity of TAM in the field of acceptance of information technology and communication (Venkatesh & Davis, 2000; Roberts & Henderson, 2000; Davis et al., 1989).

TAM was selected as basic structure of this research, and we intend to develop it to reflect the reactive and viral features and offer another structure as customer loyalty in this research. Davis (1989) offered this model to determine and predict the adaptation and application of information technology. The basis of TAM is that the perceiving of usefulness and facility in usage are the key factors for determining the adaptation of innovative technology. Davis considers the perceiving of usefulness to the extent that technology helps the improvement of performance while the perceiving of facility in usage is the belief of people about this fact that the usage of one technology is easy and simple (Davis, 1989).

According to Davis's Technology Acceptance Model:

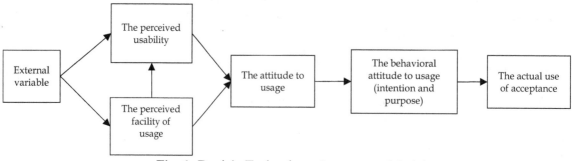

Fig. 1. Davis's Technology Acceptance Model

The proposed model of this paper is as follows,

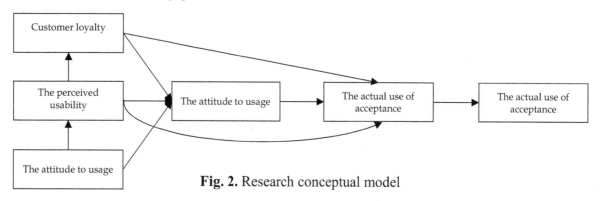

Fig. 2. Research conceptual model

3.1 Hypothesis

The proposed study of this paper considers the following hypotheses,

1) The perceived usefulness of customer is associated with his/her loyalty for involving in viral marketing.
2) Customer loyalty is associated with his/her attitude for involvement in viral marketing.
3) Customer loyalty is associated with his/her intention for involvement in viral marketing.
4) The perceived facility of usage of customer is associated with his/her perceived usefulness for involvement in viral marketing.
5) The perceived usefulness of customer is associated with his/her attitude for involvement in viral marketing.
6) The perceived facility of usage of customer is associated with his/her attitude for involvement in viral marketing.
7) The perceived usefulness of customer is associated with his/her intention for involvement in viral marketing.
8) The perceived facility of usage of customer is associated with his/her intention for involvement in viral marketing.
9) The intention of customer is associated with his/her actual usage (acceptance) in viral marketing.

3.2 Research Methodology

Research methodology of this study is Descriptive-survey in which the relationships of variables are analyzed based on research purpose.

3.3. Classification Based on Objectives

The method of this research based on its objective is practical since its findings can be used in the face of market practices.

3.4 Statistical Population

The statistical population of this study consists of 14400 civil engineers and architects who are the member of Engineering Council of Isfahan.

3.5 Statistical Sample

A) Sample size

Therefore we could use the following formula to calculate the minimum number of sample size,

$$n = \frac{N \times z_{\alpha/2}^2 \times p \times q}{\varepsilon^2 \times (N-1) + z_{\alpha/2}^2 \times p \times q}, \tag{1}$$

where N is the population size, $p = 1 - q$ represents the yes/no categories, $z_{\alpha/2}$ is CDF of normal distribution and finally ε is the error term. Since we have $p = 0.5, z_{\alpha/2} = 1.96$ and $N=14400$, the number of sample size is calculated as $n=762$.

3.5 The method and tools of data collection

The data of this research was collected in field. An anonymous questionnaire was used to collect data and achieve the objectives which were completed by civil engineers and architects of the members of Engineering Council of Isfahan. The research questions were put in the format of Questionnaire items. Each item of questionnaire, based on the major objective and considered questions and the answer of each question, is a step to realization the main objective of the research. This questionnaire includes 71 items as explained in Table 1.

Table 1
Variables and numbers of items of questionnaire

Row	The questioned variable	The number of item of questionnaire
1	The perceived usefulness	1-4
2	The perceived facility of usage	5-7
3	Attitude to usage	8-10
4	Behavioral intention to use (desire to purchase)	11-13
5	Customer loyalty	14-17
6	Actual usage (acceptance)	18-20

In this research, the measurement is Ordinal Scale and the employed spectrum is Likert Scale (from completely agree with 0 score to completely disagree with 5 score). The research questionnaire validity was assessed by experts and managers. Thus, it has suitable validity or it is valid, in another word. Cronbach's alpha coefficients was used for assessment of reliability of the questionnaire. Cronbach's alpha coefficients was measure 0.95 by computer and SPSS software, Distributing all the questionnaires, Cronbach's alpha coefficients was measured for the fully completed questionnaires and analyzed. The results were achieved as Table 2. Considering the fact that the minimum Cronbach's alpha coefficients for research questionnaires is 0.70%, the achieved Cronbach's alpha coefficients is more than that and suitable.

Table 2
Cronbach's alpha coefficients

Row	The questioned variable	Cronbach's alpha coefficients
1	The perceived usefulness	0.871
2	The perceived facility of usage	0.838
3	Attitude to usage	0.889
4	Behavioral intention to use (desire to purchase)	0.891
5	Customer loyalty	0.722
6	Actual usage (acceptance)	0.906
7	Total Questionnaire	0.941

3.6 Research Variables

The research variables can be classified as follow:

Latent exogenous variables which there is one exogenous variable in this research which is the perceived facility of usage. Latent endogenous variables include: the perceived usefulness, Customer loyalty, attitude to usage, behavioral tendency to usage (intention), and actual usage (acceptance). The observed variables related to Exogenous variables include the perceived facility of usage (Q5, Q6, Q7, Q8) and observed Latent endogenous variable include the perceived usefulness(Q1, Q3, Q3, Q4),customer loyalty (Q17, Q16, Q15, Q14), attitude to usage (Q10, Q9, Q8), behavioral tendency to usage or intention (Q13, Q12, Q11) and actual usage or acceptance (Q20, Q19, Q18).

3.7 Data Analysis Method

For analyzing the data and testing the research hypothesis of this research, inferential statistics and structural equation modeling were used. Structural equation modeling is statistical models for analyzing linear equations between Latent variables (not observed) and obvious variables (observed). Researchers can approve or disapprove the adaptability of these Hypothetical structures, which is generally called model (with less accuracy) and causative models, with contesting data by the use of these models (Houman, 2008). For analyzing the statistical data of this study, first the data was extracted from the questionnaires and set in the mother table. Then, all the data was analyzed by computer and SPSS and LISREL software.

The necessities of usage of Structural equation modeling

A) Since the major goal of Structural equation modeling is to analyze latent variables, specifically the analysis of causative relation of these variables, this method has more ability compared with other analytical methods.
B) Structural equation modeling can estimate the interconnected relationship between internal dependent and independent variables.
C) There are some software packages such as LISREL to estimate the parameters of models rapidly and accurately, and evaluate the constructed model.

3.8 Assessment of Research Model

When the data of sample group is changed into correlation matrix or covariance, and it is described by a series of regression equation, this model can be processed and analyzed (by some available software) in the societies which the samples are driven. Some assessments of parameters of that model including coefficient of the path and error sentences and some measures for its suitability to the sample data is achieved (Houman, 2008). Fig. 3 illustrates the standard model which is achieved by LISREL software.

As it is indicated in the diagram, seven latent variables (the perceived facility of usage, the perceived usefulness, customer loyalty, the attitude to usage, behavioral attitude to usage and actual use) and their measurement indicators are shown.

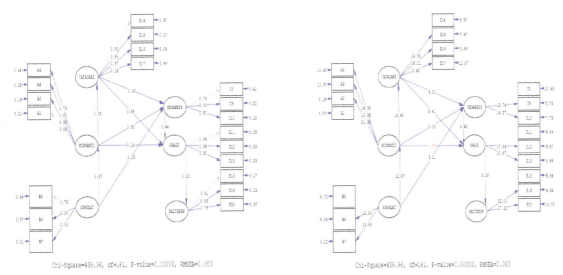

Fig. 3. Standard Research Model by the use of LISREL software

Fig. 4. Model in Significant state with t-value

3.9 Analysis of model congruency

For analyzing the fitness of this model, some indicators such as Chi-Square, Root Mean Square Error of Approximation (RMSEA), P-value, indicators of GFI and AGFI were used. Among the Fitness indexes, generally, RMSEA is an Optimal Index and CFI is considered as the best index. Fitness indexes are generally between zero and one. The coefficients which are more than 90% are considered acceptable though it is optional as p=0.05. In this research, the measured amount for index RMSEA equals to 0.080 and for parameters of GFI=0.86, IFI=0.97, CFI=0.97, and Chi-Square =2.732 which indicate acceptability of this model. The offered indexes and their comparison with the optimal model shows a suitable fitness of the model. One of the important things in this model fitness is that fitness index confirms the structure of the model but it never indicates that this is the unique valid model.

3.10 The results of research hypothesis

In this section, the significance of the numbers achieved by the model is studied; in terms of significance of numbers, it can be said that as we are testing the hypothesis by 0.95 assurance and 0.5 percent error, the numbers which are significant for *t* are more than -1.96 and +1.96. This means that if in this test a number is between -1.96 and +1.96, it is insignificant. In model number 1, the numbers achieved for *t* test are meaningful, and we can analyze the causative factor (measurement indicators with latent variable) and effects (latent variables with each other). According to what is mentioned in the table and figure, the achieved model has suitable status. Thus, according to the model in significance level (Fig. 3) and Standard estimation model (Fig. 4), the analysis or research hypothesis is based on Table 3.

Table 3
Regression weights- Loading factor model

Predictors variables		Instant predictor variables	Estimated values	Standard values	Error	T statistics	R^2	Test Result
The perceived facility of usage	↘		0.30	0.33	0.09	3.21		Confirmed
The perceived usefulness	→	Attitude to usage	0.36	0.39	0.12	3.08	0.84	Confirmed
Customer loyalty	↗		0.25	0.26	0.08	3.30		Confirmed
The perceived usefulness	↘		0.18	0.18	0.07	1.89		Confirmed
Customer loyalty	→	Behavioral attitude to usage	0.40	0.39	0.09	5.41	0.93	Confirmed
Attitude to usage	↗		0.46	0.44	0.10	4.52		Confirmed
The perceived facility of usage	→	The perceived usefulness	0.86	0.87	0.07	12.57	0.75	Confirmed
The perceived usefulness	→	Customer loyalty	0.78	0.83	0.06	13.40	0.69	Confirmed
Attitude to usage	→	Behavioral attitude to usage	0.46	0.44	0.10	4.52	0.93	Confirmed
Behavioral attitude to usage	→	Actual usage	0.26	0.21	0.08	3.26	0.24	Confirmed
The perceived usefulness	→	A1	1.00	0.89	--	--	0.79	
The perceived usefulness	→	A2	1.12	0.98	0.05	21.69	0.81	
The perceived usefulness	→	A3	0.89	0.67	0.07	12.85	0.45	
The perceived usefulness	→	A4	0.89	0.73	0.06	14.86	0.54	
The perceived facility of usage	→	B5	1.00	0.75	--	--	0.56	
The perceived facility of usage	→	B6	1.10	0.80	0.09	12.90	0.63	
The perceived facility of usage	→	B7	1.07	0.83	0.08	13.50	0.69	
Attitude to usage	→	C8	1.00	0.76	--	--	0.59	
Attitude to usage	→	C9	1.25	0.88	0.08	15.74	0.78	
Attitude to usage	→	C10	1.27	0.91	0.08	16.27	0.82	
Behavioral attitude to usage	→	D11	1.00	0.84	--	--	0.71	
Behavioral attitude to usage	→	D12	1.04	0.85	0.06	17.64	0.72	
Behavioral attitude to usage	→	D13	1.10	0.88	0.06	18.67	0.77	
Customer loyalty	→	E14	1.00	0.80	--	--	0.63	
Customer loyalty	→	E15	1.08	0.90	0.06	16.86	0.80	
Customer loyalty	→	E16	1.00	0.87	0.06	16.21	0.76	
Customer loyalty	→	E17	0.21	0.15	0.09	2.42	0.22	
Actual usage	→	F18	1.00	0.91	--	--	0.83	
Actual usage	→	F19	1.05	0.93	0.05	22.00	0.87	
Actual usage	→	F20	0.94	0.79	0.05	17.23	0.63	

3.11 Results based on hypotheses

In this research, the relation of customer loyalty and acceptance of viral marketing based on TAM model was analyzed among the civil engineers and architects of members of Engineering Council of Isfahan. According to the analysis or research result data, the analysis of each of the hypothesis is as follow:

1. The perceived usefulness of customer is related to customer for engaging in viral marketing. Since Factor variable path of the perceived usefulness of customer is calculated on the variable of customer loyalty with t value, this statistic is significant with 0.95. Thus, the first hypothesis is confirmed. Thus, the perceived usefulness of civil engineers and architects of engineering council of Isfahan is related to their loyalty for engaging in viral marketing. Thus, as the perceived usefulness is more, it can be expected that their royalty for involvement in viral marketing increases.

2. Customer loyalty is related to his/her attitude for involvement in viral marketing.
Since the factor variable path of customer loyalty to his/her attitude for involvement in viral marketing is calculated with t value, this statistic is significant with 0.95. Thus, the second hypothesis is confirmed and the loyalty of civil engineers and architects of engineering council of Isfahan is related to their attitude for engaging in viral marketing. Thus, Construction companies can effect on their attitude for engaging in viral marketing by providing some conditions to increase their loyalty.

3. Customer loyalty is related to his intention for involvement in viral marketing. Since Factor variable path of customer loyalty to his intention for involvement in viral marketing is calculated with t value, this statistic is significant with 0.95.Thus, the third hypothesis is confirmed. Thus, the loyalty of civil engineers and architects of engineering council of Isfahan is related to their intention for engaging in viral marketing. Thus, Construction companies can effect on their intention for engaging in viral marketing by providing some conditions to increase their loyalty.

4. The perceived facility of usage of customer is related to his/her perceived usefulness for involvement in viral marketing. Since Factor variable of path of the perceived facility of usage of customer to his/her intention for involvement in viral marketing is calculated with t value, this statistic is significant with 0.95.Thus, the fourth hypothesis is confirmed. Thus, as the perceived facility of usage increases, they expect to understand more usefulness in engaging in viral marketing. This finding is in parallel with Pavlov et al.'s studies (2005) which showed that facility of usage is effective on the perceived usefulness in electronic commerce.

5. The perceived usefulness of customer is related to his/her attitude for involvement in viral marketing. Since Factor variable path of perceived usefulness of customer to his/her attitude for involvement in viral marketing is calculated with t value, this statistic is significant with 0.95 and the fifth hypothesis is confirmed. Thus, the perceived usefulness of civil engineers and architects of engineering council of Isfahan is related to their attitude for engaging in viral marketing. This finding is in parallel with Davis studies (1989) which showed that perceived usefulness of customer from a technology is effective on their attitude toward that technology.

6. The perceived facility of usage of customer is related to his/her attitude for involvement in viral marketing. Since Factor variable path of perceived facility of usage of customer to his/her attitude for involvement in viral marketing is calculated with t value, this statistic is significant with 0.95 and the sixth hypothesis is confirmed. Thus, the perceived facility of usage of civil engineers and architects of engineering council of Isfahan is related to their attitude for engaging in viral marketing. This finding is in parallel with Davis studies (1989) which showed that perceived facility of usage of customer from a technology is effective on their attitude toward that technology.

7. The perceived usefulness of customer is related to his/her intention for involvement in viral marketing. Since Factor variable path of perceived usefulness of customer to his/her intention for involvement in viral marketing is calculated with *t* value, this statistic is significant with 0.90 and the seventh hypothesis is confirmed. Thus, the perceived usefulness of civil engineers and architects of engineering council of Isfahan is related to their intention for engaging in viral marketing. This finding is in parallel with Pavlov et al.'s studies (2005) which showed that perceived usability in ecommerce is effective on the intention of using it. On the other hand, this finding is matched with the finding of Yang et al. (2011) which emphasized the role of perceived usefulness for resending electronic messages.

8. The perceived facility of usage of customer is related to his/her intention for involvement in viral marketing. Since Factor variable path of perceived facility of usage of customer to his/her intention for involvement in viral marketing is calculated with *t* value, this statistic is significant with 0.95 and the eighth hypothesis is confirmed. Thus, the perceived facility of usage of civil engineers and architects of engineering council of Isfahan is related to their intention for engaging in viral marketing. This finding is matched with the finding of Yang et al. (2011) which was based on resending text messages. On the other hand, the chain of attitude, intention, and doing the action or resending messages is confirmed by Palka et al. (2009).

9. The intention of customer is related to his/her actual usage (acceptance) in viral marketing. Since Factor variable path of intention of customer to his/her actual usage for involvement in viral marketing is calculated with *t* value, this statistic is significant with 0.95 and the ninth hypothesis is confirmed. Thus, the intention of civil engineers and architects of engineering council of Isfahan is related to their actual usage for engaging in viral marketing. That indicates that the intention of the people is effective on their practical involvement in viral marketing. This finding is matched with the finding of Yang et al. (2011) which both was based on resending text messages. On the other hand, the chain of attitude, intention, and doing the action or resending messages is confirmed by Palka et al. (2009).

The confirmation of hypotheses 4, 5, 6, 7, 8 and 9 have resulted to the approval of technology Acceptance Model. Thus, the findings of this study are matched with the studies of Davis (1989), Venkatesh and Davis (2000) and Roberts (2000). Thus, according to the results of the hypotheses, we can find that the loyalty of civil engineers and architects of Engineering Council of Isfahan is related to their acceptance of viral marketing and their practical involvement in viral marketing.

4. Research Limitations

1. There have been a lot of researches related to viral marketing. It is not claimed in this research that all these studies have been explored.
2. The other limitation of this research is related to its domain. This research is limited to send and receive of text messages based on email. Although email is one of the most common tools of viral marketing, other tools are also considered. Each tool can have several aspects in terms of research.
3. The case study of this research is related to Engineering Council of Isfahan. Thus, the results cannot be generalized for all the users of this industry or other fields of this industry.
4. For collecting the data, a questionnaire was used but it seems that combination of quantitative data of questionnaire and qualitative data of calculations could lead to more valid and reliable results, and decrease Unintended biases.
5. Technology acceptance model used in this research is very common, and it was confirmed several times by researchers. Surely, not limiting the research to this model and using other technological models with new variables can be more efficient.

4.1 Recommendation for further research

1. Today, the expanding influence of Internet and electronic interactions causes that companies increase their advertising and marketing plans. Therefore, investment on viral marketing as a solution with high potentiality is recommended. Although, studies have revealed that large multinational corporations use releasing of viral marketing extensively, it seems that small corporation especially in Iran use this method less, it is necessary to pursue this method more.
2. This showed that customers, attitude toward their intention to engage in viral marketing is positive, so the company must respond to this demand and with planning and designing campaigns for viral marketing, take advantage of the benefits of this level of willingness of consumers. In other words, other opportunities must be provided for clients who are involved in viral marketing and support of active consumers in different ways is strongly recommended.
3. This loyalty is a factor in the challenging virtual environment (Eckler & Rodgers, 2010) affecting consumer involvement in viral marketing identified in the message content. As a result, companies that are designing viral marketing campaigns, have to seriously and actively seek to strengthen customer loyalty by creating and maintaining a closer relationship with customers. In this case, there must be better attitudes and more willing to engage customers in the shop viral content, and therefore the chances of success greatly increases in viral marketing campaigns.
4. Since this study showed that the perceived usefulness of consumers could predict their attitudes for engagement in viral marketing and their intention, it is recommended to the designers of viral marketing camps to increase the performance and usefulness of viral contents from the perspective of customers. This means that customers should understand that involvement in this case is beneficial for them. This requires special attention in designing viral content in a way that customers would not feel that their involvement is wasting of time or merely in the scope of benefits of company. On the other hand, another negative aspect of viral marketing is creating negative attitude in customers as they think that they are abused. Thus, avoiding such a kind of feeling, the designers of viral contents spend enough time and cost to provide useful content for them. On the other hand, this research confirmed that the perceived facility of usage is effective on the perceived usefulness of that. So, to make a viral content more practical and useful for the users, it is suggested that its involvement must be easy.
5. This research showed that the perceived usefulness is effective on the attitude of customers for engaging in viral marketing. Thus, it is reemphasized that it must be easy to access. These contents shall be opened easily and rapidly, read it and send it. Thus, the designers must know that it must be accessible with the fewest clicks. It must have low capacity, and it must be shown easily by common software. In brief, designers must increase the perceived usefulness, their attitude and customer loyalty by innovative methods on that specific field and specific customer.

Acknowledgement

The authors would like to thank the anonymous referees for constructive comments on earlier version of this paper.

References

Ajzen, I. (1991). The theory of planned behavior. *Organizational behavior and human decision processes*, *50*(2), 179-211.

Davis, F.D. (1989). Perceived usefulness, Perceived ease of use, and user acceptance of information technology. *MIS Quarterly, 13*(3), 319-340.

Day, G. S. (1969). A two–dimensional concept of brand loyalty. *Journal of Advertising Research, 9*, 29-35.

Eckler, P., & Rodgers, S. (2010). *Viral Marketing on the Internet.* Wiley International Encyclopedia of Marketing. John Wiley & Sons Ltd.

Fishbein, M., & Ajzen I. (1975). *Belief, attitude, intention, and behavior: an introduction to theory and research*. Reading, USA: Addison-Wesley.

Ho, J. Y., & Dempsey, M. (2010). Viral marketing: Motivations to forward online content. *Journal of Business Research*, *63*(9), 1000-1006.

Houman, H.A. (2005). Structural equation modeling using LISREL. In Persian.

Hubona, G.S., & Burton J.A. (2003). Modeling the user acceptance of E-mail. *Proceedings of the Thirty-sixth Annual Hawaii International Conference on System Sciences (HICSS)*.

Jacoby, J., & Chestnut, R.W. (1978). *Brand Loyalty: Measurement Management*. New York: John Wiley & Sons.

Jan Nesar Ahmadi, H., & Ghafari, M. (2007). Viral Marketing, cell-to-cell movement, Tadbir publication, 183, 48-46. In Persian.

Maghsoudi, M.H. (2003). The relationship between customer satisfaction with the efficiency and effectiveness of processes, Tehran: *Proceedings of the Fourth Conference on Quality Management*. In Persian.

Masouleh, S., Pazhang, M., & Moradi, J. (2012). What is Impulse Buying? An analytical network processing framework for prioritizing factors affecting impulse buying. *Management Science Letters*, *2*(4), 1053-1064.

Oliver, R. L. (1999). Whence consumer loyalty?. *the Journal of Marketing*, *63*, 33-44.

Palka, W., Pousttchi, K., & Wiedemann, D. G. (2009). Mobile word-of-mouth–A grounded theory of mobile viral marketing. *Journal of Information Technology*, *24*(2), 172-185.

Pavlov, O. V., Melville, N. P., & Plice, R. K. (2005). Mitigating the tragedy of the digital commons: The problem of unsolicited commercial e-mail.*Communications of the Association for Information Systems*, *16*, 73-90.

Roberts, P., & Henderson, R. (2000). Information technology acceptance in a sample of government employees: a test of the technology acceptance model. *Interacting with Computers*, *12*(5), 427-443.

Venkatesh, V., & Davis, F. D. (2000). A theoretical extension of the technology acceptance model: Four longitudinal field studies. *Management science*, *46*(2), 186-204.

Yang, H., Liu, H., & Zhou, L. (2012). Predicting young Chinese consumers' mobile viral attitudes, intents and behavior. *Asia Pacific Journal of Marketing and Logistics*, *24*(1), 59-77.

Strategic analysis of the mobile services value chain in Iran's capital market and development of a mechanism to promote it

Bahareh Ghodoosi[a]*, Alireza Moshkforoush[b], Ali Abdollahi[c] and Mohammadesmaeil Fadaeinejad[c]

[a]*Department of IT Management, E-Learning Course, Tehran, Shahid Beheshti University, Iran*
[b]*Department of Management, E-Learning Course, Isfahan, Isfahan University, Iran*
[c]*Department of Management and Accounting, Tehran, Shahid Beheshti University, Iran*

CHRONICLE	ABSTRACT
Keywords: Services value chain Mobile services Capital market SWOT method Environmental opportunities	The goal of the present study was to strategically analyze the value chain of the services based on cell phone in Iran's capital market and to present solutions for its upgrade. Nowadays, due to focusing on the customer and his needs, services are of great significance to create value for the customers. On the other hand, given the growing trend of online users, the capital market's future belongs to the online business. This research was concerned with a strategic analysis of the aforesaid services value chain. By using SWOT method, the data related to the strengths, weaknesses and threats, as well as environmental opportunities, were collected through using two questionnaires and interviews with users, specialists, and experts in technical and regulatory domains. At the end, by using descriptive statistical methods of analysis, suggestions for upgrading every part of the chain have been presented. Regarding the analyses, the weakness in communication networks and the existing infrastructure for the purpose of information transfer could be regarded as the greatest barrier to the services; also, due to the substructure problems, sometimes the users could be faced with problems such as inaccessibility to the information and inability in conducting their transactions. However, it should be noted that the companies providing these services have been successful in presenting efficient software and useful information for their users, as well as giving them deep satisfaction. Given the existing high capacity in this competitive market and the growing number of online users, it is predicted that the capital market could have the potential to be greatly prosperous and serve as an appropriate market for newcomers' activity.

1. Introduction

Today, electronic services are developed by expanding some concepts such as electronic business (E-business) and mobile commerce (m-commerce). M-commerce is making a revolution in the business world by the innovation technology. According to researches, mobile users were 4 billion until 2010 around the world, with 90% of community in the developed countries (Gereffi & Fernandez-Stark, 2010). Technological development in wireless communications and cellular phone and the growing number of users have led to changing the personal lifestyle and configuring business in recent years.

---
* Corresponding author.
E-mail address: bahare.ghodoosi@gmail.com (B. Ghodoosi)

According to these changes, some companies have focused on electronic services (Al-Debei et al., 2013). In recent decades, companies have tried to improve electronic devices and services, as well as reasonable prices and high quality all over the world. Smart phones are one of these improvements. Smart phones have made significant amount of values in electronic services by new technologies (Dedrick et al., 2011).

With the appearance of four-generation mobile (4G), data services were improved by mobile cell phone. Today, most telecommunications companies try to present variable services for achieving more benefits instead of only voice services (Lu et al., 2007). Many researches have been conducted on cell phone services with new technology and the value chain (Barnes, 2002; Camponovo & Pigneur, 2002; Prtm, 2003; Tsalgatidou & Pitoura, 2001). Researchers have firstly studied the marketing aspect of cell phone services (Al-Debei et al., 2013). After that, they have been concerned with designing the mobile network and improving the value of it (Tsalgatidou & Pitoura, 2001; Tan, 2001; Varshney & Vetter, 2002; Varshney, 2003). Using new technologies in mobile have two effects on businesses. Simplification of connections between employees, customers and suppliers is the first effect, leading to profitability and efficiency in companies. The second effect is the dynamic of business processes by changing access to data and making the chance of transaction for users (Lin et al., 2007).

Iran is one of Middle East countries with a growing number of mobile users. Many companies have started to also increase the added value to improve mobile services. Therefore, investigation of the weakness of mobile services for increasing the chain value of these services is very important. In this study, the effect of mobile services on the capital market in Iran was investigated by using a questionnaire and interviewing with users and experts (De Vellis et al., 1991; Kurttila et al., 2000). Then, according to results, some suggestions are presented to improve the value chain of the systems. Mobile services in this study mean some features through which the user can be archived by installing the marketing software on mobile. On the other hand, SWOT method is applied to analyze the value chain of services.

2. Research methodology and design

In this study, as the number of users was relatively big, the sampling method had be used to determine the number of interviewees. The possibility percentage of the occurring application of software was 84% in the statistical society. The confidence level in this primary study was chosen to be 95%. The number of samples could be calculated by the following equation:

$$n = \frac{z_{\alpha/2}^2 P(1-P)}{d^2}, \tag{1}$$

,where $z_{\alpha/2}$ is the alpha level's z-standard score for normal distribution (1.96), P is possibility percentage (84) and d is the confidence level, which is equal to 0.05. According to Eq (1), the number of samples was calculated to be 206. For reducing the possible errors, 25 percent of all samples were added to samples and increased to 257. After the distribution of the questionnaire among people, because of the incompleteness of some answers, they were rejected. Finally, the number of samples for analysis became 240 people.

The questions of the questionnaire included five sections covering the aim of this study. The components of each section were recognized according to the analysis by SWOT method and the questions were drafted. The Likert scale was used to answer the questions. In this scale, the agreement of responder with each question was determined based on the scale, from 1 (very low) to 5 (very much). The number of questions for each section is shown in Table 1.

Table 1
Classification of questions in six sections

Number of rows	Sections	Number of questions
1	Users	1-3
2	Services	4-20
3	Technology	21-26
4	Communication networks	27-32
5	Legislative	33-37
6	Competitive market	38-40

A conceptual model for this study is shown in Fig. 1.

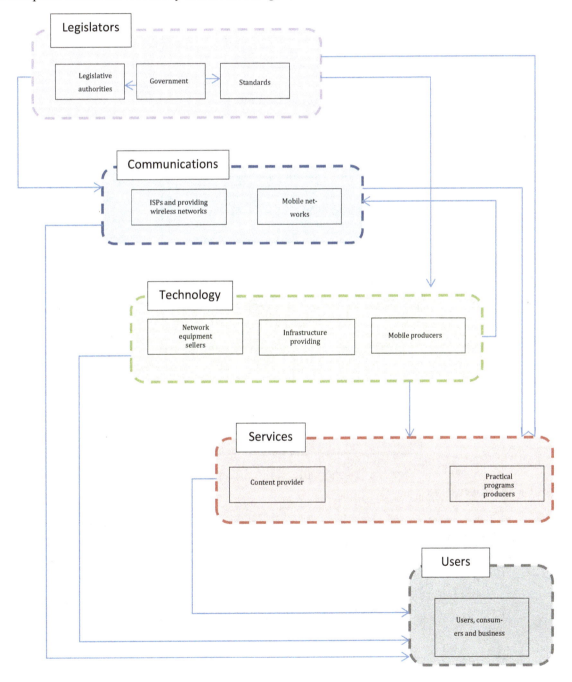

Fig.1. A conceptual model for investigating value chain of mobile services in Iran's capital market

To validate the questionnaire, Cronbach's alpha criterion was used. This criterion could show if other samples were chosen for answering to questions, would result to be the same as before. If the number of questions is shown by K and each question by Y_i, $Xi = Y_1 + Y_2 + \ldots\ldots Y_i$ Cronbach's alpha can be calculated by the following equation (De Vellis & Dancer, 1991):

$$\alpha = \frac{K}{K-1}(1 - \frac{\sum_{i=1}^{K} \sigma_{Y_i}^2}{\sigma_X^2}) \qquad (2)$$

, where σ_{Y_i} and σ_x are standard divisions of each question and whole questions, respectively. For more information and points, experts were interviewed. The obtained data were analyzed by the SWOT method or other statistical analyses. The statistical tests used in this study included the binomial test and the Friedman variance analysis test. For pros and cons, the binomial test was used. The binomial test included two groups with questions in the Likert scale; first group was less or equal to 3 and the second one was more than 3. Fig. 2 shows the schematic of the research program.

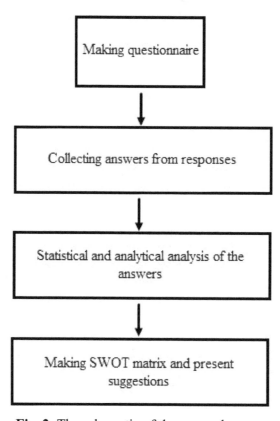

Fig. 2. The schematic of the research program

3. Results and discussion

According to Table 1, questions were divided to six sections including users, services, technology, communication networks, legislative and competitive market. Table 2 shows the average and standard division of each section.

Table 2
Statistical indicators for each component

Component	Sample numbers	Average	Standard division
Users	240	3.62	0.56
Services	240	3.66	0.43
Technology	240	3.08	0.4
Communication networks	240	2.75	0.76
Legislative	240	3.3	0.6
Competitive market	240	3.22	0.53

According to Table 2, services were the strongest component and communication networks could be regarded as the weakest one in the value chain. Details of the analysis of each section are shown in the following section.

3.1 Analyzing of components for the users section

The results for the first component are shown in Table 3. According to Table 3, the significance level for the first component was less than 0.05. On the other hand, the frequency of the second group was more than that of the first group. Therefore, this component could be considered as an opportunity.

Opportunity: Using stock services software by mobile could lead to improving the users' efficiency in their jobs.

The significance level for the second and third components was more than 0.05. Moreover, these two components were in the middle level and could be considered as threat, but the amount of this threat was not too much.

Threat: Users have enough knowledge to work with the software.

Table 3
Statistical indicators for users' components

No of components	Component	Group	Levels	Numbers	Percentage of observation	Validity
1	Using stock mobile software leads to improving efficiency	First group	Less or equal to 3	44	18	0.000
		Second group	More than 3	196	82	
2	Users have enough knowledge to work with software	First group	Less or equal to 3	124	52	0.784
		Second group	More than 3	116	48	
3	Users know safety tips for protecting their privacy	First group	Less or equal to 3	124	52	0.784
		Second group	More than 3	116	48	

As can be seen in Table 3, the majority of responders emphasized on the positive effects of using stock software on mobile, believing that this capital market software could improve the efficiency of user's works. But, for user's knowledge and their awareness of safety tips, percentages in the first and the second groups were almost the same.

Given the increase in the number of online users in the stock market, it could be inferred that users would want to do online deals without brokers. In future, brokers could play the role of consultants in the capital market. But some users did not have enough knowledge about capital market rules and the safety tips for protecting from privacy information. Therefore, the companies that produced software could play an important role in informing users by inperson or virtual training.

3.2 Analysis of components for the services section

The results for the services section are shown in Table 4. For the components 10 and 14, the significance level was less than 0.05 and the frequency of the first group was more than that of the second one. Therefore, they belonged to the weak point. The weak point means that software was not able to be installed on the variable mobile with variable operating systems. On the other side, Strengths mean that software could have a user-friendly application, considering the privacy of users; so it could be useful information, as well as updating the information.

The significance level for the components 9, 11, 12, 13 and 15 was more than 0.05 and it was in the middle level. Therefore, they could not be taken as strengths. On the other hand, for the components 4, 5, 6, 7, 8, 16, 17, 18, 19 and 20, the significance level was less than 0.05. The frequency of the second group (more than 3) was more than that of the first group (less or equal to 3) for these components. So, they included the strengths.

Table 4
Statistical indicators for services components

No of components	Component	Group	Levels	Numbers	Percentage of observation	Validity
4	the ease of use with software	First group	Less or equal to 3	48	20	0.000
		Second group	More than 3	192	80	
5	the quality of being software user-friendly	First group	Less or equal to 3	60	25	0.000
		Second group	More than 3	180	75	
6	The ease of learning software	First group	Less or equal to 3	68	28	0.000
		Second group	More than 3	172	72	
7	Harmonizing services with user needs	First group	Less or equal to 3	92	38	0.013
		Second group	More than 3	148	62	
8	High capacity for protecting privacy and user's information	First group	Less or equal to 3	64	27	0.000
		Second group	More than 3	176	73	
9	Low cost to buy the software	First group	Less or equal to 3	116	48	0.784
		Second group	More than 3	124	52	
10	High speed of software to provide information and services	First group	Less or equal to 3	160	67	0.000
		Second group	More than 3	80	33	
11	Novelty in the provision of services	First group	Less or equal to 3	108	45	0.315
		Second group	More than 3	132	55	
12	Good support service for software	First group	Less or equal to 3	108	45	0.315
		Second group	More than 3	132	55	
13	Ability to merge and integrate web, mobile and computer for the users' comfort	First group	Less or equal to 3	120	50	1
		Second group	More than 3	120	50	
14	High ability to install software in different mobiles with different operating systems	First group	Less or equal to 3	192	80	0.000
		Second group	More than 3	48	20	
15	Availability of information for using software	First group	Less or equal to 3	100	42	0.082
		Second group	More than 3	140	58	
16	Provision of useful output information for the user	First group	Less or equal to 3	68	28	0.000
		Second group	More than 3	172	72	
17	Correlation of the provided information with the user's need	First group	Less or equal to 3	72	30	0.000
		Second group	More than 3	168	70	
18	Update of the provided information	First group	Less or equal to 3	36	15	0.000
		Second group	More than 3	204	85	
19	High precision and trust in the provided information	First group	Less or equal to 3	88	37	0.004
		Second group	More than 3	152	63	
20	Comprehensiveness of the provided information	First group	Less or equal to 3	92	38	0.013
		Second group	More than 3	148	62	

According to the pervious table, the ease of working with software and the high capability for protecting privacy and user's information were the most desirable ones and more than 70 percent of respondents agreed with these components. On the other side, the speed of software in the provided services had the most dissatisfaction in the answers. After that, the cost of buying software and the integrity between web and mobile were the two components causing the most satisfaction.

The services section was divided to "software producers" and "content producers". In the "software producers" section, software has a good design, creating trust in the user for protecting privacy. But the capability to integrate web, mobile and computer, and the ability to install software on different mobiles with different operating systems can be considered weak in supporting the services section. The speed of the available software is the main weak point of them. The strength of this section is the ease of learning and using the available software. Therefore, companies working in this filed can make a comparative market by supplying various software with better and innovative supported services.

3.3. Analysis of components for the technology section

According to the results for the technology section, as shown in Table 5, the significance level for the components 21, 23 and 26 was less than 0.05, but for the question 23, the frequency of the second group was more than that for the first group. Therefore, this component could be an opportunity. Opportunity is the ease of work with smart phones. For the components 21 and 26, the frequency of the first group (Less or equal to 3) is less than that of the second group (more than 3). Therefore, these components could be taken as threats. Threat is inadequate for the variations of mobile models and brands and weaknesses in the infrastructures for communication between software producers companies and stock exchange database.

Table 5
Statistical indicators for technology components

No of components	Component	Group	Levels	Numbers	Percentage of observation	Validity
21	Accessibility of the convenient mobile for installing software	First group	Less or equal to 3	164	68	0.000
		Second group	More than 3	76	32	
22	Low cost of buying the convenient mobile	First group	Less or equal to 3	140	58	0.082
		Second group	More than 3	100	42	
23	Ease of work with the convenient mobile	First group	Less or equal to 3	80	33	0.000
		Second group	More than 3	160	67	
24	Good support services for mobiles	First group	Less or equal to 3	124	82	0.784
		Second group	More than 3	116	48	
25	Low cost of necessary equipment for software producers	First group	Less or equal to 3	132	55	0.315
		Second group	More than 3	108	45	
26	Existence of the convenient infrastructure for communication between software producers	First group	Less or equal to 3	152	63	0.004
		Second group	More than 3	88	37	

According to Table 5, the highest point belonged to the ease of using mobile. But, the most dissatisfaction was for the absence of the convenient mobile and the necessary infrastructure for communication between software producers companies and the stock exchange database.

According to the results of this section and experts' comments, preparing and installing the equipment can be too expensive for companies. On the other hand, absence of enough knowledge for using these equipment is one of the weak points. It is the reason for problems for newcomers. Therefore, installing the convenient infrastructures and supervision can be an important subject that supervisory authority should consider. The strength of this section is good user's knowledge for working with smart phone.

3.4. Analysis of components for the communication networks section

The results for the communication networks section are shown in Table 6. According to the results for the components 27, 28, 29, 31 and 32, the significance level was less than 0.05. For the components 27, 28, 29, 31 and 32, the frequency for the first group (less or equal to 3) was more than that for the second group (more than 3), so it could be regarded as a threat. In this section, threat means the inappropriate coverage of mobile in all parts of the city, inaccessibility to internet by mobile in all parts of the city, absence of competition between different mobile operators for providing cheaper and better services, absence of convenient supported services by operators and the high mobile internet cost. The component number 30 was in the middle level; therefore it was not a threat. As shown in Table 6, this section caused the most dissatisfaction among the users. Except the component number 30, more than 60 percent of respondents were dissatisfied with other components.

Communication networks could be regarded as the most inefficient section, causing a lot of problems for the user. Absence of coverage by mobile networks in all parts of the city was one of problems. On the other hand, the cost of mobile internet was high, making a competition between mobile operators. It seemed that increasing the competition between mobile operators could improve mobile services.

Table 6
Statistical indicators for communication networks components

No of components	Component	Group	Levels	Numbers	Percentage of observation	Validity
27	Convenient coverage of mobile network in city	First group	Less or equal to 3	156	65	0.001
		Second group	More than 3	84	35	
28	Access to internet by mobile in all parts of the city	First group	Less or equal to 3	184	77	0.000
		Second group	More than 3	56	23	
29	The low cost of using internet by mobile	First group	Less or equal to 3	144	60	0.035
		Second group	More than 3	96	40	
30	Installing a new generation of mobile network for access to high speed internet	First group	Less or equal to 3	116	48	0.784
		Second group	More than 3	124	52	
31	High competition between different operators for providing cheaper and better	First group	Less or equal to 3	156	65	0.001
		Second group	More than 3	84	35	
32	Good support services of mobile networks	First group	Less or equal to 3	204	85	0.000
		Second group	More than 3	36	15	

3.5 Analysis of components for legislative section

Table 7 shows the results for legislative section. The significance level for 33 and 37 components was less than 0.05. The frequency of the first group (less or equal to 3) was more than that of the second group (more than 3); so, these could be taken as the threat. Threats can consist of the absence of certain standards in all fields and lack of support by government in providing convenient facilities. For the questions 34, 35 and 36, the significant level was more than 0.05. They were in the middle level; therefore, they could not be taken as an extreme opportunity.

Table 7
Statistical indicators for legislative components

No of components	Component	Group	Levels	Numbers	Percentage of observation	Validity
33	Existence of certain standards in all steps	First group	Less or equal to 3	160	67	0.000
		Second group	More than 3	80	33	
34	Existence of rules for providing stock services by mobile	First group	Less or equal to 3	120	50	1
		Second group	More than 3	120	50	
35	Application of useful rules to protect privacy and the confidential information of users	First group	Less or equal to 3	112	47	0.523
		Second group	More than 3	128	53	
36	Supervision of the stock of software producers	First group	Less or equal to 3	120	50	1
		Second group	More than 3	120	50	
37	Government support from this field by providing the convenient facilities	First group	Less or equal to 3	164	68	0.000
		Second group	More than 3	76	32	

According to Table 7, the lowest point belonged to providing convenient facilities by government. For the rules and quality of supervising the stock for software producers, the satisfaction was on the middle level. The stock exchange with comprehensive supervision on software producer companies could create good satisfaction in the users. But the absence of collaboration and convenient integration between supervisory authorities and software producer companies could cause some problem for the users.

The responders point to weak supported by government in this field. Given the capital market in Iran and the potential of this filed, government could make convenient infrastructure and provide various facilities to help boom the market and the user could take part in this field.

3.6 Analysis of components for competitive market section

The significance level for the component 39 was less than 0.05 and the frequency for the first group was more than that for the second group. Therefore, it could be considered as an opportunity. Opportunity could be defined as low competition between companies providing software. For thequestions38 and 40, the significance level was more than 0.05 and the frequency of these components was in the middle level. So these components could not take as an extreme opportunity. The results for the competitive market section are shown in Table 8.

Table 8
Statistical indicators for the competitive market components

Component No	Component	Group	Levels	Numbers	Percentage of observation	Validity
38	The ease for newcomers to enter to this field	First group	Less or equal	120	50	1
		Second group	More than 3	120	50	
39	High competition between software producing companies	First group	Less or equal	168	70	0.000
		Second group	More than 3	72	30	
40	Existence of original segments for presenting services based on mobile in the capital market	First group	Less or equal	100	42	0.082
		Second group	More than 3	140	58	

According to Table 8, the competition between companies is not as a threat and in this field, there are some original segments in which newcomers can work. The competition in this market in low, and few companies work on this filed. According to responder's answers and experts' comments, entering for newcomers is easy, but competition with big companies is too hard. Therefore, newcomers, by using nobility in productions and entering the original filed, can make a new market.

Friedman test was carried out on all components to determine the priority of opportunities, threats, strengths and weak points. The Friedman test is a non-parametric statistical test used to detect differences in treatments across multiple test attempts.

3.7 SWOT analysis

After that, SWOT analysis was conducted on all sections to present convenient suggestions for each section. SWOT analysis is a structured approach to evaluate an organization with respect to its internal and external environments. By identifying factors in a SWOT matrix, action plans can be developed to augment strengths, eliminate or minimize weaknesses, exploit opportunities and identify threats (Kurttila et al., 2000). In SWOT analysis, the external environment and the internal resources of the organization can be investigated and summarized in key subjects. By interacting between these components, four strategies (WT, ST, OT and SO) can be defined. SO strategy is the operation of the external opportunity by internal strength. Improving internal weak points by considering the existing opportunities is the WO strategy. ST strategy is decreasing the effects of threats from the external environment by using organization strength. Defensive mode can be seen in companies using the WT strategy. The aim of the WT strategy in this study is reduction of internal weak points and prevention of external environment threats. On the other hand, 15 experts reviewed the provided strategies and their suggestions were investigated for final solutions. The matrix of SWOT analysis is shown in Table 9.

Table 9
SWOT matrix

Always white	Strengths (S)	Weak points (W)
Opportunities	SO strategy	WO strategy
Threats	ST strategy	WT strategy

According to Table 9, the SWOT matrix for suggestions in different sections can be defined as shown Table 10.

Table 10
Final SWOT matrix

	Weak points (W): - Low speed in presenting services - Disability in installing software on different mobiles with different operating systems	Strengths (S): - Providing updated and exact information for the users - Protecting the privacy and information of users in software - Good design of software (to ease learning software by users) - Proportioning the presented services from software and the users' need - The low cost to buy software - Novelty in the presented services - Convenient supported services for software	
WO strategy: - Designing software systems according to different platforms - Improving network and communication infrastructures in companies		SO strategy: - Designing systems for the supervision of users and customer's relationship management (CRM) - Classification of the way software services presented to users in proportion to service-level agreement (SLA) - Presence of innovation systems and services based on mobile, such as using genetic algorithm and automatic order based on mobile - Designing decision support (DSS) systems based on mobile - Integration of systems based on mobile with other companies' package software - A culture improving the use of mobile services in the capital market	Opportunities (O): - Optimistic view of users to make use of software to improve efficiency - Existing pristine segments in the presence of mobile services in the capital market - Ability of users to use new smart phones - Installing new generation mobile network for accessing the high speed internet - Effectiveness of laws to protect privacy and information of users
WT strategy: - Review of chain value models based on mobile in Iran's capital market with the supervision of legislators - Using the outsourcing method for better and cheaper infrastructure		ST strategy: - The use of the capability of mobile for teaching users (providing educational software) - Cooperation with companies and operators that present services as strategic co-operation - Presenting integrated solution according to software, hardware and network infrastructure - Making various communication networks to provide interface software for communication with databases	Threats (T): - Absence of convenient supported services for different mobile operators - Absence of access to internet in different parts of the city - Absence of coverage by mobile network in different parts of the city - Absence of effective competition between different operators to provide better and cheaper services - Inefficient support by government from this field - Limiting the convenient mobile to use the software - Absence of the convenient standard in all fields (from infrastructures to software design) - Absence of the convenient infrastructure for communication between software producers and database - High cost of using internet by mobile - High cost of buying convenient mobile on which software can be installed at - High cost of providing equipment for software producers - Low knowledge of users for using the software

Therefore, solutions according to priority can be summarized in Table 11.

Table 11
Prioritize of suggested solutions

Priority	Solution
1	Classification of the way software services presented to users in proportion to service-level agreement (SLA)
	Integration of systems based on mobile with other companies' package software
2	The use of the capability of mobile for teaching users (providing educational software)
	Review of chain value models based on mobile in Iran's capital market with the supervision of legislators
	A culture improving the use of mobile services in the capital market
3	Presence of innovation systems and services based on mobile, such as using genetic algorithm and automatic order based on mobile
	Cooperation with companies and operators that present services as strategic cooperation
	Presenting integrated solution according to software, hardware and network infrastructure
	Making various communication networks to provide interface software for communication with databases
	Designing software systems according to different platforms
4	Designing decision support (DSS) systems based on mobile
	Providing interface software for communication with databases
	Improving network and communication infrastructures in companies
	Designing systems for the supervision of users and customer's relationship management (CRM)
5	Using the outsourcing method for better and cheaper infrastructure

4. Conclusion

This study focused on the mobile services value chain in Iran's capital market. Therefore, the effect of mobile services on the value chain in Iran's capital market was investigated by preparing the questionnaire and interviewing with the experts.

Based on the results obtained in this study, communication networks can be considered as the weakest section for mobile services in the capital market. Therefore, cooperation between the operators could improve communication networks, making a comparative market leading to be better services. Positive section refers to the "users", which contained the most points. The users believed that using software for doing online deal could lead to increasing efficiency in the capital stock. But user training is an important subject that software producers should be taken in to account. In the technology section, the absence of the convenient infrastructure could be a main problem. So, installing new equipment to make the convenient infrastructure and considering users for providing the appropriate mobile could be suggested for this section. Stock and exchange organization could also make use of a good supervision on software producer companies. But government supports could lead to booming capital market and increasing the value chain in this filed. The competition between software producer companies is too low. On the other hand, few companies have been able to work up in this filed until now. Because of the existence of original segments in the capital market software, newcomer companies can work up in original filed, thereby making a good comparative marketing.

References

Barnes, S. J. (2002). The mobile commerce value chain: analysis and future developments. *International Journal of Information Management, 22*(2), 91-108.

Camponovo, G., & Pigneur, Y. (2002, July). Analyzing the actor game in m-business. *In Proc. First International Conference on Mobile Business, Athens*.

Al-Debei, M. M., Al-Lozi, E., & Fitzgerald, G. (2013). Engineering innovative mobile data services: Developing a model for value network analysis and design. *Business Process Management Journal, 19*(2), 336-363.

Dedrick, J., Kraemer, K. L., & Linden, G. (2011). The distribution of value in the mobile phone supply chain. *Telecommunications Policy, 35*(6), 505-521.

Gereffi, G., & Fernandez-Stark, K. (2010). The offshore services value chain: developing countries and the crisis. *Durham: Center on Globalization Governance and Competitiveness - Duke University. Commisioned by CORFO.*

Kurttila, M., Pesonen, M., Kangas, J., & Kajanus, M. (2000). Utilizing the analytic hierarchy process (AHP) in SWOT analysis—a hybrid method and its application to a forest-certification case. *Forest Policy and Economics, 1*(1), 41-52.

Lin, C. H., Shih, H. Y., & Sher, P. J. (2007). Integrating technology readiness into technology acceptance: The TRAM model. *Psychology & Marketing, 24*(7), 641-657.

Lu, Y., Dong, Y., & Wang, B. (2007). The mobile business value chain in China: a case study. *International Journal of Electronic Business, 5*(5), 460-477.

Prtm, U. (2003). *The ecology of mobile commerce: charting a course for success using value chain analysis*. Mobile Commerce: Technology, Theory, and Applications, 122.

Tsalgatidou, A., & Pitoura, E. (2001). Business models and transactions in mobile electronic commerce: requirements and properties. *Computer Networks, 37*(2), 221-236.

Tan, K. C. (2001). A framework of supply chain management literature. *European Journal of Purchasing & Supply Management, 7*(1), 39-48.

Varshney, U. (2003). Mobile and wireless information systems: applications, networks, and research problems. *Communications of the Association for Information Systems, 12*(1), 11.

Varshney, U., & Vetter, R. (2002). Mobile commerce: framework, applications and networking support. *Mobile networks and Applications, 7*(3), 185-198.

De Vellis, R. F., & Dancer, L. S. (1991). Scale development: theory and applications. *Journal of Educational Measurement, 31*(1), 79-82.

# Impact of Mobile advertising on consumer attitudes in Algeria: case study of Ooredoo

Amina Merabet[a*], Abderrezzak Benhabib[b] and Abderrezzak Merabet[c]

[a]Lecturer, Tlemcen university, Algeria, BP: 226 Tlemcen Algeria
[b]Professor, Tlemcen university, Algeria, BP: 226 Tlemcen Algeria
[c]Student, Tlemcen university, Algeria, BP: 226 Tlemcen Algeria

CHRONICLE	ABSTRACT
Keywords: Mobile advertising Attitude towards mobile advertising Brand attitude Purchase intention	Mobile advertising is a perfect tool to build a relationship based on proximity between brand and consumer. It is tactile, interactive, and personalized. As few studies have focused on this concept, particularly in the Algerian context, we aim in this research to show the role of mobile advertising on consumer attitudes. After a literature review, an empirical study is conducted among 150 students in Tlemcen city. Results, using regression analysis, show that attitude towards mobile advertising had no influence on the attitude towards brand and purchase intention.

1. Introduction

Today Smartphones have penetrated every daily life aspects of Algerians. Indeed, they have reinvented the mobile phone by allowing multiple uses. Advertisers and practitioners specializing in mobile marketing have understood the opportunity offered by these new technologies that help consumers receive personalized and contextualized ads on diverse mobile media. However, if the first effectiveness results of mobile marketing campaigns seem quite encouraging, some studies exhibit lower efficiency of mobile advertising through some mediator variables in advertising effectiveness, particularly as attitude toward mobile advertising. In Algeria, few studies have focused on the influence of mobile advertising on consumer attitudes. Consequently, this study attempts to clarify how mobile advertising influences the attitudes of Algerian consumers. Thus, our objectives are twofold: First, we try to summarize the current state of knowledge on mobile advertising and second, we test causal relationship between mobile advertising and Algerian consumer attitudes.

* Corresponding author.
E-mail address: aminamerabet1982@gmail.com (A. Merabet)

2. Literature review

2.1 Definition of advertising

Advertising is the favorite instrument of communication. It is *"a nonpersonal communication of information usually paid for and usually persuasive in nature about products, services or ideas by identified sponsors through the various media"* (Bovee & Arens, 1994). According to Krugman (1975), advertising success depends on three elements, namely: information, rational stimulus and intensity. Good advertising must have at least one of these elements. Advertising plays a very important role to develop a products or services. On the one hand, it informs customers of the existence of a new product on the market and helps them to find the best products. Second, it increases business sales, changes attitudes and behavior of consumers towards a product. In addition, it strengthens firm credibility.

2.2 Definition of mobile marketing

Many definitions exist of mobile marketing. According to Scharl et al. (2005), mobile marketing involves the use of a wireless medium to provide consumers a personalized information that promotes products, services or ideas and thus brings benefits to all stakeholders. According to the Mobile Marketing Association (MMA) (2009), mobile marketing *"is a set of practices that enables organizations to communicate and engage with their audience in an interactive and relevant manner through and with any mobile device or network."*

This latter definition includes all aspects of mobile marketing. First, the concept of "*practice*" includes all the marketing processes and activities such as promotions, relationship management, CRM, customer services, loyalty, social marketing. Second, the concept of "*engagement*" in turn, implies a junction in communication and a social interaction between firms and consumers.

2.3 Definition of mobile advertising

According to Li (2004), "Mobile *advertising refers to any communication about products, services and ideas that involves the use of mobile devices for promotional purposes"*. This definition includes not only telephony terminal but also all mobile devices. Although mobile device are different, they have in common the ability to contact consumers in personalized manner wherever they are. Advertisers use more and more the mobile communication medium because it is:

- Powerful: (high mobile penetration rate),
- Personal: mobile is the ideal communication tool One to One,
- Relevant: the mobile allows very precise targeting of marketing campaigns,
- Low cost.

2.4 Attitude

Understanding consumer behavior is not easy as it is a key factor in the development of business strategies. Among most of the different consumer behavior models developed up to now, attitude is the variable that retain most attention. Attitude is a key factor in the study of consumer behavior because it is one of the main elements that influence consumer behavior as well as purchase intention.

Since the 20s, researchers have been interested in the concept of attitude that was thought off as the basis of all behavior (Allport, 1935; Campbell, 1963; Doob, 1947). Allport (1935) defines it as *"a mental and neural state of readiness, organized through experience, exerting a directive and dynamic influence upon the individual's response to all objects and situations with which it is related"*. For Kotler et al. (2006), *"an attitude sums up the feedback (positive or negative), emotional reactions and predispositions toward an object or idea"*. This means that attitudes enable an individual to establish consistent behavior with respect to a class of similar objects. All these definitions highlight the characteristics of consumer attitude as:

• An attitude is built and results from the evaluations of experiences,
An attitude is durable:
• The attitude is based on a set of predispositions that can be favorable or unfavorable to an object or class of objects.

Baker and Churchill (1977) consider that the structure of Attitudes can be described in terms of three components: cognitive (beliefs), affective (feelings) and conative (behavior).

2.5 The influence of m-advertising on consumer attitudes

Starting from the idea that m-advertising is a form of advertising, persuasive advertising models can thenceforth be applied. Several authors have attempted to explain the effectiveness of persuasive advertising from the early theories of persuasion based on the hierarchy of effects to the more recent Elaboration Likelihood Model (ELM) (Petty & Cacioppo, 1981, 1986), and other extension works (Grossbart et al., 1986). In Algeria, also some researchers have tried to explain this phenomenon (Merabet & Benhabib, 2012, 2014). Furthermore, other studies in the field of mobile advertising are based on the Technology Acceptance Model (TAM) of Davis (1986) by considering mobile advertising as an innovation. This model has been widely used to predict buying intentions (Hoffman & Novak 1996; Yang, 2005).

3. The conceptual model

3.1 Variables

3.1.1 The attitude towards the brand (Ab)

The previous definitions could be extend to the brand or ad. Howard (1989) defines attitude towards a brand as "*the degree of satisfying the needs the consumer thinks this brand may provide*". It represents all the assessments made by the consumer on the ability of different brands or products to satisfy needs (Assael, 1984).

3.1.2 The attitude toward mobile advertising (Aad)

The attitude toward advertising has been recognized as a central element in the advertising persuasion process. According to Lutz (1985), attitude toward advertising is "*a predisposition to respond favorably or unfavorably to a particular advertisement during a particular exposure*". For Derbaix (1995), In general, the Aad is a personal and global assessment of an advertising stimulus-related to an exposure situation.

3.1.3 The purchase intention (Purchase intent) (PI)

The purchase intention is a very complex concept. Some researchers consider it as a component of the attitude that is on the conative dimension (Greenwald 1968; Kothandapani 1971; Ostrom, 1969), others consider it as an independent variable (Bagozzi, 1981). According to Duhaime et al. (1996), purchase intention is a step of the decision-making process where the consumer expresses its preference for a product based on its experience, beliefs and attitudes.

3.2. Hypotheses

Several researchers have shown the positive influence of the attitude toward the **ad** on the attitude toward the brand and purchase intention. Therefore, we can formulate the following hypotheses:

H₁: There is a causal link between consumer attitudes towards mobile advertising in general and their attitude towards a brand.
H₂: There is a causal link between consumer attitudes towards mobile advertising in general and their buying intentions.

On the basis of the seminal work of Fishbein and Ajzen (2011), which assumes that in general, attitudes would lead to intentions which, subsequently, would lead to actual behavior, many researchers have been interested in the link between consumer attitudes and intentions of future behavior (e.g., Oliver, 1980; Berger & Alwitt, 1996). According to their work, we shall check these links and therefore formulate the following hypothesis:

H₃: There is a causal link between consumer attitudes toward a brand and their intentions for future behavior toward that brand.

The above hypotheses can be illustrated in our research framework shown in Fig. 1 as follows,

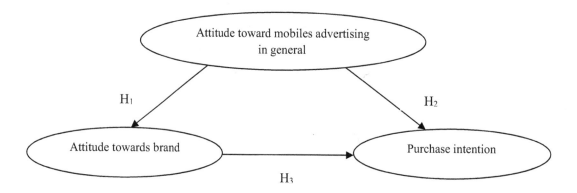

Fig. 1. The conceptual model

4. Methods

To test our hypotheses, an experiment was necessary in this study.

4.1 Brand selection

We choose a telecommunication provider, namely **Ooredoo** brand, widely known for its mobile advertising campaigns.

4.2 Sample

The sample consists of 150 student of Tlemcen University (Algeria).

4.3 Scale selection

Many scales have been developed to measure the attitude toward mobile advertising. We select items from the scales developed by the following authors (Sing & Vij, 2008; Mehta, 2000).

- The scale of Grossbart et al. (1986) is used to measure Ab with three items.
- PI is measured by the probability scale of Axelrod (1968).

4.4 Testing measurement models

At first and in accordance with the Churchill procedure, we conduct principal components analysis with varimax rotation to test the different structures of constructs used in this research, excluding purchase intention scale as it consists of a single item. To determine the number of factors to retain, we consider the most usual rule of Kaiser (selected factors corresponding to Eigen values above the unit). Only items with communality greater than 0.5 and the absolute value of their correlation to an axis are greater than 0.6 are retained. Then, the Cronbach's alpha is used to assess the reliability of these constructs. The estimated coefficients can be described as acceptable as they are all above 0.70. In a second step, we conduct a confirmatory factor analysis with a bootstrap procedure. The validity of each scale is checked by means of absolute, incremental and parsimony indices. In general, all adjustment indices are considered good and acceptable (see Table 1)

Table 1
Results from Exploratory analyses

Item	Communalities	Factor loading	% explained variance	KMO	Bartlett's Test of Sphericity	Eigen values	Cronbach Alpha
Aad1	0,811	0,9					
Aad2	0,605	0,778					
Aad4	0,526	0,629	60,39	0,514	p=0,000	1,81	0,645
Ab1	0,5	0,887					
Ab2	0,787	0,803					
Ab3	0,645	0,703	64,1	0,592	p=0,000	1,92	0,702
PI2	0,772	0,879					
PI3	0,772	0,879	77,2	0,600	p=0,001	1,54	0,704

5. Findings

To test a causal relationship between a dependent variable and one or more independent variables, it is necessary to use an explanatory analysis. Our model can be tested using a simple and multiple regression model. We chose the regression analysis because it is characterized by its simplicity and can explain a quantitative variable by several other independent quantitative variables.

5.1 Effect of Aad on Ab

As Tables (2-4) show, the results obtained postulate that the Aad does not influence the Ab.

Table 2
Summary of models (Relation Aad→ Ab)

Model	R	R square	Adjusted R square	Std. error of the estimation
1	0,194[a]	0,038	0,012	2,30043

a. Predicted value: (Constants), Aad

Table 3
ANOVA[b] (Relation Aad→ Ab)

Model		Sum of squares	ddl	Mean of squares	D	Sig.
1	Regression	7,879	1	7,879	1,489	0,230[a]
	Residual	201,096	38	5,292		
	Total	208,975	39			

a. Predicted value: (Constants), Aad
b. Dependent Variable : Ab

Table 4
Coefficients[a] (Relation Aad→ Ab)

Model		Unstandardized Coefficients		Standardized Coefficients	t	Sig.
		A	Erreur standard	Bêta		
1	(Constant)	11,017	1,486		7,412	0
	Aad	0,169	0,139	0,194	1,22	0,23

a. Dependent Variable : Ab

5.2 Effect of Aad on PI

The results indicate that the relationship (Aad-PI) is not significant (see Table 5, Table 6 and Table 7)

Table 5
Summary of models (Relation Aad→ PI)

Model	R	R square	Adjusted R square	Std. error of the estimation
1	0,055[a]	0,003	-0,023	2,21859

a. Predicted value: (Constants), Aad

Table 6
ANOVA[b] (Relation Aad→ PI)

Model		Sum of squares	ddl	Mean of squares	D	Sig.
1	Regression	0,558	1	0,558	0,113	0,738[a]
	Residual	187,042	38	4,922		
	Total	187,6	39			

Table 7
Coefficients (Relation Aad→ PI)

Model		Unstandardized Coefficients		Standardized Coefficients	t	Sig.
		A	Erreur standard	Bêta		
1	(Constant)	6,132	1,433		4,278	0
	Aad	0,045	0,134	0,055	0,337	0,738

a. Dependent Variable : PI

The results of the hypotheses H1 and H2 could be explained by the fact that the Algerian mobile users perceive mobile advertising as intrusive, and have negative perceptions about them.

5.3 Effect of Ab on PI

The results show that Ab influence purchase intention.

Table 8
Summary of models (Relation Ab→ PI)

Model	R	R square	Adjusted R square	Std. error of the estimation
1	0,502[a]	0,252	0,232	1,92162

a. Predicted value: (Constants), Ab

Table 9
ANOVA[b] (Relation Ab→ PI)

Model		Sum of squares	ddl	Mean of squares	D	Sig.
1	Regression	47,28	1	47,28	12,804	,001[a]
	Residual	140,32	38	3,693		
	Total	187,6	39			

a. Predicted value: (Constants), Ab
b. Dependent Variable : PI

Table 10
Coefficients[a] (Relation Ab→ PI)

Model		Unstandardised Coefficients		Standardised Coefficients	t	Sig.
		A	Erreur standard	Bêta		
1	(Constant)	0,524	1,725		0,303	0,763
	Ab	0,476	0,133	0,502	3,578	0,001

a. Dependent Variable : PI

6. Conclusion and discussion

Experts predict a significant growth of mobile advertising market in the coming years in Algeria that remains largely under-exploited. In fact, it is a perfect tool to establish a closer relationship between the brand and the consumer. Nevertheless, the understanding of the effectiveness of this specific form of communication is still in its infancy. After a short review of the literature on mobile advertising and its effects on consumer attitudes, we tested the influence of attitude towards mobile advertising on the attitudes of the Algerian consumer. The results obtained among a sample of 150 students using a regression analysis, showed firstly, the existence of a direct positive link between Ab and PI, and secondly, confirm our conclusions about the direct role of Ab on IP and support the existing literature. Thus, a consumer who has a positive attitude towards a brand is more likely, for example, first to buy the products offered by this brand, second, to consume again the product and third, recommend it to his friends. Furthermore, the results show that attitude towards mobile advertising has no influence on the attitude toward the brand and purchase intention. One explanation for this may be sought in the work on the intrusiveness of mobile advertising. Researchers agree on the fact that individuals are increasingly anxious to preserve their privacy. Mobile advertising therefore can present several risks of rejection. Hence, the need for a precise segmentation by firms. Brands must also build a relationship with their customers based on loyal clients in order to have permissions to send messages or applications through their mobile.

References

Allport, G. W. (1935). Attitudes. In C. Murchison (Ed.), Handbook of social psychology. (pp. 798-844).
Assael, H. (1984). *Consumer behavior and marketing action*. Kent Pub. Co..
Bagozzi, R. P. (1981). Attitudes, intentions, and behavior: A test of some key hypotheses. *Journal of Personality and Social Psychology, 41*(4), 607-627.
Baker, M. J., & Churchill Jr, G. A. (1977). The impact of physically attractive models on advertising evaluations. *Journal of Marketing Research*, 14(4), 538-555.
Berger, I. E., & Alwitt, L. F. (1996). Attitude conviction: a self-reflective measure of attitude strength. *Journal of Social Behavior and Personality*, 11(3), 555.
Bovee, C. L., & Arens, W. F. (1994). *Contemporary advertising*. Irwin Professional Publishing.
Campbell, D. T. (1963). From description to experimentation: Interpreting trends as quasi-experiments.
Davis, F. (1986). Perceived usefulness, perceived ease of use, and user acceptance of information technology. *MIS Quarterly, 13*(3), 319-339.
Derbaix, C. (1995). *L'impact des réactions affectives induites par les messages publicitaires : hune analyse tenant compte de l'implication. Recherche et Applications en Marketing, 10*(2), 3-30.
Pecheux, C., & Derbaix, C. (1999). Children and attitude toward the brand: A new measurement scale. *Journal of Advertising Research, 39*(4), 19-19.
Doob, L. W. (1947). The behavior of attitudes. *Psychological Review, 54*(3), 135.
Duhaime, C.P., Kindra, G.S., Laroche, M., & Muller, TE. (1996). Le comportement du consommateur, Editor Gaétan Morin, 2nd edition, 669.

Fishbein, M., & Ajzen, I. (2011). *Predicting and changing behavior: The reasoned action approach*. Taylor & Francis.

Greenwald, A. G. (1968). On defining attitude and attitude theory. *Psychological Foundations of Attitudes*, 361-388.

Grossbart, S., Muehling, D. D., & Kangun, N. (1986). Verbal and visual references to competition in comparative advertising. *Journal of Advertising*, *15*(1), 10-23.

Hoffman, D. L., & Novak, T. P. (1996). Marketing in hypermedia computer-mediated environments: Conceptual foundations. *The Journal of Marketing*, *60*(3), 50-68.

Howard, J. A. (1989). *Consumer behavior in marketing strategy*. Prentice Hall.

Kothandapani, V. (1971). Validation of feeling, belief, and intention to act as three components of attitude and their contribution to prediction of contraceptive behavior. *Journal of Personality and Social Psychology*, *19*(3), 321.

Kotler, P. (2006). *Marketing-Management* (pp. 20-28). Poeschel.

Krugman, H. E. (1975). What makes advertising effective. *Harvard Business Review*, *53*(2), 96-103.

Lendrevie, J., & Lévy, J. (2012). *Mercator 2013: Théories et nouvelles pratiques du marketing*. Dunod.

Li, H. (2004). Responses to mobile advertising: a diary study of mobile phone users. In *Proceedings of the conference-American Academy of Advertising* (pp. 248-249). Pullman, WA; American Academy of Advertising; 1999.

Lutz, R. J. (1985). Affective and cognitive antecedents of attitude toward the ad: A conceptual framework. *Psychological processes and advertising effects*, 45-63.

Mehta, A. (2000). Advertising attitudes and advertising effectiveness. *Journal of advertising research*, *40*(3), 67-72.

Merabet. A., & Benhabib, A. (2014). The moderating role of brand familiarity and product involvement in the relationship between brand personality and persuasive advertising elaboration. *European Academic Research, 2(*3), 3965-3994.

Merabet, A., & Benhabib, A. (2012). Brand Personality: Antecedents and Consequences. *Indian journal of marketing*, *42*(10), 11-21.

Myers, J., Aaker, D.A., & Betra, D. (1996). *Advertising Management*. Englewood Cliffs, NJ : Prentice-Hall).

Ostrom, T. M. (1969). The relationship between the affective, behavioral, and cognitive components of attitude. *Journal of Experimental Social Psychology*, *5*(1), 12-30.

Oliver, R. L. (1980). A cognitive model of the antecedents and consequences of satisfaction decisions. *Journal of Marketing Rresearch*, *17*(4), 460-469.

Petrof, J. V. (1993). *Comportement du consommateur et marketing*. Presses Université Laval.

Petty, R. E., & Cacioppo, J. T. (1981). *Attitudes and persuasion: Classic and contemporary approaches*. Dubuque, IA: Wm. C. Brown.

Petty, R. E., & Cacioppo, J. T. (1986). *Communication and persuasion: Central and peripheral routes to attitude change*. New York: SpringerVerlag.

Scharl, A., Dickinger, A., & Murphy, J. (2005). Diffusion and success factors of mobile marketing. *Electronic commerce research and applications*, *4*(2), 159-173.

Singh, R., & Vij, S. (2008). Public attitude toward advertising: An empirical study of Northern India. *The ICFAI Journal of Marketing Management*, *7*(1), 49-66.

Yang, K. C. (2005). Exploring factors affecting the adoption of mobile commerce in Singapore. *Telematics and informatics*, *22*(3), 257-277.

www.mmaglobal.com

The effect of firm's logo on its performance: Evidence from oil industry

Jafar Jafari[a*]

[a]MA in Marketing, Department of Management, Central Branch, Islamic Azad University, Tehran, Iran

CHRONICLE	ABSTRACT
Keywords: Logo Company's Performance Likeness/Description Benefits Benefits Functional Benefits Aesthetic Tendencies	Nowadays, trade mark is one of the most important components of the products in both consumers and producers' perspectives. In this study, two separate but related mechanism through which the trademark is supposed to create value for customers, were investigated. Likeness/ description and functional-aesthetic benefits were taken into consideration. This research shows the positive effects of logo on customer commitment regarding the performance. Commitment reflects customers' desire for cooperation by considering the effects of a logo. Logo will help customers easily identify and select a brand. This research proves that, from the customer's perspective, trademarks contain meaning, and thus include brief information on the struggle for marketing. In case of the purpose, this study is an applied research and in terms of data-gathering it is a descriptive – survey one. Since the population of the survey was unlimited, initial investigations indicated that 384 questionnaires should be distributed based on Morgan table. Using structural equation modeling, the survey results showed that descriptive-cognitive, functional benefits and aesthetic tendencies had significant influences on customer commitment in regards of performance.

1. Introduction

A good brand will add benefit and value to goods and generates some advantageous for consumers and consumers will also adhere to names which create value for them. According to Kotler, (2009) brand can be defined as "a name, term, sign, symbol or combination of them intended to identify a product or service to a seller or a group of sellers and distinguishes the goods or services from that of a competitor". A brand is an important medium to create a positive image in customer's minds, which results in difference with available products (Kotler, 2009). Trademarks resolve the lack of recognition by the clients. It is essential to note that the positive image of the brand with the marketing efforts of the firm is not eternal and the emergence of more new products with attractive logos will affect it. As mentioned, customers are able to establish a significant relationship with a brand logo. Brand is an intangible asset which has considerable influence on performance (Woo et al., 2008).

* Corresponding author.
E-mail address: j.jafari1985@yahoo.com (J. Jafari)

For example, the ancient Chinese used symbol of the dragon to express imperial power. In addition to be a means of distinguishing, logo helps to convey meanings and information about the product or service. Good logos can result in a good reputation and form positive customers' attitudes, their goal of purchasing and loyalty. In fact, previous studies about branding suggest that logos work as a visual display of the original meaning of the brand and public image. Logos could affect the economic value of a company (Walsh et al., 2010).

Oliver (1999) defines loyalty as a strong commitment to repurchase a product or a premier service in the future and referring to the same product or brand, despite the impact of competitors and their marketing efforts for selling products (Rahimi Helari & Hosseini, 2012). This research proves that in customers' view, logo represents its meaning and therefore it is a brief information on the struggle for marketing. The reason for the importance of the topic is that brands have the ability to provide cognitive explanations, and logos are important tools for communication between the brand and the people. Due to increasing car productions and machineries, and consequently production of needed oil derivatives, there exists a gap of research regarding logos of these products to identify their benefits and performance. We hope that this research will be fruitful in the respective industry.

Müller et al. (2013) studied the brand revitalization by investigating the impacts of logo similarity and type of logo on brand modernity and brand loyalty and highlighted the importance of certain logo characteristics in describing logo attitude and presenting the effects on brand modernity, brand attitude, and finally, brand loyalty.

Shukla (2011) studied how interpersonal influences and branding cues could shape consumer luxury purchase intentions based on a sample of British and Indian consumers. He reported that normative interpersonal influences were significant across nations but the role of informational interpersonal effects was significant only among Indian consumers. He also reported that British consumers depended increasingly on branding cues, brand image was a significant moderator between normative interpersonal influences and luxury purchase intentions in both countries.

2. Literature Review

2.1. Concepts and theories

Brand bears a connotation more than a product or a service. Nowadays, many goods and services, especially in petrochemical and oil and its derivatives, are not different significantly and it is the brand that makes the basic distinctions. The resulting image of the brand, its performance advantages and descriptive-cognitive benefits, come from brand logo and can be effective on customer commitment and performance of the bank. Therefore, this paper conducts a survey in respect of the different kinds of logos and their effects; those who have used mere signals for logos and those who used just names or a combination of the two. Building a positive attitude of a bank logo can affect consumer attitudes and identity and should be kept in mind that a positive attitude appears from a good experience of a product. Brand awareness benefits include a descriptive-cognitive benefits, functional benefits and brand image. As awareness of the brand and its relationship with customers' perception of quality increases, it starts to increase customer loyalty which promotes the performance.

2.1.1. Likeness / descriptive Benefits

Brand has the ability to help us describe the definition of the concerned consumer. It will differentiate the customers from others, for instance, a brand may represent various parts of the identity of customers; such as core beliefs/values or a life cycle which they believe in (Van den Bosch et al., 2005). Also, logos connect people to each other who share similar values and beliefs.

Since logos represent trademarks, they could potentially be the source of connections for customers through strengthening the brand's core values. In other words; a trademark logo is an essential tool for communication between brands and people which, in turn, help customers feel the sense of belonging. Besides, since logos build a form for trademark, they enhance their credibility and tend to incite customers. Logos have the potential to express their communications and empower them. Hence, the customers' desire for more efforts and investment to continue their relationships with the trade show will be increased (Thomson et al., 2005). Engendering a symbolic relationship with a brand is essential, but there would be a stronger affinity with the trademark that fostered relationships with customers.

2.1.2. Functional benefits

The researchers suggest that the brand can be managed to reduce uncertainty in people's lives and enable them to facilitate the efficient control in obtaining the desired results. Therefore, the brand may have an effective sense to help people perform their daily activities well. Logos are visual display of a trademark which reminds functional advantage to customers. For instance, consider Red Bull logo that two opposing striker bull with the sun shining in front of the brand ensures that this product gives life to the mind and body. Customers are normally familiar with companies, which could meet their requirements because they make their life easier and they will not shift to competitor companies as long as they are happy with the service they receive. This study aims at logos with functional benefits which encourage customers to compensate and being dependent to the respective trademark. As a result, trademark has the potential to empower commitment among customers. In this way, logos strength the relations with customers (Walsh et al., 2010).

2.1.3. Aesthetic tendencies

Throughout history, beauty and design trends have been of human interest and imagination have taken them in their hands. Handicrafts and admiring objects with attractive shapes have a long history. Thus, previous researches on logo emphasized on aesthetic aspects. In addition to visual delight, aesthetic tendencies in logo can foster emotional bond with customers. Trademarks with aesthetic attraction facilitates communication with customers. For instance, the Walt Disney Company's brand logo with an image of a fairy castle may contain a substantial effect on customers. Similarly, Hello Kitty with a funny image of a white kitty fosters a deep relationship with clients around the world based on the funny design. Therefore, aesthetic tendency is the key factor which exhibits the power of a firm to form mutual relationship with potential customers and will result in customer loyalty (Woo et al., 2008).

2.2. Theoretical framework

Brand bears a connotation more than a product or a service. Nowadays, many goods and services, especially in petrochemical and oil and their derivatives, are not different significantly and it is the brand that makes the basic distinctions. The resulting image of the brand, its performance advantages and descriptive-cognitive benefits, come from brand logo and can be effective on customer commitment and performance of the bank. Creating a positive attitude of a bank logo can influence consumer attitudes and identity and should be kept in mind that a positive attitude comes from a good experience of a product. Brand awareness benefits include a descriptive-cognitive benefits, functional benefits and brand image (Park et al., 2013).

2.3. Conceptual Research Model

Initial conceptual model based on the research accomplished by Park et al. (2013) is given by Fig. 1 as follows:

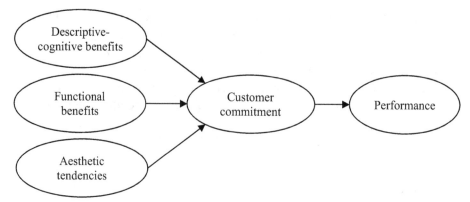

Fig. 1. Conceptual model of the research based on the study accomplished by Park et al. (2013)

2.4. Research Hypotheses

Based on the conceptual model, the researchers' hypotheses are:

1. Descriptive-cognitive benefits of a logo on customer commitment are impressive.
2. The functional benefits of a brand logo on customer commitment are impressive.
3. Aesthetic tendencies of a brand logo influence customer commitment.
4. Customer commitment influences the oil companies' performance.

3. Methodology

The present study is considered functional according to the fact that the results of it can be applied by managers and officials of oil companies. Regarding data collection, the study is a descriptive – survey one, also it can be categorized as cross-sectional survey type as well. Survey method is a way to obtain information on attitudes, beliefs, opinions and behaviors of members of population through study. We call it a cross-sectional study as it is a type of observational study that involves the analysis of data collected from a population, or a representative subset, at one specific point in time. The population of this study includes all Sepahan Oil Company's customers in Tehran. Due to some limitations such as time and budget limitation and distribution of customers and consumers of petroleum products in all parts of Tehran, sampling was implemented. Due to the fact that the population size is not specified, 384 cases were chosen based on Kerjesy and Morgan table. Sampling method was simple random.
In order to collect necessary information for the study, the following methods were used:

- Books, articles and Persian and English websites,
- Data associated with similar researches

In this study, questionnaire was used to collect field data. In this section, 16 questions were raised to assess the effectiveness of contextual factors and criteria related to Sepahan Oil Company's logo. In order to check the validity of the questionnaire, professors' opinions were taken into consideration. Also, Cronbach's alpha was used to assess the reliability of the results. Following is the result.

Table 1

Reliability by Internal Consistency Method (Cronbach's alpha)

Variables	Number of Questions	Cronbach's alpha
Cognitive-descriptive benefits	3	0.72
Functional benefits	3	0.84
Aesthetic tendencies	3	0.74
Customer commitment	3	0.73
Performance	4	0.82

SPSS 22 and LISREL 9.1 software were used for data analysis.

4. Findings

4.1. Normality test of basic variables

In order to confirm the normality of data, Skewness and Kurtosis tests have been applied to determine the distribution of the data. The results of the tests show that the research's variables were normally distributed. Skewness and Kurtosis values of all variables were within the range of ±1. The Skewness of cognitive-descriptive benefits variable is -0.231, functional benefits is -0.320, aesthetic tendencies is 0.415, customer commitment equals to 0.309 and performance variable is 0.309. Also, Kurtosis values of all variables are between +1 to -1, which indicates that the distributions of the basic variables were not significantly deviant from the normal distribution. So, variables' distribution may be rendered as normal or near to normal.

Table 2
Skewness and kurtosis values to assess the normality of variables

Variable	Skewness	Kurtosis
Cognitive-descriptive benefits	-0.231	-0.303
Functional benefits	-0.320	-0.294
Aesthetic tendencies	0.415	0.474
Customer commitment	0.309	-0.312
Performance	-0.449	-0.585

4.2. Correlation of variables

The results show that all relationships among variables were approved (P<0.05). There exists a positive relationship between variables of cognitive-descriptive benefits and functional benefits (r = 0.25). There exists a positive relationship between variables of cognitive-descriptive benefits and aesthetic tendencies (r = 0.24), a positive relationship between variables of cognitive-descriptive benefits and customer commitment (r = 0.39), a positive link between performance relationship and cognitive-descriptive benefits (r = 0.27), a positive relationship between functional benefits and aesthetic tendencies (r = 0.12), a positive relationship between functional benefits and customer commitment (r = 0.55), a positive link between functional benefits and performance relationship (r= 0.37), a positive relationship between aesthetic tendencies and customer commitment (r=0.33), a positive relationship between aesthetic tendencies and performance relationship (r = 0.11), a positive relationship between customer commitment and performance (r =0.43). The strongest relationship between was between the functional benefits and customer commitment with the correlation of 0.55.

Table 3
Correlation matrix of variables

Variable					
Cognitive-descriptive benefits	-				
Functional benefits	0.25**	-			
Aesthetic tendencies	0.24**	0.12*	-		
Customer commitment	0.39**	0.55**	0.33**	-	
Performance	0.27**	0.37**	0.11**	0.43**	-

** Correlation at a significance level of less than 0.01
* Correlation significant at the level of less than 0.05

4.3. SEM

Fig. 2 and Fig. 3 shows the model in standard coefficients and t-values, respectively. As we can observe, most coefficients are meaningful when the level of significance is one percent.

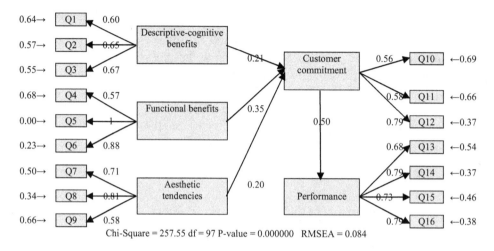

Fig. 2. The results of standard coefficients

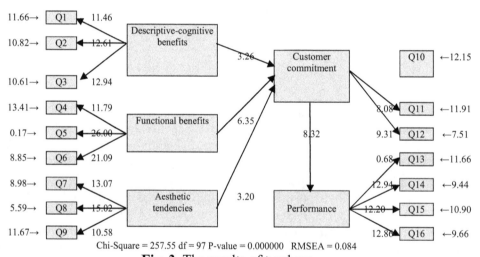

Fig. 3. The results of t-values

Fitted model indexes are listed in the Table 4 and by assessing all fitted indexes, it may be concluded that all achieved fitted indexes were acceptable and data were appropriately fitted to the model.

Table 4
Model's fitting indexes

Type of index	Indexes	Favorable amount	Result	Analysis
Absolute	Chi-Square	>0.05 P	< 0.05 P	Lack of good fitting
	GFI	> 0.9	0.91	Well fitted
	RMSEA	< 0.08	0.084	Approximately fitted
Relative	CFI	> 0.9	0.92	Well fitted
	NFI	> 0.9	0.89	Approximately fitted
	IFI	> 0.9	0.9	Well fitted
Concise or thrifty	AGFI	> 0.5	0.56	Well fitted
	PGFI	> 0.5	0.55	Well fitted
	df Chi-Square	2≤index≤3	2.65	Well fitted

4.4. Research hypotheses test

Table 5 presents the summary of testing the hypotheses of the survey. As it can be seen, the relationships and conceptual model show that all of the hypotheses have been confirmed.

Table 5
Research hypothesis test, standard coefficient and significance level

Hypothesis	Standard coefficient	Sig.	Result
Effects of cognitive-descriptive benefits of logo on customer commitment	0.21	$P < 0.01$	Confirmed
Effects of functional benefits of logo on customer commitment	0.35	$P < 0.01$	Confirmed
Effects of aesthetic tendencies of logo on customer commitment	0.2	$P < 0.01$	Confirmed
Effects of customer commitment on oil Company	0.5	$P < 0.01$	Confirmed

5. Discussion and conclusion

5.1. Discussion

First hypothesis test

The results suggest that at confidence level of 99%, cognitive-descriptive benefits of logo have a significant relationship with customer commitment ($P<0.01$). The positive standardized coefficient equals to 0.21. So, the first hypothesis of the research which stated that cognitive-descriptive benefits of logo affect customer commitment, is confirmed at 99% confidence level.

Second hypothesis test

The results show a significant relationship between functional benefits of logo and customer commitment ($P<0.01$). The results show a direct relationship or positive relationship between these two variables. Standardized coefficient of functional benefits of logo on customer commitment equals to 0.35. Totally, the results suggest that the research's second hypothesis which stated that functional benefits of logo affect customer commitment, is confirmed at 99% confidence level.

Third hypothesis test

The results suggest that at confidence level of 99%, aesthetic tendencies of logo have a significant relationship with customer commitment ($P<0.01$). The positive standardized coefficient equals to 0.20. So, the third hypothesis of the research which stated that aesthetic tendencies of logo affect customer commitment, is confirmed at 99% confidence level.

Fourth hypothesis test

The results show a significant relationship between customer commitment and Oil Company's performance ($P<0.01$). The results show a positive relationship. Standardized coefficient equals to 0.50. Totally, the results suggest that the research's fourth hypothesis which stated that customer commitment affects Oil Company's performance is confirmed at 99% confidence level.

5.2. Conclusion

Within the petroleum and petrochemical industry, having a strong, effective and communicative brand can be a competitive advantage. In other word, it should illustrate the benefits which the respective product brings to the customers and consumers. This study has performed an empirical investigation to study the role of the Sepahan Oil Company's trade show on the performance of the Company. The results showed that the managers should always consider their products' trademark from three perspectives of cognitive-descriptive benefits, functional benefits and aesthetic tendencies, and visual sign in a brand logo as an up-to-dated ongoing position. This study determined that managers need to continually review and consider brands as a powerful and influential tool in customer relationship management. A client's rapid detection of a brand logo does not mean that customer spends his/her time and resources to establish and maintain communications with a brand. Visual signs as a brand logo give a good opportunity to repeat presentation. This study found that brands with a logo were performing better than logos which were formed merely by name. According to the conducted research and achieved confirmation for all hypotheses, it is suggested that future studies would focus on factors affect descriptive-cognitive benefits (such as color, font and set of elements associated with a logo) to identify the relationships between and customers' behavior.

Acknowledgement

The authors would like to thank the anonymous referees for constructive comments on earlier version of this paper.

References

Kotler, P. (2009). *Marketing management: A south Asian perspective*. Pearson Education India.
Müller, B., Kocher, B., & Crettaz, A. (2013). The effects of visual rejuvenation through brand logos. *Journal of Business Research, 66*(1), 82-88.
Oliver, R. L. (1999). Whence consumer loyalty?. *The Journal of Marketing, 63*, 33-44.
Park, C. W., Eisingerich, A. B., Pol, G., & Park, J. W. (2013). The role of brand logos in firm performance. *Journal of Business Research, 66*(2), 180-187.
Rahimi Helari, M., & Hosseini, S.M. (2012). Effect of brand equity on consumer response (Case study Iranol Brand). *MBA thesis in Shahid Beheshti University*.
Shukla, P. (2011). Impact of interpersonal influences, brand origin and brand image on luxury purchase intentions: Measuring interfunctional interactions and a cross-national comparison. *Journal of world business, 46*(2), 242-252.
Thomson, M., MacInnis, D. J., & Park, C. W. (2005). The ties that bind: Measuring the strength of customers' emotional attachment to brands. *Journal of Consumer Psychology, 15*(1), 77–91.
Van den Bosch, A. L. M., de Jong, M. D. T., & Elving, W. J. L. (2005). How corporate visual identity supports reputation. *Corporate Communications, 10*(2), 108–116.
Van Riel, C. B. M., & Van den Ban, A. (2001). The added value of corporate logos. An empirical study. *European Journal of Marketing, 35*(3/4), 428–440.
Walsh, M. F., Winterich, K. P., & Mittal, V. (2010). Do logo redesigns help or hurt your brand? The role of brand commitment. *The Journal of Product and Brand Management, 19*(2), 76–84.
Woo, J. J., Chang-Hoan, C., & Hyuck Joon, K. (2008). The role of affect and cognition in consumer evaluations of corporate visual identity: Perspectives from the United States and Korea. *Journal of Brand Management, 15*(6), 382–398.

Integrating technology acceptance model and organizational innovativeness in the adoption of mobile commerce

Maruf Gbadebo Salimon[a*], Jibril Adewale Bamgbade[b], Ajulor Olusegun Nathaniel[c] and Tijani A. Adekunle[d]

[a,b]School of Business Management, Universiti Utara Malaysia, Malaysia
[c]Faculty of Liberal Arts, Houdegbe North American University, Benin Republic
[d]Faculty of Social Sciences, Lagos State University, Ojo, Lagos, Nigeria

CHRONICLE	ABSTRACT
Keywords: Adoption M-Commerce Organizational innovativeness TAM	The primary objective of this paper is to consider the influence of perceived usefulness, perceived ease of use, business innovativeness and product innovativeness on the adoption of mobile commerce. For the model of this study to be tested empirically, data were collected from mobile commerce users in Nigeria. A total of 405 questionnaires were used for the analysis via PLS-SEM. The results of the study revealed a positive and significant relationship between perceived usefulness, perceived ease of use, business innovativeness and product innovativeness. The results of this study provide some guides for mobile commerce practitioners.

1. Introduction

The rate of competition in the contemporary business environment is getting higher. In order to survive in this tough terrain, organizations have started to improve the process through which products and services are delivered with the objectives of retaining their customers (Wei et al., 2009). The need to improve this process has also been warranted by the proliferation of internet technology that ushered in Mobile Commerce (m-Commerce) (Thakur & Srivastava, 2013; Wei, et al., 2009). Today, m-commerce, which emanates from e-commerce has almost reached a climax in terms of the rate of adoption in Asia countries, while its acceptance in African nations seems to be lagging (Digital-Capital, 2014). Report from Digital-Capital (2014) reveals that Asian countries account for nearly half of the global m-commerce revenue, which stood at us$230 billion, while sales revenue from m-Commerce in developing countries is still at very low ebb. It has also been advocated that despite the tremendous benefits which users of m-Commerce can derive from its usage, the rate of adoption in a country like Nigeria is still low (Osakwe & Okeke, 2016) as m-Commerce is still at the infant stage in developing countries

* Corresponding author.
E-mail address: salimonmg@gmail.com (M. G. Salimon)

generally (Wei et al., 2009; Wong & Hiew, 2005). For instance, experience has also indicated that many customers are still reluctant to accept this new technology notwithstanding that it has much potential in developing countries (United Nations, 2002). Despite the low rate of adoption of m-Commerce in developing countries, strong empirical evidence to validate this seems to be very scarce as most past studies were conducted in developed and emerging nations such as USA, China and Taiwan (Wei et al., 2009). In fact, majority of the previous studies based their concepts on traditional and original TAM (Davis et al., 1989) and other models such as theory of planned behavior (TPB) while the concept of organizational innovativeness which can improve the rate of adoption among customers has been ignored, completely. Recently, facts have begun to emerge that TAM is the most parsimonious model due to its simplicity and capacity in explaining over 40% adoption behavior of technology (Rana et al., 2013; Venkatesh et al., 2003; Yousafzai et al., 2010). However, series of studies have argued that except that TAM is extended by integrating other variables in line with the content and context of the study, its predictive capacity may reduce (Alalwan et al., 2016; Riquelme & Rio, 2010; Shareef et al., 2014). In view of this, this study is extending original TAM by incorporating concept of organizational innovativeness as evidence has shown that apart from lack of usefulness and ease of use that constitute a barrier towards adoption of m-Commerce (Liao et al., 2007; Khalifa & Shen, 2008; Wei & Chong, 2009), lack of innovation among organizations offering the service is also an impediment to the rate of success of this technology based service. To the researchers' best knowledge, this study is the pioneer research that has extended TAM by incorporating the concept of organizational innovativeness to explain m-Commerce adoption especially in developing countries. This is a major contribution to the body of knowledge as majority of previous mobile commerce studies have only considered customer innovativeness (e.g., Lam et al., 2008; Bhatti, 2015; Chong, 2013; Nysveen et al., 2005; Kam-Sing Wong, 2012), while organizational innovativeness has been totally ignored.

The remainder of the article proceeds as follows. The literature review and theoretical background based on the conceptual framework (Fig. 1) of this study are discussed in the next section. The third section introduced our research method while the conclusion and limitation of the study are discussed in the final part.

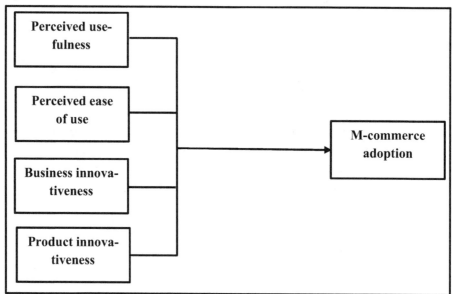

Fig. 1. Conceptual model

2. Literature Review and theoretical background

2.1 Mobile Commerce Adoption

M-Commerce is one of the emerging Information System (IS) based services. It is in the category of e-marketing, e-learning, and other related e-commerce internet based technology trends. Because of its newness, series of definitions have been advanced but no consensus has been reached among scholars about how it should be defined. Moshin et al. (2003) for instance, asserted that a line of difference can hardly be drawn between m-commerce and e-commerce as the former is a representation or an extension of the latter and which indicates that it is a form of e-commerce being used through wireless devices (Varshney & Vetter, 2002; Ashraf et al., 2016). Zhang et al. (2012) while corroborating Moshin et al. (2003) equally argued that m-commerce extends e-commerce as it affords business activities to be performed wirelessly using mobile devices. However, Feng et al. (2006) opined that m-commerce is a new invention which gives room for business opportunity and has different dimensions of mobility and broad reachability beyond e-commerce. Wei and Chong (2009) defined m-commerce as "any transaction, involving the transfer of ownership or rights to use goods and services, which is initiated and/or completed by using mobile access to computer-mediated networks with the help of mobile devices".

Despite lack of consensus about its definition, ample evidences are available about how the m-commerce positively influences the ways businesses are done across industries as it is increasingly becoming a significant strategy which organizations are employing to achieve improved performance (Chong, 2013). For instance, Thakur and Srivastava (2013) empirically proved that m-commerce affords organizations to offer personalized services to their customers while its ubiquities are assisting individual users to have instant access to usage without time and place restrictions (Chong, 2013). The prolific nature of m-commerce across the industries in the 21st has helped the practitioners generate over $1.3 trillion revenue globally while the figure is projected to reach $1.8 trillion in 2016 (Nassoura, 2013). Even though the advantages of m-commerce have been highlighted by many previous researchers, the rate of usage by individual users is still very low (Chong, 2013; Drossos & Giaglis, 2006) while arguments still exist among scholars about specific factors that can be used to effectively predict its adoption. Predicting users' adoption behavior is essential for the growth of m-commerce, but empirical studies to validate this seem to be sparse (Chong, 2013) while most previous scholars have used various fragmented factors with a large of them employing TAM as the main model (e.g. Chong et al., 2011; Wei et al., 2009). Importantly, known scholars such as Venkatesh and Bala (2008), Yousafzai et al., (2010), Venkatesh et al. (2003) proved that TAM is robust and parsimonious as it is capable of explaining over 40% variance of users' attitude and behavior. In spite of its robustness, Barki (2007) for instance argued that since the main constructs of TAM are perceived usefulness and perceived ease of use, the model cannot fully guide m-commerce providers on what motivates users to either adopt or reject m-commerce and if there are other precise factors that are pertinent to m-commerce such as organizational innovativeness in our case. In this view, this study is extending original TAM by integrating organizational innovativeness and through which m-commerce can be predicted effectively.

2.2. Perceived Usefulness (PU)

Perceived Usefulness is one of core constructs of TAM. Basically, scholars from the field of information science (IS) and other related studies have generally acknowledged the importance of PU as it determines the acceptability or otherwise of new innovation like m-commerce (Amin et al., 2013; Wei et al., 2009). It is often seen as a subjective probability that when individuals use a system, their tasks would be accelerated (Jahangir & Begum, 2008). Rouibah et al. (2011) refer to PU as the degree to which customers believe that adopting IT will yield important value for them. Amin et al. (2014) see PU as the general perception and evaluation done by mobile users with respect to the usability of 3G phones. Davis (1989, pg. 320) consideres PU as the "degree to which a person believes that using a particular system would enhance his or her job performance". Succinctly, this study defines PU as the benefits which users of mobile commerce may derive from the usage of the m-commerce. Such benefits or values may include facilitation of the process in locating a store, purchasing/selling of services and products, paying utility bills, executing banking transactions and even joining social networks (Khalifa & Shen, 2008; Nassuora, 2013; Hsu & Wang, 2011; Hanafizadeh et al., 2014; Yadav et al., 2016). Without these values, users will not be willing to adopt information system like m-commerce while the objectives of expending huge amount on m-commerce facilities may not be achieved by the service providers (Pikkarainen et al., 2004). This therefore indicates the users will rapidly adopt m-commerce if the service providers are able to provide superior benefits over other alternatives (Tsu Wei et al., 2009; Yadav et al., 2016) and this will further signifies the success and acceptance of the platform. Based on this, the following hypothesis is formulated

H1. Perceived usefulness has a positive and significant relationship on adoption of m-commerce

2.3. Perceived Ease of use (PEU)

PEU is another main construct of TAM which denotes the degree to which an individual perceives that using a new technology would not be hard. According to Davis (1989), perceived ease of use "is the degree to which a person believes that using a particular system would be free of effort". Amin et al., (2014) defined PEOU as the overall perception of users relating to the convenience of purchasing a mobile system via their mobile phone. In essence, a system may be deemed useful, but perceived to be difficult as such a system is not configured to 'ease' the task of the users. A system may also be regarded to be too complex if the resultant-benefits are being outweighed by the efforts applied in using the system. It therefore connotes that users would be wary of the efforts required to operate a new system like m-commerce and the more complexity involved in the process the more the users would avoid the system (Aboelmaged & Gebba, 2013). A number of complexities such as small display screen, difficulty in inputting data, internet connectivity, can constitute a barrier that may inhibit ease of browsing, information identification and performance of other transactions which could make individual users to have memorable experiences (Curran & Meuter, 2005; Deb & Lomo-David, 2014; Kleijnen et al., 2004; Porter & Donthu, 2006, 2005; der Heijden et al., 2003). This is also in line with the arguments of Chong et al. (2010) as issue of designing an interface that is not interactive enough, especially for a mobile-based application can reduce the functionalities and accompany benefits of mobile system. Perceived ease of use has been confirmed to be instrumental in many studies such as electronic banking adoption (Salimon et al., 2016) internet usage (e.g., Abedalaziz et al., 2013; Teo et al., 2003), mobile instant messaging (e.g., Lauricella & Kay, 2013), social networking (Bilgihan et al., 2016) and a host of others. Based on this, the following hypothesis is formulated

H2. Perceived ease of use has a positive and significant relationship to adopt m-commerce.

2.4 Business innovativeness

One of the first studies that conceptualized innovativeness is Rogers and Shoemaker (1971. p. 27), where innovativeness was referred to as "the degree to which an individual is relatively earlier in adopting new ideas than the average member of his social system". The main focus of this conceptualization was the apparent degree of innovativeness in behavioural patterns. Innovation literature has also demonstrated that business innovativeness is an important model for e-commerce adoption in firms, because even established firms are expected to continuously innovate to mitigate the threat of changes and competition resulting from the emerging IT environment (Lin & Hsia, 2011). Firms' business innovativeness entails value-added activities in the production processes and presenting new goods and services using new business ideas (Dess & Lumpkin, 1997; Knight, 1997). In addition, in the present competitive era, firms need to continuously create new products, discover new marketing approaches, and fashion out new production lines in order to improve their competitive performance and retain their customer base (Thakur et al., 2012). These strategies will allow firms to attain value addition for their customers, stimulate higher profitability and market share, and an improved organizational image. However, firms' good strategies alone are not enough for them to cope in the present dynamic business environment. It is expected that firms' business innovativeness should incorporate operational flexibility to survive within the present competitive market. However, the environment is taking a new dimension with the recent diversity in customer's behavioral patterns, their innovation attributes, and risk adoption levels (Lee et al., 2010). While previous studies have indicated how business innovativeness enhances firms' financial performance (e.g., Akgün, et al., 2014), assists in developing firm's core competencies and capabilities (Damanpour, et al., 2009), and improves firm's efficiency to detect and utilize available resources (Habtay, 2012), its influence on consumers' adoption of m-commerce has been largely ignored. A number of IS researchers have suggested that m-commerce is one of the most important models that could easily get prompted by technological innovation, as it is an emerging platform for the expansion of access to transactions through mobile or handheld devices, and by operating wireless communication technologies (Lin, 2011). In this manner, business innovativeness is becoming more challenging as investing in such innovation not only requires a good understanding of the market diversities, but also a conscious recognition of the evolving user's preferences, which exerts a huge influence on firm's performance (Robinson et al., 2005; Belanche, et al., 2012). Thus, business innovativeness is posited to result in more positive attitude toward the adoption of m-commerce, leading to the following hypothesis:

H3. Business innovativeness has a significant and positive relationship with m-commerce adoption.

2.5 Product innovativeness and m-commerce adoption

Organizational success and sustained competitive advantage are some of the outcomes of organizational innovativeness. However, in spite of the continuous efforts in product design and marketing, most new products have recorded incessant failure (Srinivasan et al., 2009). While there has been several innovation studies, the literature mainly focused on organizational innovations in terms of product development and characteristics (Shmueli & Koppius, 2010; Greenhalgh et al., 2004; Rogers, 1995; Wejnert, 2002). To date, much of the literature on mobile commerce adoption placed emphasis on customer innovativeness without much effort being directed towards firm innovative capacities. Whereas, product success is largely dependent on firms' ability to constantly stimulate innovative ideas, and compete favorably with customer-oriented products with stylish yet aptly functional contents (Gecevska et al., 2010). In spite of the imperative for firms to continually develop e-commerce delivery processes for competitive advantage (Patricio et al., 2008), we remain largely uninformed about the effect of firms' product innovativeness to aid consumer decision making to adopt mobile transactions.

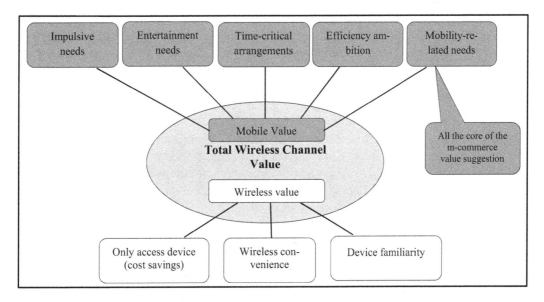

Fig. 2. Mobile commerce value elements (adapted from Anckar & d'Incau, 2002)

Several innovativeness dimensions have also been examined to influence mobile transaction adoption. In particular, Yang (2005) demonstrated the direct effect of innovativeness on mobile commerce in the South East Asian countries, just like Leung and Antypas (2001) highlighted how product efficiency is improved in firms through mobile commerce by offering new avenues through which interaction with customers are perfected. Five factors for wireless services were listed by Anckar and d'Incau (2002) in their study on mobile commerce value creation, as illustrated in Fig. 2.

Thus, in spontaneous needs, plans and decisions are not essential for m-commerce adoption like purchase decisions that involve small amounts of money. The entertainment needs digital games and music. Time-criticality in mobile purchases requires the platform to satisfy consumers' time-critical needs with prompt and to-the-point interactions. In addition, as many customers nowadays prefer more effective ways of doing simple everyday activities, m-commerce efficiency needs and ambitions become a necessary time saver for purchases like mobile banking and travel reservations. According to Clarke (2008), mobility-related needs such as routing and tracking, location-based services and roadside services are not only of exclusive value in the entire mobile settings, but also constitute an essential part of mobile commerce value proposition. Since m-commerce offers a direct avenue to communicate with consumers via a mobile handheld, without space and time constraints, firms should utilize mobile commerce and communication as an innovative and interactive platform for business success. As innovation generates more marketing opportunities for firms, mobile media platforms should be utilized thanks to its superiority over the traditional communication (Chowdhury et al. 2010). Product innovativeness is likely to be associated with m-commerce adoption, resulting in the following hypothesis:

H4. Product innovativeness has a significant and positive relationship with m-commerce adoption.

3. Methods

3.1. Sample and Procedure

We employed mall intercept method to collect the data of the study from users of mobile commerce in a popular shopping mall in Lagos State, Nigeria using self-administered questionnaires. In using the mall intercept, the researcher first approached the potential respondents in order to ask for their consent of participation after which the questionnaires were administered. This method was used due to its veracity of having access to likely respondents within a short period of time, as it equally assists the researchers to have personal interactions with the respondents to screen the respondents and as well as stimulate their interest to participate in the research and its common use in marketing research (e.g. Grace & O'cass, 2005; Maronick 1995; Prakash & Venkatachalam, 2016).The questionnaire has two sections: The first section requires the respondents to provide answers to demographic information, while the second part asks some questions on the variables of the study. The questionnaire made use of a five-point Likert scale, which ranged from "strongly agree" to "strongly disagree".

All items measuring the latent constructs were adapted from previous studies that have validated the items. The items of mobile commerce adoption were adapted from Khalifa and Shen (2008), Luarn and Lin (2005), and Thakur and Srivastava (2013), perceived usefulness items were adapted from Khalifa and Shen (2008) and Wei et al. (2009), perceived ease of use items were selected from Amin et al. (2014), Lee et al., (2015) and Wei et al., (2009) while business innovativeness and product innovativeness items were also adapted from Kamaruddeen et al. (2012). Out of 430 questionnaires that were collected, 25 were discarded due to inappropriate fillings and which implies that only 405 questionnaires were used for the analysis indicating a response rate of 94 per cent.

Based on the demographic information, 57.2 per cent 42.8 percent were males and females respectively. With regards to their age range, majority of the respondents (36.5 per cent) were aged between 25 and 29 years old, 27.0 per cent of the respondents were aged between 30 and 34 years old and 15.8 per cent of the respondents were aged between 35 and 39 years old. This was followed by 10.8 per cent between 45 and 50 years old and 9.9 per cent between 40 and 44 years old. In terms of employment, 48.0 per cent of the respondents were private companies employees, 44.0 per cent were government employees, 8.0 per cent belongs to others. In terms of the marital status range, married respondents contributed largely to the sample (62 per cent), followed by single (34.6 per cent) and divorced respondents (3.4 per cent) (see Table 1).

Table 1
Demographics of respondents

	Frequency	%
Gender		
Male	232	57.2
Female	173	42.8
Age		
Age 20 and below 30	148	36.5
Age between 30 and 34	109	27.0
Age between 35 and 39	64	15.8
Age between 40 and 44	40	9.9
Age between 45 and 50	44	10.8
Employment Status		
Private Employment	195	48
Government Employees	179	44
Others	31	8
Marital Status		
Married	251	62
Single	140	34.6
Divorced	14	3.4

4. Data Analysis and Results

4.1 Assessment of measurement Model

In order to analyze generated hypotheses, the researchers employed Partial least squares structural equation modelling (PLS-SEM). The PLS-SEM is regarded as a covariance based technique that contemporary academic researchers use in prediction or in the development of theory (Hair et al., 2017; Lowry & Gaskin, 2014). In using the PLS-SEM, a two-step analytical approach is suggested by Anderson and Gerbing (1988). In the first-step, a measurement model was evaluated while in the second-step, a structural model was equally analyzed.

For the purpose of analyzing the measurement model, factor analysis was performed in order to establish the fitness of the model. Hair et al. (2014) argue that reliability and validity are the two important criteria that are used to evaluate the theoretical soundness of a model. Measuring the reliability requires that the internal consistency reliability be established first. This criterion can be achieved through assessment of the values of composite reliability (CR) for each construct. Construct validity which is the second criterion that must be established before further analysis can be performed comprises convergent validity and discriminant validity (Hair et al., 2010). Convergent validity refers to the degree to which a measure positively correlates with another measures of the same variable (Hair et al., 2014). This therefore suggests that items of the same construct must share a degree of variance or converge. It has been suggested that for convergent validity to be ascertained, it is mandatory that the outer loadings of the items and as well as average variance extracted (AVE) must be considered (Hair et al., 2014). Hair et al. (2017) argue that the loadings and AVE must not be less than 0.50 and 0.70 respectively. Fig. 2 shows the result of the measurement model of the study. As shown in Table 2, all the values of loadings, and average variance explained (AVE) are greater than 0.50 while that of composite reliability and Cronbach alpha are higher than 0.70. This therefore implies that the measurement model of this research is theoretically sound while the convergent validity has been established. Discriminant validity based on empirical standards refers to the degree to which a particular construct in the model is quite different from other constructs (Hair et al., 2014). This shows that the construct is unique by capturing the phenomenon which other constructs in the model do not capture. The discriminant validity can be ascertained by ensuring that AVE for each set of variables is greater than the squared correlations values of other constructs. Table 3 shows that this threshold has been achieved following Fornell and Larcker's (1981) approach.

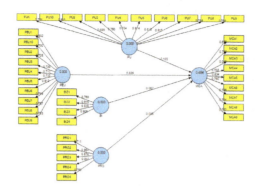

Fig. 3. Measurement model

Table 2
Factors Loading Significance

Constructs and items	Loading
Business innovativeness	AVE: 0.741; α: 0.882; CR:0.919
BIZ1	0.769
BIZ2	0.915
BIZ3	0.846
BIZ4	0.906
Perceived ease of use	AVE: 0.571; α: 0.916; CR:0.930
PEU1	0.802
PEU2	0.725
PEU3	0.736
PEU4	0.710
PEU5	0.732
PEU6	0.812
PEU7	0.789
PEU8	0.757
PEU9	0.783
PEU10	0.700
Product innovativeness	AVE: 0.666; α: 0.874; CR:0.908
PRO1	0.711
PRO2	0.854
PRO3	0.878
PRO4	0.837
PRO5	0.789
Perceived usefulness	AVE: 0.600; α: 0.925; CR:0.937
PU1	0.731
PU2	0.699
PU3	0.760
PU4	0.704
PU5	0.814
PU6	0.815
PU7	0.817
PU8	0.798
PU9	0.790
PU10	0.803
Mobile commerce adoption	AVE: 0.588; α: 0.912; CR:0.928
MCA1	0.675
MCA2	0.738
MCA3	0.803
MCA4	0.758
MCA5	0.834
MCA6	0.790
MCA7	0.795
MCA8	0.731

Table 3
Results of construct reliability and validity

		1	2	3	4	5
1	Business innovativeness	*0.86*				
2	Mobile commerce adoption	0.553	*0.767*			
3	Perceived ease of use	0.603	0.527	*0.756*		
4	Product innovativeness	0.705	0.575	0.629	*0.816*	
5	Perceived usefulness	0.610	0.632	0.693	0.652	*0.77*

Diagonal elements are the square roots of the AVE of each construct. For adequate discriminant validity, diagonal elements should be greater than the corresponding off-diagonal elements.

4.2 Assessment of Structural Model

The assessment of structural model is required as it shows the relationship between latent constructs that the researchers hypothesized. In order to ascertain the significant value of loadings, as well as that of path coefficients, a bootstrapping of 5000 subsamples was performed (Hair et al., 2017). Fig 4, and Table 4 reveal the result of the structural model.

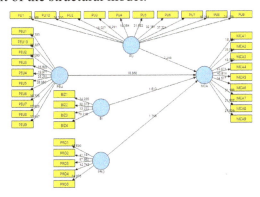

Fig. 4. Structural Model

Table 4
Testing results of main effect structural equation model

Hypotheses	Beta	SE	t- value	p-value	Decision
Business innovativeness	0.067	0.045	1.610	0.07	Supported
Perceived ease of use	0.829	0.047	18.666	0.00	Supported
Product innovativeness	0.086	0.049	1.756	0.04	Supported
Perceived usefulness	0.122	0.055	2.246	0.01	Supported

Dependent variable: Mobile commerce adoption

Table 4 shows the PLS outputs of the structural model as it is equally depicted in Fig. 2 which reveals the path coefficients, and coefficient determinants (R^2) of each construct. As shown in the table, perceived usefulness was significantly related to mobile commerce adoption (β = 0.122, t.2.246) thereby supporting H1. Perceived ease of use was also a significant predictor of mobile commerce adoption (β = 0.829, t.18.666), likewise business innovativeness (β = 0.067, t.1.610), and product innovativeness (β = 0.086, t.1.756), making H2, H3, and H4 to be supported.

4.3 Predictive Relevance of the model (Q2)

Hair et al. (2014) suggest additionally step to ascertain the theoretical soundness of a model by using the StoneGeisser's Q2 measure (Geisser, 1974; Stone, 1974). The Q2 value assists the researcher to establish the predictive power of the model apart from the coefficient of determination (R^2) as it shows the degree to which the values observed are recaptured by the structural model and its approximating yardsticks' (Luqman et al., 2016). The value of Q^2 in the structural model that is higher than zero for a given reflective-construct is an indication that the model's path has predictive relevance required for a given endogenous variable (Hair et al., 2014). For researchers to establish the predictive relevance, blindfolding procedure is required employing D = 7 omission distance (Hair, et al., 2012) and this will assist the researcher to obtain the Q^2 value which is based on the 'cross-validated redundancy' that is integrated in the PLS-SEM (Hair et al., 2014). As shown in Table 5, the Q2 value of 0.399 is higher than zero indicating that the model in this study has required predictive relevance.

Table 5
Predictive Relevance of the Endogenous Construct

Endogenous constructs	R^2	Q^2
MCA	0.694	0.399

4.3 Effect Size (F^2)

The purpose of effect size (F^2) is to assess the contribution of exogenous construct to the value of coefficient determinant (R2) of the endogenous construct. As shown in Table 6, perceived ease of use and perceived usefulness show large to small effect size.

Table 6
Effect Size

	MCA (dependent variable)	
	f^2	*Effect size*
Business innovativeness	0.003	None
Perceived ease of use	0.77	Large
Product innovativeness	0.01	None
Perceived usefulness	0.02	Small

5. Discussion

This study employs TAM and organizational innovativeness to explain adoption of mobile commerce in a developing country, Nigeria. In this instance, TAM was extended by incorporating business innovativeness and product innovativeness with perceived usefulness and perceived ease of use. The study hypothesizes four relationships. The First hypothesis (H1) which states a positive relationship between perceived usefulness and mobile commerce adoption was supported. Previous studies have equally proved that perceived usefulness is an important factor that can accelerate the rate of adoption of IS/IT such as mobile commerce (Wei et al., 2009; Yadav et al., 2016), e-commerce (Guriting & Ndubisi, 2006; Jahangir & Begum, 2008) and e-banking (Aboelmaged & Gebba, 2013; Tan et al., 2010). These findings have shown that the adoption of mobile technology is majorly anchored on the perception of usefulness by the consumers as the consumers would only increase the rate of usage if, for instance, they can retrieve required information with urgency, perform the transaction seamlessly and achieve their daily and other mobile commerce transaction objectives (Wei et al., 2009).

The second hypothesis (H2) which states a positive relationship between perceived ease of use and mobile commerce adoption was also accepted. A number of scholars have equally reported that the easiness that is associated with IS/IT based services such as social networking (Wamba, et al., 2017), e-government (Carter et al., 2016; Susanto & Aljoza, 2015), e-insurance (Leeet al., 2015) and mobile banking (Safeena et al., 2011) is a core determinant of adoption of these latest technology trends. The essence of these findings indicate that the absence of face-to-face interaction that is common in an internet enabled services platforms such as mobile commerce requires such platform to be easily used with regards to user friendliness as this will reduce the difficulty that may be associated with the usage of the services (Chong et al., 2010). This has been initially reiterated by Pikarrainen et al. (2004) that a system that is regarded to be easily learned and used is likely to be accepted than otherwise.

The third hypothesis (H3) which states a positive relationship between business innovativeness and mobile commerce adoption was also accepted. This relationship has been previously confirmed by a number of studies indicating that innovativeness in all its ramification can improve business performance, such as adoption of mobile commerce (Aragon-Correa et al., 2007; Erdem et al., 2011; Garcia-Morales et al., 2008; Noruzy et al., 2013; Samad, 2012; Yıldız et al., 2014). The finding indicates that continuous changes in customer needs coupled with a competitive business environment require business organizations to be innovative in their approaches through new methods and systems (Yıldız et al., 2014). Experience has shown that any organization that resists innovation will likely fizzle out since its performance will continue to decrease while businesses that are innovative will improve in performance (high rate of mobile commerce adoption).

The fourth hypothesis (H4) states a positive relationship between product innovativeness and mobile commerce adoption was supported. Product innovativeness which indicates novelty, perceived newness, uniqueness or originality of products has equally been found to improve performance in different studies (e.g., Henard & Szymanski, 2001). The result points to the fact that mobile commerce companies that can introduce new attributes which users perceived to be unique, perhaps with functionality, ease of use and usability will attract more patronage thereby increase the rate of adoption of new innovation such as mobile commerce. In line with the argument of Anckar and d'Incau (2002) embedding mobile commerce wireless value that will take care of impulsive needs, saves cost and gives convenience will make the rate of adoption to be increased.

6. Conclusion

Mobile commerce is one of the current waves of information technology. However, for the purpose of coping with the high velocity of changes that are taking place in the contemporary global competitive market, and especially in the mobile commerce industry, it is highly important that mobile commerce providers should place priority on ensuring that the platform is reconfigured and strengthened for the purpose of serving the current users effectively and to attract a large number of potential users. For instance, to increase the rate of adoption, our findings regarding the perceived usefulness with respect to the benefits of mobile commerce; perceived ease of use concerning easiness that surrounds the usage; business innovativeness and product innovativeness regarding the incorporation of wireless value (cost savings access device, wireless convenience, device family familiarity) and mobile value (impulsive needs, entertainment needs, time-critical arrangements, efficiency ambition and mobility related needs) (see Fig. 2) should be seriously considered as these will perform a critical role in the transformation of m-commerce.

The findings of this research with respect to PU and PEU therefore indicate that while designing m-commerce platforms, it is essential that the designers ensure that the platforms are useful, and easily used. This therefore points to the fact that m-commerce designers should provide improved and variety of services, design the platform to meet the needs of the users while the users face less physical and mental rigor when using the platform. The usefulness of mobile commerce against any other platform such as e-commerce is that users can also use the platform to perform other internet based functions such as reading news, sending email, or watching videos apart from the core uses of the platform. Configuring the platform to comply with this ensures that the users are equally attracted largely. Aside, the easiness that the designers may embed with the platform may ease the difficulty that will likely be associated with the physical characteristics of mobile devices with respect to tiny display screen, strain in inputting data and others that can inhibit m-commerce adoption. In particular, it is important that a reminder be sent to mobile commerce managers and practitioners that innovation as discussed in this study would not just arrive overnight but comes through insight that inspires change which can be initiated through product or business process (Wong, 2012). In this regard, it is imperative for mobile commerce providers to be flexible by ensuring that their mind is opened while permitting their product and process engineers to think, dream, and initiate new ideas as long as organization's resources allow as this is the greatest way to encourage innovation that would improve the rate of adoption of mobile commerce.

This study extended TAM by adding product business innovativeness and product innovativeness which previous researchers have largely ignored. By adding these variables, the simplicity of TAM has been retained while its parsimony is equally improved. By the integration of organizational innovations concept with TAM, this study presents a considerable improvement in predictive ability of the proposed model. Asides, this study used PLS-SEM to predict and understand important constructs which can improve the m-commerce adoption.

7. Limitation of the study

This research has a number of limitations despite that it is expected to contribute to the body of knowledge and practice in the mobile commerce industry in Nigeria. First, the study is quantitative and cross-sectional nature in nature; it only captured and analyzed a limited number of factors that can influence mobile commerce adoption in a developing country. In this regard, a qualitative and longitudinal research should be done to have a broad comprehension and perspective of other factors that are not covered in this study. In line with the recommendations of previous researchers, coming studies can incorporate factors such as security-privacy, consumer self-efficacy, perceived risk and trust (Chong, 2013; Faqih & Jaradat, 2015) for the purpose of understanding and predicting adoption of mobile commerce effectively. Second, this study was conducted in a developing country where the level of technology usage and organizational innovation is still coming up. In this regard, the generalization of our findings should be applied with caution, especially to other developed and developing countries. In this regard, further studies may be conducted in other developing countries based on multi-countries comparison using the model of this study. If this is done, the veracity of our model can further be ascertained.

References

Abedalaziz, N., Jamaluddin, S., & Chin, H. L. (2013). Measuring attitudes toward computer and internet usage among postgraduate students in Malaysia. *The Turkish Online Journal of Educational Technology*, *12 (*2), 200-214.

Aboelmaged, M. G., & Gebba, T. R. (2013). Mobile Banking Adoption: An Examination of Technology Acceptance Model and Theory of Planned Behavior. *International Journal of Business Research and Development*, *2* (1), 35–50.

Akgün, A. E., Ince, H., Imamoglu, S. Z., Keskin, H., & Kocoglu, İ. (2014). The mediator role of learning capability and business innovativeness between total quality management and financial performance. *International Journal of Production Research*, *52(*3), 888-901.

Alalwan, A. A., Dwivedi, Y., Rana, N. P., & Williams, M. D. (2016). Consumer adoption of mobile banking in Jordan: examining the role of usefulness, ease of use, perceived risk and self-efficacy. *Journal of Enterprise Information Management*, *29 (*1), 118-139.

Amin, M., Rezaei, S., & Abolghasemi, M. (2014). User satisfaction with mobile websites: the impact of perceived usefulness (PU), perceived ease of use (PEOU) and trust, *Nankai Business Review International*, *5 (*3), 258-274.

Anckar, B., & D'incau, D. (2002). Value creation in mobile commerce: Findings from a consumer survey. *Journal of Information Technology Theory and Application*,*4(*43), 43-64.

Anderson, J. C., & Gerbing, D. W. (1988). Structural equation modeling in practice: A review and recommended two-step approach. *Psychological Bulletin*, *103(*3), 411-423.

Aragon-Correa, J.A., Garcia-Morales, V.J. & Cordon-Poza, E. (2007). Leadership and orgaizational learning's role on innovation and performance: Lesson from Spain. *Industrial Marketing Management*, 36 (1), 349-359.

Ashraf, A. R., Thongpapanl, N., Menguc, B., & Northey, G. (2016). The role of m-commerce readiness in emerging and developed markets. *Journal of International Marketing*, 25 (2), 25-51.

Barki, H. (2007). Quo vadis TAM? *Journal of the AIS*, 8 (1), 211–218.

Bhatti, T. (2015), Exploring factors influencing the adoption of mobile commerce. *The Journal of Internet Banking and Commerce*, *12 (*3), 1-13.

Bilgihan, A., Barreda, A., Okumus, F., and Nusair, K. (2016). Consumer perception of knowledge-sharing in travel-related Online Social Networks. *Tourism Management, 52* (1), 287-296.

Carter, L., Weerakkody, V., Phillips, B., & Dwivedi, Y. K. (2016). Citizen adoption of e-government services: Exploring citizen perceptions of online services in the United States and United Kingdom. *Information Systems Management, 33 (*2), 124-140.

Chong, A. Y. L. (2013). A two-staged SEM-neural network approach for understanding and predicting the determinants of m-commerce adoption. *Expert Systems with Applications,* 40 (4), 1240-1247.

Chong, A. Y. L., Chan, F. T. S., & Ooi, K. B. (2011). Predicting consumer decisions to adopt Mobile Commerce: Cross country empirical examination between China and Malaysia. *Decision Support Systems*, 53(1), 34–43.

Chowdhury, H. K., Parvin, N., Weitenberner, C., and Becker, M. (2010). Consumer attitude toward mobile advertising in an emerging market: An empirical study. *Marketing,12(*2), 206-216.

Clarke III, I. (2008). Emerging value propositions for m-commerce, *Journal of Business Strategies, 25(*2), 41-57.

Curran, J. M., & Meuter, M. L. (2005). Self-service technology adoption: comparing three technologies, *Journal of Services Marketing, 19 (*2), 103-113.

Damanpour, F., Walker, R. M., & Avellaneda, C. N. (2009). Combinative effects of innovation types and organizational performance: A longitudinal study of service organizations. *Journal of management studies, 46 (*4), 650-675.

Davis, F. D. (1989). Perceived usefulness, perceived ease of use and user acceptance of information technology. *MIS Quarterly, 13(*3), 319–340.

der Heijden, H., Verhagen, T. & Creemers, M. (2003). Understanding online purchase intentions: contributions from technology and trust perspectives. *European Journal of Information Systems, 12* (1), 41-48.

Dess, G. G., Lumpkin, G. T., & Covin, J. G. (1997). Entrepreneurial strategy making and firm performance: Tests of contingency and configurational models. *Strategic Management Journal, 18*(9), 677-695.

Drossos, D., & Giaglis, G. M. (2006). Mobile advertising effectiveness: An exploratory study. In IEEE international conference on mobile business. Copenhagen, 26–27th June.

Erdem, B., Gökdeniz, A. & Met, Ö. (2011). The relationship between innovation and business performance: A case study of five star hotels' managements in Antalya. *Faculty of Economy and Administrative Sciences Journal, 26* (2), 77-112.

Faqih, K. M., & Jaradat, M. I. R. M. (2015). Assessing the moderating effect of gender differences and individualism-collectivism at individual-level on the adoption of mobile commerce technology: TAM3 perspective. *Journal of Retailing and Consumer Services, 22*(1), 37-52.

Feng, H., Hoegler, T. & Stucky, W. (2006). Exploring the critical success factors for mobile commerce. *Proceedings of the International Conference on Mobile Business (ICMB'06)*, Copenhagen, Denmark.

Fornell, C., & Larcker, D. F. (1981). Evaluating structural equation models with unobservable and measurement error. *Journal of Marketing Research, 18*(1), 39- 50.

Garcia-Morales, J.V., Llorens-Montes, F.J. & Verdu-Jover, A.J. (2008). The effects of transformational leadership on organizational performance through knowledge and innovation. *British Journal of Management, 19*(1), 299-319.

Gecevska, V., Chiabert, P., Anisic, Z., Lombardi, F., & Cus, F. (2010). Product lifecycle management through innovative and competitive business environment. *Journal of Industrial Engineering and Management, 3(*2), 323-336.

Grace, D., & O'cass, A. (2005). Examining the effects of service brand communications on brand evaluation. *Journal of Product & Brand Management, 14(*2), 106-116.

Greenhalgh, T., Robert, G., Macfarlane, F., Bate, P., & Kyriakidou, O. (2004). Diffusion of innovations in service organizations: systematic review and recommendations. *Milbank Quarterly, 82*(4), 581-629.

Guriting, P. & Ndubisi, A.O. (2006). Borneo online banking: evaluating customer perceptions and behavioral intention. *Management Research News*, 29(1/2), 6-15.

Hair, J. F., Anderson, R. E., Babin, B. J., & Black, W. C. (2010). *Multivariate data analysis: A global perspective* (Vol. 7). Upper Saddle River, NJ: Pearson.

Hair, J. F., Sarstedt, M., Ringle, C. M., and Mena, J. A. (2012). An assessment of the use of partial least squares structural equation modeling in marketing research. *Journal of the Academy of Marketing Science*, 40(3), 414-433.

Hair Jr, J., Sarstedt, M., Hopkins, L., & G. Kuppelwieser, V. (2014). Partial least squares structural equation modeling (PLS-SEM) An emerging tool in business research. *European Business Review*, 26(2), 106-121.

Hair Jr, J., Hult, F., & GTM, R. C., & Sarstedt, M.(2017). *A primer on partial least squares structural equation modeling. (PLS-SEM)(2nd edition ed.)* Sage Publications, Thousand Oaks.

Hanafizadeh, A., Behboudi, M., Koshksaray, A.A. & Tabar, M.J.S. (2014). Mobile-banking adoption by Iranian bank clients. *Telematics and Informatics*, 31(1), 62-78.

Habtay, S. R. (2012). A firm-level analysis on the relative difference between technology-driven and market-driven disruptive business model innovations. *Creativity and Innovation Management*, 21 (3), 290-303.

Henard, D. H., & Szymanski, D. M. (2001). Why some new products are more successful than others. *Journal of marketing Research*, 38(3), 362-375.

Hsu, C.L. & Wang, C.F. (2011). Investigating customer adoption behaviors in mobile financial services. *International Journal of Mobile Communications*, 9(5), 477-494.

Jahangir, N., & Begum, N. (2008). The role of perceived usefulness, perceived ease of use, security and privacy, and customer attitude to engender customer adaptation in the context of electronic banking. *African Journal of Business Management*, 2 (2), 32-40.

Kamaruddeen, A. M., Yusof, N. A., Said, I., & Pakir, A. H. K. (2012). Organizational factors and innovativeness of housing developers. *American Journal of Applied Sciences*, 9 (12), 1953-1966.

Kam-Sing Wong, S. (2012). The influence of green product competitiveness on the success of green product innovation: Empirical evidence from the Chinese electrical and electronics industry. *European Journal of Innovation Management*, 15(4), 468-490.

Khalifa, M., & Ning Shen, K. (2008). Explaining the adoption of transactional B2C mobile commerce. *Journal of Enterprise Information Management*, 21(2), 110-124.

Kleijnen, M., Wetzels, M., & Ruyter, K. D. (2004). Consumer acceptance of wireless finance. *Journal of Financial Services Marketing*, 8(3), 206-217.

Knight, G. (1997). Cross-cultural reliability and validity of a scale to measure firm entrepreneurial orientation. *Journal of Business Venturing*, 12(1), 213-225.

Lauricella, S., & Kay, R. (2013). Exploring the use of text and instant messaging in higher education classrooms. *Research in Learning Technology*, 25(1), 1-12.

Lam, S. Y., Chiang, J., & Parasuraman, A. (2008). The effects of the dimensions of technology readiness on technology acceptance: An empirical analysis. *Journal of Interactive Marketing*, 22(4), 19-39.

Lee, V. H., Lam, S. Y., Ooi, K. B., & Safa, M. S. (2010). Structural analysis of TQM and its impact on customer satisfaction and innovation. *International Journal of Modelling in Operations Management*, 1(2), 157-179.

Lee, C. Y., Tsao, C. H., & Chang, W. C. (2015). The relationship between attitude toward using and customer satisfaction with mobile application services: an empirical study from the life insurance industry. *Journal of Enterprise Information Management*, 28(5), 680-697.

Leung, K., & Antypas, J. (2001). Improving returns on m-commerce investments. *The Journal of Business Strategy*, 22(5), 12-13.

Liao, C. H., Tsou, C. W., & Huang, M. F. (2007). Factors influencing the usage of 3G mobile services in Taiwan. *Online Information Review*, 31(6), 759-774.

Lin, H. F. (2011). An empirical investigation of mobile banking adoption: The effect of innovation attributes and knowledge-based trust. *International Journal of Information Management*, *31*(3), 252-260.

Lin, L. M., & Hsia, T. L. (2011). Core capabilities for practitioners in achieving e-business innovation. *Computers in Human Behavior*, *27*(5), 1884-1891.

Lowry, P. B., & Gaskin, J. (2014). Partial least squares (PLS) structural equation modeling (SEM) for building and testing behavioral causal theory: When to choose it and how to use it. *IEEE Transactions on Professional Communication*, *57*(2), 123-146.

Luarn, P., & Lin, H. H. (2005). Toward an understanding of the behavioral intention to use mobile banking. *Computers in Human Behavior*, *21*(6), 873-891.

Luqman, A., Razak, R. C., Ismail, M., & Alwi, M. A. M. (2016). Predicting continuance intention in mobile commerce usage activities: The Effects of Innovation Attributes. In *8th International Conference on Humanities and Social Sciences held on* (pp. 1-29).

Maronick, T. J. (1995). An empirical investigation of consumer perceptions of "made in USA" claims. *International Marketing Review*, *12*(3), 15-30.

Moshin, M., Mudtadir, R., & Ishaq, A.F.M. (2003). Mobile commerce – the emerging frontier: exploring the prospects, application and barriers to adoption in Pakistan. *International Workshop on Frontiers of IT, Islamabad*.

Nassuora, A. B. (2013). Understanding factors affecting the adoption of m-commerce by consumers. *Journal of Applied Sciences*, *13*(6), 913.

Noruzy, A., Dalfard, V. M., Azhdari, B., Nazari-Shirkouhi, S., & Rezazadeh, A. (2013). Relations between transformational leadership, organizational learning, knowledge management, organizational innovation, and organizational performance: an empirical investigation of manufacturing firms. *The International Journal of Advanced Manufacturing Technology*, *64*(1), 1073-1085.

Nysveen, H., Pedersen, P. E., & Thorbjørnsen, H. (2005). Explaining intention to use mobile chat services: moderating effects of gender. *Journal of Consumer Marketing*, *22*(5), 247-256.

Osakwe, C. N., & Okeke, T. C. (2016). Facilitating mCommerce growth in Nigeria through mMoney usage: A preliminary analysis. *IJIKM*, *11*.

Pikkarainen, T., Pikkarainen, K., Karjaluoto, H. & Pahnila, S. (2004). Consumer acceptance of online banking: an extension of the technology acceptance model. *Internet Research*, *14* (3), 224-35.

Porter, E. & Donthu, N. (2006). Using the technology acceptance model to explain how attitudes determine internet usage. *Journal of Business Research, 59* (9) 999-1007.

Prakash, K., & Venkatachalam, S. M. (2016). Consumer perception towards private label brands. *PARIPEX-Indian Journal of Research*, *5*(7).

Rana, N.P., Dwivedi, Y.K. & Williams, M.D. (2013). Evaluating alternative theoretical models for examining citizen centric adoption of e-government. *Transforming Government: People, Process and Policy, 7* (1), 27-49.

Riquelme, H.E. & Rios, R.E. (2010). The moderating effect of gender in the adoption of mobile banking, *International Journal of Bank Marketing*, *28*(5), 328-341

Robinson, L., Marshall, G.W. & Stamps, M.B. (2005). Sales force use of technology: Antecedents to technology acceptance. *Journal of Business Research, 58*(12), 1623-31.

Rogers Everett, M. (1995). *Diffusion of Innovations*. New York, 12.

Rouibah, K., Abbas, H., & Rouibah, S. (2011). Factors affecting camera mobile phone adoption before e-shopping in the Arab world. *Technology in Society*, *33*(3), 271-283.

Safeena, R., Hundewale, N., & Kamani, A. (2011). Customer's adoption of mobile-commerce a study on emerging economy. *International Journal of e-Education, e-Business, e-Management and e-Learning*, *1* (3), 228-233.

Samad, S. (2012). The influence of innovation and transformational leadership on organizational performance, *Procedia-Social and Behavioral Sciences. 57*(1) 486-493.

Shareef, M.A., Kumar, V., Kumar, U. & Dwivedi, Y. (2014). Factors affecting citizen adoption of transactional electronic government. *Journal of Enterprise Information Management*, *27*(4), 385-401.

Shmueli, G., & Koppius, O. R. (2010). Predictive analytics in information systems research. *MIS Quarterly, 35*(3), 553–572.

Srinivasan, S., Pauwels, K., Silva-Risso, J., & Hanssens, D. M. (2009). Product innovations, advertising, and stock returns. *Journal of Marketing, 73*(1), 24-43.

Susanto, T. D., & Aljoza, M. (2015). Individual acceptance of e-Government services in a developing country: Dimensions of perceived usefulness and perceived ease of use and the importance of trust and social influence. *Procedia Computer Science, 72 (1),* 622-629.

Tan, G. W. H., Chong, C. K., Ooi, K. B., & Chong, A. Y. L. (2010). The adoption of online banking in Malaysia: an empirical analysis. *International Journal of Business and Management Science, 3*(2),169-193.

Teo, T. S. H., & Pok, S. H. (2003). Adoption of WAP-enabled mobile phones among Internet users. *The International Journal of Management Science, 31*(6), 483–498.

Thakur, R. & Srivastav, M. (2013). Customer usage intention of mobile commerce in India: An empirical investigation. *Journal of Indian Business Research, 5*(1), 52-72.

Thakur, R., Hsu, S. H., & Fontenot, G. (2012). Innovation in healthcare: Issues and future trends. *Journal of Business Research, 65* (4), 562-569.

Tsu Wei, T., Marthandan, G., Yee-Loong Chong, A., Ooi, K. B., & Arumugam, S. (2009). What drives Malaysian m-commerce adoption? An empirical analysis. *Industrial Management & Data Systems, 109(*3), 370-388.

United Nations (2002). E-Commerce and Development Report 2002, available at: www.r0.unctad. org/ecommerce/ecommerce_en/edr02_en.htm (accessed May 25).

Varshney, U. & Vetter, R. (2002). Mobile commerce: framework, applications and networking support. *Mobile Networks and Applications, 7*(1), 185-98.

Venkatesh, V., Morris, M., Davis, G., & Davis, F. (2003). User acceptance of information technology: Toward a unified view. *MIS Quarterly, 27*(3), 425–478.

Venkatesh, V., & Bala, H. (2008). Technology acceptance model 3 and a research agenda on interventions. *Decision Sciences, 39*(2), 273–315.

Venkatesh, V., Morris, M., Davis, G., & Davis, F. (2003). User acceptance of information technology: Toward a unified view. *MIS Quarterly, 27*(3), 425–478.

Wei, T. T., & Chong, A. Y. (2009). What drives Malaysian m-commerce adoption ? An empirical analysis. *Industrial Management & Data Systems, 109*(3), 370–388.

Wejnert, B. (2002). Integrating models of diffusion of innovations: A conceptual framework. *Annual Review of Sociology, 28*(1), 297-326.

Wong, C.C. and Hiew, P.L. (2005). Diffusion of mobile entertainment in Malaysia: drivers and barriers. *Enformatika,* 5(1), 263-6.

Yadav, R., Sharma, S. K., & Tarhini, A. (2016). A multi-analytical approach to understand and predict the mobile commerce adoption. *Journal of Enterprise Information Management, 29(*2), 222-237.

Yang, K. C. (2005). Exploring factors affecting the adoption of mobile commerce in Singapore. *Telematics and Informatics, 22*(3), 257-277.

Yıldız, S., Baştürk, F., & Boz, İ. T. (2014). The effect of leadership and innovativeness on business performance. *Procedia-Social and Behavioral Sciences, 150*(*1*), 785-793.

Yousafzai, S. Y., Foxall, G. R., & Pallister, J. G. (2010). Explaining internet banking behavior: Theory of reasoned action, theory of planned behavior, or technology acceptance Model. *Journal of Applied Social Psychology, 40*(5), 1172–1202.

Zhang, L., Zhu, J., & Liu, Q. (2012). A meta-analysis of mobile commerce adoption and the moderating effect of culture. *Computers in Human Behavior, 28*(5), 1902- 1911.

Identifying and ranking the factors affecting the adoption of biofuels

Saeed Azizi[a*], Fattaneh Alizadeh Meshkani and Reza Agha Mousa

Department of Management and Accounting, South Branch, Islamic Azad University, Tehran, Iran

CHRONICLE	ABSTRACT
Keywords: Biofuel Green product Adoption	This paper presents an empirical investigation to determine the important factors influencing on adoption of biofuels from consumer's perspective. The study designs a questionnaire in Likert scale and distributes it among 211 randomly selected people who use green products in city of Tehran, Iran. Cronbach alpha is calculated as 0.812, which is well above the acceptable level. Using principle component with Varimax rotation, the study has determined five important factors including social commitment, product usefulness, infrastructure, management approach and customer oriented, which influence the most on adaptation of biofuels.

1. Introduction

One of the most essential questions in today's day-to-day activities is to learn more on how to take care of the environment. Every day, more news appear about the effects of global warming on people's lives. These days, we hear more from media on unpleasant incidents such as shortage of water supply, starvation, air pollution, etc. Fossil fuels are blamed as the most important causes of air pollution and Biofuel is an alternative solution to reduce the burden of fossil fuels. During the past several decades, many have argued as to whether or not it is possible to reach a replacement of environment friendly fuels, which would be also cost effective. In other words, many have tried to answer a simple question "Does it pay to be green?" (Hart & Ahuja, 1996). Bhat (1999) investigated the relationships between the environmental performances and financial performances of some U.S. firms. The environmental performance in this survey was measured in pollution in pounds per sales revenue while the financial performance was computed in terms of profit margins and stock market performance. Bhat performed an indebt investigation into more than 230 firms and found that lower pollution per sales revenue had a positive effect on the profit margins and stock performance. Pollution in their survey was also determined to maintain a direct effect on environmental compliance, spills and different other legal infractions. Stefan and Paul (2008) investigated the relationship between emissions reduction and

---

* Corresponding author.
E-mail address: saeedazizi1363@yahoo.com (S. Azizi)

company performance on data from S&P 500 firms. They reported that "efforts to prevent pollution and reduce emissions drop to the 'bottom line' within one to two years of initiation and that those firms with the highest emission levels stand the most to gain". Orsato (2006) presented a model for categorizing generic kinds of competitive environmental strategies to help managers determine and rank areas of organizational action, and to optimize the overall economic return on environmental investments and making them into sources of competitive advantage. King and Lenox (2001) performed a survey and reported that despite the fact that there are some evidences on relationship between lower pollution and higher financial valuation, a firm's fixed characteristics and strategic position may create some barriers on this association. Biofuels extracted from low-input high-diversity mixtures of native grassland perennials may give more usable energy, bigger greenhouse gas reductions, and less agrichemical pollution per hectare than alternative ones such as corn grain ethanol or soybean biodiesel (Tilman et al., 2006) and the primary objective of the present survey is to learn how to cope with this type of fuels.

2. The proposed study

This paper presents an empirical investigation to determine important factors influencing on adoption of biofuels in consumer's perspective. The study designs a questionnaire in Likert scale and distributes it among 211 randomly selected people who use green products in city of Tehran, Iran. Cronbach alpha is calculated as 0.812, which is well above the acceptable level. Table 1 presents the results of KMO and Bartlett's tests. Table 2 demonstrates the results of the summary of communalities. Table 3 presents the implementation of principal component analysis after rotation. Fig. 1 demonstrates Scree plot of the factors in our survey.

Table 1
KMO and Bartlett's Test

Kaiser-Meyer-Olkin Measure of Sampling Adequacy.		.756
Bartlett's Test of Sphericity	Approx. Chi-Square	2596.94
	df	595
	Sig.	.000

Table 2
The summary of communalities

Question	Variable	Initial communalitie	Extracted communalitie	Question	Variable	Initial communalities	Extracted communalities
q1	Distribution channels	1	0.567	q19	Public awareness	1	0.788
q2	Attention to environment	1	0.798	q20	Technical feasibility	1	0.614
q3	Organization's social responsibility	1	0.733	q21	Financial feasibility	1	0.778
q4	Customers' knowledge	1	0.628	q22	Fast commercialization	1	0.56
q5	Attention to green social programs	1	0.669	q23	Supply of raw material	1	0.681
q6	Customization	1	0.688	q25	Quality life	1	0.671
q7	Business strategy	1	0.647	q26	Logistics	1	0.695
q8	Green distribution	1	0.691	q27	Government support	1	0.74
q9	Public transportation	1	0.719	q28	High cost of R & D	1	0.515
q10	Fair prices	1	0.669	q29	Product life cycle	1	0.556
q11	Profitability for customers	1	0.705	q30	Customer expectation	1	0.669
q12	Subjective norms	1	0.726	q31	Perceived usefulness	1	0.678
q13	Green purchase behavior	1	0.551	q32	Social marketing	1	0.6
q14	Technical equipment	1	0.642	q34	Fossil fuel resources	1	0.606
q15	Market analysis	1	0.529	q35	Fossil fuel prices	1	0.596
q16	Customer information	1	0.625				
q17	Green development	1	0.698				
q18	Globalization	1	0.654				

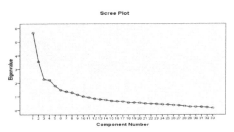

Fig. 1. The results of Scree plot

As we can observe from the results of Fig. 1, after eight components, the figure becomes flat. Therefore we initially extract eight factors.

Table 3
The results of principle component analysis after Varimax rotation

	Component							
	1	2	3	4	5	6	7	8
VAR00002	.388					.616		
VAR00003						.667		
VAR00004						.675		
VAR00007		.485		.389		.553		
VAR00008		.943						
VAR00009					.959			
VAR00010			.914					
VAR00011	.593		.465					
VAR00012								.969
VAR00013	.858							
VAR00014							.956	
VAR00015	-.383				.543			
VAR00016	-.523				.509			
VAR00018					.669			
VAR00019					.733			
VAR00020					.680			
VAR00021		.485		.389		.553		
VAR00022		.943						
VAR00023				.959				
VAR00024			.914					
VAR00025	.593		.465					
VAR00026								.969
VAR00027	.858							
VAR00028							.956	

Extraction Method: Principal Component Analysis.
Rotation Method: Varimax with Kaiser Normalization.
a. Rotation converged in 7 iterations.

As we can observe from the results of Fig 2, the survey has detected five important factors as the most important factors influencing on Biofuels adoption the study including social commitment, product usefulness, infrastructure, management approach and customer oriented, which influence the most on adaptation of biofuels. Table 4 demonstrates the results of examining different factors and as we can observe the effects of all factors have been confirmed.

Table 4
The results of the effects of different influential factors

Alternative	Estimate	P	Accept the	Alternative	Estimate	P	Accept the
q2	0.904	P<0.001	Accept	q14	0.738	P<0.001	Accept
q19	0.868	P<0.001	Accept	q1	0.422	P<0.001	Accept
q9	0.736	P<0.001	Accept	q26	0.38	P<0.001	Accept
q3	0.835	P<0.001	Accept	q35	0.496	P<0.001	Accept
q13	0.395	P<0.001	Accept	q20	0.733	P<0.001	Accept
q30	0.762	P<0.001	Accept	q22	0.61	P<0.001	Accept
q31	0.666	P<0.001	Accept	q15	0.429	P<0.001	Accept
q34	0.755	P<0.001	Accept	q25	0.48	P<0.001	Accept
q11	0.6	P<0.001	Accept	q6	0.636	P<0.001	Accept
q10	0.63	P<0.001	Accept	q12	0.686	P<0.001	Accept
q16	0.536	P<0.001	Accept	q4	0.519	P<0.001	Accept
q27	0.698	P<0.001	Accept	q29	0.459	P<0.001	Accept

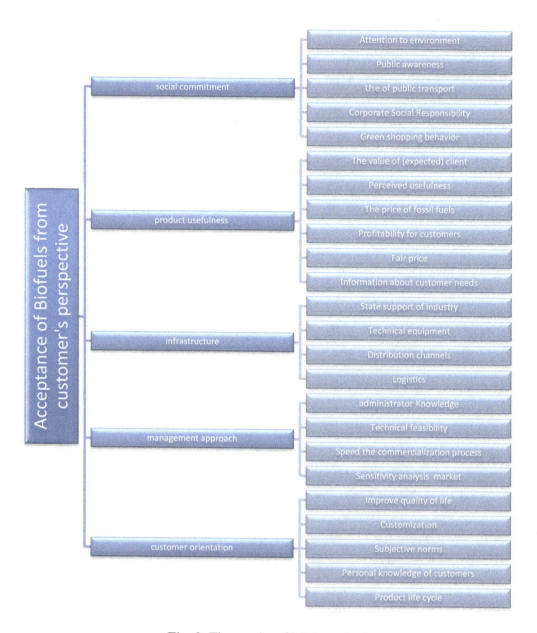

Fig. 2. The results of PCA method

3. Discussion and conclusion

In this paper, we have presented an empirical investigation to study the effects of various factors influencing on the adaptation of biofuels in Iran. The survey has detected five factors. The first factor, social commitment, consists of five sub-factors. Attention to environment appears to be one of the most important items, which must be considered in both governmental as well as public sector (D'Souza et al., 2008). To reach this objective, it is essential to raise public awareness, which is also the second factor detected in our survey. There is no doubt that public transportation plays essential role for reaching better environment system. Of course, this should be accompanied with a good corporate social responsibility and green shopping behavior, which are other important factors and it must be considered as social commitment. The findings of this part of the survey are consistent with findings reported by Gan et al. (2008).

Product usefulness is the second factor in our survey, which consists of six factors. The value created by client is the most important factor followed by the perceived usefulness. In order to reach this objective, it is necessary to see cheaper prices of biofuel products and increase consumer's profitability. Government may intervene in pricing alternative fuel products and provide necessary information for customer. Infrastructure is the third most important factor influencing on biofuel adaptation with four sub-factors. Any fuel change must be supported by industry and technical equipment must be available. In addition, it is necessary to have appropriate channels with effective logistics (Gurau & Ranchhod, 2005).

Management approach is another factor in our survey, which consists of four sub-factor. The first step for management team to adopt biofuel is to setup an appropriate administrate knowledge. It is also necessary to determine whether or not the new fueling system is technically feasible (Hu et al., 2008; Brennan & Owende, 2010). On the other hand, technology now changes rapidly and it is important to cope with the changes and perform an analysis on how to cope with market change.

Customer orientation is the last component of our survey with five sub-factors. Improving the quality of life would be first objective of the survey followed by appropriate customization of the product and subjective norms. Moreover, any customer orientation must be accompanied with sufficient personal knowledge of customers. Finally, product life cycle is the last important factor influencing the most on customer orientation. In fact, a short life cycle for a particular fuel product may discourage customer for green fuel usage. Development of biofuel may offer other advantages such as reduction on poverty in agriculture (Peskett et al., 2007). However, others argue such claims. According to Car (2011), in the forest products marketing literature, many people study the environmental perspectives of business strategy as the nexus between economic growth and sustainable development. Car (2011) presented a three-stage evolutionary framework driven by the government regulations, environmental standards, private initiatives, environmental NGOs and consumers. The study suggested that an environmental marketing strategy may create competitive opportunities for companies, but some environmental practices, such as forest certification, might not improve competitive performance unless they are located with the firm's resources and the external environment as part of the strategy. This part of Car's findings are consistent with findings of this study in terms of management approach.

Acknowledgement

The authors would like to thank the anonymous referees for constructive comments on earlier version of this paper.

References

Brennan, L., & Owende, P. (2010). Biofuels from microalgae—a review of technologies for production, processing, and extractions of biofuels and co-products. *Renewable and sustainable energy reviews*, *14*(2), 557-577.

Bhat, V. N. (1999). Does it pay to be green?. *International Journal of Environmental Studies*, *56*(4), 497-507.

Cao, X. (2011). *Does it pay to be green? An integrated view of environmental marketing with evidence from the forest products industry in China* (Doctoral dissertation, University of Washington).

D'Souza, C., Taghian, M., Lamb, P., & Peretiatkos, R. (2006). Green products and corporate strategy: an empirical investigation. *Society and business review*, *1*(2), 144-157.

Gan, C., Wee, H. Y., Ozanne, L., & Kao, T. H. (2008). Consumers' purchasing behavior towards green products in New Zealand. *Innovative Marketing*, *4*(1), 93-102.

Gurau, C., & Ranchhod, A. (2005). International green marketing: A comparative study of British and Romanian firms. *International Marketing Review*, *22*(5), 547-561.

Hart, S. L., & Ahuja, G. (1996). Does it pay to be green? An empirical examination of the relationship between emission reduction and firm performance. *Business strategy and the Environment*, *5*(1), 30-37.

Hu, Q., Sommerfeld, M., Jarvis, E., Ghirardi, M., Posewitz, M., Seibert, M., & Darzins, A. (2008). Microalgal triacylglycerols as feedstocks for biofuel production: perspectives and advances. *The Plant Journal*, *54*(4), 621-639.

King, A. A., & Lenox, M. J. (2001). Does it really pay to be green? An empirical study of firm environmental and financial performance: An empirical study of firm environmental and financial performance. *Journal of Industrial Ecology*, *5*(1), 105-116.

Orsato, R. J. (2006). Competitive environmental strategies: when does it pay to be green?. *California management review*, *48*(2), 127-143.

Peskett, L., Slater, R., Stevens, C., & Dufey, A. (2007). Biofuels, agriculture and poverty reduction. *Natural resource perspectives*, *107*, 1-6.

Stefan, A., & Paul, L. (2008). Does it pay to be green? A systematic overview. *The Academy of Management Perspectives*, *22*(4), 45-62.

Tilman, D., Hill, J., & Lehman, C. (2006). Carbon-negative biofuels from low-input high-diversity grassland biomass. *Science*, *314*(5805), 1598-1600.

Permissions

All chapters in this book were first published in MSL, by Growing Science; hereby published with permission under the Creative Commons Attribution License or equivalent. Every chapter published in this book has been scrutinized by our experts. Their significance has been extensively debated. The topics covered herein carry significant findings which will fuel the growth of the discipline. They may even be implemented as practical applications or may be referred to as a beginning point for another development.

The contributors of this book come from diverse backgrounds, making this book a truly international effort. This book will bring forth new frontiers with its revolutionizing research information and detailed analysis of the nascent developments around the world.

We would like to thank all the contributing authors for lending their expertise to make the book truly unique. They have played a crucial role in the development of this book. Without their invaluable contributions this book wouldn't have been possible. They have made vital efforts to compile up to date information on the varied aspects of this subject to make this book a valuable addition to the collection of many professionals and students.

This book was conceptualized with the vision of imparting up-to-date information and advanced data in this field. To ensure the same, a matchless editorial board was set up. Every individual on the board went through rigorous rounds of assessment to prove their worth. After which they invested a large part of their time researching and compiling the most relevant data for our readers.

The editorial board has been involved in producing this book since its inception. They have spent rigorous hours researching and exploring the diverse topics which have resulted in the successful publishing of this book. They have passed on their knowledge of decades through this book. To expedite this challenging task, the publisher supported the team at every step. A small team of assistant editors was also appointed to further simplify the editing procedure and attain best results for the readers.

Apart from the editorial board, the designing team has also invested a significant amount of their time in understanding the subject and creating the most relevant covers. They scrutinized every image to scout for the most suitable representation of the subject and create an appropriate cover for the book.

The publishing team has been an ardent support to the editorial, designing and production team. Their endless efforts to recruit the best for this project, has resulted in the accomplishment of this book. They are a veteran in the field of academics and their pool of knowledge is as vast as their experience in printing. Their expertise and guidance has proved useful at every step. Their uncompromising quality standards have made this book an exceptional effort. Their encouragement from time to time has been an inspiration for everyone.

The publisher and the editorial board hope that this book will prove to be a valuable piece of knowledge for researchers, students, practitioners and scholars across the globe.

List of Contributors

Ayad Hendalianpour and Jafar Razmi
School of Industrial Engineering, College of Eng, Tehran University, Tehran, Iran

Arefe Rameshi Sarvestani
Department of Mathematics, Shahrood University of Technology, Shahrood, Iran

Aakash Kamble
School of Industrial Engineering, College of Eng, Tehran University, Tehran, Iran

Aatish Zagade
Department of Mathematics, Shahrood University of Technology, Shahrood, Iran

Reza Koohjani Gouji, Reza Taghvaei and Hossein Soleimani
Department of Marketing, Malayer Branch, Islamic Azad University, Malayer, Iran

Raja Ahmed Jamil and Syed Rameez ul Hassan
Department of Management Sciences, University of Haripur, Pakistan

Asdaq Farid
College of Business Administration, Chonnam National University, South Korea

Naveed Ahmad
COMSATS Institute of Information Technology, Abbottabad, Pakistan

Virender Chahal
Research Scholar Department of Mechanical Engineering, Deenbandhu Chhotu Ram University of Science and Technology, Sonipat, Haryana, India

M.S. Narwal
Associate professor, Department of Mechanical Engineering, Deenbandhu Chhotu Ram University of Science and Technology, Sonipat, Haryana, India

Hadi Pazoki Toroudi
Department of Industrial Engineering, Ghaemshahr Branch, Islamic Azad University, Ghaemshahr, Iran

Mahsa Sadat Madani
Department of Industrial Engineering, TaJan University, Ghaemshahr, Iran

Fatemeh Sarlak
Department of Industrial Engineering, College of Engineering, University of Tehran, Tehran, Iran

Samar Rahi and Feras MI Alnaser
University Sultan Zainal Abidin, Terengganu, Malaysia

Mazuri Abd. Ghani
Senior Lecturer, University Sultan Zainal Abidin, Terengganu, Malaysia

Daniel Osezua Aikhuele
Faculty of Manufacturing Engineering, Universiti Malaysia Pahang, 26600 Pekan, Malaysia

Haftu Hailu
Public Service and Human Resource Development Ministry: Ethiopia Kaizen Institute, Addis ababa, Ethiopia
Ethiopian Institute of Technology Mekelle, Mekelle University, Tigray, Ethiopia

Abdelkadir Kedir and Getachew Bassa
Ethiopian Institute of Technology Mekelle, Mekelle University, Tigray, Ethiopia

Kassu Jilcha
Addis Ababa University, Addis Ababa Institute of Technology, Addis Ababa, Ethiopia

Torsten J. Gerpott
Chair of Strategic and Telecommunications Management, Mercator School of Management, University of Duisburg-Essen, Lotharstr. 65, D-47057 Duisburg, Germany

Peyman Ghafari Ashtiani
Department of Management, Arak Branch, Islamic Azad University, Arak, Iran

Atefeh Parsayan and Moein Mohajerani
Master of EMBA, Department of Management, Arak Branch, Islamic Azad University, Arak, Iran

Bahareh Ghodoosi
Department of IT Management, E-Learning Course, Tehran, Shahid Beheshti University, Iran

List of Contributors

Alireza Moshkforoush
Department of Management, E-Learning Course, Isfahan, Isfahan University, Iran

Ali Abdollahi and Mohammadesmaeil Fadaeinejad
Department of Management and Accounting, Tehran, Shahid Beheshti University, Iran

Amina Merabet
Lecturer, Tlemcen university, Algeria, BP: 226 Tlemcen Algeria

Abderrezzak Benhabib
Professor, Tlemcen university, Algeria, BP: 226 Tlemcen Algeria

Abderrezzak Merabet
Student, Tlemcen university, Algeria, BP: 226 Tlemcen Algeria

Jafar Jafari
MA in Marketing, Department of Management, Central Branch, Islamic Azad University, Tehran, Iran

Maruf Gbadebo Salimon and Jibril Adewale Bamgbade
School of Business Management, Universiti Utara Malaysia, Malaysia

Ajulor Olusegun Nathaniel
Faculty of Liberal Arts, Houdegbe North American University, Benin Republic

Tijani A. Adekunle
Faculty of Social Sciences, Lagos State University, Ojo, Lagos, Nigeria

Saeed Azizi, Fattaneh Alizadeh Meshkani and Reza Agha Mousa
Department of Management and Accounting, South Branch, Islamic Azad University, Tehran, Iran

Nayna Abhang

Index

A

Ad Effectiveness, 13, 16, 19
Adoption, 71-73, 78-81, 83, 90, 92, 139-140, 170, 179-184, 186-197
Aesthetic Tendencies, 171, 173-175, 177-178
Analytic Network Process (ANP), 64
Attitude, 15-16, 19-20, 70, 72-79, 98, 100, 103-108, 111, 129, 142-145, 147-150, 163-166, 169-170, 172-173, 181, 183, 191-192

B

Biofuel, 195, 199-200
Brand Affections, 18
Brand Attitude, 16, 20, 163, 172
Buying Decision Satisfaction, 36-37, 39-43

C

C&rt, 1, 3, 5, 9-10, 12
Capital Market, 151-153, 155, 158-161
Celebrity Endorsements, 13
Company's Performance, 171, 177
Consumer Behaviour, 20, 136
Contemporary Business Environment, 179
Corporate Image, 21-23, 25-30, 34-35
Critical Success Factor, 96-97
Cultural Values, 36-39, 41-43, 45-46
Customer Attraction, 21-24, 29-30, 32-33
Customer Integration, 112
Customer Loyalty, 25, 35, 38, 68, 78, 81, 139-145, 147, 149, 172-173
Customer Relationship Management (CRM), 1-2, 11

D

Decision Tree, 1, 3-12
Dual Mediation Hypothesis, 13-16

E

Electronic Business, 151, 162
Emotional Values, 36, 38-39, 41-44
Empirical Pricing Research, 112
Environmental Opportunities, 151

F

Factor Analysis, 74, 96, 101, 167, 185
Functional Benefits, 171-178

Fuzzy Shannon's Entropy, 83, 85, 87-88, 92

G

Green Product, 192, 195

I

Ideal Solution, 82-83, 85, 87-89
Implementation Limitations, 82-83, 90, 92
Impulse Buying, 13-15, 17, 19-20, 38-39, 42-43, 45, 47, 150
Infrastructure, 26-27, 151, 153, 157-158, 160-161, 195, 197-199
Innovative Business Strategy, 82
Intention, 13-20, 38, 40, 45, 70-79, 81, 125, 140-144, 147-150, 163-170, 192-194
Internet Banking, 70-74, 77-81, 190, 194
Irancell Telecommunications, 21, 26-27, 30, 32-33

K

Kaizen, 49, 53, 55, 58-60, 93, 96-104, 106-111

L

Lean Barriers, 48
Lean Concept, 48-49, 59
Lean Implementation, 48-53, 58, 60-62, 82-84, 89-90, 92, 94
Lean Manufacturing, 48-54, 56-63, 83, 95
Lean Product Development Practices, 82-84, 86, 90
Lean Strategies, 48-50, 54, 56-58, 60
Lean Waste, 48
Likeness/description Benefits, 171
Logo, 171-174, 177-178

M

M-commerce, 151, 179-184, 189-194
Management Approach, 195, 197-199
Millennial, 36-37, 39-41, 43
Mobile Advertising, 163-166, 168-170, 191
Mobile Marketing, 163-164, 170
Mobile Services, 22, 151-153, 157, 160-161, 192

P

Pay What You Want Pricing, 112, 135-136, 138
Peacock Shoe, 96
Perceived Usefulness, 70-74, 77-80, 140-145, 147-149, 169, 179, 181-182, 184, 186-192, 194, 196, 198

Price Setting, 112, 115-116, 118, 121-123, 126-129, 131-133
Product Mix Planning, 64
Product Selection, 64
Product Usefulness, 195, 197-198
Profitability, 1-2, 4, 24, 64-65, 68, 78, 100, 107, 126, 152, 182, 196, 198-199
Purchase Intention, 13-19, 38, 163-166, 168-169

R
Rate of Competition, 179

S
Services Company, 21-23, 26-27, 30, 32-33
Services Value Chain, 151, 161-162
Smes, 1-4, 8-10, 58, 61, 79, 95

Social Commitment, 195, 197-198
Strategic Analysis, 151
Structural Equation Model (SEM), 70, 76
Swot Method, 151-152, 154
Systematic Model, 82-85, 89-90, 92

T
Technology Acceptance Model (TAM), 70, 80, 139-141, 165
Trademark, 171, 173, 178

V
Viral Marketing, 139-142, 147-150
Voluntary Customer Payments, 112, 118

W
Word of Mouth, 36-39, 41-45, 47

CPSIA information can be obtained
at www.ICGtesting.com
Printed in the USA
BVHW062301280519
549552BV00002B/34/P